Dancing Revolution

MUSIC IN AMERICAN LIFE

*A list of books in the series appears at the end of this book.*

# DANCING REVOLUTION

*Bodies, Space, and Sound in American Cultural History*

CHRISTOPHER J. SMITH

UNIVERSITY OF ILLINOIS PRESS
Urbana, Chicago, and Springfield

Publication of this book was supported by a grant from the H. Earle Johnson Fund of the Society for American Music.


1 2 3 4 5 C P 5 4 3 2 1
∞ This book is printed on acid-free paper.

Library of Congress Cataloging-in-Publication Data

Names: Smith, Christopher J. (Christopher John), 1959– author.
Title: Dancing revolution: bodies, space, and sound in American cultural history / Christopher J. Smith.
Description: Urbana: University of Illinois Press, 2019. | Series: Music in American life | Includes bibliographical references and index. |
Identifiers: LCCN 2018059613 (print) | LCCN 2019013274 (ebook) | ISBN 9780252051234 (ebook) | ISBN 9780252042393 (hardback) | ISBN 9780252084188 (paper)
Subjects: LCSH: Dance—United States—History. | Dance—Social aspects—United States—History. | Popular culture—United States—History. | BISAC: MUSIC / Ethnomusicology. | SOCIAL SCIENCE / Ethnic Studies / African American Studies.
Classification: LCC GV1623 (ebook) | LCC GV1623 .S65 2019 (print) | DDC 792.80973—dc23
LC record available at https://lccn.loc.gov/2018059613

Cover illustration: Paul Colin, *Josephine Baker*, 1927

*Dedicated to Angela Mariani*

# Contents

# Preface

I am profoundly grateful for the opportunity to write this book. I thank all the people, events, experiences, and processes that have made it possible.

It may seem curious that a person such as myself, trained as an instrumental musician and a historian, should choose to write about dance and semiotic meaning—especially in light of the fact that dance is something at which I am much more adept as witness than participant![1] On the other hand, there are some signposts in my own personal biography that point toward the present volume: I have been a vernacular musician, engaged in apprenticeship-based teaching and learning, for many more decades than I have been a cultivated one (for the "cultivated versus vernacular" locution, thank you, H. Wiley Hitchcock, RIP).[2] I have been a community musician far longer than I have been an inhabitant of academia; for helping me breach those gates, deep thanks to George W. Buelow, J. Peter Burkholder, Thomas J. Mathiesen, David N. Baker, Bob Prins, Dianthe Myers-Spencer, Joseph Dyer, and Austin B. Caswell. I have been a dance musician, engaged with the subtle, un-notated intangibles of "lift" and "groove," for as long as I have been conscious of the beauty of music: thank you, Martin Grosswendt, Geoff Bartley, Larry Baeder, Paul Rishell, Joshua Levin-Epstein, Tony Allen, and other early and influential funky brethren and sistren. I have been a proponent of artistic community ever since I encountered it, as a disaffected early-adolescent product of a dysfunctional middle-class suburban upbringing, in the folk and acoustic coffeehouses of Massachusetts: thank you, Me & Thee Coffeehouse, and Saturday Night in Marblehead Coffeehouse (both Marblehead), and Nameless

Coffeehouse (Cambridge). I have been a political activist (at first nascent, later conscious, but always engaged) ever since my mother (Bobby Smith Thomas, RIP) took me and my siblings to hear Dr. King speak in Lynn, Massachusetts, around 1964.

That I found my way to the worlds of vernacular expressive experience—as player, dance-sympathizer, scholar, teacher, and advocate—is the most significant artistic, emotional, psychological, political, and ethical event in my life. Without vernacular culture's capacity to build community—its ability, as Bob Dylan said, to "teach you everything you need to know about life, if you let it"—genetics, experience, biography, and psychology suggest that I would probably be dead or addicted.[3] Hence, these art forms, and the human relationships and experiences they made possible, without hyperbole saved my life.

It's important to me to give back to them.

In the existing literature regarding the phenomenon of westerners (specifically North Americans) taking on the music and dancing of the exotic Other—the "theft," for example, of the blackface "minstrel mask"—a number of explanations are tendered for these genres' attraction to members of the dominant culture, including cultural exoticism.[4] But, among these analyses of cross-class appropriation, notable for its relative de-emphasis is the idea that subaltern genres might also have appeal because engaging in them elicits a fundamental sanity, connectedness, integration (versus alienation), efficacy: in short, an enhanced experience of "self-ness," humanity, and community. Participation in such experiences (as performer or audience and in the richly ambiguous place between those two roles) serves deep-seated human desires and need. This is precisely my motivation for promulgating these art forms: because that connection, integration, "self-ness," was—most emphatically, in the formation of my professional, pedagogical, and ethical identity—my own experience.

Expressive culture, including especially participatory expressive culture (music and dance), is a tool, whose form or name or details of construction may be beautifully unique to each cultural context from which it emerged, but whose functions tend, across cultures, contexts, and epochs, to serve a consistent network of fundamental cognitive, experiential, psychological, and emotional human needs. Sometimes outsiders seek participation not in order to aggrandize or mythologize themselves but because they believe that participation can teach better ways to be: Ted Solis asks simply "Is there room for a space for critical *and* sensual involvement that doesn't reproduce exoticist voyeurism?"[5] This book seeks to create such a space.

# Acknowledgments

Sincerest thanks are due to:

My brothers, sisters, avatars, and teachers in the worldwide communities of dance musicians: Chipper Thompson, Mason Brown, Steve Cooper, Grey Larsen, Randal Bays, Martin Grosswendt, Andrew Lazaro, Grant Manhart, John White, Heather Maxwell, John Perrin, Larry "Guitar" Baeder, Mike Bevan, Dean Magraw, Dominic Spera, and the great David N. Baker;

My role models for writing about vernacular culture: Peter Guralnick, Gearoid O hAllmhurain, Ciarán Carson, Eric von Schmidt, Gary Snyder, and Henry Glassie;

The seminal dance and performance scholars I—remarkably—encountered by chance, just when I needed to: Richard Schechner, Anya Peterson Royce, and Richard Bauman; and

My champions Laurie Matheson (Director) and Julianne Laut (Outreach & Development Acquisitions Assistant) of the University of Illinois Press.

As well, I thank my scholarly colleagues in the linked fields of American vernacular musics, dance, and cultural history;

At my home institution, I thank my boss, William Ballenger, Director of the Texas Tech University School of Music; Keith Dye, Associate Dean of the TTU College of Visual and Performing Arts and subsequent Director of the School of Music; Dr. Bill Gelber of the School of Theatre and Dance, Brecht scholar, and admired artistic ally; my Musicology colleagues, Lauryn Salazar, Thomas Cimarusti, Stacey Jocoy, and Sarai Brinker; also

My colleague and musical brother-in-arms, Roger Landes: thanks for inviting me to that first Zoukfest, Rog!

My great friend, the master image-researcher, Rich Remsberg, for irreplaceable assistance and stimulating discourse—and for the art program!

The student participants in my seminars and other projects at Texas Tech University since 2000;

My teaching and research assistants at Texas Tech, including most notably the Vernacular Music Center crew during the time this book was being written: Abi Rhoades, Candice Holley, Kathryn Mann, and Marusia Pola Mayorga;

The players, singers, dancers, and audiences of the Elegant Savages Orchestra, the Celtic Choir, the Eagles' Heart Sisters, the Celtic Dance Corps; Caprock Morris; the Tech Irish Set-Dancers; the *Mother Courage* Junkyard Cabaret; the cast and creative staff of *Dancing at the Crossroads*; and the *Plunder!* oratorio crew;

The advocacy organizations with whom I have partnered in the ongoing battle to recover the centrality of bodily experience within music: The Bay Area Country Dance Society; the Country Dance and Song Society; Comhaltas Ceoltóirí Éireann: especially cherished friends in the County Clare chapter headquartered at Cois na hAbhna in Ennis; and,

Once again, the owners, management, and baristas of independent coffee roasters J&B Coffee, Lubbock, Texas, who continue to provide congenial, generous, engaging, and ethical environments for community and creativity.

This book is offered in grateful appreciation to the dancers, at the barre and in the street, who have so profoundly shaped my musical consciousness: Becky Smith, Martha Bremser, Heather Maxwell, Jayme Smith, Emily Furillo, Bridget Hall, Miss Abi Rhoades, Mats Melin, Kat Finley, Genevieve Durham, Miss Kris Olsen, Justin Duncan, Samantha Wilde, Felicia Rojas, Lesley Gomez, Aimee Dixon, Becca Rhoades, Barry Horn, Sharon Green, Anne Wharton, and my beloved sister in arms, Nicole Wesley . . . and to all the rest of them.

May all beings attain Enlightenment.

# Dancing Revolution

# Introduction

## "Callin' out, around the world . . ."

> Dance remains a greatly undervalued and undertheorized arena of bodily discourse.
>
> —Jane C. Desmond, In *Meaning in Motion: New Cultural Studies of Dance* (1997)

In the history of American political culture, popular music forms have often been deployed as tools for contestation or critique: there is, for example, a rich tradition of melodic contrafacta, for which "Yankee Doodle," "John Brown's Body," and "In the Sweet Bye and Bye" represent perhaps the most familiar tunes. Similarly, oratory and iconography, particularly in the medium of editorial cartooning, have been essential parts of American public discourse and subaltern resistance since before the Revolution.[1]

Less commonly remarked or explored has been the role of vernacular dance. Yet from the colonial period onward, participatory ways of moving the body in relation to musical sound have often been experienced as confrontational, subversive, immoral, or even revolutionary. Within the slippery, mutable historical contexts of American public life, in which class, race, gender, and political and regional identity are contested and transformed, street music and dance have taken on complex and contested semiotic meanings. To move in an "akimbo" fashion—to dance with bent arms or twisted torso, and thus to "cut" and syncopate musical rhythm—or to make "noise"—that is, unregulated or unregularized interruptive sound—in public spaces, was to be seen, intentionally or unintentionally, as transgressive, rebellious, defiant, exotic, and "Other."[2]

Movement has been a zone in which dominant cultural priorities and dictates have held sway: Wendy James links repression of subaltern identity to "attempts over three centuries to restrict, reshape, and effectively to co-opt dancing," while hip-hop scholar Tricia Rose explicitly situates contestation of public space as a component in the cycle of repression and resistance.[3] This text examines public dance—public movement, both preconceived and spontaneous, to heard sound—as an "alternative code" that has been used to "direct attention to offstage cultures" and to "validate the perceptions [and the subaltern identities] of the less powerful."[4] Our topics will thus include the complex social and symbolic dynamics that made dancing, singing, and playing in North American public settings a potentially revolutionary act; the political and legal conversations that sought to restrict such semiotic defiance; and the artistic and communicative strategies through which practitioners of street dance and "rough music" carved out sociopolitical space in various ages of the Republic.[5] My fundamental premise is that participatory vernacular dance in the United States, especially dance occurring in public or quasi-public contexts, has been a tool for contesting, constructing, and reinventing social orders. Much dance scholarship has tended toward the descriptive-historical, in the case of vernacular styles, or the analytical-critical, in the case of concert idioms.[6] The current text, however, seeks to locate deep currents and recurrent tropes in the visible behaviors and imputed meanings of "ordinary" people transforming public space through movement.[7]

In North American and Caribbean colonial history, diverse immigrant groups' distinctive movement vocabularies have been variously employed, imitated, appropriated, or condemned, because they were seen to create transformative spaces; hence, dance represents semiotic power, particularly for and to groups otherwise marginalized.[8] Public (especially urban) spaces provided the sites for danced contestation of social and political control. Public dance events within them were the locus for particularly explosive collisions of gender, sexuality, race, class, and community identity. Participatory dance culture—particularly in the venues of the street, theater, and dance hall—acted-out verbal and extra-verbal debates about what constituted permissible body behaviors and their connotations. In the new Republic, accelerating industrialization and urban growth made city streets a canvas upon which the widest diversity of American classes, genders, ethnicities, and professions interacted, in an environment that—because it was mutable, spatial, and temporary—resisted "indoor" social controls.

In this book, drawing on more than four centuries of vernacular dance encounters, I propose a historical model of street dance as both consciously irruptive and politically representative, while always acknowledging its fraught, racist, and exploitative history.[9] An early example of the kind of anxiety that lay behind this push for social controls is the blackface character of "Zip Coon," an African American dandy.[10] Robert Allen identifies the character as embodying the threatening anonymity that whites feared urban streets conferred upon free blacks:[11]

> [Zip Coon] represented the free black male who aped the dress and manner of the white dandies he passed on the street. As such, he served to reinforce the notion that any attempt to "civilize" black males outside their "native" plantation culture would result in a grotesque travesty of white culture. Laid over this caricature, however, was another: that of the white social type Dandy Jim took as his model—the overweening, self-centered, wealthy man-about-town.[12]

This derogatory caricature—in the minstrel show and on the theatrical stage, in musical prints and electronic media—reflects both the intent to delegitimate subaltern race- or class-expression, and the anxiety that underlaid that intent. In the case of Zip Coon and many analogous instances, street dance ritualized and symbolically gamed-out conflict: between ethnic or, especially, immigrant groups or social classes; between conservative and modernist social models; and between majority and subaltern identities.

Subaltern exploitation of the "crevices and crannies" within structures of social control often flowed along more indirect channels of creative expression such as music and dance.[13] Urban modernism sought to regularize or channel this irruptive impulse: for example, it was New Orleans lawmakers' desire to contain carnivalesque behaviors, formerly distributed throughout the city, that led to the concentration of masking, singing, and other noisy, festive behaviors in Place Congo, as reported in Benjamin Latrobe's iconic 1819 account.[14] At watershed moments in the history of New World cities, when new immigrant groups have entered urban spaces or dominant social classes have wished to reclaim them, geographical and legislative strictures have closed in—while in opposition, working-class groups across a wide span of identities have used street dance as an empowering rhetorical strategy.[15]

Moreover, by virtue of its mimetic quality, eschewing texts in favor of gestures and actions, movement has been usefully receptive to multivalent and even contradictory interpretations. Street dance and noise have been central to much subaltern resistance precisely because of their unspoken and ambiguous political intentions—is the movement or noise intentionally or unintentionally disruptive? Very frequently, transgressive or oppositional visual or sonic actions—"rough music" and "rough dance"—have been experienced as emblematic of resistance—regardless of whether that resistance was intended.[16]

## Methodology and Survey of Literature

However, the analysis of street dance's historical idioms and contexts presents challenges to traditional historical methods. Because vernacular culture's musical practices and movement vocabularies were comparatively poorly documented, and because the subaltern classes, ethnicities, and communities among which these art forms emerged were not considered to merit serious study, the concrete material record is sparse, indirect, and prone to bias. In the absence of musical notation or dance diagrams, therefore, some of the most extensive data is simultaneously the most indirect and challenging; these include static two-dimensional images, themselves often fictional or idealized; impressionistic prose descriptions; census, newspapers, and other primary source data, and so on.

As the following review of literature makes clear, there are lacunae in the existing scholarship on popular dance in North American culture—and, specifically, on the semiotic meanings of participatory street dance. Specialists addressing the historical and political connotations of dance-making have tended to focus upon either the contexts or the programmatic intentions of theatrical and concert performance; participatory and street idioms have been less extensively investigated. The historical address of this book is not to the sociology or political consciousness of dance criticism; rather, I am interested in street-dancers' motives and experiences: what they intended and how they were understood. I believe that there is an untold story here—one whose recurrent patterns of action and reaction, of intention and reception, can illuminate key factors in North American cultural history.[17]

Thus, although my central analytical perspective comes from historical musicology, this book also draws upon methods from ethnomusicology, historical performance practice, and cultural geography. Likewise, my analysis of such data for its communicative meaning employs tools from not only historiography and ethnography but also from kinesics, iconography, and semiotics. Scholarship based in all these disciplines has informed my critical method and the book that has resulted; the following provides a brief excursus of some of these sources.

## HISTORICAL MUSICOLOGY

A small body of scholarship on New World history engages considered and extended analysis of vernacular movement vocabularies, though that topic is rather better represented among art historians than musicologists.[18] When undertaken, musicological address to this material has often necessitated the employment of diverse tools to sift out data from indirect primary sources. For example, one of the seminal investigations of blackface minstrelsy, Dale Cockrell's *Demons of Disorder*, begins with an account from the working-class "flash" paper *The Libertine*, describing a gladiatorial dance battle in 1842, the winter of the Virginia Minstrels, between two prostitutes, Nance Holmes and Suse Bryant, competing on Boston's Long Wharf.[19] Cockrell unpacks this event as iconic of antebellum street culture's challenge to existing power, class, and economic structures. For our purposes, we may note that the body vocabularies described in this account of prostitutes, as in hundreds of period illustrations and descriptions of "low" (for which read "mulatto," "working-class," African American, or Afro-Caribbean) culture, the depicted movements, in their angularity, looseness, and spinal flexibility, directly contradict Anglo-European body ideals of line, curve, symmetry, alignment, and flow.[20] This physical contradiction was perceived by dominant culture to represent ethical and existential threat; as Dixon Gottschild puts it, "by Europeanist standards, the Africanist dancing body [was] vulgar, comic, uncontrolled, undisciplined, and, most of all, promiscuous."[21] Yet, in the syncretic aesthetics of the creole New World, these same bent, twisted, "sprung" postures—so repugnant to European dance aesthetics—conveyed strength, energy, authority, and vitality.[22]

William J. Mahar's *Behind the Burnt Cork Mask: Early Blackface Minstrelsy and Antebellum American Popular Culture* is one of the standard contemporary texts on minstrelsy. Mahar deals primarily with the pre–Civil War history of blackface troupes, and in particular with the parodic European and light-classical sources of minstrel texts and theatrical entertainments, but he also provides a particularly useful articulation of "the sometimes contradictory American beliefs and attitudes about race, gender, and class" that swirled around blackface minstrelsy; his analysis of "beliefs and attitudes" directly informs this book's approach.[23]

### ETHNOMUSICOLOGY

For our purposes, ethnomusicology's willingness to situate musical behaviors within culture-specific contexts of understanding and meaning provides an effective complement to historical analysis. While the discipline's traditional emphasis upon the fieldworker's physical presence and experience contrasts musicology's engagement with records of past objects, ethnomusicology provides useful tools for thick description of music-and-dance performance and the ways they literally embody webs of meaning within communities' contextual frames of perception.[24] However, recovering *past* contexts inaccessible to fieldwork has been a challenge.[25] Fortunately, ethnomusicology and historical musicology, once occupying contrasted topics dictated by geography or ethnicity, have found a venue for cooperation through their shared engagement with *contexts of performance*, whether distanced by chronology or geography. Historical musicology has thus opened its doors to methodologies addressing a range of cultures, locations, genres, and experiences from around the world, while ethnomusicology has acquired historiographic tools that facilitate investigation of past experiences: folklore/folklife, oral history, cultural geography, and the study of material culture.

### HISTORICALLY INFORMED PERFORMANCE

Though not so commonly cited as a methodological source by cognate disciplines, the field of historically informed performance (HIP) and its sensitivity to expressive behaviors' meaning within past social and geographical contexts links directly to the subdiscipline of historical ethnomusicology. Tools borrowed from this world of historical performance, an area of activity that directly integrates historiographic, contextual, and behavioral methods with analytical perspectives drawn from both parent disciplines, have been crucial to my own "historical ethno/musicology."[26] Existing as it does at the nexus where historical and contextual analysis meet, historical performance draws upon both musicology and cultural history, but—in service of developing actual performance events—also addresses the reconstruction of physical behaviors around music and dance. Thus, historical performance provides useful additional perspectives, in its ability not only to interpret distant contexts' interpretive frames but also to reconstruct possibilities for physical conduct, specifically in the acts of performance. In terms of the recovery of historical movement; its interface of bodies, instruments, and spaces in historical contexts; and its emphasis upon participants' *actions*—most notably, in the brilliantly idiosyncratic synthesis of analysis, inference, and experiment promulgated by my own teacher, Thomas Binkley—the craft of historical performance has strongly informed the present work.[27]

## ICONOGRAPHY

The majority of iconographic analysis within the study of historical music has tended toward the interpretation of images' symbolic meaning as intended by artists and understood by viewers. That is to say, most study of musical iconography—a discipline borrowed from art history—has emphasized unpacking the semiotic and metaphorical messages built into images of music making for what they tell us about a period's, or an artist's, symbolic perceptions around that music-making.

Less commonly, but more immediately, "music iconography" can also be understood as the study of the contextual, rather than purely metaphorical, data contained—and sometimes hidden—within images, and of what that data can tell us about actual musical conduct. As a kind of frozen, two-dimensional replacement for the in-person data of ethnography's fieldwork observation, historical-informed analysis of period images provides useful models for precisely the same sorts of reconstruction.

On the other hand, there are challenges in employing iconographic data to reconstruct music-and-dance behavior. These include the necessity of establishing a given artist's historical reliability—that is, the accuracy of the data an image contains—and that of reanimating the frozen moment to yield three-dimensional movement. In the former case, historical musicology's primary source rigor provides a useful counterbalance: a musicologist can assess the legitimacy of an image's accuracy in the same way we vet a prose or notational source, through consideration of its consistency with other available data and our understanding of the period's contextual expectations. Similarly, in the recovery of the kinesthetic information contained within a static image, the lessons of historical dance iconography provide useful corollary evidence.[28] Permutations of iconographic analysis, joined with elements of semiotics and performance analysis, play out in the discipline of film studies and inform my commentary on Josephine Baker, the Marx Brothers, Spike Lee's *Bamboozled*, and Sir Mix-a-Lot's "Baby Got Back."[29]

## CULTURAL GEOGRAPHY

The discipline of cultural geography—the study of human communities operating within specific physical landscapes—provides a particularly fruitful meeting-place for aspects of musicology, ethnomusicology, and folklore relevant to the current study. Though applications of its methodology specifically to music have been relatively few, it provides highly effective tools for examining the ways that spaces channel conduct and, in turn, the ways that conduct can impose layers of semiotic association upon physical landscapes. In this arena, an often-cited exemplar is Ruth Finnegan, *The Hidden Musicians: Music-Making in an English Town*, which provides a relatively complex and multilayered view of the social economies of musical subcommunities in the planned Midlands city of Milton Keynes in England. Finnegan's willingness to engage with the full range of musical activity, both professional and avocational, shapes some of my own work on temporary or momentary participation in street dance.[30]

However, my own thinking has been even more heavily influenced by folklorist Henry Glassie's *Passing the Time in Ballymenone*, a magisterial study of a small community in Fermanagh in Northern Ireland, which includes lengthy, detailed, very sensitive exegeses of everything from terrain maps of relationships and crop rotations, to descriptions of the making of butter and buildings and the harvesting of turf and potatoes for fuel and food.[31] In its insistence upon a holistic view of "pattern languages," the interplay of form, function, and material culture that is distinctive to specific communities operating within and impacting upon specific landscapes, *Ballymenone* is a strong influence upon this book's investigation of street communities moving within urban cityscapes.[32]

Cultural geography thus contributes to the present study through its ability to demonstrate how landscapes—especially in specific locations or historical moments—facilitate certain types of cultural expression and exchange.[33] Its methods help reveal street music-and-dance behaviors to be shaped by topographical and cognitive terrain as much as by webs of social meaning.[34] The necessary corollary to cultural geography's methods is to find other persuasive circumstantial data—as, for example, first-person reports or retained stylistic characteristics—that support interpretations of genres' contact via simple geographical proximity.

### KINESICS AND THE PSYCHOLOGY OF GROUP PERFORMANCE

The challenge of understanding the cultural specifics versus the psychological/cognitive universals of movement experience—that is, of *kinesics*—is an especially central one, especially in the case of historical repertoires and contexts.[35] Lack of direct quantitative evidence has sometimes led historians or critics of popular dance toward presumptions of inhering genetic inheritance or to qualitative assertions of inherited cultural meaning and cognitive perception, which, while quite possibly accurate, are difficult to theorize, measure, or concretely articulate.[36] In contrast, anthropological methodologies have been rather more successful at explaining the human rewards of dance; Judith Lynne Hanna for example, in a classic work, and grounding her argument in part in the psychology of catharsis, has argued persuasively that group dance provides demonstrable communal bonds and rewards.[37]

Moreover, either simple observation, or imitative participation, entails engagement with and internalization of the Other's psychological experience as well as bodily vocabularies. Dance scholar Rebecca Sachs Norris, for example, suggests that shared movement enhances internalization, commenting, "Sometimes we intentionally copy others in order to take on their experience."[38] Thus, analysis of imitative movement vocabularies, which have been an integral part of diverse immigrant experiences in the New World, provides the opportunity to investigate new and shared psychological experiences.

Semiotics, a discipline that originates in literary criticism and theories of communication but which is widely employed in the performing arts—especially music—plays a very significant role in the current study.[39] This is especially true in those case studies that implicate African American and Afro-Caribbean body consciousnesses: recognition that these movement traditions employ "signifyin'"—that is, the intentional imitation, distortion, exaggeration, and/or parody of music-and-dance vocabularies precisely through reference to others'—is a powerful tool for reading past the surface details of images and performances.[40] As Gates and Borshuk demonstrate, understanding "signifyin'" as a political and strategic act is a way to understand the semiotic tactics of resistance historically employed by subaltern communities.[41] For my purposes, therefore, *movement semiotics* will be taken to mean "the analysis of situational and contextual communicative symbols," whether those symbols appear in visual or sonic media.

## Organization

Within a format of roughly chronological historical examples, this book finds patterns of intention and reception emerging through occurrences of participatory public dance. From the evangelical public ecstasy of the First Great Awakenings (ca. 1730–1745); through the creolized theatrical and festival dance of cities as diverse as New Orleans, Albany, Kingston, New York, Port-au-Prince, and Bristol; to the movement vocabularies of utopian religious like Shakers and Ghost Dancers; the meetings of race, aesthetics, late colonialism, and modernism in Jazz Age perceptions of African American dance; the Civil Rights–infused integrating popular dance of the post–World War II period; the 1960s cultural revolution's street protests and their outgrowth in the Women's and Gay Rights movements, and the hip hop nation: street dance is herein theorized as inherently social and political. Thus, cutting across and linking the chronological divisions of the case studies, we discover a series of topics, critiques, and tropes whose recurrence reveals the long history of participatory dance's social and political power. This Introduction introduces the thesis and delineates the scope of the problem. I include a summary of my argument and of its potential impact upon scholarship, a survey of relevant existing literature, and a discussion of methodological models and potential impact, introducing Borshuk's idea of "performance as resistance [and] dance as the embodiment of disruptive play."[42]

Chapter 1 explores the transgressive body vocabularies of the evangelical Great Awakening of the late eighteenth century, when "hellfire preachers" like Jonathan Edwards of Massachusetts espoused a radical democratization of religious experience. Particularly attractive to Presbyterians, and early Baptists and Methodists, and, on the frontiers, radically inclusive of women and slaves, the Awakening countenanced "noise," "enthusiasm," and censorious opposition to existing power structures. This outsider status played out in physical as well as cognitive spaces: barred from churches and other mainstream edifices, Edwards and George Whitefield preached in fields and in the streets, and the "hysteria" they elicited and learned to control became a physical manifestation of their rhetoric of apocalyptic opposition.[43] Though the most notable evangelical preaching eschewed dance, its movement tactics would be borrowed, codified, and exploited in street protests by other subaltern groups, most notably the Sons of Liberty, in the decades before the American Revolution. The expressive and transgressive power of sacred dance would be still more heightened when Presbyterian preaching met Afro-Caribbean and Native American body vocabularies in the Cumberland Plateau around 1800.[44] The Cumberland revivals are framed, at this stage in the book's argument, as a danced ritual of group cohesion, a cognitive process by which the group identity described by the anthropologist Victor Turner as *communitas* can be evoked, maintained, and exploited.[45] *Communitas* provides the means to theorize not only sacred ritual—the movement vocabularies of the Catholic Mass or of Afro-Catholic *candomblé*, for example—but also secular rituals of group identity, including dance.

Chapter 2, "A Tale of Two Cities I: Akimbo Bodies and the English Caribbean," investigates the bodily meanings and meetings of Caribbean syncretic festival, with particular emphasis upon ways that certain geographical and demographic contexts—specifically, in Jamaica, New York City, and England—served as centers of cultural migration and exchange. Music, dance, and noise, as part of theatricalized ritual, are analyzed as points of overlap in the encounter and synthesis of European and African bodily behaviors and framed as one of the most significant inspirations for blackface minstrelsy.[46] The chapter analyzes attempts to contain creolization's revolutionary impulse through theatricalized performances of Afro-Caribbean street ritual, including Jamaican *Obi* and Afro-Dutch Pinkster, and locates the creole synthesis of body vocabularies through investigation of period iconography and the career of the African American actor Ira F. Aldridge. Close analysis of iconography and biography reveals the revolutionary impact of an intentionally angular, asymmetrical, and akimbo aesthetic, and the tensions between creole/colonial body vocabularies and bourgeois body morality. We discover that the stage and the salon, no less than the street, were sites for revolutionary movement.[47]

As an intentional contrast to the balance of the chapters, which address a limited number of complex case studies in comparative depth and detail, Chapter 3, "Spaces, Whistles, Tags, and Drums: Irruptive Noise," employs a series of shorter vignettes, cutting across time periods and social contexts, to identify the "sonic akimbo": abrupt, interruptive, human-generated noises that contest the sonic norms of spaces and experiences. These include street vendors' cries, blackface minstrels' whistles, frontiersmen's whoops and hollers, street protesters' sirens and bullhorns. The chapter thus provides a parallel, in the medium of sound, to the analysis of street dance's interruptive movement impulses, and confirms the study's overall integration of music and dance examples. Though not a primary focus of this book—whose topic is the ways bodies moving in public space were intended or perceived to contest social and political hierarchies—noise nevertheless provides a useful counterpoint to some of the text's central tenets about subaltern resistance.[48] If we think of group dance, especially group dance drawing upon the "akimbo" movement vocabularies of the African Caribbean, as interruptive of Anglo-European social norms, then we may view "noise" as similarly disruptive of sonic space. More specifically, we can test the validity of seeing noise in the New World as revolutionary by looking at the history of its legislation or prohibition in either sounding or visual realms. In such historical cases, we identify "noise" (control of whose very definition was itself a product of social and political dominance—the music of subaltern communities was far more likely to be labeled as "noise" than the music of elites) as connoting interruption or resistance and frequently mapped by dominant culture onto subaltern movement vocabularies as connoting the same things.

Chapter 4, "A Tale of Two Cities II: Festival and Spectacle in the French Caribbean," looks at two more geographic loci for creolization—Port au Prince in Haiti and New Orleans in Louisiana—to uncover in their parallel urban histories the bodily cultural exchanges between Anglo-Celtic and Afro-Caribbean worlds, which are the bedrock of North American expressive culture. Of particular focus in this chapter is the temporary nature and psychological impact of "the spectacular": that is, group performance that, taking over physical and sonic landscapes, presents a defiant, highly fluid, and intentionally temporary zone of carnivalesque, topsy-turvy liminality. This chapter is particularly heavily focused upon historical and demographic primary source evidence: who danced, in which sacred and secular contexts, in Haiti and Louisiana (during a period when the two were especially closely linked by language and emigration), and what those people said and thought about the meaning of that dancing. Again in the interests of diverse expository approaches, the chapter takes a longer historical perspective, linking eighteenth- and nineteenth-century sources to contemporary twenty-first-century experiences and perceptions of street festival and dance community solidarity (Mardi Gras Indians and Carnivale *Rara* troupes) in both locations.

Though, in the history of a North American social imperative dominated by Anglo-European conceptions of body versus intellect, dance was most typically treated warily and with suspicion, certain anomalous historical moments provide examples of utopian communities, formal or informal, for which dance was a tool of social unity and revitalization. Chapter 5, "Utopian Movements and Moments: Shakers and Ghost Dancers," explores two syncretic religious sects wherein dance played a central role in community identity—and in turn elicited outsiders' disdain or castigation.[49] I identify a recurring ethos of unity, "fraternity," and group experience and a consistent set of metaphorical and kinesic tools intended to evoke this liminal group experience and then tie these to other cross-cultural examples of dance as community transformation. We also trace a hidden thread of Afro-Caribbean and Native American movement vocabularies and aesthetics (previously introduced in Chapter 2) as a generative catalyst for these nineteenth-century utopian dances.

Chapter 6, "Blackface Transformations I: Modernism, Primitivism, and Race," is the first of a pair of essays, drawing particularly upon the methodologies of iconography and film studies, which explore the impact of urbanizing and globalizing contexts and electronic media upon the meanings of African American vernacular dance. Central topics in this chapter include analysis of primitivist images of Josephine Baker and a blackface-plus-dance film sequence from the Marx Brothers to make the argument that their masking behaviors intended and were received as carrying revolutionary connotations. Primarily focusing upon pre–World War II electrical media, the chapter also provides an introduction and historical framework to understand its followup, which addresses the post–World War II world.

Chapter 7, "Blackface Transformations II: Voyeurism, Identity, and Double-Consciousness," likewise draws upon iconography, film studies, and semiotics in two more examples of electronically mediated "masking"—that is, the assumption or manipulation of the "blackface mask"—that intentionally subvert the voyeuristic white gaze. In this chapter, I investigate the richly detailed first-person descriptions of Lindy Hop in *The Autobiography of Malcolm X* (1966), reading those passages for their cultural/political subtextual argument. I follow this with an extended analysis of the blackface comedy and tap-dance sequences in Spike Lee's *Bamboozled* (2000), which intentionally juxtapose explicitly racist caricature and performative virtuosity, precisely in order to problematize the paradoxical viewer responses of discomfort and pleasure. I suggest that, in both of these examples, Malcolm X and Spike Lee—cultural commentators from within the African American community—were using dance, and specifically the rhythmic, athletic, and virtuosic dance that racism presumed resulted from blacks' "natural rhythm," in order to problematize the paradox of black creativity's virtuosity as it has flourished "behind the minstrel mask."

Chapter 8, "Body and Spirit in a Post-1960s World: Hippies, Queens, Punks, and B-boys," carries on from the previous chapter to explore the impact of the 1960s Civil Rights revolutions upon a wide range of subsequent activist groups and their public conduct: marching, singing, and dancing in political contexts, music festivals, street theater, and street protests. It employs, in contrast to previous chapters, an intentionally loose and more widely inclusive definition of "street dance"—essentially (as the chapter states) "bodies moving in concert in physical spaces"—to unpack examples from four post-1960s, politically active subaltern communities. These include: (1) dance as both festival/spectacle, and political protest, in late Sixties rock festivals and, most specifically, street protests at the 1968 Chicago Democratic National Convention; (2) dance as gender-bending political "camp" in the street protests surrounding the 1969 Stonewall Uprising, a watershed in the nascent Gay Rights movement; (3) dance and the politics of liberation in the aggressively antihegemonic world of 1980s U.S. punk rock, especially focusing upon dance protests opposing Gulf War I and led by the straightedge Washington, D.C., collective band Fugazi; and (4) the complexity of space-, place- and movement-based resistance strategies manifested in early hip hop culture, with a primary emphasis upon the South Bronx. All four of these case studies build upon methods employed, and genres explored, in previous chapters, and demonstrate the applicability of those approaches to a wider range of more diverse (and more contemporary) dance languages. Chapter 8 also finalizes the transition from historical to contemporary considerations and the summary of major insights, which will be completed in the final chapter.

Chapter 9, "Street Dance and the Dream of Freedom," links to wider considerations in historical, musical, choreographic, and political scholarship and culture. It suggests the applicability of this book's methodology to analogous analysis of movement vocabularies, and their semiotic intentions and reception, in other historical/cultural contexts. I suggest that transgressive movement has been a particularly effective tactic for subaltern communities whose speech and movement have been otherwise circumscribed by dominant elites, and that it is therefore a particularly suitable target for recovering subaltern communities' under-documented historical experience.

The book's fundamental takeaway point is that, in multiple eras of American cultural history, subaltern resistance to dominant control has literally been "embodied" through the phenomena of participatory dance. The epigram "If I can't dance, I don't want to be part of your revolution" (apocryphally attributed to Emma Goldman, but more probably coined by proto-feminist Alix Kates Shulman) is thus revealed as not just a personal statement of bodily liberation but as an acute, evocative, precise, and sophisticated political analysis—as is, itself, the very act of "dancing in the street."[50]

# CHAPTER 1

# Sacred Bodies in the Great Awakenings

This chapter explores the ecstatic experiences and transgressive body vocabularies associated with Pentecostal Protestantism, rooted in the First Great Awakening of the 1730s and manifested through public worship in the cross-cultural dance synthesis of syncretic communities on the early-nineteenth-century frontier. These examples are contextualized by a brief investigation of the role of kinesthetics and cognition in street dance and in transport experience, for both participants and observers, and the ways in which kinesthetics and cognition collapse the boundary between the two. The experiences of bodies moving in cultural landscapes are relevant here because they help us understand both the strategy and political impact of group motion in the street and also its experiential tactics and religio-psychological appeal.[1] These considerations further illuminate our understanding of the kinesthetic appeal of participation in sacred, utopian, popular, and political dance. Sachs Norris says, "Because the wish to belong is essentially human, *there is often a joy in giving oneself to the experience of worship or communal dance*."[2]

In such circumstances, as we will see in the case of the Cumberland Revival on the Kentucky frontier, movement becomes a sacred tool. Because it is both a sonic and a kinesthetic phenomenon, rhythm can be *enacted* in sounding or visual realms, by sound or by bodies in motion, in a way that melody, for example, is more constrained. Dance is, in turn, one part of the range of kinesthetic bodily responses evoked by rhythm, and its "interactional rhythms" structure both sounding music and bodily functions.[3] Thus, elements of dance theory that address cognition and psychology can help us understand the central functional role played by dance in transformational and utopian worship.

In the mid–eighteenth century, impassioned preachers like Jonathan Edwards (1703–1758), author of the prototypical and widely influential hellfire-and-brimstone sermon "Sinners in the Hands of an Angry God" (1741), and George Whitefield (1714–1770) pioneered an emotional, extravagant, and graphic style of extemporaneous speech.[4] They saw themselves not as revolutionaries but as reformers, reclaimers of a more direct and rigorous experience of sanctity that they still believed possible within the frame of Protestant theocracy, and they explicitly condemned dance.[5] In the 1740s, it was left to defiant outsiders—itinerant preachers like the notorious James Davenport (1716–1757)—to take the new style of evangelical preaching out of sanctified spaces, into the streets and meadows, and to translate its improvisational emotionalism from speech into movement and song. The visible and audible elements of the resulting physical ecstasy, as detailed by eyewitness reporters like the Reverend Joseph Fish, evoked horrified fascination:

> [Davenport] not only gave an unrestrained liberty to noise and outcry, both of distress and joy, in time of divine service, but promoted both with all his might by extending his own voice to the highest pitch, together with the most violent agitations of body, even to the distorting of his features and marring his visage: as if he had aimed, rather, at frightening people out of their senses, than, by solid argument, nervous reasoning and solemn addresses, to enlighten the mind, and perswade them as reasonable men, to make their escape unto Christ. And all this, with a strange, unnatural singing tone, which mightily tended to raise or keep up the affections of weak and undiscerning people, and consequently, to heighten the confusion among the passionate of his hearers. Which odd and ungrateful tuning of the voice, in exercises of devotion, has, from thence, been propagated down to the present day, and is become one of the characteristicks, of a false spirit, and especially of a separate; that sect being almost universally distinguished by such a tone.[6]

The "unrestrained liberty" with which a preacher like Davenport "extend[ed] his own voice" and "agitated" his body, the "distorting of his features" and "strange, unnatural singing tone" of his voice, simultaneously violated standards of religious decorum and transformed Pentecostal public address, especially in the culturally remote frontiers. Because New England was still dominated by a moneyed Anglican theocracy, there was little space or desire for Davenport's fundamental public-space challenges to social hierarchy (Edwards and Whitefield, for example, both explicitly condemned the "extremity" of his crowd-based worship), and his challenge lasted less than a year in 1743.[7] However, the radical democratization of religious experience implicit in Edwards's and Whitefield's midcentury rhetoric, and explicated in Davenport's bodily challenge (discussed later), played out much more extensively, and with much more lasting impact, upon the southern and western frontiers, in the period between the American Revolution and the War of 1812. Particularly attractive to frontier Presbyterians and to early Baptists and Methodists, and radically inclusive of women and slaves, the theology of preachers like Edwards, Whitefield, and Davenport countenanced "noise," "enthusiasm," and—in some cases—censorious opposition to existing power structures.[8] The "hysteria" the radical preachers elicited and learned to control became a physical manifestation of the rhetoric of apocalyptic opposition; their street tactics would be borrowed, codified, and exploited by the Sons of Liberty in the decades before the American Revolution.[9]

The democratized bodily experience of the Great Awakening's ecstatic public speech, song, emotional expression, and conduct; its literal invasion of public and sacred spaces and, metaphorically, of the assembled bodies (groups and individuals) themselves; and its appeal to frontier sectarian and minority populations, all connect it to later public conduct.[10] Edwards himself, though he opposed dance, specifically countenanced noise and was castigated by power elites for his "censoriousness and extemporaneous and itinerant preaching."[11] Inflammatory public speech (sermonizing) was regarded as transgressive, and, while only the most radical evangelicals engaged in ecstatic body behaviors, the very fact of large crowds moving in public spaces—especially when they left the rural countryside and entered urban streets and buildings, under the influence of renegades like Davenport—was itself a kind of danced rebellion. This rebellion reached much further, birthing the "Shaking Shakers" among others, in the first years of the nineteenth century.

It was not Edwards and Whitefield who brought syncretic body practices into Protestant religion; those hellfire preachers, with the exception of a few like Davenport, roundly condemned dance in worship as had the Anglican theocracy. Rather, an unremarked source for "physical enthusiasm" in late-eighteenth-century evangelism was a carryover from Afro-Caribbean dance and worship practices traveling westward from Virginia and Georgia, and possibly eastward from the Mississippi Basin, into the Cumberland Plateau.[12] The meeting of Afro-Caribbean and Anglo-European worship practices, which leads to the Shakers (only the best-known of the dancing congregations), is rooted in the sacramental season of frontier camp meetings, on the western watershed between the Appalachians and the Ohio's tributaries in the last part of the eighteenth century, when Ulster Scots Presbyterianism met Afro-Caribbean and Native American body religions.

Here are the factors that shaped that meeting.

## Prologue

The reforming New England preachers of the First Great Awakening, though employing literally inflammatory rhetoric to rekindle religious enthusiasm, *opposed* sacred dance and bodies-in-motion activity.[13] James Davenport provided a test case for their pushback against the liberation of movement as a religio-political strategy; the very fact that Whitefield and others condemned Davenport confirms that they sought theological reform but stopped short of bodily revolution. We may note that their fundamental objection to Davenport was not that he used rhetorical and theatrical techniques borrowed from other evangelists, but that he extended their usage far beyond Anglican zones of control and, most notably, reinjected them into urban contexts.[14] Whitefield had revolutionized dramatic preaching by speaking extemporaneously to outdoor crowds at camp meetings in the open air—but Davenport brought those same crowds back into the center of urban life in cities like New London and New Haven.

The parading, singing, preaching, and dancing "enthusiasm" of these crowds, and the Anglican theocracy's attempt to contain them, are precisely the basis for Davenport's relevance to this book. His audiences were not contained or sequestered; like the street protestors of the 1960s, discussed later, they *moved* freely, impulsively, and unpredictably through urban cityscapes. In addition, their demographics skewed young, male, and unmarried; they provide, therefore, a link to the Francophone night-visiting custom of "charivari" or "rough music," which came down the Mississippi and evolved a Deep South variant called "shivaree," and they are a prototype both in sociology and in behavior to the transgressive, "noisy" personnel and street tactics of the Sons of Liberty in the 1760s and '70s, and the audiences and behaviors associated with urban blackface from the 1820s onward.[15] When Davenport's followers in March 1743 made, at his instruction, a bonfire of books on Christopher's town wharf in New London, he prefigured the street tactics of a range of later dance revolutionaries.[16] In his relationship with the theocratic establishment, Davenport thus occupies the same (perhaps unintended or uncontrollable) oppositional "Trickster" posture as would minstrelsy's George Washington Dixon (1801?-1861), who not only performed and wrote for the blackface stage from the 1820s, but also edited various scandalous, scurrilous, and/or subversive "flash" newspapers from the 1830s.[17] In this sense, Davenport in 1740s Connecticut represents a democratizing sacred-context challenge to orthodox hierarchies that was every bit as transgressive as Dixon's 1820s secular version of the same.

## THE FRONTIER

The ecstatic body languages, which are mostly absent from the First Revival, and were castigated by Edwards and Whitefield when employed by the iconoclastic Davenport and his followers reappeared along the trans-Appalachian frontier, especially the southwest watershed of the Cumberland Plateau. These movement practices, which we will subsume under the general umbrella term of *sacred dance*, appear immediately in the wake of the Haitian Revolutions of the 1790s, when the flight of colonialists, their extended families, and their black and mixed-race households to other Francophone locations (notably New Orleans and Charleston) transformed maritime/riverine spaces all over eastern North America.[18] The admixture of Afro-Caribbean cultural influences and practices was widespread, though underreported, and directly impacts the dance practices and communal ecstasy of the Cumberland Revivals ca. 1800–1801.[19]

## KINESTHETICS AND THE COGNITIVE TRANSFORMATIONS OF ECSTASY

Group dance has cognitive and kinesthetic as well as aesthetic implications. The scholar Judith Lynne Hanna, cited already in Chapter 1, situates dance's communicative efficacy "in its capacity to fully engage the human being."[20] Scholarship like Hanna's and that of Mary M. Smyth, grounded primarily in ethnographic or anthropological methodologies, suggests that engaging with dance as either participant *or* observer literally evokes cognitive, kinesthetic, and neuromuscular responses.[21] Hence, our understanding of dance as an essential part of the sacred traditions that combined to yield the Cumberland revival—and subsequently as a central practice for the Shaker and Ghost Dance sects which each in their own way reflected the influence of the revivals—is greatly enriched when we recognize that participatory dancing yields what the swing-dance specialist Paul Jordan-Smith calls *cathexis*—a "raising of energy."[22] The Cumberland Revivalists danced the way they did as a result of both inherited and exchanged cultural perceptions—what dance "meant" and that meaning's relevance to the sacred—and of cognitive connections because it was physically pleasurable and because it forged cathexis: an emotional experience of communal connection.

## LOCALE AND CULTURE CONTACT

These body practices appear within the southwest Appalachian immigrant population of Anglo-Scottish Presbyterians, for whom the summertime festivals of "sacrament season" had been a feature of religious congregation ever since early-eighteenth-century Scotland, and were shared with the various mixed-race groups they encountered.[23] On the Kentucky frontier, Presbyterian practices met the evangelizing preaching and radically egalitarian message of salvation central to Baptist and Methodist revivalism. They also met Afro-Caribbean sacred dance, most particularly the complex of worship behaviors known collectively as the *ring-shout*—walking in a circle, singing, hand-clapping—accounts of which recur across many locations and several centuries.[24] The diversity of these communities, and the collapse of social distinction between them during frontier revivals, played out in democratized movement practices; Ellen Eslinger, describing the Cumberland revival, says this leveling "had the effect of reducing the contrast between rich and poor and creating a special, if temporary, community.[25] As with movement vocabularies, the exchange between disparate groups, and frontiers' distance from cultural elites, explain how they become sites for evolving, individualizing, improvisational, oral/aural-tradition vocal hymnody.[26] In both movement and sound, frontier experience yielded an expanding heterogeneity of regionalized approaches.

Moreover, the motives, political identities, and movement vocabularies of those who undertook the western migrations differed from those coastal elites who sponsored them. Since the seventeenth century, diverse immigrant groups had been coming over the Mountains and into the Cumberland, often bringing African American slaves with them, and contending for space with the native Shawnee, Cherokee, and Yuchi peoples. The wealthy Virginians who financed and encouraged exploration into the region of the Cumberland did so both because they sought to establish a tough Presbyterian emigrant buffer against the resident Indians and the Frenchmen adventuring eastward from the Mississippi and because they wished to ensure that the slavery that had created their colonial wealth would be continued in the new western territories. When, therefore, in 1775, Daniel Boone (1734–1820) led his first party of Scots-Irish settlers through the Cumberland Gap and into the western watershed of the southern Appalachians, he brought with him farmers, hunters, women, children, and slaves.

But the experience of black-white contact west of the mountains would be decidedly different than that found in the tobacco and rice plantations of the Tidewater. Throughout the upland South, the diversified nature of frontier homesteads meant that slaves tended to be held in lower numbers (only 1–2 to a household was not uncommon) and therefore to experience much closer day-to-day contact with their subsistence-farmer owners. It was nearly impossible, on the frontier, to source white wage laborers, who were better served to homestead for themselves (land was essentially free for the asking), and so slaves, rather than white laborers, remained essential to the region's economy and central to its culture. Many of those slaves brought essential skills, and not a few were family relations of their owners; for example, Monk Estill (ca. 1750–1835) hunted, fished, and farmed with his white father James Estill, taught Daniel Boone to make gunpowder, and fought at the Battle of Little Mountain (1782) with such conspicuous bravery that he became the first freed slave in Kentucky history.[27]

Monk Estill also played the fiddle, for listening and dancing. Though there is no record or list of the music he brought with him into Kentucky, it was likely the repertoire of dance melodies common throughout both North and South in the colonial period: English, Scottish, and occasionally French tunes, played on "German" (wooden) flute and, and especially the fiddle, by white and black musicians alike.[28] But something happened to the music of people like Monk Estill in Kentucky; something precipitated by frontier isolation and self-reliance (as occurred, for example, with frontier hymnody's divergence from "scientific" practice) but also by the communities encountered there: not only French, Creole, and Native American populations from the west, but also Atlantic immigrants who were present before Boone crossed into the Cumberland.

One early immigrant population, the so-called "mysterious" Melungeons, were inhabitants of the southern end of the South Fork of Licking River by the 1760s; e.g., they preceded the Anglo-Scots migration of ca. 1790 and were already established in close proximity to Cane Ridge, in the uplands, by the time Boone's immigrant parties arrived through the Cumberland Gap.[29] Many romantic or mythographic claims have been made for their origins, but in fact *Melungeon* in this context was simply a convenient, rather generic label for a multiracial person.[30] Some were likely descendants of free people of color or mixed-race unions, others of escaped slaves fleeing west over the mountains; more recent scholarship suggests that still others were the descendants of black and white indentured servants from seventeenth-century Virginia.[31] In the Cumberland, free and mixed-race people of color, like the "Maroons" of Jamaica or the "Black Creeks" of Florida, found that, leaving plantation zones, they could escape some of the racial strictures of the Virginia and North Carolina Tidewater.[32] Such communities are also sometimes described as *mulattos* (meaning, loosely, a person of mixed European and African ethnicity), another very imprecise term but whose very imprecision, like the romantic folklore about them, reflects the diversity of the Melungeons' creole background.

Recent—and very intriguing—scholarship suggests that the tri-racial genetic inheritance of the Melungeons may actually reach back to seventeenth-century South Carolina—that they are the descendants of Afro-Celtic *Barbadians* who had gradually been shunted aside and eventually displaced in that island's transition to a sugar economy.[33] Identified in the western counties of North Carolina and Virginia by the 1750s, and farther west across the mountains at Hancock County Kentucky by 1790, their presence on the frontier suggests that the Afro-Celtic movement synthesis in Kentucky worship significantly predates Boone's settlement of the territory itself.

We know that, on the one hand, black slaves were a significant part of the western-immigration settlement patterns; but we know, on the other, that reporting on free people of color was incomplete and misleading, both in terms of available data and the imprecise definitions attaching to terms like *mulatto*, *Melungeon*, and *Indian*. It is therefore extremely difficult to know whether some others of those early mixed-race populations in Kentucky might have come from the West, as opposed to simply preceding Boone's settlers from the East. The presence of French-speakers among the Kentucky settlers is not itself definitive: French and "Creole-French" "was also understood and used by free black and colored mariners who traveled back and forth from Virginia to the West Indies" from the 1750s, but the tributaries that flowed north from the Cumberland to meet the Ohio were also well-known to Native Americans and to French traders before the influx of Virginians, so a western cultural influence, traveling eastward from the Mississippi Valley, is not unlikely.[34] Demographic evidence therefore suggests that diverse multiethnic cultural influences could have come into the Cumberland both from the East, with very early frontier settlers, and from the West, via Spanish and "French" creoles.[35] The region's multiracial character only intensified at the end of the century.[36]

### TRANSPORT AND COMMUNICATIONS

In the antebellum period, both river and coastal travel by water were absolutely essential, not only to trade, travel, and communications but also to cultural exchange. On boats, ships, wharves, and levees, diverse transient populations came into contact. Particularly in the period immediately after the American Revolution, a vast expansion of trade and the networks of trade made river travel and canal development central both to the new nation's economies and to its consciousness. Water-borne populations and their mutation of white-black hierarchical norms were responsible for new modes of expression, especially of dance and music.[37]

In the specific case of the Cumberland Plateau, in Kentucky and Ohio, flatboats were an essential part of early riverine economics. Crudely built with simple tools and primarily designed to transport goods—timber, hides, corn, and other frontier products—from the uplands to market towns, they traveled downstream only, being broken up and sold after arrival and disbursement, with their crews making their way back upriver by other means. Early settlers from Kentucky were therefore aware of the feasibility of trading to the West "as soon as the Spanish authorities opened the Mississippi." Afro-Caribbean musical influences from the Mississippi and Ohio thus did not directly come upstream into Kentucky via the river in the pre-steamboat era (e.g., before ca. 1840); rather, upcountry flatboatmen (who, exemplified by the semi-legendary "Mike Fink," were one source and inspiration for early minstrelsy: "Old Dan Tucker" originated as an Ohio River song) encountered the Afro-Caribbean music on the river landings and brought those influences back into the hills. Thus, for the 1800–1801 Revivals and the syntheses of religious dance that occurred within them, no less than for the secular roots of minstrelsy, the Ohio River tributaries' ports were significant sites of expressive transmission, importation, and exchange.[38]

## The Roots of the Sacred and Secular Synthesis

All these factors quickened to catalyze the fervor of the nineteenth century's first wave of evangelical revival, between the years 1797–1802, among frontier populations in central Kentucky at open-air religious revivals convened by itinerant Presbyterian and Methodist preachers like James McGready, Richard McNemar,

David Rice, and Barton Stone. George Whitefield himself had preached to crowds of 20,000–30,000 in Scotland in the 1740s; his theatrical, emotional delivery was continued among frontier Protestant communities for whom conventional Anglicanism was distant in space, time, and spiritual relevance. The impact of charismatic itinerant preachers was felt all along the southern frontier, from Logan County southwest of Bowling Green, north through the Cumberland to Danville, and finally to the northward-flowing tributaries of the Ohio, the Licking, and the Big Sandy Rivers, around Lexington and Paris. While by no means inevitable, it is certainly explicable why the new syntheses of sacred Pentecostal dance might appear in the same frontier zones of cultural exchange—especially along the rivers.

We know that members of the Cane Ridge congregations were inspired and instructed by the revival experience and that they later carried that experience north of the Ohio to found the first Shaker communities, for whom dance was likewise an essential and well-known spiritual tool. Cumberland worship (and therefore music and dance repertoires) was thus a direct influence on Midwestern Shaker practices throughout most of the nineteenth century. The sect had originated as the "Shaking Quakers," an offshoot of Quakerism in northwest England during the same 1740s period that was the launchpad for the First Great Awakening and the revivalism of George Whitefield, and they had practiced "free ecstatic worship" (probably speaking in tongues, possibly movement) under the charismatic leader Mother Ann Lee (1736–1784).[39] But in the 1820s, the later "Era of Manifestations" (discussed later), the Shakers experienced a transformation of theology and dance practices fueled by "manifested" visions of deceased saints and of sanctity in the bodies and voices of the members.[40] In this period—which this chapter suggests was informed by the example of the Cane Ridge celebrants—it would be newly claimed that "heavenly spirits came to earth, bringing visions, often giving them to young Shaker women who danced, whirled, spoke in tongues, and interpreted these visions through their drawings and dancing."[41] The ubiquity and extended detail of these dream gifts (images, songs, and anecdotes) markedly increased in this era, and suggests the possible influence of visionary experience drawn from both Afro-Caribbean and Native American theologies.

The large summer religious and social festival called "sacrament season" in the Scots Presbyterian tradition had been carried to the New World and then to the Appalachian frontiers with frontier immigrants in the eighteenth century. The opportunity for ethnic/cultural/dance exchange at "sacrament season," in the South and West, parallels the demonstrable exchange that occurred at analogous interracial festivals like Pinkster and Negro 'Lection Day in the North and East: Melvin Wade says, "the[se] festivals . . . collapsed social boundaries more so than did any other social event in colonial New England, deriving their participants and spectators across lines of race, sex, class, and generation," suggesting that they yielded temporary, liminal zones, outside the realm of day-to-day social and racial boundaries, in which movement exchange was heightened and centralized.[42] Variegated gatherings in warm weather, at traditional holidays in the agricultural calendar, open to observation and participation by a very wide diversity of ethnicities and economic classes and situated at a (physical or experiential) distance from cultural and political elites, provided fertile ground for the exchange of English, French, Dutch, Haitian, Jamaican, Presbyterian, Catholic, and African American songs, tunes, dances, and experiences. The revivals were as transgressive as more secular festivals, and likewise eroded boundaries between black and white participant behaviors.[43]

Moreover, charismatic and theatricalized performance—by preachers, players, singers, and/or dancers—was influential in the sacred revivals as it would later be in the secular manifestations of blackface, and danced physicality played into both. In some cases, these semilegendary, quasi-trickster preachers actually interacted with their secular counterparts: particularly rich and engaging examples are the self-mythologizing stories of the itinerant preacher Peter Cartwright, who in one autobiographical anecdote claimed to have met and "whupped" the semilegendary riverman Mike Fink.[44] In their accounts, the efficacy and attraction of movement was made explicit: Richard McNemar, a Presbyterian who preached at Lone County and was later one of the early architects of the Ohio Shaker congregations, was "especially indicted as encouraging physical enthusiasm" and likening leaping and dancing to biblical examples of people leaping for joy.[45] McNemar himself described his 1802 congregation at Turtle Creek as "praying, shouting, jerking, barking or rolling, dreaming, prophesying and looking as through a glass at the infinite glories of Zion."[46] By the same token, some of the western preachers were markedly effective with mixed-race congregations and even particularly targeted slaves for conversion: the itinerant cleric James Blyth (born 1765 in North Carolina), for example, "grew up in a biracial, religious household, learning to read and write from a slave and hearing the word of the Lord roll off the tongues of white Presbyterian preachers as well as those of his father's slaves."[47] It is certainly plausible that the particular success experienced by preachers like Blyth among black congregations was in part the product of their greater familiarity with Afro-Caribbean religious belief and practice, derived either from early experience (in Blyth's case) or by cross-racial frontier contacts.[48] Cumberland evangelism was thus the beneficiary and the precipitant of a further blurring of racial hierarchies; this in turn facilitated cross-cultural rhetorical and bodily exchange; and the racial and political implications of such exchange were perceived as both empowering and potentially revolutionary.

## Moving in the Spirit

In terms of the actual physical vocabularies that appear to have first flowered in Kentucky, west of the Mountains after 1790, there is strong circumstantial evidence supporting the case for Afro-Presbyterian syncretisms: most telling is the widespread appearance of the frenzied ecstatic movement called "the Jerks." The reminiscences of the itinerant Presbyterian preacher Robert Stuart (1772–1856) recount both the environment, social behaviors, and interracial complexities of the camp meetings and also of the "extraordinary bodily exercises" that emerged.[49] For example, the "falling exercise," which Stuart describes, clearly anticipates the visions and "dream gifts" associated with the later Shaker Era of Manifestations:

> *The falling exercise.*—The subject of this exercise would instantly fall down, as in a swoon. . . . This exercise was called a trance, in which the individual professed to have seen things wonderful and unutterable. . . . They would also sing in what was deemed the strains of heaven.

Stuart's detailed description of the "jerks" recalls both the convulsive nature of the bodily and facial contortions in both historical and contemporary descriptions of Afro-Caribbean syncretic possession rituals and confirms that this physical exertion, whether interpreted as revealing sanctity or sin, was seen as a religious experience:

> *Jerks.*—This bodily exercise was truly wonderful beyond description. The subject of this exercise was instantly thrown, in every muscle, and nerve, and tendon, into the most convulsive state.—His head was thrown from side to side, with such rapidity that it was impossible to distinguish his visage. . . . He would change his position with the rapidity of lightning, hopping over pews and benches, if in a church, so that the beholder would readily imagine that every joint in his body would be dislocated, or that he could not escape being bruised and mangled to death. . . . It was useless in friends to attempt to hold him; and indeed so strangely were the minds of many warped by enthusiasm, that all attempts to hold him, to prevent injury, was striving against the Spirit of God; and he was therefore generally left alone, until the paroxysm was over, by exhaustion of physical strength. . . . Another fact that proved them involuntary, is, that wicked men were instantly seized with them, while guarding against them, and when seized were cursing every jerk.

Stuart describes related behavioral categories using more perfunctory etymology, although his details on the "running exercise" and the "barking exercise" are again reminiscent of the ecstatic movement and verbal behaviors of Afro-Caribbean worship.[50] Finally, although he provides only a cursory description—nothing like the lurid detail of the "jerks"—Stuart also explicitly links Cane Ridge behaviors to the ecstatic cognitive transport of dancing.[51]

The theological connotations of the jerks and related bodily expressions ("the barks," "the running dance," and so forth) were variously interpreted: some observers saw them as affliction called down upon the unfaithful.[52] Still others, among them the later Shaker sects, saw them as symbols of sanctity or of spiritual renewal.[53] In either case, the hypothesis of a movement exchange between frontier Presbyterian ritual behaviors and Afro-Caribbean practices, specifically in the Cumberland through the medium of Mississippi and Ohio River valley exchange, is indirectly supported by the parallels between the behaviors described in the historical sources, and those appearing in more recent ethnographic reports.[54]

Also relevant is the contemporaneous documentation of Haitian ritual by Médéric Louis Élie Moreau de Saint-Méry (1750–1819). A Martinique native born at Fort-Royal, trained as a lawyer, and a keen amateur scientist and political activist, Moreau published a lengthy and ethnographically detailed account of Haiti, which sought to buttress the continuation of slavery.[55] He primed the pump for subscriptions to the projected multivolume edition by issuing several short monographs, including (most importantly for our purposes), the 62-page monograph *Danse*, published at Philadelphia in 1796. The work's detail is unparalleled in the period, and its extensive descriptions of dance, drumming, Kikongo *bambula* songs, footwork, couples dancing, and other details are widely cited.[56] Moreau also includes a very lengthy description of a *Vadoux* (vodou) ceremony, one portion of whose details closely recall the Cumberland jerks described by McNemar:

> Everyone begins to make movements, in which the upper part of the body, the head and shoulders, seem to dislocate. . . . Fainting and swooning occur in some, and a kind of fury in others, but in everyone there is a nervous trembling, which they do not seem to be able to master. They spin around endlessly. . . . Others, who are no more than deprived of their senses and have merely fallen down in place, are transported, always still dancing, into an adjoining room.[57]

Analogous dances to those described in Haiti by Moreau are documented in period descriptions of New Orleans by 1808; given the surprisingly wide spread of Haitian cultural influence on Atlantic and Caribbean ports in the years after Toussaint's revolution, it is likely that these behaviors might have arrived into New Orleans and spread northward and eastward through the Mississippi and Ohio Valleys, in the first decades of the nineteenth century.[58]

Both historical and ethnographic descriptions of Afro-Creole Haitian sacred dance thus speak directly to: first, the ecstatic public theatricality of the First Great Awakening's preaching—that is, the degree to which it sought a kind of hypnotic response—and, second, to the "merging of the satisfying and the sacred" in dance and its "further implications for those who . . . sought a direct social relationship with their gods."[59] We recognize close experiential as well as situational and sonic parallels between Afro-Caribbean (Haitian and Barbadian) and Scots-Irish ecstatic practices; history, ethnography, and anthropology thus reinforce the circumstantial evidence.[60] Ecstatic dance practices in all these interlinked subaltern frontier traditions carried subversive and transgressive connotations.[61] Especially in the African American tradition, and traditions touched by them (like the Cumberland Revivals), communitas through movement served as an indirect mode of "symbolic action" by a subaltern community.[62]

The linkage between the communitas found in Afro-Caribbean worship, the Cane Ridge synthesis and the Shakers' later codification of sacred dance, and these rituals' connection to other creolized festival and carnivalesque behaviors, are further confirmed by a particularly striking linguistic parallel in period descriptions. Since the late Middle Ages, the English language word *merry* had connoted not only "joyful" or "brisk"—the more modern locutions—but also implications of festive or transgressive (often sexual) behaviors.[63] From the *New-York Weekly Journal*'s account of the upstate New York Pinkster festival, on March 7, 1736, for example, we find festival, noise, "making merry," and the banjo all symbolically linked:

> This morning I heard my Landlord's black Fellow very busy at tuning of his Banger, as he call'd it, and playing some of his Tunes; I . . . asked what the Meaning was of his being so merry? He . . . answered, Massa, to day Holiday; Backerah no work; Ningar no work; . . . go yonder, you see Ningar play Banger for true, dance too.[64]

While the word "merry" recurs analogously, in a sacred context, in the Cane Ridge era:

> At the spring sacrament at Turtle-Creek in 1804, br. Thompson had been constrained just at the close of the meeting to go to dancing, and for an hour or more to dance in a regular manner rownd the stand, all the while repeating in a low tone of voice—"This is the Holy Ghost—Glory!" But it was not till the ensuing fall or beginning of the winter, that the Schismatics began to encourage one another to praise God in the dance and unite in that exercise; just believing that it was their privilege to rejoice before the Lord, and go forth in the dances of them that make merry.[65]

The religious suitability of dancing, singing, and "making merry" are topics of hot debate throughout the era of the Awakenings; McNemar's quotation regarding movement's meaning, sanctity, and "merry" connotations conveys its centrality to theological debates, and to experience, on the frontiers:

> Next to the new and old doctrine of the cross, the hue-and-cry was raised against the new and old manner of worship. "What! go forth in the dance? Go voluntarily without being jerked? And say they are praising God in the dance! The dances too of them that make merry—of them that serve the devil! Take their dances to serve God! Christians, read your Bibles, and you will see that these fellows are not of God, for they keep not the Sabbath."—"Think" (says brother Stone, in this letter of

> July) "Think seriously and soberly of the shocking conduct of your revelling mock-worship, and tremble." [reply] "Don't you hear that it is MUSIC and DANCING? And is not the Father entreating you to come in? Then—
>
> Brother cast your anger off,
> And every passion bury;
> Come in and share the fatted calf,
> And let us all be merry."[66]

Throughout western hemisphere zones of Afro-Caribbean and Anglo-Celtic/North European cultural contact in festival environments, and reaching a particular moment quickened in the polyglot festivals of ca. 1800 Kentucky religious revivals, a creolized synthesis of sound, movement, practice, belief, and communal experience arose, whose meanings were precisely and uniquely a product of this collision and exchange, an "authentically new thing under the sun."

## Aftermath

That creole synthesis would later shape more well-known utopian dance idioms. Though the period of Cumberland frontier revival was relatively brief (ca. 1790–1805), its influence was both widespread and long-lasting. As slavery took more substantial hold and its supporters predominated in Kentucky, religiously motivated abolitionists, including the early Shakers, pioneered north and west. Shaker societies were thus founded between 1800–1810 by alumni of the Cane Ridge revivals in western Kentucky, southern Indiana, and the free territory of Ohio.[67] By the birth of Daniel Decatur Emmett in Mount Vernon (northeast of Columbus) in 1815, Ohio was an integrating zone.[68] In the same decade, the teenaged George Washington Dixon (born Richmond, Virginia, probably in 1801) and Thomas Dartmouth Rice (born 1808 on Manhattan's Lower East Side) were touring actors with frontier companies, traveling on the riverine thoroughfares of the Ohio, the Mississippi, and their tributaries—during which travels they both appear to have encountered the creole music-and-dance frontier idioms that, by the late 1820s, had been theatricalized in the onstage persona of the blackface minstrel. Meantime, the Ohio River ports of Lexington, Covington, and Cincinnati (for example) continued to evolve their own waterfront musical syntheses, driven by the meeting of river-borne Afro-Caribbean and Appalachian mountain Anglo-Celtic styles, embodied in the music, songs, and personae of the flatboatmen and keelboatmen who delivered upcountry goods from the tributaries of the Licking and the Big Sandy north to the Ohio and then south and west to the Mississippi, and brought additional elements of Afro-Caribbean river music back upstream with them into the foothills.[69]

And the influence of the "sacred creole" synthesis of Logan County and the Cane Ridge revivals spread further—westward onto the continually expanding frontier. The First African Baptist Church of Lexington was founded around 1790 by Peter Durrett (1733–1824), a Baptist preacher and slave who had participated in the very early settlement of the Cumberland (he was known in the community as "Old Captain" for precisely this leadership); his church welcomed both slave and free congregants. The Cumberland's sacred creole practice even echoed outward and southward to the Caribbean: Samantha Futrell describes the career of the slave George Liele (born 1751), who converted in 1774 in Burke County, Georgia; saved for and purchased his own freedom; and departed to Jamaica as an evangelist in 1782—and there are many other examples.[70]

In sum: on the southern and western frontiers, far beyond the reach of East Coast theological and intellectual elites, in the context of large, outdoor, multiracial festival celebrations, a "creole synthesis" took hold in the realm of ecstatic religion and sacred music-and-dance, roughly contemporaneous with the secular variant that was later captured on the blackface stage.

# CHAPTER 2

# A Tale of Two Cities I

## Akimbo Bodies and the English Caribbean

All dance is situated in a cultural context.
—Karen E. Bond and Susan W. Stinson,
"I Feel like I'm Going to Take off!" (2001)

### Introduction

Between the Revolution and the Civil War, the Louisiana Purchase (1803) nearly doubled the nation's territory; the development of navigable waterways, culminating with the opening of the Erie Canal in 1826, accelerated economic activity and westward expansion; urbanization drove economic rifts (exemplified by the Missouri Compromise of 1820) between agrarian, slaveholding South and industrializing, free-market North; and the extension of the franchise to working-class whites, nearly complete by 1840, transformed the political landscape. New cross-cultural popular arts idioms both reflected and furthered these transformations.[1]

The contemporaneous enclosure of formerly public zones was a direct response to shifting social hierarchies and class distinctions, as modernizing trade, communications, and geopolitics transformed the demographics of the sailors, pilots, masters, and harbor workers who worked the windjammers and steamers, which in turn transported global consciousness. Such populations exhibited much greater diversity of ethnicity and experience than did land-bound society. On decks and docks, black slave or free pilots and captains commanded white or mixed-race crews, as deckhands and officers exchanged songs, tunes, dances, stories, handcrafts, and a wide array of expressive culture. In time, these more egalitarian maritime perspectives came ashore to influence and mutate social conduct in port and river cities.[2]

Dale Cockrell's seminal blackface study, *Demons of Disorder*, begins with working-class street dance in precisely these sorts of liminal zones. An 1842 account from the "flash paper" *The Libertine* describes a gladiatorial contest between two prostitutes, Nance Holmes and Suse Bryant, on Boston's Long Wharf: an event which Cockrell unpacks as iconic of antebellum street culture's challenge to existing power, class, and economics.[3] Public music and noise, its close cousin, have often elicited contested, gendered, or sexualized associations, particularly when in the hands of marginalized social groups: we may think of the charivari of medieval weddings and "shivaree" of the American South; the masked and costumed irruptions of Carnivale; the gongs and firecrackers of China's Tai-ping Rebellion; even the Vuvuzelas of twenty-first-century sporting events; in each case, "noise" becomes a tool for simultaneously creating subaltern group cohesion and contesting economic or political regulation. If we therefore understand "akimbo" motion and "rough music" as representing related, indeed often simultaneous, subaltern defiance, it becomes possible to see public dance, especially street dance in groups, as likewise a tool of resistance and change.

Cockrell and others have suggested that the roots of later twentieth-century African American idioms like ragtime and early jazz may in fact lie in the hidden economy of sex workers and the musicians who plied their trade in the nineteenth-century sexual marketplace, finding evidence to suggest the presence of thousands of brothels in towns both large and small across the young Republic, while my own research has suggested that white social and sexual adventurers had been part of that world of expressive environments since the Revolution.[4] Cockrell shows that the shuttering of red-light districts at the end of the nineteenth century closed thousands of full-time musicians out of familiar venues, sending them in search of new ones, and that this shift in turn provided the impetus for an explosion of musical visibility and creativity.[5]

Thus, in order to more completely understand the fervent initial response to theatrical minstrelsy, and the reasons for its portability, popularity, and resiliency, we need to situate the idiom within wider and earlier networks of stage and street genres. Theatrical predecessors will be discussed ahead; as for street festival behaviors implicating music and dance, while the annual festival of Carnivale (Brazil) / *Kanaval* (Haiti) / Mardi Gras (New Orleans) was best-known in the Spanish and French Caribbean, two other examples from English-speaking communities even more effectively enrich our understanding of the transition to the stage. These include the eighteenth-century Afro-Dutch spring festival of Pinkster, which originates in the German holiday of *Pfingster* or Pentecost. This festival was found across the Northeast in the early eighteenth century and is particularly well documented in New Jersey and upstate New York.[6] Dancing, athletics, music, food, alcohol, and other festival behaviors evidently exerted a powerful attraction for white onlookers and participants; from Boston in the 1760s, for example, Shane White quotes a doggerel report of whites and blacks mingling during Pinkster celebrations: "There all day long they sit & drink / Swear, sing, play paupau, dance and stink."[7] Similar festive behaviors, including music, dance, drink, feasting, and the crowning of a mock king, "Carolanus Rex," likewise appear in various newspaper accounts and in a pamphlet entitled *A Pinkster Ode*, an iconic account from Albany.[8] Quoting from another report, from around 1803, White notes the horrified fascination experienced by white observers of the festival's piebald interactions:

> "Blacks and a certain class of whites" formed "a motley group of thousands" and presented "to the eye of the moral observer, a kind of chaos of sin and folly, of misery and fun." Later, [the reporter] took a walk across Pinkster Hill to see the results of the dissipations of "depraved nature": "Here lies a beastly black and here lies a beastly white," he lamented, "sleeping or wallowing in the mud or dirt."[9]

Leaving aside the reporter's distaste for low behaviors, this detailed description confirms that voyeuristic fascination with syncretic North American public festivals began very early in the new Republic: by around 1803, in fact, a version of Pinkster was being presented in New York City theaters.[10] Similarly, the popular stage "extravaganza," *The True History of Tom and Jerry, Or, The Day and Night Scenes of Life in London*, which in British productions featured a "Descent into the East End," was modified in North American productions to feature replications of visits to syncretic festivals and urban slums.[11]

A parallel to Pinkster, also in the North, was the eighteenth-century "Negro 'Lection Day," celebrated in New England from the 1740s, as a parodic imitation of the (very loosely organized) elections for colonial governments.[12] Many similar festive events in the early Colonies and the Republic—militia muster days, seasonal holidays, and political campaigns—provided opportunity for boundary-crossing social behavior and the construction of temporarily liminal spaces. There were analogous events in the South, which demonstrate even more clearly the Caribbean origins of creolization in the early Republic: for example, the Afro-English midwinter festival of John Canoe (Junkanoo, John Koonah, or John Kooner), is found scattered throughout the Caribbean, southwest Atlantic, and northeast coastal South America.[13] John Canoe, which had roots in Yoruba masquerade, synthesized the costuming, masking, and "rough music" associated with North European night-visiting traditions like mumming and wassailing with West African festival traditions.[14] Such festivals represented syncretic events, participation in whose irruption in dance, music, masking, and social inversion temporarily subverted social controls over public spaces. Like Pinkster, it was eventually appropriated for the stage, as we will see in discussing *Obi, or Three-Finger'd Jack*, ahead.

Throughout the history of creole festivals, and of their theatrical transformation, tension has existed between the embodiment of working-class street consciousness versus elites' desire to control that irruption. Festival behaviors appeared as working-class resistance to official dicta in many historical contexts. The period reports cited earlier, and more recent examples—from the nineteenth-century confinement to Place Congo of masking and dance behaviors previously distributed throughout New Orleans, the addition of temporary bleachers and, eventually, a "Samba-drome" to Rio's downtown to channel twentieth-century Carnivale paraders, to the iron bands of Trinidad Carnival and the tamboo percussion of Haiti, to the bucket drums and plastic trumpets at various cities' bicycle-borne Critical Mass protests, to tin-can bands in Spain in 2009—all represent political elites' pragmatic desire to channel or contain subversive street behavior if it cannot be completely eradicated.[15]

Moreover, street festival originated in the Creole Atlantic and Caribbean was subversive not only because of the social or physical violence which it was feared might be committed by the masked proletariat, but also because the same behaviors engaged the white gaze and subverted bourgeois morality. The attendance of white "mechanics" at back-house brothels and concert saloons and at Manhattan's African Grove and Bowery Theaters, their subscription to "flash" papers like *The Flash* and *The Libertine*, and their blacked-up imitation of creole music and dance behaviors all testify to working-class participatory impulses as well as middle-class voyeurism. It was one thing for bourgeois reformers to tour and gawk in the Five Points or Natchez-Under-the-Hill, in company with the new corps of municipal policemen or the moralizers of religious rectitude, or even for middle-class men to secretly patronize mix-race establishments: but it was quite another for those working-class young men, seeking sex, alcohol, and music, having observed and learned these dance behaviors, to in turn imitate them in the public forum of the street. Hence, the replication of festivals—Pinkster, Jonkonnu, and so forth—in working-class and blackface theaters was a translation and ultimately a transformation of the street's irruptive energy. The "rough music" (percussion, brass, found instruments, revival song, or whistling) and "rough dance" of the street were central components of political rallies, street performance, and working-class theatrics, and of what I have termed elsewhere "the creole synthesis."[16] Dance, by virtue of its embodied interactions, was a central avenue for cross-cultural exchange.[17] To move, in a street festival or on a working-class stage, in an "akimbo" fashion—that is, to dance with bent arms or twisted torso, and thus to "cut" and syncopate musical rhythm—was to be seen, intentionally or unintentionally, as rebellious, defiant, and "Other."

These coded cultural and racial kinesthetics can be recognized; it is also possible to identify creolized movement vocabularies in nineteenth-century dance iconography, even if it is sometimes a hidden language. When, in William Sidney Mount's *Dancing on the Barn Floor* (1831), for example, we find one dancer's torso upright, the head erect, and the shoulders in line with the hips and the pelvis level, we are seeing the physical connotations of Anglo-European body aesthetics. In contrast, when we see another dancer's spine bent, the head canted forward or backward, or the shoulders twisted out of line from the hips and the pelvis tilted, we are seeing, equally clearly, Afro Caribbean body aesthetics.[18] Thus, even in iconography whose surface depicts idealized Anglo-European experience, hidden markers of Caribbean bodily vocabulary indicate the presence, breadth, subtlety, and ubiquity of the Creole synthesis.

Analogous evidence is identifiable in street dialects re-created in travelers' tales and comic theater. Of course, ethnic parody had been part of stage comedy for centuries and was a staple of the eighteenth-century ballad operas epitomized by the smash hit *Beggar's Opera* (Gay/Pepusch, 1728). However, the adaptation of shows like the *Beggar's Opera*, and of related works like *Tom and Jerry* (cited earlier), and their host of Yankee imitations, reflect the influence of the creole synthesis in New World contexts. Here, for example, is a moment of dialect from *The Saw-Mill or, A Yankee Trick* (Chatham Garden Theatre, New York, 1824), authored by W. S. Mount's musical uncle Micah Hawkins (1777–1825), a New York tavern- and shopkeeper. Aspects of creole vocabulary lie hidden within this dialog in the same way that the creole synthesis lies "hidden" within the bodies in *Dancing on the Barn Floor*:

> "Odrot [O drat] de Grand Conol [Canal], for all me. . . . Weze [Louise] Clark, I wont trape [traipse] one step furder wid you—Wont . . . I was'nt never any ting else but A weak, tick-headed, ignorant, dumb Dutch woman."[19]

Despite the fact that we moderns might read this quotation as gross caricature of African American dialect (a problem with contemporary historiography of several other works, most notably in Andrew Barton's *The Disappointment, or the Force of Credulity*, from 1767), the character speaking, the comic servant "Norchee," is explicitly identified as Dutch.[20] Despite appearances—and the presumptions of some earlier scholarship—Hawkins is sincerely seeking to capture (even if in parody) the *actual sound* of Manhattan working-class speech in the 1820s, as his painter nephew William Sidney Mount sought to do with the *actual body vocabularies* of the creole synthesis a decade later.

Theatrical representations of costume, like body vocabulary or dialect, signaled syncretic identity and ethnicity: Mount's itinerant musicians are depicted with slouch hats and ragged greatcoats, while two "tricksters" in Hawkins's *The Saw-Mill* disguise themselves as "Yankee" apprentices with "their hair being cued with eel-skins, &c. &c. [and] having in their hands broad-axes, addices, chisels, various mechanical implements, besides each one a handkerchief of wearing apparel." There were Dutch monoglot speakers on Long Island, Irish speakers in Manhattan, French and Haitian creole speakers in Charleston and New Orleans.

All these diverse (and diversely represented) verbal and physical vocabularies reflect the polyglot cultural exchanges in the young Republic.[21]

Movement was particularly rich, particularly indicative, and particularly fluid. Creolized bodies provided visible iconographic markers of boundary-crossing racial and sexual experience. Unmarried young men and the occasional woman learned body vocabularies by dancing in creolizing situations. If the young white single man, the "mechanic" or apprentice or colonial planter's son, moved in creolized ways, then when he brought those body vocabularies into contexts like the formal ball or the theatrical stage, that movement's kinesthetic specifics carried transgressive and revolutionary connotations. To dance in creolized fashion was, intentionally or unintentionally, to resist the growing dominance of middle-class values and movement aesthetics, and as Cockrell has suggested, to literally embody a boundary-crossing underground culture.[22]

Of course, integration of body vocabularies predated blackface and the nineteenth century altogether, occurs historically wherever contrasting movement aesthetics meet, and was widely distributed throughout the creolizing Caribbean.[23] And movement vocabularies were not only manifested, but also read, as definitive, on stage, in images, and in social contexts of class and race.[24] European body aesthetics prioritized a very different physical language than did Afro-Caribbean: we may cite the idealized dance manuals of Louis XIV's court, the hyperextension of line and curve in James Gillray's parody of *La valse* (1810) or William Sidney Mount's *Rustic Dance after a Sleigh Ride* (1830), and the exaggerated idealization of line and flow in George Cruikshank's caricatures on dance lessons (1835).

In the creole world—in contrast to European dance aesthetics—bent, twisted, "sprung" postures, whether static in two-dimensional frozen moments, or active in three-dimensional motions, were experienced as strong, energized, vital, and "alive."[25] For purposes of scholarship, the first step in tracing these vocabularies is simply to begin learning to see them. Analysis of visual data in light of these considerations makes it possible for us to observe the syncretization of Anglo-European and Afro-Caribbean kinesthetic experience in the depiction of individual bodies.

For that matter, we can locate the comic and irruptive connotations of creolizing body vocabularies in descriptions from period literature as well: two examples from the archetypal Yankee storyteller, Washington Irving, will suffice. The first comes from his 1820 epistolary novel *Salmagundi*, in which a character recalls a visit to the postrevolutionary court of Jean-Jacques Dessalines in Haiti, the social behaviors he saw there, and their parallels to Northeastern U.S. movement vocabularies:

> "A very pretty gentleman, truly," cried Wizard, "he reminds me of a contemporary beau at Hayti. You must know that the magnanimous Dessalines gave a great ball

> to his court one fine sultry summer's evening; Dessy and me were great cronies;—hand and glove:—one of the most condescending great men I ever knew. Such a display of black and yellow beauties! such a show of Madras handkerchiefs, red beads, cock's-tails and peacock's feathers!—it was, as here, who should wear the highest top-knot, drag the longest tails, or exhibit the greatest variety of combs, colours and gewgaws. In the middle of the rout, when all was buzz, slip-slop, clack and perfume, who should enter but TUCKY SQUASH. . . . He could whistle like a north-wester; play on a three-stringed fiddle like Apollo; and as to dancing, no Long-Island negro could shuffle you "double-trouble," or "hoe corn and dig potatoes" more scientifically.[26]

A second period description of syncretic movement vocabularies—and their mapping as indicative of class and race—comes from Irving's iconic short story, "The Legend of Sleepy Hollow" (1820), which is set (contemporaneously with the efflorescence of Pinkster) in 1790 in the Dutch settlements of upstate New York. In the context of sketching his comic and unsophisticated "foreign" (e.g., Yankee) schoolteacher, Irving uses akimbo dance vocabularies to link Ichabod Crane to black and creole communities and body conduct:

> Ichabod prided himself upon his dancing as much as upon his vocal powers. Not a limb, not a fibre about him was ideal; and to have seen his loosely hung frame in full motion, and clattering about the room, you would have thought St. Vitus himself, that blessed patron of the dance, was figuring before you in person. He was the admiration of all the negroes; who, having gathered, of all ages and sizes, from the farm and the neighborhood, stood forming a pyramid of shining black faces at every door and window, gazing with delight at the scene, rolling their white eyeballs, and showing grinning rows of ivory from ear to ear.[27]

Africa Diasporic akimbo aesthetics were perceived as revolutionary. Indeed, the simple act of bending the knee, twisting the spine, or tipping the pelvis was a transgressive and transracial signal. Movement became an embodiment of resistance, as the Brazilian theologian Cláudio Carvalhaes puts it:

> The knee bent was a certainty that final death was not close by, and that even the rigidity of the social system demonstrated through exploitation, violence and death could not hold back the aliveness of those bending knees. Moreover, these bending joints, these fighting knees that, along with the movements of hands, arms, hips, torso, head, and foot, would bring about changes in culture and would write and change history.[28]

We can see these akimbo vocabularies, in the very act of "chang[ing] culture" and rewriting history, in a period illustration from Jamaica, *A Grand Jamaica Ball!* by Abraham James.

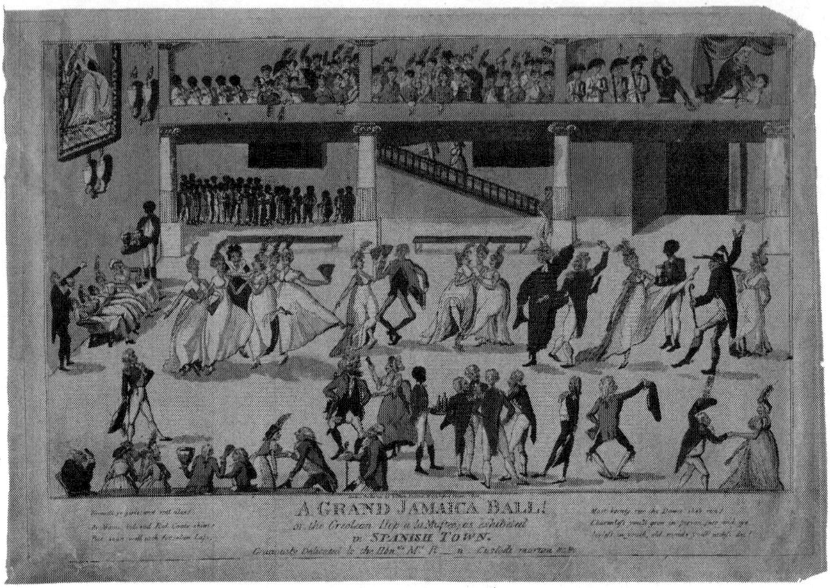


**Figure 1:** *A Grand Jamaica ball! or the Creolean hop a la muftee; as exhibeted [*sic*] in Spanish Town*, attributed to Abraham James (d. 1844).

## Spanish Town, Jamaica

The painting, labeled *A Grand Jamaica Ball! or the Creolean hop a la muftee; as Exhibeted [sic] in Spanish Town* is attributed to Abraham James (d. 1844), a solder in the 67th South Hampshire Regiment of Foot, who was transferred from Saint Domingue to Jamaica in 1798. Roger N. Buckley, whose 1984 article provides most of the biographical information, interprets James's ink-and-watercolor images as cutting Regency satire in the tradition of Thomas Rowlandson (1756–1827) and James Gillray (1756/1757–1815).[29] While we can recognize the parodic intent in his savage caricatures of Jamaica's "white plantocracy" and "the looseness displayed at public social functions," we should also consider the potential of James's images to provide actual interpretable historical-ethnographic data.[30] Like William Sidney Mount—a more sophisticated and technically skillful artist, but one analogously positioned to observe the creole synthesis of black and white body vocabularies—James was present, and sought to depict, if in heightened, parodic form, what he saw. In this light, and as with Mount's *Dancing on the Barn Floor*, the bodies captured in *A Grand Jamaica Ball* reveal hidden codes.[31]

Figure 1 depicts a dance in a colonial salon circa 1802. In terms of ethnicity (traced in facial features and skin tone), clothing, and most especially body vocabularies, it is clear that James observed a creolizing population. Not only the diversity of body vocabularies but also the subtitle and inscriptions nod to the morally ambiguous implications and locations of such conduct (Spanish Town was the nineteenth-century capital and colonial entrepôt of Jamaica):[32]

> A GRAND JAMAICA BALL!
> or, the Creolean hop a la muftee;
> as exhibeted
> in SPANISH TOWN.
> *Graciously Dedicated to the Honble Mre R___n Custonid marum &c &c.*
> *Farewell ye girls! and still alas!*
> *As Mama bids sad Red Coats shift!*
> *But soon will each forsaken Lass,*
>
> *Most keenly rue the Dance she's run!*
> *Charmless you'll grow in person, face and eye,*
> Joyless in youth, old maids you'll useless die!

The drawing, in ink and watercolor, provides a wealth of detail, but for our purposes, James's eye for movement is most relevant. Examination of even a few examples will serve to confirm the acuity of his observation, the literal mixture of Anglo-European and African American vocabularies, the social and racial connotations of those visual elements, and the presence of the creole synthesis. The full gamut of skin colors, not to mention costumes and body languages, confirm that this is a multiethnic situation. We have dark-skinned servants and musicians: the black fiddlers in the upper-left of the loft, the adult and youthful house servants to the left below the loft, the dapper waiters in short scarlet jackets and white breeches carrying trays generously laden with drink, and most notably the black cymbals player with the military wind-band in the upper right of the loft—black drummers and fifers were part of colonial armies all over the hemisphere, being prized above white players and often recruited from Haiti or Barbados into the various military services.[33]

We have swarthy mixed-race or deeply tanned Caucasian individuals (distinction between which is, in some cases, clarified by looking for the presence or absence of "creolized" body vocabularies): the gentleman dancing with a lady in the upper center of the floor, in Jim Crow style, bent-knees akimbo, in grey breeches and loose brown coat, both holding fans; the white-powdered, heavily bearded gent in the lower left of the dance floor, whose grey jacket and yellow breeches echo his partner's yellow blouse and full grey skirt; the gentleman greeting a lady at the bottom left margin, while his white-haired swarthy companion—possibly a manservant—holds his cane.

We have individuals whose costume, skin tone, and body vocabularies exemplify the Anglo European body aesthetic: the trio of elegant young officers, in red coats and white breeches, greeting a navy officer in blue, behind whom another, younger officer waits, baring his head and "making a chest," to be introduced; the red-faced senior officer, in the upper center of the dance floor, possibly drunk, whose hyper-extended arms and legs appear to be imitating the cluster of five girls, chaperoned by a wizened lady in black, in the center left. This body language, possibly reflecting partnered social dance in the process of learning, is in turn mirrored, just to the right, by the pairing of another pink-bonneted girl, daringly revealing her calf as she dances, with an elderly civilian, in tailcoat and spurred top boots, wearing a slouch hat (indoors—a social faux pas).

Perhaps most interesting are those individuals the details of whose costume, features, or complexions are *contradicted* by their body vocabularies—in other words, whose implied ethnicity appears to contrast their movement behaviors—and the impolite or even licentious connotations of those vocabularies. These would include the unpartnered young ladies slouched gracelessly—one clutching a bottle—on a bench against the left wall; the trio of young ladies, possibly sisters, dancing together and showing scandalous ankles or even calves; other young ladies, dancing alone or with akimbo partners, the drapery of whose garments reveals legs, torsos, and buttocks; finally, most explicitly (and, in terms of James's editorial intent as a serving officer, most subversively), the portly senior army officer, with white powder and gold epaulettes, assaulting a bare-breasted young woman in the right side of the loft behind curtains and under cover of the wind-band's noise.

In keeping with early-nineteenth-century caricaturists like Gillray or Hogarth, every aspect of appearance, conduct, and ethnicity is treated as fair game. And it *is* an amusing image, evocative of a whole range of comical behaviors, pretenses, and imagined social interactions, even in light of our contemporary ethic of gentler, less savage parody. But *A Grand Jamaica Ball!* is also a useful historical and thus musicological document, because it permits us, through the colliding body vocabularies depicted, to begin to recover sound and movement experience as well. The "gentleman dancing in Jim Crow style, bent-knees akimbo, in grey breeches and loose brown coat" is deeply tanned or perhaps swarthy-skinned; with the right eyes, we can see his "akimbo" body posture as indicating a creolized body vocabulary—because that is precisely what the Jim Crow bent-kneed posture was stereotyped to represent. Despite the fact that he frowns with self-regard, James clearly depicts him as a colonial, who regardless of genetic ancestry or social aspiration *moves* like a creole person.

That James (per Buckley) might disapprove such creolization, and seek to mock it with Gillray-esque savagery, should not lead us to presume his observation is therefore inaccurate. On the contrary, the likelihood is that James's visual parody is rooted in (if an exaggeration of) body behaviors he actually witnessed. Numerous elements in the image—the polyrhythms Afro Caribbean fiddlers brought to European quadrilles and cotillions (which would lead eventually to the syncretic Caribbean dances of *kwadri* and *contradanz*) and to European wind-band pieces, the polyrhythmic motion visible in akimbo bodies, and the spectrum of ethnicities and kinesthetic vocabularies—capture the cultural exchange that the creole synthesis literally embodied. When the sons of Charleston or Bristol merchants went out to Caribbean sugar plantations, when the daughters of colonial planters danced to the creolized rhythms of slave fiddlers; when those sons and daughters made their debuts, married, or inherited with their offspring in England or America—they all carried creolized accents, cuisines, bacteria, and body vocabularies with them.[34]

The liminal public "arenas" of creolized dance zones thus held the possibility of transformation precisely because what happened within them was non-normative and ultimately uncontrollable. Rituals of transformation are contextual, experimental, and admit the possibility of both failure and error.[35] The staging of rituals like *Obi* or Pinkster for colonial theatrical consumption foregrounded the rolling, cutting-and-breaking, "akimbo" languages of creole expression, and through this music and dancing, generations of blacks, whites, and creoles, and later subaltern communities (slaves, immigrants, mechanics and apprentices, women, gays and lesbians) theatricalized the movement possibilities of transformation.[36]

We can locate the irruptive conduct and transgressive connotation in other historical examples and situate both in the wider collision between Afro Caribbean and Anglo European bodily aesthetics. In the nineteenth century, an expanding American middle class sought to claim and regulate public conduct while working-class "performative strategies" contested public spaces.[37]

As part of a long chronology of resistant movement that often centered within North America's creole cultures, akimbo dance, the visual and bodily realization of participatory discrepancy, disrupted the visual and behavioral symmetry of middle-class values. Theatrical minstrelsy's quick and extensive popularity in the young United States during the 1820s represented a response by the mechanics, apprentices, and other working-class young men who were its first audiences, to seeing music and dance forms they knew from the street, the concert saloon, and the colonial salon, newly legitimized on the theatrical stage. The "minstrel mask," to use Maher's locution, permitted coded expression of white working-class identity and resentment, directed both downward toward a growing free black population increasingly competing for jobs, and upward at a growing white middle-class which increasingly sought to constrain transgressive working-class behavior and interracial contexts.[38]

This polyvalent symbolism accounts for the tumultuous response to Tom Rice's and George Dixon's first solo turns on the stages of the Lower East Side's Bowery and Chatham Theatres in the 1830s and the immediate and immense popularity of Dan Emmett's Virginia Minstrels, formed in the winter of 1842–1843. The latter were the first widely recognized troupe of blackface musicians to offer a full evening's entertainment, driven by the iconic instrumentation of banjo, fiddle, tambourine, and bones. The idiom became a cornerstone of music publishing and promotions as well as performance and provided the inspiration for vaudeville, tap dance, and much American slapstick comedy; America's first successful pop songwriter, Stephen Foster, drew heavily upon blackface styles for his compositions and upon minstrel troupes (Christy's principle among them) for promotion. The Virginia Minstrels toured the U.K. in 1844 and were nearly as popular as they had been at home; in their wake, homegrown blackface troupes and banjo-strumming soloists sprang up in imitation, and minstrelsy is widely credited with providing the first introduction of the five-string banjo in English and Irish traditional musics as well.

However, documentation on the lives, music, and careers of blackface minstrels decreases in inverse proportion to historical proximity: the earlier the documented players or performers, the sparser the available information—particularly as regards their original performance sources. Dance music, dancing, song, and comic improvisation in the pre–blackface era are least documented of all, so the evidence for their existence and inspiration must be sought in other places than the theatrical prints.

## Bristol, England

When minstrelsy first came to Britain with the touring troupes of the '40s, it connoted an even stronger whiff of black exotica, though one that was familiar in the English theatrical tradition at least since Shakespeare's day. The colonial trades in indentured servants (in the seventeenth and eighteenth centuries), sugar (eighteenth and nineteenth), and slaves (also eighteenth and nineteenth) had made commercial cities like Bristol, and then Liverpool, key zones for cross-cultural contact and expressive performance. Though the commerce was dominated by British merchant houses, the *crews* of vessels employed in the various Triangle Trades (Britain to West Africa, West Africa to the British Caribbean, the British Caribbean to New England, and then back to Britain) were, as in the southwest Atlantic, demonstrably multiethnic sites for cultural exchange.[39] As a result, cities with large transient, maritime, and working-class populations, including not only New York and New Orleans, Spanish Town (Jamaica) and Bridgetown (Barbados), Liverpool and Bristol, but also London, Glasgow, Dublin, and Belfast, were centers of trans-Atlantic blackface performance.

Creole culture, carried by water, was created by populations who exchanged expressive experiences. Land-bound rules governing race and class simply don't fully explain what went on in maritime and riverine zones.[40] Cycles of immigration or exchange and the impact of New World creole influence were especially visible in cities involved in the Caribbean trades of sugar, tobacco, and slaves. Like the Spanish Town of *A Grand Jamaica Ball*, the maritime trading city of Bristol, in the southwest of England, reveals the symbiotic relationship between nineteenth-century European and Caribbean cultures.

Thus, to explain the significance of the English story of the New York–born African American actor Ira F. Aldridge, it is necessary to understand something of Bristol's role in the Atlantic trade. While the latter lost economic power to Liverpool, whose wealth arose from her essential role in the "Middle Passage" that brought slaves from West Africa to the Caribbean and the American southeast coast, in late-eighteenth-century Bristol, in the southwest Severn Estuary, still retained the central role in Atlantic commerce it had held since the days of John Cabot and the North Atlantic salt cod fisheries. Its merchant houses and shipping lines were foundational to the British Sugar Trade, which spawned gigantic plantations in Jamaica and Barbados, created mercantile fortunes in London and Glasgow, sent thousands of indentured servants from southwest England and Ireland and slaves from West Africa to the Islands, and provided employment for captains, pilots, crews, and harbor workers whose geographic origin and polyglot linguistic experience made Atlantic culture a zone for creolization. Sons of Bristol went out to apprentice in the Islands, daughters of wealthy planters married into Bristol trading families, mixed-race colonists' children were educated in Europe, and occasionally Caribbean-born inheritors, their fortunes made, retired to landed estates in the Severn valley.[41] Music, dance, and body vocabularies exported from the British Caribbean were well known on Bristol's docks and in her dance salons.

The economics and mechanics of making money in the Sugar Colonies accelerated the rise there of expressive modes that combined African and European influences, including festivals like Kanaval and Jonkonnu, but also syncretic religions: *voudou* and *santeria* in the French and Spanish colonies and *Obeah* in the English-speaking islands. These religions, whose beliefs and practices represent a very complex mélange of cultural sources, shaped the experience of slaves and freemen in the Caribbean and also, eventually, theatrical practices in New York, London, and Bristol. Working-class theater in each of these cities involved the participation of blacks or whites in blackface, Afro-Caribbean sources, Anglo-American actors or entrepreneurs or musicians, integrated audiences, and creole folkways.

A particularly fruitful venue for discussing Bristol, on the eastern rim of this creole Atlantic, actually originates in a New York City theater. The African Grove had been founded in Manhattan in 1817 as a pleasure garden, akin to London's Vauxhall, by William Brown, a black ex–ship-steward who had been born in Haiti (date unknown) and sailed on liners out of Liverpool. Originally congregating in a "back house" (that is, on the alley) behind 38 Thompson Street and offering popular songs and dancing, by 1820 the black "*dandies and dandizettes*" of the Grove's audience had become an item for the "flash" press, those street newspapers aimed at working-class single young white men.[42] The Grove was also a favored destination for whites with a taste for exotica and erotica; it was the place Charles Mathews, the English "monopolyloguist" actor who made a specialty of regional or ethnic character types, had claimed as the source of the "rich . . . black fun" he would bring back to London stages.[43] Favorite venues for "slumming" whites, like the African Grove, Bowery, and Chatham Theaters in New York, the Cincinnati and New Orleans waterfront bars described in the postbellum era by Lafcadio Hearn, and the concert saloons like Almack's and Hill's on the Lower East Side, were zones in which racial, sexual, and expressive exchange could occur; as Fischer has it "In these clandestine pursuits, the color line broke down completely."[44]

Within just a few years, Brown's success as a theatrical impresario had led to more ambitious programming—in September 1821 he staged an all-black *Richard III*—and new quarters at Mercer & Bleecker, a few blocks west of the Lower East Side Catherine Wharf where ferries docked and black fishermen selling fried eels danced on the wharves to attract trade. This is precisely the same period in which the Bowery and Chatham Theaters, which would become the homes of blackface minstrelsy in the second half of the decade, opened a few blocks east—a proximity that may have led to commercial competition between black and white theater owners.

Period sources describe Brown's productions, Shakespearian and otherwise, as a fluid and evolving gumbo of singing, dancing, topical airs, physical comedy, and both serious and parody monologues. By January 1822, for example, he was staging his own full-length *The Drama of King Shotaway*, a melodrama with songs, dancing, and music that related the true story of a 1795 rebellion by Black Caribs on the British island of St. Vincent. In March 1823, a New York production of the English *Tom and Jerry* had opened at the Park Theater; Brown's heavily adapted version at the Grove imported transvestism (a "Mr. Jackson" danced the characteristic "African Sal") and it replaced the scene set in London's notorious East End with one set in a South Carolina slave market, during which, "a white actor was employed to auction off the cast."[45] This would have been an explosively "realistic" theatrical presentation, mimicking actual events, some recent and/or revolutionary, occurring in other maritime locales on the southwest Atlantic rim. But beyond their crucial role as a model for the fluid interaction of black and white theatrical personnel and properties that would inspire minstrelsy, the polyglot productions at the Globe are important for an additional reason: because they provided some of the first training for the most famous African American actor of the nineteenth century, who in his own professional career embodied the creole synthesis.

Ira Frederick Aldridge was born in New York City in 1807, the same year that the painter William Sidney Mount was born on the North Shore of Long Island, just east of the city, and coincidentally also the year that Parliament outlawed the British slave trade. As a child, Aldridge attended the African Free School in its second location on Mulberry Street (in what is now Chinatown), receiving his first training in performance there and at the African Grove, where he developed as a competent comic and dramatic actor, dancer, singer, and physical comedian. His centrality to Grove productions is confirmed by Charles Mathews in 1822, who claimed to have heard the blackface song "Possum up a Gum Tree" there; Aldridge later countered, rather persuasively, that Mathews had got "Possum" from his own performances of that iconic tune.[46]

"Possum up a Gum-Tree" (after London, J. Willis & Co., c1824; Nathan p47 has in A)

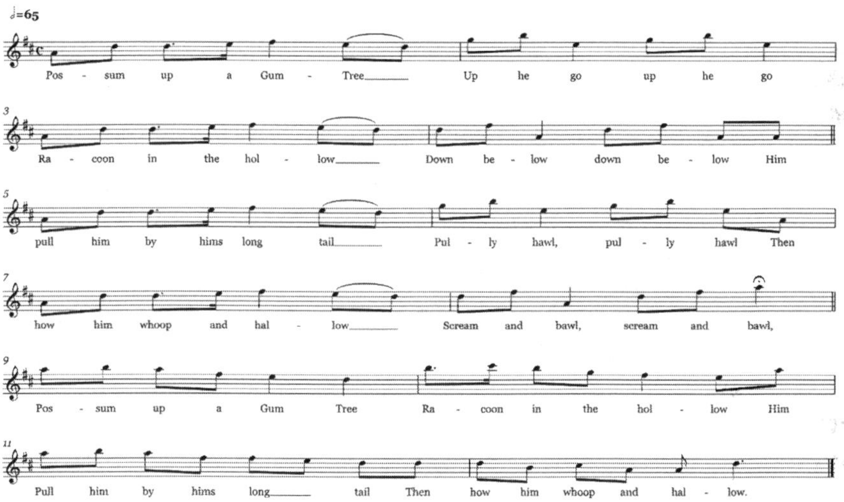


Aldridge also appears to have recognized, like a later generation of New Orleans and Chicago jazzmen, that opportunities for African American performers might be greater, and prejudice less an impediment, abroad, particularly after he and several other Grove personnel had been assaulted by a white mob outside the theater.[47] So, at the age of 17, he sailed for England, earning his passage as a ship's steward, the same fluid profession followed by the Grove's founder, William Brown. By 1825, Aldridge had become a noted theatrical interpreter of both "African" and whiteface roles in England, including archetypal "noble savage" figures such as Oroonoko in Thomas Southerne's *A Slave's Revenge* (originally 1695), Gambia in *The Slave* (1820), and Mungo in *The Padlock* (originally 1768). Period reception of Aldridge's performances evoked both romantic primitivism and "progressive" humanism; for example, the *Morning Post* of March 21, 1848, commented:

> Mr. Ira Aldridge is a *bona fide* African, of mulatto tint, with wooly hair; his features are capable of much expression, his action is unrestrained and picturesque, and his voice clear, full, and resonant. It was interesting to witness the acting of Mr. Ira Aldridge, a native of Africa, giving utterance to the wrongs of his race in his assumed character, and standing in an attitude of triumph over the body of one of its oppressors. Mr. Ira Aldridge is an intelligent actor, and his elocutionary powers are admirable. Compared with the people by whom he was last night surrounded, he might with strict justice be considered a true Roscius.[48]

In the white imagination, Aldridge could thus represent both the "noble savage" and an archetype of racial aspiration, often by crossing racial and theatrical boundaries. He played widely in Britain and Ireland, and over time across both Europe and Russia.[49] He was admired for his financial success and played for decades in most of the national capitols.[50] He died while on tour in 1867 and is buried in Lodz, Poland.

Aldridge's career, experience, and reception are rich sources of insight regarding the complex performativity of African American identity in nineteenth-century Atlantic culture but particularly useful for the present analysis is the concatenation of events that first brought him to Europe and led to his first notable success. At Bristol, in 1830, he starred at the Theater Royale in a newly authored version of another creole theatrical property, *Obi, or Three-Finger'd Jack* (originally Haymarket, 1800).[51] This melodrama, based upon the actual 1780s career of a notorious mixed-race Jamaican slave hunter, fugitive, and freedom fighter, Jack Mansong or Three-Finger'd Jack, is shot through with the complex political associations of the supernatural system called *Obeah*. First outlined by the physician Benjamin Moseley in his 1799 *A Treatise on Sugar*, an apologia for the brutality of the sugar-driven slave trade, the historical Jack's tale proved to be both financially durable and stylistically flexible, as it was capable of catering to theatrical archetypes which had been part of English colonial perceptions since Elizabethan times.[52]

A mythologized version of Jack Mansong inspired the massively popular *Obi*, which as a seriocomic pantomime to Samuel Arnold's music took audiences at the Haymarket Theatre by storm in 1800. This version of the tale theatricalized savagery and nobility but also provided a way to vent working-class tensions, providing a mask for cultural critique like the slightly later blackface theatrics of Jim Crow and Zip Coon. *Obi*'s apotheosis in the early 1820s occurred within the period between the 1789–1799 French Revolution (overlapping Toussaint's rebellion of 1799–1804) and the 1838 cessation of the slave trade, during which the British middle class experienced a kind of fearful fascination with the revolutionary furor of republican France and English rural rebellion.[53] In *Obi, or Three-Finger'd Jack*, the twin cults of *Liberté* and *Obi* focused this fascination but, crucially, were symbolically tamed and controlled through their scripted portrayal on stage.[54]

At the same time, like the rewritten Manhattan productions of *Tom and Jerry* which had replaced the exoticism of London's East End with that of a fish market on the Lower East Side or a slave market in South Carolina, *Obi*'s appeal to middle-class white voyeurism also foregrounded remarkably precise imitations of Afro-Caribbean folk ritual. These depended for their theatrical effect not only upon gothic caricature of pagan syncretic religion, but also the subtler allure of Afro-Caribbean social ritual: for example, *Obi* contains a scene (I/vi) recreating a celebration of the night-visiting festival of Junkanoo ("John Canoe"), in which a costumed and masked band of dancers travel from house to house, singing and dancing in return for rewards of money and drink.[55]

What lay, in part, beneath the exoticist voyeurism of minstrelsy's blackfaced Zip Coon, as with the Maroon guerrillas sensationalized in *Three-Finger'd Jack*, the white riots outside Manhattan's African Grove, and James's or Irving's mockery of creolizing body vocabularies, was of course fear—fear felt by a white colonial or mercantile minority toward an exploited black and white underclass. In America, akimbo street dance and the "minstrel mask" permitted carnivalesque transgression: it was a means for working-class young men to simultaneously mock the free blacks with whom they competed for work, and the white bourgeois who were rapidly distancing themselves—economically, professionally, and geographically—from the working-class street life of cities.[56] While Bristol depended upon the Triangle Trade, most of that trade's victims—the indentured or "Barbadoz'd" Irish and kidnapped West Africans—lay conveniently out of sight over the Atlantic horizon. Bristol thus saw the profits from but not the day-to-day human cost of the Sugar Trade; this left space for both exotica and ennoblement of the sort captured in *Three-Finger'd Jack*. Yet, as we have seen with *A Grand Jamaica Ball!*, this same period also witnessed the growth of a trans-Atlantic planter class, shuttling between the Sugar Islands and the British sugar ports, whose language, diets, entertainments, offspring and body vocabularies were already "creole": that is, already reflective of the process of cultural mixing that Atlantic creole culture made possible. The complex comedy, allure—and, perhaps, subtle fear—with which middle-class and elite viewers perceived the encroachment of creole behaviors is captured visually in *A Grand Jamaica Ball*, paralleled in Irving's prose accounts of "Dessalines" and Ichabod Crane, and reflected in the fascinated response to Ira Aldridge's theatrical Jack Mansong in *Obi*.

Between 1825 and his debut at London's Covent Garden in 1833 (the same year that the Emancipation Act was passed), Aldridge toured widely in Ireland and the British Isles, developing a wide repertoire that included both period and contemporary and both serious and comic roles (everything from Mungo in Dibdin's venerable *The Padlock* to the title character in *Othello*), which likewise drew upon his ability to sing, dance, and play the guitar; in 1830, for example, he first played and sang "Possum up a Gum Tree" as part of a performance of *Obi* at Coventry.[57] The sheer diversity of Aldridge's training and repertoires, in regional and provincial theaters on both sides of the Atlantic, reflect the polyglot, creole environments of Lower Manhattan and the African Grove and the conditions that led to the birth of what W. T. Lhamon has dubbed "The First Atlantic Popular Culture."[58] Playing a Jamaican character in a melodrama based upon relatively recent Caribbean historical events, which dramatized the political and economic paradoxes of the Sugar Trade, in a city—and a theater—built upon the profits of that trade and singing a song that was already emblematic of cross-dressing, blackface and whiteface ethnic exchange, Ira Aldridge literally embodied the creole synthesis on the British stage.

Certainly, the reception to his Mungo or Three-Finger'd Jack mapped onto existing British theatrical archetypes of *le sauvage*, but we should also acknowledge that Aldridge's Theatre Royal performances brought audiences one step closer to the reality of Afro-Caribbean performance and to the creole Atlantic street culture out of which his performance vocabulary arose. When the young scions of Bristol houses returned from their Caribbean apprenticeships, sometimes bringing with them dance moves or the daughters of wealthy planters encountered at "Grand Jamaica Balls"; when comic characters on Irving's Long Island or Micah Hawkins's Finger Lakes danced like "Haytians"; when the integrated crews of the Triangle Trade's ships dropped anchor in Bristol Channel and debarked for shore leave in waterfront taverns; when the young Ira Aldridge left the liner on which he'd been steward to try his luck as an actor in English working-class theaters: all these and thousands of others brought with them the seeds of the creole synthesis, back and forth across the Atlantic and Caribbean. Through collisions of ethnicity, genetics, history, observation, intermarriage, and imitation, the creolized communities of the Atlantic inhabited shifting contexts, which activated transformational cultural behaviors and expectations. That creole culture, which touched audiences at the African Grove, watercolorists at Jamaican colonial balls, sailors on the decks of Bermuda privateers, percussionists in the West Indian wind-bands recruited for colonial armies, and audiences in the working-class streets and theaters of the East, Ohio, Mississippi, and Severn river wharves, influenced North American popular music culture for the next one hundred years.

# CHAPTER 3

# Spaces, Whistles, Tags, and Drums

## Irruptive Noise

> The creation of sound and music is a powerfully productive tool for the disciplining and organizing of space around particular visual and aural aesthetic principles. . . . Sound-making is . . . capable of transgressing seemingly discrete social and spatial hierarchies, and should be factored more seriously into investigations of resistance.
>
> —Ronni Armstead, "Las Krudas, Spatia Practice, and the Performance of Diaspora" (2008)

This quotation, from the hip hop scholar Ronni Armstead, recognizes that in cases of subaltern resistance, sound, as a part of the larger social construct of music, has the capacity to challenge "social and spatial hierarchies" (e.g., dominant cultural constructs) and is therefore receptive to analysis as a political strategy.[1] In contrast to the balance of this book, which addresses a limited number of complex and individual case studies focusing primarily upon movement, this chapter employs a series of shorter vignettes, cutting across time periods and social contexts, to investigate multimedia "noise"—abrupt, interruptive, human-generated expression—which "transgresses seemingly discrete social and spatial hierarchies: which contests dominant norms for sonic spaces and visual experiences." These brief vignettes include the semiotics of whistling in Afro-Caribbean cultural traditions across three centuries, the public art of graffiti taggers and its role in 1970s hip hop consciousness (anticipating Chapter 8), and the sirens, stances, and amplified speech of twenty-first-century street protest. Though not a primary focus of this book—whose topic is the ways bodies moving in public space were intended or perceived to contest social and political hierarchies—analysis of "noise" nevertheless provides a useful counterpoint to some of my text's central tenets. This book as a whole theorizes unregulated dance, especially group dance drawing upon the akimbo movement vocabularies of the African Caribbean, as "interruptive" of North American social norms. Here, I test my thesis of noise as analogous interruptive strategy by analyzing examples of its definition, legislation, and prohibition in North America. In these historical cases, we see subaltern sound—itself a hierarchical construct, because subaltern cultures' music or visual art is often denigrated by dominant culture as "mere noise"—as connoting resistance and as mapped onto political or movement vocabularies in similar ways.[2] This chapter thus provides a parallel analysis, focusing upon shared experience in sound and visual media, to other chapters' analyses of street dance's political impulses and impact.

Noise *works* as subaltern resistance. Because portable human sound can saturate public space, because it is time-bound and elusive in a way that concrete physical or bodily structures cannot be, it has been a particularly effective and comparatively "invisible" resistance tactic.[3] As a result, the history of authority's attempts to constrain noise on legal, physical, or aesthetic grounds is a very long one: Michel de Certeau says, in a classic work of cultural geography, "It is a symptomatic tendency of functionalist totalitarianism . . . that it seeks precisely to eliminate these [contradictory] local authorities, because they compromise the *univocity* of the system."[4]

At the same time, the very disreputability of noisemakers has sometimes protected them from authoritarian forces wary of the ways that repression can backfire into legitimization; that is, the repression of subaltern public expression has sometimes inadvertently raised its visibility and strengthened its messaging. On such occasions, when officialdom avoids deploying law or force against rebellious public noise—often because of concerns that such deployment might legitimize or martyr opposition—cultural arbiters as servants of dominant culture have been recruited to delegitimize its intentional or explicit political relevance: "That's not music—it's just noise!"[5]

Subaltern peoples exploit sound as resistance precisely because of its ephemerality; conversely, as Martin Munro points out, sound is also a site for dominant classes to further extend their attempts to control both public space and subaltern identity.[6] In New Orleans, for example, at 12:01 a.m. on Ash Wednesday after Mardi Gras, police sirens literally "sweep" the noise of Fat Tuesday's carnivalesque revelry before them, just as municipal workers literally "sweep up" Bourbon Street, following along directly behind the line of police lights and sirens. Ethnomusicologist Matt Sakakeeny describes this liminal moment, the moment of transition between Carnival and Lent, thus: "The auditory violence of the police siren itself works to silence the agency of the second-liners as it drowns out the brass band's music and, thus, disrupts the unity and integrity of the crowd."[7]

Noise has been widely theorized, especially in sociology and folklore, but for our purposes, a more immediately useful perspective comes from information theory.[8] Abraham Moles, for example, describes "noise" in multiple media, and its potentially irruptive capacities, as "a signal we do not want to hear."[9] In seeking to theorize subaltern sound in public spaces as transgressive in the same way that group movement might be, Moles's definition of "noise" as "any undesirable signal in the transmission of a message" will resonate—particularly when that visual or sonic noise is manifested by those who would seek to resist.[10]

## Noise

Political, cultural, or economic elites' prerogative to define undesirable sound as "noise" has been a metric of power in the Americas for four centuries, while public sound that resisted definition or constraint has been a site for insubordinate resistance for nearly as long.[11] Yet only a few studies have framed carnivalesque noise within the historiography of American musical experience; a notable example is Dale Cockrell's *Demons of Disorder: Blackface Minstrels and Their World*.[12] In a preliminary to this text, Cockrell comments: "'noise' is implicit violence, a challenge to law's authority, as carnival is a challenge to Lent, as callithumpians were demons of disorder."[13] Cockrell's topic of blackface minstrelsy has been widely theorized as a site for carnivalesque "masking," the assumption of a disguised identity as a means of stating critical truths unsafe without that mask.[14] However, there is not so much examination of sonic or visual "noise" in blackface or other nineteenth-century idioms, despite the fact that minstrelsy's or hip-hop's akimbo body vocabularies display classic traits of rebellious grotesquerie in both movement and sound.[15]

Cockrell identifies "rough music" or *charivari* (which produces the southern U.S. expression for festive noise, the *shivaree*) as an inheritance from medieval carnival traditions, particularly linked to mobs' public expressions of rough justice against scapegoated individuals, although certainly sound is an equally integral part of West African festive behaviors that met European culture in the Caribbean.[16] Hence, certain moments may be analyzed as watershed shifts in the contestation of American public soundscapes. Such moments help frame our examination of noise as sonic resistance, and as a legitimate consideration in tandem with the "visual noise" of transgressive public dance.

The First Great Awakening itself was one such site, when the noise, no less than the size, of the vast revivals' crowds were a focus of commenters' horrified fascination.[17] As we have seen, the turn-of-the-century Cane Ridge Revivals and the modifications of Shaker worship that emerged from them were watersheds in the history of transgressive public sound, with period commentators describing the noise of conversion and worship in apocalyptic terms:

> The noise was like the roar of Niagara. . . . At one time I saw at least five hundred swept down in a moment as if a battery of a thousand guns had been opened upon them, and then immediately followed shrieks and shouts that rent the very heavens.[18]

Beyond the sacred realm of the Great Awakenings, the intentional devaluation or misinterpretation of African-based cultural expressions as "black noise" rationalized white dehumanization and control of black bodies, labor, and expressions.[19] Conversely, the infection of white soundscapes—like white movement vocabularies—with black or brown inflections was regarded as dangerous and undesirable: Jeroen DeWulf quotes a 1736 condemnation of Afro-Dutch Pinkster from *The Spy*, whose equation of racial miscegenation with dangerous noise merits citing at length:

> It was no small Amusement to me, to see the Plain partly covered with Booths, and well crowded with Whites, the Negroes divided into Companies, I suppose according to their different Nations, some dancing to the hollow Sound of a Drum . . . other-some to the grating rattling Noise of Pebles [*sic*] or Shells in a Small Basket, others plied the Banger, and some knew how to joyn the Voice it. . . . Tired with the Noise I endeavored to get out of it, and in my Way home, considering the Day, (being one of those set apart to commemorate the Resurrection of our Blessed Saviour) and the Diversions I had seen, I could not chuse [*sic*] but think that Holidays thus spent could be of very little Service, if they were not pernicious.[20]

David Wall cites the noisy African American and Afro-Caribbean festival celebrations of Negro Election Day and Pinkster as sites for similar anxiety, while a 1797 reference to "iron bands" in Kingston, Jamaica's syncretic John Canoe festival, similarly conflates class and race in a complaint about the capacity of subaltern noise to "disagreeably" impact dominant-culture soundspaces:

> The confusion occasioned by the rattling of chains and slings from the wharves, the mock-driving of hoops by the coopers, winding the postmen's horns, beating militia and negro drums, the sound of the pipe and tabor, negroe [*sic*] flutes, gombas and jaw-bones, scraping on the violin, and singing of men, women, and children, with other incidental noises, make Kingston at this time a very disagreeable residence.[21]

In addition to these ongoing festival traditions, throughout the nineteenth century the accelerated pace of urbanization and industrialization raised the ambient sound level of North American soundscapes and directly implicated class-based social tensions. By 1900, political authorities and their cultural arbiters explicitly conflated unregulated public noise with the public presence of uncontrollable subaltern bodies, most notoriously in various cities' public campaigns against the cries of street vendors, who often were—or were presumed to be—immigrants.[22]

Controlling public spaces meant containing the expressions of subaltern bodies, though the noncorporeality of sound made it a particular regulatory challenge.[23]

Paradoxically, twentieth-century noise ordinances often originated with progressive cultural elites—a confirmation of the class- as well as race-based criteria upon which "noise" was assessed; for example, a classically trained music educator, Julia Barnett Rice, in 1906 founded the Society for the Suppression of Unnecessary Noise in New York, which "forbade musical instruments on the street with certain exceptions."[24] The best known of the new ordinances, enacted by New York City health commissioner and NYC police chief Thomas Bingham's notorious "General Order 47," targeted noise control, but engaged in selective, anti-immigrant enforcement; in practice, "vendors, musicians, and shouters . . . were the only targets actually pursued by the police."[25] And both sides recognized the semiotic power of noise in this contestation of public space: in response, peddlers and street sellers continued to employ noise as resistance; as Vaillant says, "Even as they found themselves subjected to a kind of aural profiling, street sellers also found ways to make 'noise' and deploy sound as a weapon of the weak as well as the powerful."[26]

In roughly the same period of early-twentieth-century urbanization, labor activists and strikers led by the Industrial Workers of the World (IWW) developed a particularly rich repertoire of noise-driven public strategies.[27] When mine- and mill-owners sent sponsored Salvation Army Brass bands to play hymns on street corners to drown out IWW speakers, "Wobbly" songwriters supplied new contrafact texts, to be sung along with the competing Sally Ann bands' music: this is the origin, for example, of the Joe Hill contrafact "The Preacher and the Slave," a/k/a "Pie in the Sky," sung to the tune of "In the Sweet Bye and Bye."[28] Wobbly organizers learned how to exploit the power of massed song no less than of massed bodies: the journalist Ray Stannard Baker's 1912 description of the Lawrence Massachusetts textile strike is particularly evocative:

> It is the first strike I ever saw that sang. I shall not forget the curious lift, the strange sudden fire of the mingled nationalities at the strike meetings when they broke into the universal language of song. And not only at the meetings did they sing, but in the soup houses and in the streets. . . . They have a whole book of songs fitted to familiar tunes—"The Eight Hour Song," "The Banner of Labor," "Workers, Shall the Masters Rule Us?"[29]

A similar watershed moment in the history of North American rebellious noise lies in the first glimmerings of the post–World War II Civil Rights movement, when public sound—songs, chants, or raised voices—again became a site of dominant versus subaltern contest. During the War, black working-class activists exploited the mutability of sound in public space as veiled protest: on the segregated Birmingham buses in 1943, for example, "the negroes . . . started ringing the [request-for-stop] bell for the entire block [though] no one would alight when he stopped."[30] There were times when it was safer to sing metaphorically than to speak semantically, to resist sonically rather than physically, and by the early 1960s, public song was a widely recognized and deployed resistance strategy in the Civil Rights movement—though the roots of that strategy are in the late-1940s activities of activists like Zilphia Horton and Guy Carawan, and, before that, in the international Popular Front.[31] Noise was both deployed as a tactic and legislated as unlawful: a 1969 lawsuit, for example, protested the arrest under an antinoise ordinance of Richard Grayned for too loudly leading a demonstration outside a black high school in Rockford, Illinois, and there are many other similar examples of selective and constraining enforcement.[32] And sound as subaltern resistance extended even beyond the realm of speech and song.

## Whistles and Shrieks

Within the contexts of legislated and normalizing sounds, the whistle—as both a musical object and as a physical action of the larynx, lips, and tongue—has carried irruptive connotations in New World and North American culture since, at latest, the seventeenth century. Whether mimetic—often an imitation of birdsong or human technologies—or connotative and communicative—as with samba whistles or the double-tongued blast signaling urban taxi-drivers—the whistle has been interruptive, unexpected, ubiquitously available across social groups and economic classes, and paradoxically elusive, because nearly invisible. Indeed, as Raymond Smilor put it, "Amid the everyday din, identifying the source of [its] racket was often no easy task."[33] Though certainly part of European carnival traditions, whistles and whistling as festive and spectacular phenomena are found even more widely throughout the Afro-Caribbean.[34] The physical act of whistling in such traditions is particularly associated with the Yoruba *orisha* Eshu-Elegba, the trickster god of chance, misrule, and the ambiguous crossroads; the *orisha* who "opens the way" for the other gods at vodou ceremonies. Eshu-Elegba (known, in the American South, as the "Legba" who haunts the Delta blues crossroads) carries a tobacco pipe and whistle, which are emblematic of his "disobedience and disregard for authority."[35]

Afro-Caribbean whistling enters North American public spaces via the maritime and riverine trades, especially in cities influenced by Francophone festival behaviors like New Orleans, Charleston, Mobile, and Memphis.[36] We can trace the continued presence of notable whistlers through the medium of runaway-slave notices, which in addition to habits of speech, dress, conduct, or language, would often mention special musical skills, including whistling.[37] It is worth noting that whistling was regarded as potentially rebellious: for example, Radano argues that controlling *sounds* slaves made was part of a larger project to control their bodies, suggesting that it was only when *"the auditory culture of slaves became conceptualized* as part of the effort of whites to recover their [runaway] property" that slave owners even began to reflect upon the sound of slave sound.[38]

In fact, whistling was so closely associated with African American culture that it became an essential part of the repertoire of antebellum blackface minstrels—as it had been for the musicians they learned from—and would be for their successors. As I have commented elsewhere, "Virtuoso whistling linked sonic transgression—that is, the making of a loud, unexpected, nearly invisible, intrusive sound in public spaces—and blackface's own irruptive character."[39] However, whistling both pre- and postdates the era(s) of minstrelsy. Washington Irving makes explicit the connection between whistling and the Caribbean's akimbo creole body vocabularies. In the early epistolary novel, *Salmagundi*, his narrator includes whistling in the expressive arsenal of the African American character, "Tucky Squash," saying "He could whistle like a northwester."[40] Likewise, Mark Twain—who had a very deep awareness of African American contributions to the antebellum North American soundscape—also employs the whistle's slippery physiognomy to blur racial boundaries and connotations, specifically citing, in the opening of *Tom Sawyer*, the pleasurable attraction of African American whistling:

> Within two minutes, or even less, he had forgotten all his troubles . . . because a new and powerful interest bore them down and drove them out of his mind for the time. . . . This new interest was a valued novelty in whistling, *which he had just acquired from a negro*, and he was suffering to practice it un-disturbed. It consisted of a peculiar bird-like turn, a sort of liquid warble, produced by touching the tongue to the roof of the mouth at short intervals in the midst of the music. . . . Diligence and attention soon gave him the knack of it, and he strode down the street with his mouth full of harmony and his soul full of gratitude.[41]

The transgressive connotations of whistling carry on into other works influenced by blackface minstrelsy: not only in Twain's *Huckleberry Finn*, whose overall structure is indebted to the tripartite shape of the minstrel show, but also and very centrally within Harriet Beecher Stowe's novel, *Uncle Tom's Cabin*.[42] In that now dated but nevertheless highly influential and resilient abolitionist fable, whistling is included in the attributes of the iconic character "Topsy"; her diminutive stature; "wooly" hair; ragged clothing; distorted expressions, speech, and bodily patterns; and her whistling are all archetypal of minstrelsy's "pickaninny" caricature, and would be borrowed by later popular entertainment figures, from the *Our Gang* films' Allen "Farina" Hoskins (1920–1980) to Josephine Baker's comic "End Girl" (discussed later).[43] Stowe's first introduction of Topsy emphasizes irruptive noise, including whistling, as well as subversive bodily and facial vocabularies, and hints at the "double-consciousness" that both conceal:

> The black, glassy eyes glittered with a kind of wicked drollery, and the thing struck up, in a clear shrill voice, an odd negro melody, to which she kept time with her hands and feet, spinning round, clapping her hands, knocking her knees together, in a wild, fantastic sort of time, and producing in her throat all those odd guttural sounds which distinguish the native music of her race; and finally, turning a summerset or two, and giving a prolonged closing note, as odd and unearthly as that of a steam-whistle, she came suddenly down on the carpet, and stood with her hands folded, and a most sanctimonious expression of meekness and solemnity over her face, only broken by the cunning glances which she shot askance from the corners of her eyes.[44]

These subversive, subaltern associations carry into the era of modern media; one of the first great stars of early acoustic recording was the street entertainer George W. Johnson (ca. 1846–1914), the "Whistling Coon" (*sic*), born the son of slaves in Maryland, who recorded his eponymous novelty whistling for wax cylinders.[45] He was discovered "down by the Hudson, busking among the ferry goers," and eventually built a career creating one-off wax cylinders of his signature pieces, recording whistled performances "with alacrity and an unnerving accuracy."[46]

Gilded Age vaudeville, which inherited a number of blackface tropes and provided the most immediate staging ground for the architects of early audio and film recording, yielded various performers for whom whistling was a notable career association.[47] Most iconically in the late vaudeville period, Al Jolson, who in *The Jazz Singer* (1927) played the Jewish son of a cantor donning blackface, employed whistling as part of his onstage act from 1909 onward. It was a sonic version of the minstrel mask that reached back over one hundred years.[48] African American whistling was understood to be powerful, iconic, subversive, and potentially defiant; there is a cruel historical irony in the fact that the teenaged Emmett Till (born 1941) was lynched and murdered by Roy Bryant and J. W. Milam for having allegedly whistled at a white woman on the street in Money, Mississippi, in August 1955.[49]

## Graffiti Taggers in Three-Dimensional Space

"Loud, public celebration of an object that signifies one's alien status is an act of defiance and self-possession."[50] This quotation, from hip hop scholar Tricia Rose, reminds us that the very act of performing subaltern identity in public spaces, via music, movement, or visual "noise," is an act of resistance. Graffiti—the inscription of visual symbols, characters, or pictures on physical objects or (especially) public edifices, in the absence of official approval—is an ancient manifestation of visually noisy "defiance and self-possession," dating back to the classical world and practiced very widely in imperial cultures, including Greek, Roman, Mayan, and medieval European. It has likewise been equivalently widespread in the modern era, as for example in the complex symbolic vocabularies of U.S. hobo culture and in the "Kilroy was here" tagline and graffito, whose caricatured face became emblematic of the experience of U.S. Army troops during WWII's Second Front.[51]

However, a very significant shift in graffiti's clientele, media, techniques, and ubiquity came in the late 1960s with the increased availability of the permanent wide-nibbed marker and the new aerosol spray can, which provided a small, light, cheap, and portable means of painting on flat surfaces.[52] In this same period, as youth gangs in Philadelphia, New York, Detroit, and Chicago began using graffiti to mark their physical territory, young artists developing individual painting styles began "tagging" urban locations with personal symbols, competing to display the geographic breadth of their markings. The iconic late '60s tagger is TAKI 183, a Greek-American teenager in the Bronx, who combined a diminutive of his name and his West 183rd Street address, in a symbol that became legendary. As a foot messenger, "Demetrius" (long since retired from tagging, he still goes by the single first name) was able to post all over the city. His model—a simple, distinctive, and personalized *nom de plume*, scrawled in permanent marker—was imitated by a host of others. In turn, as other artists took up the can and began spreading their own tags, they evolved individualized, often stylized, approaches to "writing." The ubiquity of subway cars, and the cars' capacity as a mobile platform for writers' artwork, made them a favored target, and tagged subway cars became the locus of dominant authority's attempts to control the visual expression of subaltern identity.[53]

Graffiti writing was understood, very early in its history, to be a defiance, if not defilement, of public ownership; John Lindsay was only the first of several New York mayors (most notoriously, Rudolf Giuliani) to attempt to crack down on taggers, as early as 1972. By the 1980s, precisely as graffiti was reaching an apotheosis of both style and execution, with taggers plotting sophisticated entry into security-guarded depots and developing whole car-sized murals of great complexity, the New York City Transit Authority's "Clean Train Movement" was seeking to eradicate these pieces, which have subsequently been reinterpreted as a rich and vital urban art form.[54]

Developing concurrently with but initially independently of hip hop, the art of graffiti "writers" or "taggers" thus became part of the cluster of artistic expressions that coalesced hip-hop aesthetics: music, dance, speech, technology, and so forth, and, along with dance, it became the predominant visual language of the movement.[55] As with the 1970s B-boy street dancing that moved into Manhattan clubs, by 1979 the first downtown galleries were assembling shows of graffiti art, in the endless cycle of new urban art forms birthed on the subaltern fringes and then swept into the dominant media mainstream. Just as B-boy dancing and hip hop music (discussed later) became known worldwide and were adopted by self-identified minority communities in the 1990s as Jamaican reggae had been in the 1970s, graffiti transformed conceptions of public visual discourse and "spawned a *truly* avant-garde visual culture," one adopted by downtown artists like Basquiat and Keith Haring and, eventually, by Madison Avenue itself.[56]

However, long before tagging was thus mainstreamed, the early writers, especially those who saw allies in the youth-gangs-turned-hip-hop-crews like the Young Lords and the Zulu Nation, understood the irruptive public intent at the heart of graffiti's aesthetic. Fab 5 Freddy (Fred Brathwaite, born 1959 in Brooklyn), one of the canniest of the 1970s artists, who later became a filmmaker and helped break MTV's color bar with the series *Yo! MTV Raps*, explicitly linked the sonic and visual in a confrontational aesthetic that was graffiti's core message:

> A big part of this hip-hop culture in the beginning was putting things in your face, whether you liked it or not. That was the graffiti, that's like a break dance battle right at your feet, you know what I'm saying? Or this music blasting loud, whether you wanted it or not.[57]

In the twenty-first century, graffiti art, like hip-hop sound and movement, remains a defiant street idiom, sometimes deployed under conditions of considerable personal risk within contested public space—just as it was in early 1970s Philly and the Bronx.[58] In its subversive, often literally masked, and always temporary contestation of public space, graffiti was—and still is, in some parts of the world—a transgressive visual "noise," which pushes back against hegemonic control.

In closing, I therefore provide a more extended paraphrase, from de Certeau's classic study, which can be mapped onto this chapter's discussion of noise and space; whistling and shrieking; graffiti, hegemony, and the hip-hop nation:

> The space of a tactic is the space of the other. Thus it must play on and with a terrain imposed on it and organized by the law of a foreign power. It does not have the means to *keep to itself* . . . it is a maneuver "within the enemy's field of vision," as von Buelow put it, and within enemy territory. . . . What it wins it cannot keep. This nowhere gives . . . a mobility that must accept the chance offerings of the moment, and seize on the wing the possibilities that offer themselves at any given moment. It must vigilantly make use of the cracks that particular conjunctions open in the surveillance of the proprietary powers. . . . *In short, a tactic is an art of the weak*. . . . [Dominant culture's] strategies are actions which, thanks to the establishment of a place of power . . . elaborate theoretical places (systems and totalizing discourses) [that] privilege spatial relationships. . . . [Subaltern] Tactics are procedures that

> gain validity in relation . . . *to the circumstances which the precise instant of an intervention transforms into a favorable situation, to the rapidity of the movements that change the organization of a space.*[59]

So: the mobile and portable noise of graffiti, or a boom box, is a "tactic" that can temporarily invade the public space "organized by the law of a foreign power"; that is, the laws of dominant elites. Noise, graffiti, and street dance itself, as subaltern tactics ("maneuvers . . . within enemy territory"), cannot permanently conquer and hold urban space ("What it wins it cannot keep"). Instead, subaltern interruption must be imaginative, mobile, and improvisational (must "seize on the wing the possibilities that offer themselves at any given moment"), dance circle by dance circle, noise by noise, corner by corner, graffito by graffito, moving and flowing through the "cracks that particular conjunctions open in the surveillance": railroad underpasses, nighttime train yards, ghetto sidewalks, after-hours subway cars, unlit commercial parking lots. The "systems and totalizing discourses" of dominant culture "privilege spatial relationships" within public spaces, while subaltern tactics use music to intercede "in relation . . . *to the rapidity of the movements that change* [or contest] *the organization of a space*."[60] Subaltern noise(s) in the dominating signal chain—sirens and whistles, bent limbs and distorted faces, slashes of aerosol paint and low-fidelity recorded sound—thus manifest the capacity to wrest agency, however temporarily, from the hands of the autocracy.

CHAPTER 4

# A Tale of Two Cities II

## Festival and Spectacle in the French Caribbean

"Well, Indian ain't for everyone. But if it's for you, it'll make you strong."
—"Albert Lambreaux," HBO's *Tremé*

This quotation from the fictional "Big Chief Albert Lambreaux" (Clark Peters) in HBO's *Tremé* is an ode to New Orleans street culture, recognizing the powerful sense of subaltern group identity manifested in the fraternal organizations called the Mardi Gras Indians—neighborhood-based social networks of a sort that recurs in parallel in a wide variety of New World creole contexts.[1] Because the west Atlantic and Caribbean were first sought, occupied, populated, and exploited for essentially mercantile reasons—as sources of raw materials (silver, gold, and quicksilver in Central America; timber and pelts in North America), and of agricultural fortunes (sugar, rice, tobacco, cotton)—and only subsequently as centers for permanent emigration and new settlement, maritime and riverine exchange between port cities, both within the Americas and between the Americas and Europe, yielded a particularly rich syncretic Caribbean culture. As we have seen, the Sugar Trade, the engine that originally drove mercantile development and precipitated African chattel slavery, transformed both English-speaking Caribbean colonies and European cities, and this transformation extended into Spanish and French zones as well. The foundation and exploitation of these entrepôts and routes not only brought African labor to the Caribbean, and Caribbean wealth to North America and Britain, but vastly accelerated the exchange of expressive cultures that diverse peoples carried and traded. Thus we have seen the port cities of Kingston in Jamaica and Bridgetown in Barbados and of London and Bristol in England, as nodes in a complex network of Atlantic economic and cultural exchange: places in which all manner of Afro-Protestant syncretic festivals like Pinkster and Negro Election Day and theatricalizations of syncretic rituals like Jonconnu and *Obeah* became sites for observation, imitation, and appropriation.

This chapter returns to the riverine/maritime model to look at two other cities, this time situated within the French Caribbean orbit, and to investigate ways that syncretic Afro-Catholic subaltern behaviors, both sacred and secular—most notably the network of spectacular street music, dance, and social noise revolving around Carnival—interacted with dominant cultures' need to control and constrain public dancing.[2] Given that the celebration of Carnival at a particular season reflects a primary influence from the Catholic calendar, and that the referenced syncresis is particularly strong in Francophone ports, New Orleans—which was a French settlement, then briefly a Spanish possession, then (even more briefly) a French commodity, before its transfer to American (that is, English-speaking northern Protestant) control in 1803—is one obvious choice for investigation.[3] It was at the same time the point of entry via the Mississippi for most of the inner Continent's trade and travel both upstream and down—a crucial strategic site occupied in April 1862 by the U.S. Navy and continuing under armed garrison for the duration of the Civil War and indeed into the early 1870s) and a magnet for French travel, emigration, and cultural exchange from all over the Caribbean and southwest Atlantic. Moreover, its history of municipal contestation over public space, dance, and noise is both venerable and highly contemporary—some of the ordinances cited in this chapter were instituted as recently as 2013.

Other candidates for the southern node in this paired Tale of Two (Catholic Caribbean) Cities might include Havana, a locus for the annual Flota de Indias which, for over 200 years, brought enormous, empire-subsidizing cargoes of silver from the mines of Central and South America to the court of Spain, and thus served as a prize target for Elizabethan and Georgian privateers. Havana was also crucially important in the history of the African Caribbean because it served a strategic purpose—it sat astride the trade winds and was a good spot for controlling access to the Gulf, as a base for fighting piracy and privateersmen, and as a major port for slavers and—eventually—the Cuban sugar trade. Havana is likewise directly implicated in at least two periods of New Orleans history: the relatively brief (1779–1801) but impactful period in which the latter was a Spanish possession and during which Havana-based artists began touring through New Orleans; and, shortly thereafter, as a crucial haven and way station for planters, household servants, and slaves escaping the Haitian revolution.[4] Sublette describes a "sort of musical Fertile Crescent . . . stretching from New Orleans across Cuba and over to wealthy Saint-Domingue," and—further to the discussion in Chapter 2 of Abraham James's comic watercolor *A Grand Jamaica Ball*—specifically cites the influence of military bands.[5] The most extensively cited direct connection between the two cities' French colonial populations is in the Jacobin period that opened in 1789 with the French Revolution and accelerated after 1804, as the gradual and growing success of slave rebellion in Saint Domingue ramped up the urgency with which *colons*, their families, and their domestic servants sought to depart.[6] These refugees, who came from an educated elite and whose slaves carried valuable technical skills in everything from sugar manufacture to musical performance, often went to relations or business associates, or at the least to other expat communities, in other port cities; the Francophile presence in Charleston and Havana, for example, increased during this period.

But an earlier, more continuous, and significantly more complex relationship existed between the Catholic colonial cities of New Orleans and Port-au-Prince, in Saint-Domingue (later Haiti). It might seem incongruous to employ the term Jacobin (originally applied in the 1790s to Breton and then Parisian revolutionaries) to reference black, white, and mixed-race individuals in the Caribbean as much as two generations after the death of Robespierre; but, as we have seen in the discussion of Ira F. Aldridge and *Obi, or Three-Finger'd Jack* in Chapter 2, slave owners, including planters in the French Caribbean, were exceptionally conscious of the perceived risk that Jacobin revolutionary rhetoric might equally elicit black rebellion. So great was this concern that the Black Codes in various periods explicitly prohibited the (previously lucrative) transshipment of slaves from Saint-Domingue to French-speaking New Orleans, precisely because of fears that such slaves might carry the "contagion" of Jacobin thought into Louisiana.[7]

Yet despite these restrictions and the paranoia that elicited them, there was still very extensive and influential exchange between Francophone Caribbean cities. In addition to commercial travelers and planters and their households (which often included mixed-race offspring of planters' liaisons), both slaves and free *gens du coleur* from Saint-Domingue, especially artisans, dancers, and musicians, found employment on their masters' or their own behalf in French Louisiana.[8] There were black and mixed-race musicians in the orchestras that played in New Orleans theaters and dance halls (the numbers of which latter experienced explosive growth in the second half of the eighteenth century), and notable soloists based in Saint-Domingue as well as Havana were appearing on operatic stages there by the 1790s.[9] *Gens de coleur*, as the male offspring of liaisons between Creole mistresses and white fathers, often received more extensive education, sometimes in music, even sometimes training in Paris, while creole women were an essential part of a surprisingly complex and subtle power exchange via black-white sexual liaison, called *placage*. Though sexual exploitation of black women by white owners was a recurrent evil throughout the New World, Shirley Thompson suggests that "*Placage* gave free women of color [especially in a tri-cultural city like New Orleans] a unique opportunity to gain social and economic status."[10] Ritualized performances of this boundary-crossing, tri-cultural status often focused around street and social dance.

## Social Dance in New Orleans

In Chapter 2, we discussed the amateur caricaturist Abraham James's *A Grand Jamaica Ball! or the Creolean Hop a la Muftee; as Exhibeted* [*sic*] *in Spanish Town* (approximately 1802) and unpacked the image as revealing not only savage satire but also—perhaps even against the artist's parodic intentions—actual movement vocabularies. We suggested that, just as costume and skin tone in the image contain a series of semi-coded messages about conduct and class, so physical postures and relationships in this portrayal of public dancing reveal "creolized" body languages.[11] Balls and dances, which were central to colonial society in both the British and the French Caribbean (including New Orleans), were simultaneously lucrative and liminal: public spaces in which profit could be generated while social strata were reinforced, contested, or transgressed.[12] James found Jamaican colonial society's movement vocabularies inelegant and disgusting, but Emily Clark's subtle and detailed description of public dances in the last part of the Spanish *cabildo* in New Orleans elegantly identifies much more complex cultural negotiation and exchange:

> The dance hall became an unlikely site of resistance [to Spanish *Codes Negres*] by the city's diverse population. The city opened a public dance hall in 1792 and restricted admission to "blancos," or whites. . . . [However] the city's large population of free blacks, who made up more than a quarter of the city's free population, constituted a significant portion of the customer base . . . ; provision was quickly made for them to have use of the hall on Saturday nights. This attempt at segregation soon failed and became even more socially transgressive. Male "blancos" and enslaved people of African descent made their way to the public ballroom, where the interracial gatherings became known as "tricolor balls."[13]

Here, the term *tricolor* punned on the flag of the Napoleonic Empire, which would take control of the city in 1800 after the Treaty of San Ildefonso, and upon the three racial identities recognized in the *Codes Noirs*: "Negro," "white," and *gen de coleur* (literally, a "free man of color" or Creole). It simultaneously referenced the integration of identities—social, verbal, and sexual—for which the New Orleans balls, like waterfront fronts, concert saloons, and working-class theaters elsewhere, were a principle venue. Clark continues:

> In 1796 the Cabildo explicitly banned slaves from attending the dances [but] the order was rescinded in the face of unanticipated opposition. Some slaveholders complained that the prohibition against slaves at the dances was having a bad effect on slave morale, *generating a greater threat to the colonial peace and economy than integrated dances*. The colonial governor responded by proposing that "blancos" be prohibited from attending the Saturday night revels. But in 1800, "blancos" were still mixing on the dance floor with free and enslaved people of color; slaves used forged notes of permission and stole to dress extravagantly and gambling flourished on the premises. The Cabildo

> evicted the dance hall managers, but the two men simply bought their own premises and continued their lucrative business. At the new ballroom, their private guards refused entry to whomever they pleased, including city officials.[14]

There is a subtle underclass resistance going on here: that is, when "slaveholders complained that the prohibition against slaves . . . generat[ed] a greater threat . . . than integrated dances," they implicitly admitted that they were otherwise powerless to prevent such integration. Throughout the nineteenth century, theaters and ballrooms would remain the sites for semiotic contestation of space and identity, especially by white males seeking "colored entertainments," and as a result, for the blurring of racial and sexual boundaries.[15] Within these spaces, the Orleanais in particular "delighted in the openness which made it possible to participate in social functions even without formal introduction," while "dance clearly ruled as the quickening passion of the place."[16] Dance was the engine, the attraction, and the mechanism for cultural exchange at many levels of intimacy, intensity, and longevity.

The Louisiana Purchase brought an additional veneer of "American" (that is, English-speaking) rule to what was already a multicultural (French-Spanish-Caribbean-African-Native American) city, within which preferences in public dancing were even more strongly linked to aspects of cultural self-identification. The following passage from Pierre Clément de Laussat's *Memoires* . . . recounts a confrontation over characteristic social dances' patriotic associations circa 1803:

> An unfortunate potential for trouble broke out between the French and Anglo-Americans at the regular public ball. Two quadrilles, one French, the other English, formed at the same time. An American, taking offense at something, raised his walking stick at one of the fiddlers. Bedlam ensued. . . . [The Governor] resorted to persuasion rather than to rigorous measures in order to silence the American [and] the French quadrille resumed. The American interrupted it again with an English quadrille and took his place to dance. Someone cried, "If the women have a drop of French blood in their veins, they will not dance." Within minutes, the hall was completely deserted by the women.[17]

Though this melodramatic and indeed theatrical anecdote occurs not technically in the street but within a dance hall, it highlights several elements that are crucial to understanding the interplay of street and social dance in Caribbean history: most specifically language, dance types, national or ethnic identifications, and their collision within and contestation of public spaces.[18]

Such semiotic conflict only intensified after the diaspora of colonial families and their servants out of Haiti following the Revolution: Sublette holds that Spanish occupation of New Orleans, though relatively brief (less than 40 years), was a powerful conduit for the transmission of its creole expressive arts.[19] This Haitian cultural influence was felt all over this diaspora, and its impact upon Francophone North American cities like New Orleans and Charleston was even more increased after Saint-Dominguais refugees were expelled from Cuba in 1809.[20] Fiehrer confirms that "Saint-Domingue slaves represented almost a third of the 1810 slave population of New Orleans and its precincts," and explicitly cites their impact upon Orleanais movement vocabularies:

> Distinctive music and dances such as the *passepied* and *contredanse*—accompanied by small orchestras whose techniques, most notably those of the early Cuban *danza*, are direct forerunners of primitive or early jazz (from *jaser*-to chatter). Slave dances—the *bomba* and *tumba*—informed many of the later popular dance styles, essentially the *calenda*—a slave version of *contredanse* that evolved.[21]

In addition to the more formalized theatrical of the theaters, balls, and salons, the street itself became a central locus for intercultural exchange. The multiethnic market of *Place Congo* in New Orleans, which brought slaves, free blacks, and native Americans from the surrounding countryside, and working-class whites together in a rich mélange described by Benjamin Latrobe and (retrospectively) George Washington Cable, in fact resulted from attempts by city authorities to *contain* carnivalesque music, dancing, and masking, formerly distributed throughout many neighborhoods in the close quarters of this walking city, to a single location more readily controlled.[22] As early as the 1750s, there were a number of neighborhoods or plazas known as points of congregation or *places Congo* utilized by slaves and free blacks; hence, the singular *Place Congo* on the northern boundary of the Vieux Carré represents not an apotheosis of the city's cultural syncresis but, in fact, a symbol of its containment.[23] Matt Sakakeeny, a particularly acute observer of Caribbean creole culture, suggests that the Congo Square dances might actually reflect an act of synthesis across formerly distinctive African linguistic groups and therefore the final emergence of a truly pan–African *American* dance culture.[24]

## Street Dance in New Orleans

Throughout the eighteenth century, continuing into the brief but influential period of Spanish occupation (1763–1801) and even into the "American" period after the Louisiana Purchase (1803), shared traditions of danced street festival behavior, occurring in culturally resonant geographical spaces, flowed between Port-au-Prince and New Orleans, and led to a particularly strong element of African retentions in those port cities.[25] The result of this mobile, free-flowing exchange, rooted in both European and African festival dynamics, was a set of dance practices that Breunlin and Regis describe as "embodied knowledge . . . experienced at ground level."[26] We can find movement exchange and cultural synthesis through examination of this "embodied knowledge," in the dance practices embedded at the heart of Haitian and New Orleanian festive behaviors.

We have already alluded to the rich variety of syncretic identities originating through contact between Native, European, and African ethnic groups in the Caribbean and southwest Atlantic and disseminated via the river systems that were fed by those two seas. In New Orleans, the neighborhood associations and social clubs called the Mardi Gras Indians, which appear to date in their present-day form from the late nineteenth century, are the literal living embodiment of traditions of music, dance, and masking attributed to cultural exchange between Afro-Caribbeans and Native Americans across the porous boundaries of city versus countryside.[27] This fluid dynamic of Caucasian versus African versus Native identity links the Mardi Gras Indians to the pan-Caribbean phenomena of Maroons, Melungeons, Black Seminoles, Black Creeks, *Kriyos*, and other indigenous/African syncretic communities: Richard Brent Turner has posited an especially interesting and complementary theory that the costume, dance, creole catchphrases, social hierarchies, and street tactics of the Indians may reflect both the presence of expatriate Haitian vodouistes and an ongoing thread of festive behavior as antislavery resistance.[28] Regardless, under whatever name it was known ("maroon," "Indian," and so forth), this syncretic neighborhood culture was perceived by authorities to represent a very real and present threat to public order.[29] Other multiethnic working-class communities elsewhere in the Caribbean were likewise sequestered and controlled as potential sites for resistance.

## Street Dance in Port-au-Prince

A modern Haitian tradition closely paralleling that of the New Orleans Mardi Gras Indians is the masking, costume, and spectacular behaviors that revolve around the twentieth-century parades of *Rara*, a combination of drumming, singing, and dancing music.[30] The form, which reflects the impact of Fon slaves brought to Haiti in the Middle Passage, is essentially a secularization and making public of a sacred and comparatively private network of symbolic behaviors associated with the syncretic religion of *vodou*. Dance and music (especially singing and drumming) have been especially essential to vodou since the early colonial period: in fact, the iconic account of Moreau de St Méry from 1797 describes *vaudoux* as a danced religion.[31] Rara's shift from, as Michael Largey puts it, "the temple to the street," originates in various syncretic practices associated with hill-country rural communities of maroons: small villages, comparatively isolated (by jungle, swamp, or hills), retaining relatively extensive elements of original foodways/folkways, often quasi-secretive and thus hospitable to escaped slaves, not infrequently the source of rural rebellion.[32] As a "a public ritual through which poor Haitians in a range of locations remember history, create publicity, and negotiate power under conditions of insecurity," modern Rara therefore represents, like the expression of the New Orleans Indians, an urban adaptation and synthesis of older syncretic practices and, also like Indian culture, a subaltern challenge to dominant ideals of order.[33] The masked invasions of unfamiliar neighborhoods made the parades of Raraistes and Mardi Gras Indians a semiotic threat, a moment when "the popular classes confront the power-holders" and "conjure up nightmares about mass uprising."[34]

Of course, stylistic distinctions exist between Haitian Rara and New Orleans Indians: Rara parades are particularly focused upon Easter Week, beginning as early as Ash Wednesday, as opposed to the Indians' calendar, which has them marching throughout the year, with Mardi Gras only one of the focal holidays.[35] On the other hand, the yearlong ritual of costume-building and music rehearsal is a central part of both traditions' social-cohesion strategies, cited in period commentaries from the mid–nineteenth-century onward.[36] Both Rara and Indian dancers make use of decorated staffs and wands to extend the body's akimbo line and, drawing upon their shared tradition of Kongo stick-fighting, as a prop intensifying the mock combat of their dancing.[37] Similarly, percussion, including both membranophones (various tambourines, especially) and idiophones (scrapers, shakers, rattles), supports the foot mobility common in both traditions, though Rara much more prominently features the Fon-influenced bamboo or metal natural trumpets called *vaksen*, which play hocketing, polyrhythmic patterns reminiscent of West and Central African panpipe and drumming repertoires. Whistling occupies an analogously crucial role in both Indian's and Rara's strategic occupation of sonic space: as with Carnivale parades in Rio and Bahia, the Rara Grand Marshal's whistle is used not only to signal physical movement but also to trigger enhanced expressive intensity.[38]

What links these two traditions most integrally is the syncretic cultural history of the Catholic Caribbean, where West African festival and sacred behaviors collided with the Catholic Church's calendar, pantheons of saints, and emphasis upon communal tools—music, movement, costume, color, aromas, psychoactive comestibles—to elicit transformative cognitive experience.[39] Rara and the Indians likewise share an association with working-class demographics whose masking, movement, noise, and irruption into public spaces was and is perceived as potentially revolutionary.[40] Though the physical vocabularies differ, mimetic ritual-combat content and space-claiming function is consistent across both repertoires.[41] The means of temporarily invading or "occupying" hostile urban space that we have seen elsewhere—percussive "noise," chanting of stylized or secret linguistic patois, literal or implicit masking, the swirl of costumed movement, the foot-borne travel which slips through de Certeau's cracks in urban spaces to escape the forces of containment, the sense of shared group *communitas* created by moving and singing together—are all consistent with the street dance we have referenced throughout this book.[42]

Though she is speaking specifically of Rara, McAlister provides an excellent summary of a "performative orality" that echoes more widely across diverse New World Afro-creole expressive arts as "part of a cultural complex that includes *public verbal wordsmithing, displays of masculinity, and competitive performances of dance and movement* [which serve to] sustain possibilities and postures of survival for the long-suffering, disenfranchised majority classes."[43] This "embodied practice" is a cultural and communicative tradition that was literally enacted, transmitted, and retained through knowledge carried in the body, and it foregrounds, in George Lipsitz's words, "an African sensibility about the interconnectedness of art and the interconnectedness of human beings.[44] Afro-Caribbean festive art forms of the Francophone world have resisted, eluded, or disappeared from the historiography of more conventional literacies precisely because of the process-oriented, multivalent, temporary, oppositional embodiment that results from the "interconnectedness" that Lipsitz describes:

> [Participants] collectively author an important narrative about their own past, present, and future. Drawing upon the tools available to them—music, costumes, speech, and dance—they fashion a fictive identity that gives voice to their deepest values and beliefs. . . . But their collective narrative goes beyond literature and folklore, it draws upon a myriad of contradictory images and icons to fashion a syncretic unity.[45]

The physical, semiotic, and racial boundaries of New Orleans and Port-au-Prince were literally porous: cultural mixing happened along their geographic and experiential edges.[46] The "syncretic unity" that Lipsitz describes emerged, throughout the Afro-Caribbean New World, precisely as a result of the complex boundary-crossing exchange, realignment, and re-creation of identity which the sufferings of the Middle Passage demanded for survival.[47]

For the purposes of our present argument, it is the Rara and Indian parades' capacity to "occupy" public spaces through the strategic deployment of movement and sound—dance and music—that is particularly significant. Like the psalm-singers of James Davenport's New Haven and New London uprising and the "jerking" sacred dancers of the Cane Ridge revivals; the revelers of Pinkster, Jonkonnu, and the *Grand Jamaica Ball*; the "whistles, sirens, and shrieks" of blackface; the Shakers and Ghost Dancers; the nightclub and theater *primitifs* of the Jazz Age; and the hippies, yippies, drag queens, punks, and B-boys of the twentieth century, the *Raraistes* and the Mardi Gras Indians employ movement and sound to push back against the forces that contain and constrain shared subaltern expression in public spaces. That resistance can be intentional, strategic, and (sometimes) explicit—dominant classes' recurrent attempts to contain it are sufficient evidence of festive behavior's perceived efficacy for cultural resistance, its "collective [if temporary] ownership of the streets."[48] The historical perception of the threat to public order, which these working-class fraternal groups were perceived to represent, is confirmed by the long history of conflict between them and the representatives of middle-class order.[49] The impulse toward containment—a product of dominant-class anxiety regarding the unfettered movement of (particularly masked or otherwise anonymized) working-class invaders—recurs repeatedly in the history of street dance: contemporary Rio *Carnivale*, antebellum blackface theater, and Jim Crow–era Civil Rights activities have all experienced a dynamic of push back, reproach, and containment.[50]

Contestation of group identity within public spaces is persistent throughout the scholarship on Haitian and New Orleanian festival behaviors.[51] The very act of parades moving through urban neighborhoods demonstrated the porous boundaries between spectator and participant, and indeed between classes, and continues to transform the communal identities of the participants, "creating relationships that *would not otherwise be possible in everyday life*, which is dominated by the moral economy of the postindustrial city."[52] Particularly in the wake of Haiti's contemporary struggles with natural and political catastrophe, the Orleanais experience of Hurricane Katrina and the post-Katrina diaspora from NOLA's working-class black neighborhoods, street cultures like the Indians and the Raraistes remain an essential part of rebuilding and reclaiming their cities' polyglot heritage, "creating a safe space for people from different neighborhoods and of different class, ethnic, and racial affiliations to come together in a celebration of conviviality and solidarity."[53] Syncretic Afro-Caribbean street festivals, and the movement and sound which are their motivating force and central ritual of connection, serve not just as symbols suitable for a twenty-first-century tourist replication—a sort of Creole Disney World—but as actual tools for rebuilding community, reestablishing cultural history and subaltern identity, and—once more—reclaiming the streets where they were born.

# CHAPTER 5

# Utopian Movements and Moments

## Shakers and Ghost Dancers

Of course crisis is often an occasion which heightens or enables movement.

Randy Martin, *Critical Moves: Dance Studies in Theory and Practice (1998)*

This epigraph captures an essential element of socially defined movement, one particularly relevant in the history of subaltern dance in the New World.[1] As we have seen, cultural narratives of the English-speaking colonies and early United States were, with the exception of a few especially polyglot locations like New Orleans, historically dominated by Protestant dichotomies of body versus intellect, sin versus sanctity. In these semiotic paradigms, dance was treated warily, as a morally ambiguous phenomenon to be isolated from spiritual and philosophical arenas. When mapped onto dominant-versus-subaltern social dynamics, the fact that subaltern minorities like Afro-Caribbeans and Native Americans extensively employed dance, precisely for its transformational cognitive effects, only increased the suspicion with which such expression was met by mainstream society. Yet, at certain "crisis" moments utopian dance was a tool of social unity and revitalization for religious communities as well. The dominant culture's negative, paranoid, or uncomprehending responses to these communities of sacred dance only confirm the potentially irruptive impact of such practices and their parallel resonances throughout the nineteenth century.[2]

This chapter focuses on two such examples: the complex narrative of historical meanings assigned to Shakers and Ghost Dancers, two communities that sought to recover an idealized past or build a utopian future particularly through the agency of sacred dance. Precisely because their dancing pushed back against dominant cultural narratives, Shakers' and Ghost Dancers' movement identities elicited disdain, incomprehension, castigation, or persecution. This chapter thus speaks most directly to utopian dance as a reaction to and strategy for coping with marginalization and persecution in a changing world.[3]

Throughout the history of both millennial Shakers—whose story is longer and more complexly diverse than has conventionally been understood—and animist Ghost Dancers—whose late-nineteenth-century manifestation, culminating in the massacre at Wounded Knee (1890), was only one of a long series of Native American dance rebellions—we can identity a recurrent trope of shared movement as a tool for unity, "fraternity," and transformation of group consciousness. In some cases, we discover a hidden thread of Afro-Caribbean movement vocabularies and aesthetics as a generative catalyst for utopian dances, as well as a complex history of interaction between the two groups—but in all the cases cited, we will find movement to be an integral part of the construction of ecstatic experience.[4] Sacred movement has been employed precisely because it is perceived to have a theological and/or a cognitive impact; it has thus served as a tool of sectarian communities' unification and group cohesion, particularly in adverse conditions.[5] Our task is to see, in the long and complex history of these two movements, wider patterns of sacred dance experience in U.S. history as resistance, transgression, or revolution.

And so this chapter will proceed to tell two stories in tandem, addressing both unique origins and timelines (the Shakers begin in mid-eighteenth-century England, while the earliest roots of Native American danced utopia are known as far back as the late sixteenth century) and also unremarked influences—most notably, of Afro-Caribbean dance upon the early Shakers, and of Protestant millenarianism upon the various manifestations of Ghost Dance. I will begin by exploring the early roots of both movements: the Kentucky revivalism (see Chapter 1) which inspired Shaker adaptation of Afro-Caribbean movement elements, and the early-nineteenth-century Native American prophetic dance rebellions, which culminated, tragically, at Wounded Knee.

## Shaker Roots

For the purposes of this chapter's analysis, I will frame dance within the lives of Shakers—celibate religious communards originating as a splinter group of English Quakers—in four distinct periods of activity, while focusing upon only two. From their origin in mid-eighteenth-century England as "the Shaking Quakers," the sect incorporated, within a tightly controlled social structure that significantly constrained interactions between body and mind and between genders, the space for spontaneous song and movement as an expression of sacred experience. In their first period, under the foundational leadership of the charismatic visionary Mother

Ann Lee (1736–1784), worship services thus included uncontrolled, spontaneous, and not particularly theorized motion of the limbs and body.[6]

A second, significantly underdocumented period of contact, development, and synthesis occurs approximately in 1790–1810, particularly in the southwestern frontier territories on the western slope of the Appalachians (discussed in Chapter 1). Here, ecstatic Presbyterian Pentecostalism met indigenous and mixed-race movement aesthetics from Afro-Caribbean, Afro-Indian, and Native American sources. This in turn inspired an elaboration and centralization of ecstatic movement as part of Shaker practice: some of the first Shaker communities in the free territory of Ohio, north of the River, were in fact fired by direct contact with the Cumberland revivalists. Elements of this syncretic sacred dance aesthetic later migrate farther, most notably to the North American West, and—in the persons of African American converts and missionaries—back to the Caribbean.

The third period of Shaker activity is also the best known: the Era of Manifestations circa 1830–1850, situated in the "Burned-Over Districts" (so called because they were regions repeatedly subjected to the "fires" of religious revivalism) of western New York, Pennsylvania, and Ohio. Visionary and charismatic personalities like Mother Ann Lee and other "Founders" had been supplanted by regularization of doctrine, codification of ecstatic song and dance, the construction of new communities, and an increase incidence of "manifestations" (visions of and bequests—drawings, songs, and dances—from departed spirits, most notably), which became new emblems of sanctity. Though this era is not my primary focus, I will suggest in passing that its increased complexity of supernatural apparatus reflects in part the influence of Afro-Caribbean, especially Haitian, possession religions.[7]

The fourth and final era, which will link to the parallel narrative of Ghost Dancers, is the late influence of Shaker practices among indigenous peoples in the North American West and Pacific Northwest, particularly as these practices were adapted and resyncretized between approximately 1870 and the post–Wounded Knee (1890) period.

## Period I: The "Shaking Quakers"

The roots of the Shakers lie in industrializing mid-eighteenth-century Lancashire, when a schismatic group called the Wardley Society, preaching sexual abstinence and revivalism, came to be known as the "Shaking Quakers" because of the centrality, in their worship, of ecstatic speech, song, and movement. Under the influence of the millenarian Camisards, French Huguenots who had come to England after 1706 in the wake of a failed religious rebellion, the early Shakers were already known for "dancing in extravagant postures" and "engaging in ecstatic worship with singing, shouting, dancing, visions, and prophecies."[8] Wild stories about their transgressive (especially dance and sexual) behaviors were promulgated—though these stories are essentially unconfirmed, and reveal more about dominant-culture prejudices than about the sectarians themselves.

Ann Lee (born in Manchester 1736), the unlettered daughter of a blacksmith, joined the Society at the age of 22 and, like other members, was subjected to verbal, legal, and physical persecution by outsiders. In 1770, after a revelation as the second coming of Christ, she became leader of the sect; under her leadership, a small group made the decision in 1774 to immigrate to North America, as previous religious minorities had done.[9] Though their early experience in the New World is not documented, it is known that as strict pacifists, they remained neutral during the American Revolution, and that they had settled by 1779 in Watervliet, New York, on the Hudson River north of Albany.[10] This location is telling, because the region was a hotbed of pan-ethnic cultural exchange in the years prior to and during the Revolution: for example, the Afro-Dutch seasonal holiday of Pinkster (from Dutch/German *Pfingster* or Pentecost) begins in this period and spreads south down the River to New York, New Jersey, and Long Island by 1800—in turn inspiring early blackface theatricals in New York City.

At the same time, the midcentury Anglican Great Awakening (Chapter 1) and Baptist New Lights revival were paving the way for millenarians of many types.[11] Despite this, the Shakers elicited curiosity and voyeuristic critique, as had been the case in England.[12] Shaker aesthetics of this early period were made more concrete and comprehensible through the medium of the physical communities they built, particularly their meeting houses: tributes to functional design and logical craftsmanship.[13] These meetinghouses, whose standard patterning was set by around 1785, were concrete and specific manifestations of a worldview that structured spaces and consciousnesses to serve the performance of community.[14] In their movement aesthetic no less than in their architectural design, the Shaker vision of the meanings of communal dance responded to and influenced—mostly unconsciously—a range of external cultural dynamics uniquely available in the North American context.

## Period II: Scots-Irish and Native Americans on the Western Watershed

In Chapter 1 we explored the swift and dynamic synthesis and transformation of Presbyterian Pentecostalism in the Cumberland revivals of ca. 1790–1803, when, on the southwestern watershed of the Appalachians, Scots-Irish immigrants met a diversity of Afro-Caribbean, Native American, and creole belief systems and movement vocabularies. Seeking land and/or religious freedom, these immigrants brought with them the Presbyterian practice of "Sacrament Season," which had evolved during the mid-seventeenth-century Scottish Reformation as a replacement for the Catholic Feast of Corpus Christi (itself an outgrowth of pre-Christian midsummer festivals). With its Pentecostal framework intact, the Sacrament Season yielded immersive experiential environments, which included "outdoor preaching, large numbers of people often traveling, long vigils, dramatic conversions, [and a] carnival-like atmosphere."[15]

On the frontiers, especially in the unsettled environment of the war and postwar years, Anglicanism's influence waned, and, after the 1794 Battle of Fallen Timbers (near present-day Toledo, Ohio) ended the Indian threat, Scots Presbyterian immigration exploded: by the time Kentucky achieved statehood in 1792, its population topped 73,000, over 10 percent of whom were slaves.[16]

Most of the rivers in the Cumberland Plateau flow north toward the Ohio, which in turn accounts for the influence of river-borne (especially Afro-Caribbean) culture upon the region (see Chapter 1); coupled with the impact of ethnic groups already resident in the Plateau (especially the so-called "Melungeons," who were themselves the descendants of Afro-Caribbean settlers from coastal South Carolina, and Barbados before that). The Cumberland was a place of extensive and rich cultural exchange. This played out in many arenas, including sacred-movement vocabularies, in the rhetoric around ecstatic experience and—as with the Shakers—in the spaces created as sites for that experience.

The largest and most impactful of the Cumberland revivals were at Cane Ridge, Kentucky, near present-day Lexington, where in 1791 a meetinghouse measuring fifty by thirty feet was constructed. The building itself was built to seat 350 and could accommodate up to 500 in the crowded summer festival seasons, but the large numbers associated with such revivals soon overrode traditional social strictures and required renovations that literally reconfigured a formerly segregated space.[17] The Cumberland revivals, like First Great Awakening that preceded them and the Shaker communities that emerged from them, were spaces in which dominant-culture racial separations were relaxed and in which cultural exchange was enhanced.[18]

Less remarked in the history of the Shakers on the southwestern frontiers, however, is the concrete impact of both Afro-Caribbean and Native American—and creole—movement and belief systems upon their dance practices. In the period after 1800, while slaves and free people of color were converted to Shaker practices—as they had been to Pentecostalism in the Cumberland—the influences went both ways, including songs, dream-visions, and movement vocabularies.[19] As has been stated, Native American references in Shaker theology would be more explicit in the third period, the "Era of Manifestations," when the influence of Midwestern spiritualism and the waning of the Founders' direct influence led to an increase in claims of visions, visitations, and gifts from the dead. But the exchange of Shaker and Native American dance practices had already been put in motion during the period of the Cumberland Revivals.

## Ghost Dancers at the Margins

Native American sacred dance was a topic of reportage, description, and attempted explication from the first European contact with indigenous peoples—and not only of reportage but also of influence and (witting or unwitting) imitation and appropriation.[20] Similarly, cultural interchange and social interaction between African Americans and Native Americans had been going on throughout the hemisphere since the earliest days of the Middle Passage—and earlier, if one considers the participation of black Africans as both slaves and free men in the early expeditions of Spanish conquistadores. Often, this colonial contact brought transformative or threatening cosmological conflict; in the U.S. Southeast, these apocalyptic visions were crystallized in the first decade of the nineteenth century.[21] Dance played a central role in both imagining and responding to such prophecies.[22]

As we have seen, new migration brought Scots-Irish settlers and their slaves into the Cumberland in the 1790s, and despite—or perhaps because of—the attendant conflict, there was extensive exchange and intermarriage between Natives, Africans, and Europeans. From a very early date, for example, the Creek of northern Alabama (who were already practitioners of a form of slavery, revolving around the assimilation of women and children captured in battle) found themselves accommodating blacks as escapees, refugees, or chattel.[23] There had likewise been ongoing native exchange with French and Spanish traders in the Southeast as early the seventeenth century; in fact, a growing intercultural market for slaves throughout the Caribbean led the Creek to trade captured women and children as far afield as Charleston and the Sugar Islands.[24] They also interacted with French Canadian explorers on the southern tributaries of the Ohio, while Africans living among them assisted as linguists in trading at the entrepot of Mobile, and fought alongside them during the Yamasee War (1715–1716).[25]

The sense of natives' cultural vulnerability increased in the wake of white settlement over the course of the eighteenth century, when longstanding enmity between Cherokee and Creek people in the southwestern Appalachians was exacerbated by their service on opposite sides as allies to the French and English during the Seven Years' War. That unrest opened the door for white settlers from North Carolina to claim Cherokee land in the 1770s, while the continued economic and demographic ferment of the post-Revolutionary period further increased conflict between indigenous peoples and settlers from "over the mountains." After 1783 the cessation of British claims, and the revocation of George III's 1763 prohibition against settlement west of the mountains, accelerated white settlement and meant that the Creek, like the Cherokee, interacted even more extensively with both Scots Presbyterian and African-creole sacred practices.[26] A not-insignificant percentage of political and military leaders among these groups were actually of mixed blood, advantaged by their enhanced language skills and understanding of European social priorities; mixed-race offspring participated fully as members of these communities, and Creek chieftains with Scots-Irish antecedents fought on the Loyalist side during the American Revolution.[27]

At precisely the same period and locations, and very much as a result of the turmoil which war, settlement, and relocation crystallized, a whole series of Native American prophetic movements arose in response to white colonization.[28] Just as Shaker millenarianism appeared in the wake of significant socioeconomic change (the early stages of the Industrial Revolution in the English Midlands, rekindled in the uneasy days of the America Revolution in upstate New York), there arose on the post-Revolutionary frontier a "Native American Great Awakening," which Sullivan describes as "a great chain of prophet-led nativist resistance, proceeding from the earliest stirrings and florid rebellions among the Delaware, Shawnee, Cherokee, and Creek [ca. 1810] to the relentless removal policies of the Jackson [1829–1837] and Van Buren [1837–1841] administrations."[29] In this period, both Cherokee Ghost Dancing (1811–1812) and the Creek War (1813) were a result of tensions between Native Americans and encroaching white settlers (and those Natives who supported compromise or conciliation, as opposed to resistance), and both carried utopian and/or apocalyptic theological implications.[30]

While millenarian dance revivals arose in different locations among different indigenous peoples at different times, they were most often and demonstrably a result of recurrent patterns of traditional/spiritual convictions directly responding to perceptions of existential threat: Martin calls them "religious revolts . . . in creative contact with history."[31] The short-lived Creek Rebellion of 1813, for example, followed a series of prophetic visions and visitations from spirits at Rocky Mountain, conjoined with a series of nearly simultaneous natural events (an earthquake on the New Madrid Fault, the Great Comet of 1811, and a series of fierce hailstorms). A more worldly influence from the North was indigenous resistance to the 1809 Treaty of Fort Wayne, which had ceded enormous tracts of native territory illegally to the Territory of Indiana. Seeking to mobilize a coalition of tribes to resist these concessions, the Shawnee leader Tecumseh (1768–1813), in October 1811 traveled to and addressed a gathering of Creek, employing powerfully apocalyptic oratory in which dance is a theological toil of rebellion:

> Oh! Muscogees, brethren of my mother, brush from your eyelids the sleep of slavery; once more strike for vengeance; once more for your country. The spirits of the

> mighty dead complain. Their tears drop from the weeping skies. Let the white race perish. They seize your land; they corrupt your women; they trample on the ashes of your dead! Back, whence they came, upon a trail of blood, they must be driven. . . . This is the will of the Great Spirit, revealed to my brother, his familiar, the Prophet of the Lakes. He sends me to you. *All the tribes of the north are dancing the war-dance. . . .* Tecumseh will soon return to his country [but] my prophets shall tarry with you. They will stand between you and the bullets of your enemies.[32]

Lawrence Sullivan, calling the rebellion "a religious drama that powerfully displayed the Muskogees' deepest concerns at a critical fissure," situates dance at the center of sacred revolt; he describes the revival of Creek spirit dancing not as a "recovery" of an older folkway (despite the revivalist language implicit in Tecumseh's speech), but rather as the importation of a foreign resource—Shawnee dance—as a way to deal with existential threats and a changing world:

> Dance played an essential role in the Muskogee millenarian movement. Men and women dramatically expressed and transformed their social, natural, and spiritual relations by incorporating dance into their daily lives. In this case, *it was not a dance from their own rich repertoire, but one coming from outside contacts. . . .* Dancing was deemed the most efficacious way to socialize prophetic visions.[33]

Sullivan quotes period reports that make explicit the conflicting symbolism of indigenous versus European dance: movement, transmitted from outside by visionary prophets of rebellion, became an expression of "competing value systems and competing ideological systems."[34] Martin makes the important point that, on the North American continent, Native Americans, Europeans, and Africans were "brought into a new world" of cognitive experience and suggested that from this contact, this attempt to learn to "live and love" in a new cosmological space, there emerged "a new kind of anticolonial warrior, a dancer guided by fresh contact with the sacred."[35] For Native Americans subjected to psychological and physical displacement in the early nineteenth century, dance became a theological strategy and a revolutionary tactic.[36]

Despite the sad cycle of U.S. government repression, containment, and relocation of Native American groups—which would recur again in the West, leading to the late apotheosis of Greasy Grass, Ghost Dance, and Wounded Knee—their influence was also felt in Anglo-American millenarianism throughout the nineteenth century.[37] Native Americans entered the symbolic vocabulary of both Shakers and spiritualism, co-opted as icons of antiquity or authenticity, at precisely the same historical moment that their actual impact east of the Mississippi was evaporating.[38] Most saliently for our discussion, in light of the earlier syncretic practices that arose in the Cumberland Revivals, indigenous symbolic constructions form a hidden thread running through the fabric of the Shaker Era of Manifestations, for it is in precisely this era that the borrowed apparatus of sacred gifts (of songs, dances, or visual images) and communion with the dead—especially the spirits of the departed Founders—revitalize Shaker practice.[39] Simpson has provided a useful summary of the synthesis of European Protestant and animist Afro-Caribbean beliefs; examining that summary, we can also locate parallel behaviors in millenarian Native American dance religions, which include "the belief that there are supernatural beings . . . who are concerned with the immediate fate of those who worship them," as well as "multiple rites for the dead" and "sorcery, dreaming, and healing."[40] "Sorcery, dreaming, and healing" would continue, in fact, to be essential theological tools shared among Shakers and Native Americans alike.

## Period III: The Era of Manifestations

The third period of Shaker experience, the Era of Manifestations (roughly 1837 through 1845), though most noteworthy and most significant in shaping public perceptions of the sect, in fact represents a brief apotheosis, followed by a long gradual twilight in response to post–Civil War urbanization and industrialization. In the early stages of this era, which followed the decease of influential Founders like Mother Ann Lee, in 1805 Shaker leader Mother Lucy Wright had "open[ed] the gospel" and "authorized missionary expeditions in the Ohio Valley" and elsewhere to the frontier, from the original communities in New York and Pennsylvania.[41] In this period, Shaker centralization of power and doctrine moved away from the relatively undocumented and freely interpreted practices of communities led by Founders and shifted into a historical moment when Shakerism evolved "from an apocalyptic sect into a millennial church."[42] Doctrinal and organizational tensions between eastern establishment and western frontier Shaker settlements soon followed; among these disputants, dance was a significant point of contention.[43] That dancing directly borrowed elements of cosmology and terminology associated with Afro-Caribbean and Native American styles; description of Shaker movement vocabularies from the Era of Manifestations clearly recall those same influences as had been felt in the Cumberland revivals:

> As the shaking took on a measure of regularity in form, so too did the elaboration of the shaking into "the step manner" of motion, the "travel," "circle," "round," etc. There were also the "drumming step," the "shuffle," "turning shuffle," "chain regular," "walking," "square order shuffle." . . . This "step manner" was not a continual progress forward, such as we call a march. It was a mode of shaking the feet which carried the shaker forward and backward within a very short space on the floor, somewhat in the manner of a slightly complicated way of marking time before one begins to start forward in a march.[44]

While this language recalls the variants of the Jerks, a more subtle reading of the descriptions, particularly of the various "shuffles," also reminds us of period potrayals of the Afro-Caribbean ring-shout, and Native American circle dances that are described as early as the 1680s.[45]

At the same time, beyond its (mostly unremarked) cultural influences, the theology of Shaker dance was also paradoxical, internally contradictory, and fruitfully ambiguous.[46] Yet its constituent elements—the utopian, apocalyptic, or millenarian Afro-Caribbean and Native American theologies that shaped its movement languages—continued to echo throughout the century, just as Shakerism continued to interweave with adjacent subaltern traditions.[47] In the Era of Manifestations, "messages from the dead, and these often in the form of songs or anthems or hymns or dance tunes, at times were 'received' in 'unknown tongues'"; sacred dances and dance tunes were gifts from the Founders, received in ecstatic trance, accompanied by visions of the departed and gifts of sacred visual patterns and designs.[48]

Still later, in the urbanizing and industrializing mid–nineteenth century, outside pressures transformed the sect further, even as it drew attention from fascinated outsiders (see for example the primitive painting by "C. Winter" reproducing blackface minstrels parodying Shaker dance, reproduced in Hans Nathan, *Dan Emmett and the Rise of Early Negro Minstrelsy* [Norman: University of Oklahoma Press, 1962, 95]) and from sympathetic contemporaries in other utopian and abolitionist circles. By the 1840s, when the Shakers had reached a peak of public visibility, all manner of sacred and secular dance, clothing, and other "worldly" attractions were flashpoints of contention between and among community members and outsiders.[49] In the wake, then, of the Cane Ridge Revivals, the "opening" of Ohio, Indiana, and Illinois, and especially during the Era of Manifestations, Shaker doctrine and practices were spun off and into other utopian and religious communities. Repeatedly throughout the century, these subaltern dance idioms shaded over into rebellion.[50] Persons of mixed ethnicity and cultural experience, and their dancing, were widely represented in numerous indigenous and slave revolts, in both North America and the Caribbean, and that apocalyptic movement vocabulary continued into the late-nineteenth-century rise and fall of the archetypal Ghost Dance: a dance of desperation in the face of cultural crisis.[51]

## Period IV: Apotheosis and Fall of the Ghost Dance

Thus, in order to understand the late-nineteenth-century Ghost Dance, probably the best-known Native American dance rebellion in American popular history, it is necessary to situate the movement within a chronology nearly as long as colonization itself, and to analyze it as a reflection of a complex series of exchanges between European and indigenous belief systems. In the New World—whether at

Wounded Knee, Charleston (1822: Vesey's rebellion), Rocky Mountain (1813: the Creek rebellion), or Bwa Kayiman (1791: the first Haitian slave rebellion)—subaltern dance had literally embodied resistance. That these resistance movements frequently arose in response to unsupportable or terrifying sociocultural change only made them more urgent; in an archetypal passage, a few weeks before the 1890 Wounded Knee massacre, the Lakota leader Little Wound, while insisting to the local Indian Agent that the syncretic Ghost Dance presented no threat, absolutely and categorically refused to commit to its cessation:

> I understand that the soldiers have come on the reservation. What have they come for? We have done nothing. Our dance is a religious dance, and we are going to dance until spring. If we find then that the Christ does not appear, we will stop dancing, but, in the meantime, troops or no troops, we shall start our dance on this creek in the morning.[52]

Inspired by a series of visions and predictions preached by the Christian-educated Northern Paiute leader Wovoka (a/k/a "Jack Wilson," ca. 1856–1932), the later western/northwestern manifestation of Ghost Dance arose and spread very swiftly in 1889–1890 among northern Plains people. This millennial dancing was self-evidently syncretic, combining elements of indigenous and Euro-Christian theology: while "Jack Wilson's" vision drew on a tradition of dancing to restore identity and to invoke the spirits, it was also directly shaped by the European encounter.[53] Aspects of this dance's elements—use of ritual ablutions, circular choreographies, and range of possession experiences—reach back to both Tecumseh's revolutionary dance and to the "Jerks" we have encountered early in the Cumberland.[54] Martin confirms the links between Wovoka's movement and the earlier dances of rebellion:

> The Sioux Ghost Dance movement also centered upon a dance that came from outside. . . . This suggests that one of the vital ways to symbolize a pan–Native American identity was to borrow an expressive practice from a group perceived to be more distant from and less dependent upon European Americans.[55]

The perceived life-or-death urgency of the dance was further exacerbated in February 1890 by the U.S. government's violation, under pressure from eastern settlers, of the terms of Sioux treaties; the Great Reservation was to be broken up and its inhabitants resettled on small farms. Despite sympathetic responses from eastern intellectuals like Charles Eastman, William James, John Dewey, and Jane Addams, who correctly understood Wovoka's dance as symbolic resistance to the imposition of physically and spiritually impossible living conditions, opportunistic Bureau of Indian Affairs officials and purveyors preferred to fan the flames of popular hysteria regarding the dance's perceived threat, insisting that it was both a prelude to violent uprisings and a "revolting" expression of resistance.[56]

In late December 1890, after the murder of the leader Sitting Bull by a tribal policeman, a group of Hunkapapa and Miniconju who had briefly escaped from the Pine Ridge Reservation surrendered to elements of the U.S. Seventh Cavalry and were then moved as prisoners to a camp at Wounded Knee Creek, preparatory to their surrender of weapons and return to the reservation. On December 29th, the morning of the handover, only a few weapons were proffered for confiscation, while a violent search of the encampment yielded only a few more. During this search, the shaman and prophet Yellow Bird broke into the steps of the Ghost Dance and danced in a circle around the negotiators. A shot—reputedly from a deaf Lakota warrior who did not understand the terms of the surrender—rang out, and the troopers of the Seventh Cavalry, George Armstrong Custer's outfit, which had been decimated at Greasy Grass in 1876, began firing into the crowd with repeater carbines and Hotchkiss guns (a variant of the multishot Gatling gun). Over 300 men, women, and children were killed, some shot in the back as much as two miles from the Creek.[57]

In the wake of this cold-blooded execution, white opinion was largely unsympathetic; only a few voices questioned the Seventh's actions or the inevitability or necessity of violent "pacification."[58] Stortz says that this condemnation of Native expression arose from willful white incomprehension of the Ghost Dance, describing it as "a confrontation between various kinds of power and authority."[59] When cosmologies, "which are socially articulated by certain structural differences," clash in situations of massively unequal technological or economic power, the disenfranchised may have recourse only in the realm of the symbolic.[60]

On the other hand, though Wounded Knee was a shattering manifestation of the U.S. government's willingness to engage in de facto genocide when placed under pressure by an expanding population, economics, or simple greed, it would be a mistake to believe that the massacre "ended" the Ghost Dance. A better construction might be to see Wounded Knee as precipitating another cycle of adaptation and syncretism between Native American animism and Pentecostal revivalism, which later continued in the Indian Shaker movement; certainly, intersections and exchange between Native American and Euro-American belief systems and syncretic religion continued through the balance of the twentieth century. [61] More broadly and philosophically, perhaps it can be possible to begin to see Afro-Caribbean possession religion, Cane Ridge revivalism, millenarian Ghost Dancing, and the Shaker geometries of ecstasy as all part of a grand, sometimes painful, inadvertent, or brutal, but nevertheless heroic experiment in seeking to make sense, on this North American continent, of what it means to rediscover, live, and move within sacred spaces that unite body, mind, and spirit.

We are, of course, still working on that.

# CHAPTER 6

# Blackface Transformations I

## Modernism, Primitivism, and Race

Even as it moved into theaters and electrical media, street dance maintained the capacity to carry resistance messages; indeed, performers learned to manipulate the specialized semiotics of the theater and soundstage, as blackface minstrels had done, for purposes of subaltern critique. The following description, for example, comes from a *Chicago Defender* article by Mark Hellinger about white hecklers ("some southern society in New York City for a reunion") crashing a Bill Robinson performance in *Blackbirds of 1928*, and details Robinson's performative response:

> Robinson stepped to the footlights. "Keep playing boys," he said softly. The music went on. Bill Robinson danced. Slowly. Tap. Tap. Tap. Tap. And as he danced he spoke. "What you men have done tonight," he murmured, "is a disgrace to your race. You down there. You. And you. And you." Tap. Tap. Tap. Tap. "If I stepped down the street," he continued, "entered the New Amsterdam theatre and waved a bill before a chorus girl, I'd be mobbed. If I did a thing like that I'd deserve whatever punishment I received." Tap. Tap. Tap. "For 30 long years I've been dancing and trying to entertain everyone to the best of my ability. The thing that happened here tonight has never been done before. I consider you—and you—and you the lowest men I have ever played before." The audience went wild. For five solid minutes they applauded. One by one the "gentlemen" reached for their hats and disappeared into the night.[1]

As we have seen, aspects of blackface practice—both its surface caricature and its subversive subtexts—held sway in North American entertainments from the heyday of the Virginia Minstrels in the 1840s all the way into the Jazz Age (and minstrelsy continued in private settings long after its gradual erasure from public forums in the 1940s). Its related creole body languages influenced ragtime, "coon" songs, cartoon animation, and early jazz dance; these dance vocabularies, though originating in working-class contexts—often, zones of transgressive behavior that facilitated black-white cultural exchange—were borrowed, imitated, stolen, and swept up into the maw of popular culture, from which they fanned out again into social dancing.[2] We can therefore expect to identify the hidden codes of the creole synthesis and thus of subaltern movement in a variety of primary source descriptions, photographs, and film.

## Josephine Baker

One notable twentieth-century exponent of "akimbo" aesthetics in the pre–Civil Rights era, whose body vocabularies were notoriously influential in North American and continental European semiotic fields, was the remarkable Josephine Baker (1906–1975). Baker's theatricalization of street dance vocabulary, played out in stage and film contexts, was perceived and intended as transgressive and liberating of racist boundaries; as Michael Borshuk, whose article "An Intelligence of the Body" strongly influences my own analysis, says, she "constructed herself within a network of injurious representations and exploited her position within this matrix to subversive effect."[3]

Born in St Louis to an unmarried mixed-race (African American / Native American) mother, Baker lived and danced on the streets in her early teens before being recruited into a vaudeville troupe at 15 and eventually heading to New York, where her appearance in the seminal 1921 Eubie Blake / Noble Sissle Broadway stage show *Shuffle Along* was a career breakthrough.[4] Though considered too young, too small, and too dark-skinned to star as a dancer, she found a place for herself as the "end girl," which role was, like that of minstrelsy's "end men" Tambo and Bones, *Uncle Tom's Cabin*'s character Topsy, or the Little Rascals' Buckwheat, essentially comic and parodic.[5] The "end girl" was caricatured as a small, young, or incompetent imitator of the more statuesque and conventionally "beautiful" chorines. Baker, in fact, played Topsy in blackface in *The Chocolate Dandies* (1924), and, as Dalton and Gates point out, evoked a response not dissimilar to that of Dickens to the character-dancer Master Juba eighty years before: e. e. cummings, for example, described her as a "vital, incomparably fluid nightmare which crossed its eyes and warped its limbs in a purely unearthly manner."[6]

Baker's pratfalls, "novelty" dance, and exaggerated facial expressions, all reminiscent of the blackface minstrels, permitted her to mock conventional notions of beauty, grace, and poise. Added to the gender-bending that her appropriation of minstrelsy's cross-dressed "wench" roles recalled (discussed later), her trickster persona connected directly with analogous parody in earlier cakewalk and blackface dance and reached back to the "participatory discrepancies" of Afro-Caribbean aesthetics and social critique.[7] In so doing, as Brooks puts it, "Baker was able to create dissonant humor. This dissonance, one might argue, emerged out of that end space," which akimbo space had been part of both the European carnivalesque, and of the Afro-Caribbean festive since the earliest colonization.[8]

Like Ira Aldridge, Baker found her greatest successes in Europe, as a character dancer and film star and, eventually, impresario and civil rights activist, but I am interested particularly in her early career and the body strategies she used to carve out an identity on the 1920s stage, a semiotic zone that was integrating swiftly and unpredictably.[9] One of her most distinctive bits of "business" was a cross-eyed expression; as Brooks points out, this gesture not only made her early career ("I was the only chorus girl making $125 a week, and all because I could cross my eyes!") but also "situates Baker in relation to other eccentric performers who made their bodies move in unexpected ways."[10] The akimbo nature of bodily motion and facial gesture, which provide a visual counterpoint to the sounding "participatory discrepancies" of polyrhythm and syncopation, thus links Baker to a transgressive and rebellious performance tradition. It likewise foreshadows her contributions to the complex oppositional semiotics of the proto–Civil Rights movement (Baker worked with the French Resistance in the Second World War and was, in fact, invited by Coretta Scott King to become a leader of Dr. King's organizations in the wake of his 1968 assassination).

An anonymous commentator on her Broadway performances captured the complex contradiction and appeal of Baker's subtly skewed movement vocabulary:

> She was the little girl on the end. You couldn't forget her once you'd noticed her, and you couldn't escape noticing her. She was beautiful but it was never her beauty that attracted your eyes. She had a trick of letting her knees fold under her, eccentric wise. And her eyes, just at the crucial moment when the music reach[ed] the climactic "he's just wild about, cannot live without, he's just wild about me" . . . her eyes crossed. . . . Nothing very beautiful about a cross-eyed coloured girl. Nothing very appealing. But it was the folding knees and the cross-eyes that helped bring back the choruses for those unforgettable encores.[11]

The account of Parisian painter Paul Colin, for whom she modeled in the late '20s, reveals the voyeurism that underlaid white fascination with Baker:

> She was part boxing kangaroo, part rubber woman, part female Tarzan. She contorted her limbs and body, crossed her eyes, shimmied, puffed out her cheeks, and crossed the stage on all fours, her kinetic rear end becoming the mobile center of our outlandish maneuvers. Then, naked but for green feathers about her hips, her skull lacquered black, she provoked both anger and enthusiasm.[12]

Beyond the primitivism that saturates Colin's description, most striking about both New York and Parisian reports is that it was *movement*—specifically unpredictable, unconventional, akimbo movement—that served as the vehicle for Baker's contestation of theatrical norms.[13] In Paris, like other African American expatriates, Baker created a public movement persona that played on overlapping tropes of "American-ness," "blackness," "primitivism," and eroticism (of the sort that would drive 1920s modernist experiments like Krenek's *Jonny Spielt Auf* and Milhaud's *Le boeuf sur le toite*) and which made her an iconic star.[14] Additionally, in the Americas, her akimbo eyes, body, and music—her persona's "cutting and breaking" of behavioral norms—aggressively exploited explicit prejudice, while embodying implicit resistance: a paradoxical multi-valence consistent with blackface's own.[15] Judith Bettelheim thus aptly describes Baker performance of sexuality as "an oppositional practice."[16]

**Figure 2:** Paul Colin (1892–1985); *La Revue Nègre*, 1925. Alamy.

We might put forth as an example for analysis a particular image in Paul Colin's *Le Tumulte Noir* portfolio, from 1927. Colin had been Baker's lover and a member of the artistic staff at the Théâtre des Champs-Élysées where *La Revue Nègre* was staged, and his 1925 poster for the *Revue*, which includes two caricatured grinning faces and a sleek full-body portrait of Baker, was hugely influential (it was reproduced, borrowed, and imitated—including by Nazi propagandists—and prints now sell for $322,000 and above). In the 1927 portfolio, which consists of hand-colored lithographs of the sketches Colin made while, as Dalton and Gates suggest, she danced for him, one image may suffice as example.

**Figure 3:** Josephine Baker. Paul Colin. *Palm Skirt*, 1927. Lithograph with pochoir coloring on paper. National Portrait Gallery, Smithsonian Institution. © 1997 Estate of Paul Colin / Artists Rights Society (ARS), New York / ADAGP, Paris.

Entitled *Palm Skirt*, and colored with shades of brown, black, and green *pochoir*, Colin depicts Baker, nude except for the eponymous skirt, which barely covers but also exaggerates the arch and lift of her rear end.[17] The perspective is from behind and to her left, so that we see her rear and right side, with arms, legs, and torso in brown silhouette against the matte gray background. Particularly notable and focal are the akimbo lines of her body: the backward curve of her supporting left leg and calf is balanced by the bent knee and lifted toes of the right, while the left thigh sweeps upward to the palm skirt and her outthrust buttocks. The deeply arched back further emphasizes the long line of her torso (as will the "Gonna push away troubles" choreography employed by Ivie Anderson in *A Day at the Races*, discussed later). Her shoulders are lifted and her two deeply bent arms frame the highlights on her "lacquered" hair: Baker in her early career affected a short, slicked-back hairstyle that emphasized the movements of her head and its varied poses atop her long neck. Her left arm is raised, elbow upward, and bent over her head, with the forearm and extended, crooked fingers further exaggerating the akimbo posture of the limb and its half-framing of her head. Her right elbow is raised as well, but at an angle upward and far out to the right, with the forearm extending backward toward, and framing, her naked breast and nipple, and an inverted hand (with lighter-colored palm) and bent fingers again exaggerating the akimbo details. Cutting back subtly against her arms' various angles are the downward arc of her hairstyle's elongated sidelocks, and the significant lateral exaggeration of her long eyelashes, seen in silhouette.

While eschewing unnecessary claims for the documentary accuracy of Colin's image—and after all, documentary accuracy was not his mandate—we should remember that Baker modeled for him by dancing. So his visual model was a dancing body in motion. Moreover, the portrait's visual syncopation and geometric cutting-and-breaking of Anglo-European aesthetics' flowing lines are consistent with both the descriptive, photographic, and filmed evidence of Baker's performances and the transgressive impulse of the creole synthesis itself. Thus, the "static" image of *Palm Skirt* can be understood as a two-dimensional, but nevertheless revealing and effective, representation, just like *A Grand Jamaica Ball!* (see Chapter 2), of Afro Caribbean akimbo aesthetics in moving body and sounding rhythm.

We may also comment that, even in the more "realist" medium of photography, Baker's own carefully deployed body vocabulary echoes that which is captured in *Le Tumulte Noir*. Two particularly iconic photographs, both well-known in the period and in both of which Baker employs akimbo body vocabulary, were shot by the photographer Lucien Walery (1863–1935): *Banana Skirt*, for the 1927 Folies Bergere production *Un Vent de Folie*, and *Girdle of Bananas*, for the 1926 *La Folie du Joir*.[18]

In *Girdle*, Baker, slightly more modestly clad (in addition to the eponymous girdle, she wears a sheer bikini top that covers her breasts but focuses attention on

**Figure 4:** *Girdle of Bananas*, 1926.

her nipples), faces the camera. Her right, supporting, leg is straight, knee locked, and carries straight upward to her right hip, which is cocked very aggressively up, back, and to her right. Her left leg is bent, with the toes touching the floor—in fact, her outthrust right hip carries into her backward-arched spine, tilting her torso forward so completely that she is able comfortably to rest her left hand, elbow straight, on her left knee. Continuing the akimbo aesthetic, her right hand, palm upward, is supported by her sharply bent right elbow, which rests on her right hip. Dropping and turning her chin to rest nearly on her right shoulder, she grins insouciantly at the lens.

The effect, in fact, is that we are seeing, from the front, elements of the posture that Colin depicts in *Palm Skirt*, particularly Baker's emphasis of her cocked hip and outthrust buttock and the use of her arms to frame and mirror akimbo aesthetics. The principle contrasts to the lithograph are, most notably, the straight-on perspective, which reveals the fullness and muscularity of her bare belly and, again, the vitality and power of her gaze—a gaze denied in the rearward perspective of

**Figure 5:** *Banana Skirt*, 1927.

Colin's print. The overall impact of Walery's photograph—over which, as subject, Baker could exert far more control than Colin's lithographs—is a strong, sensual, rooted, self-aware embodiment of polyrhythmic consciousness.

The 1927's *Banana Skirt* photograph, also by Walery, utilizes a different posture but conveys comparable power and agency. Here, in a studio setting highly reminiscent of the 1926 image, Baker faces to her left, along a line perpendicular to the camera's line of sight. Planted on her left foot, she slightly lifts, in a more relaxed fashion, her sandaled right. In this somewhat more upright posture, the visual emphasis is not so strongly upon her hips or rear end, but rather on her lifted arms, backward-arched shoulders, and prominent belly. Again turning and dropping her chin, she smiles somewhat more mysteriously at the lens, while her two arms, in contrast to the images previously discussed, trace similar angles to one another: elbows down, forearms canted sharply upward, both index fingers pointed from her closed fists and arched thumbs toward the camera's right. The downward "V" shapes of her elbows echo, at a 90-degree angle, the slighter angles of her bent

**Figure 6:** *Baker Dancing the Charleston*, 1926.

knees. The posture, angles, and effect here are possibly less inviting—though no less confident—than the previous portraits: here, the effect is of cooler, more independent, possibly more mysterious sensuality.

The third and final piece of photographic evidence in our analysis of Baker's akimbo body vocabulary is a still photo taken on the stage of the Folies Bergere in 1926. Titled *Baker Dancing the Charleston*, and again shot by Walery, it purports to capture her midperformance, although there is a strong possibility that it was taken in an onstage posing session, not a performance.

She holds the characteristic Charleston posture—heels together, toes splayed outward, knees widely separated to yield a "diamond-shaped" lower body, arms crossed and palms on opposite knees. So far, this image is consistent with many other artists' and amateurs' renditions of the Charleston's crisscrossing arm-and-leg choreography—and, for that matter, Abraham James's portrayal of creole dance in *A Grand Jamaica Ball!* What distinguishes Baker's embodiment of this trope is, once again, a subtle but intentional bit of facial choreography: with her shoulders dropped in the hands-on-knees posture, and a characteristic wide grin and tight, shiny hair, she looks sharply to her right in a "glancing out of the corner of her eyes" expression. While this might be argued as coincidental in a snapshot of another dancer in midperformance, given Baker's meticulous and virtuosic use of akimbo facial expressions, as far back as her first distinctive performances, we must recognize this "corner of the eye" expression as another manifestation of the "cutting and breaking" we have found throughout her body—and Body—of artistic work.

## The Marx Brothers in *A Day at the Races*

The boundary- and race-crossing akimbo in Baker's performances, as captured in static images and evoked by period language, is reflected similarly in period films, which add both movement and sound to the palette. My discussion moves next, therefore, to a sequence of moviemaking that likewise reveals both the historical continuity of akimbo body languages and the transgressive, shape-shifting freedom they connoted: a swing-dance sequence from the Marx Brothers' *A Day at the Races*.[19]

Though this sequence comes from a 1937 film, we should remember that the Brothers cut their teeth much earlier in live vaudeville, beginning as early as 1905.[20] This means that, like the "buffo" touring actors who were among the first blackface practitioners one hundred years before, the Brothers would have been professionally familiar with a wide range of comic ethnic character types and characteristic dances, including but not limited to those associated with blackface. Their physical humor, their fast-paced dialog—driven by malapropisms, insults, and puns—and their dance vocabularies may reasonably be read as influenced by blackface theatrics.

Although the dance sequence in *Day at the Races* is a carefully staged and edited entertainment object, multiple factors argue for its relevance in a discussion of participatory street dance. First, Whitey's Lindy Hoppers had been formed only two years previously; this is the first of their several film performances. It is unlikely that many members of a white working- and middle-class film audience, with the exception of white live-jazz fans frequenting clubs in large black urban centers (New York, Los Angeles, Detroit), would have yet seen swing dancing of such improvisational virtuosity.

Second, the dance sequence in *Races* represents a relatively direct and immediate translation of street vocabularies known in black clubs to film; the troupe began in a nightclub and, as we will see, translates that venue's body vocabulary onto the screen.[21] They may be dancing on a Hollywood soundstage, but they are employing the practices and body vocabularies of the Cotton Club. Third, the demographics of Whitey's team themselves reflected the transracial nature of the "Uptown" clubs' clienteles: two of the founding members, Ruthie Rheingold and Harry Rosenberg, were working-class whites—though, significantly, they were kept out of publicity photos and the *Day at the Races* sequence precisely in order to observe Hollywood's color bar.[22] The film's challenge to race-based norms is additionally confirmed by the fact that, in some markets, the entire dance sequence was removed before screening; Stevens and Stevens suggest that this was because Harpo is depicted dancing with a black community, but in a more global sense, the scene challenges clear-cut ethnic identity, suggesting that those who censored the sequence understood its transgressive intentions precisely.[23] Finally, and most relevantly, dance is employed at this particular point in the narrative specifically because of its capacity to mask identity, cross boundaries, and syncopate bodily and societal norms.

At this time, as in some other eras of American popular culture, dance music was a relatively viable context in which to explore or act out black-white cultural exchange: Brian Harker observes, for example, that Louis Armstrong's jazz trumpet vocabulary significantly evolved during his time in Chicago playing onstage for "eccentric" dancers in "black-and-tan" (that is, quasi-integrated) nightclubs, and a little later, the Greek American percussionist Johnny Otis (born Ioannis Veliotes, 1921–2012) was "passing" as black in order to appear with jump-blues bandleaders like Harlan Leonard (ca. 1944–1945).[24] Similarly, clarinetist Benny Goodman led the integration of swing bands with a quartet that included, eventually, black pianist Teddy Wilson (1935), vibraphonist Lionel Hampton (1936), and guitarist Charlie Christian (1939); while off the bandstand, the influence of black composers and arrangers was crucial in the swing revolution (the iconic example is that of Fletcher Henderson selling his arrangements to Glenn Miller and others). So the idea of dance-music performance as a zone in which integrative experiments could occur was very much in the air, and visible in popular media.

The *Races* sequence "All God's Chillun Got Rhythm" features the great vocalist Ivie Anderson (1905–1949) of Duke Ellington's band, and Whitey's Lindy Hoppers, from the Cotton Club, where the Ellington orchestra had held a residency from 1927–1931 and to which, in 1937, the orchestra had just returned. The songwriting team of Bronislau Kaper and Walter Jurmann (music) and Gus Kahn (lyrics) had actually composed the song itself (which Anderson later that year released as a 78) with her in mind.[25]

In this scene, which immediately precedes the film's climax of conflict and opposition (at approximately 1:23:40 in a 1:49:00 running time), the Brothers, having been revealed as a fake doctor, jockey, and sanitarium attendant, are hiding from authorities who want to arrest them and confiscate their horse. Over the course of the sequence (approximately 7:20), the Brothers, through a blackface trope that subverts authoritarian recognition, engage dancing as a transformative, cross-racial, participatory experience. The sequence carves out protected public space; invokes sacred and secular movement vocabularies; frames African American dance as virtuosic and celebratory; and enables, at the climax, re-integration within the community.

Set in a barnyard, the sequence begins with the Brothers in hiding from pursuers. Harpo momentarily startles the two young lovers (played by Allan Jones and Maureen O'Sullivan) with a tin whistle fanfare and a tootled invitation for them to join him in the dance. A shift of mood from the rather saccharine tenor song, "Tomorrow Is Another Day," is heralded by the sound of "tribal" drumming (a low tom-tom pattern). Responding to the off-screen drumming, Harpo leads the young extras of the children's choir in a danced circle, the tin whistle taking on a pentatonic, syncopated, blues-inflected improvisational character; the clockwise processional, like a ring-shout or *bamboula,* delineating the space in which the danced ritual will play out.[26] The intentionality of this delineation is confirmed by the camera tracking the parade, which reinforces the idea of a ritual space whose very invocation represents a potential threat to dominant authority.[27]

Following the vamped musical introduction, a quick cut brings the camera low, framing a circle of children on their knees shooting craps as the full band enters and the choral vocalists begin "All God's Chillun Got Rhythm." Central is a three-way call-and-response on the phrase "Who dat man?" between vocal soloist, chorus, and Harpo's tin whistle.

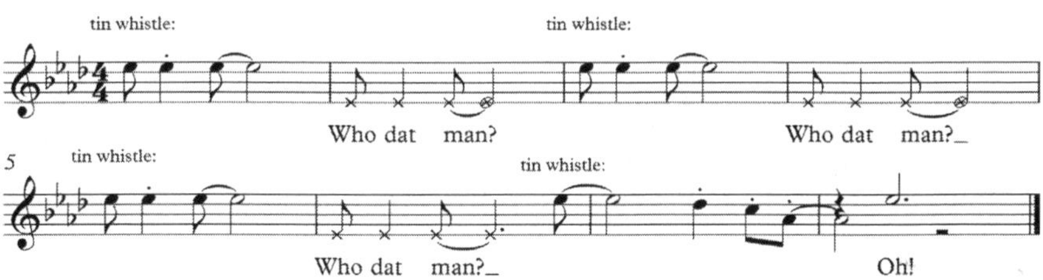


As the dance continues, the text links "Gabriel," whose Old Testament horn is emblematic of transformative musical sound (he blows, and "the walls come a-tumbling down"), to a physical choreography that frames Harpo as pied piper for the song's refrain.

A shift of tempo, tonality, and mood is signaled by a "hallelujah," borrowed from the sacred vocabulary, interrupting the "Who dat man" refrain, while the camera traverses to a cabin interior, portraying a vocalized spiritual as emblematic of African American experience. Visual details and elements of performance practice evoke the naiveté or "primitive" simplicity of old-time religion, reinforced by the use of rubato lining-out vocal textures reminiscent of evangelical congregational song practices. Within the domesticity of the cabin interior, as an extended family prepares for Saturday night, one extra engages in a very ancient bit of blackface business, employing a derby hat as a means to elongate and elaborate expressive physical gestures; such gestural heightening (the carrying of "something in hand"—a hat, bandana, or umbrella) is employed widely in street dance throughout the Caribbean.[28]

**Figure 7:** Limb extension via "object in hand": *A Day at the Races* (1937).

A tootled interruption from Harpo's whistle, and the repeated refrain of "Who dat man?" shifts us away from the cabin exterior; the sung "Gabriel" line returns us to the carnivalesque parade, which Harpo leads, tin whistle singing, toward another structure, a juke joint packed with band and musicians; in a marvelous bit of stage design, this "house is [quite literally] rocking" on its foundations. Another modulation and a military tattoo on trumpet, and the focus shifts again, to a heroic shot of vocalist Ivie Anderson, who will carry the sequence through the balance of the song, singing "Come on let's jamble / Let's jam what amble."

Harpo's whistle interruption again elicits the "Who dat man?" visual and sung response, and a spoken "why it's Gabriel!" again unites this third community—the juke joint crowd—with the at-home spirituals singers and the playing children, to the tune of Harpo's whistle.

Throughout this sequence, the physical body vocabularies on display, from Harpo, the adult dancers and singers, and—quite beautifully and un-self-consciously—the young extras of the "Crinoline Choir" cut, syncopate, and inflect time.[29] In the shout chorus, Harpo skips on one foot (alternating left and right) on beats 3 and 4 as he leads the danced parade, literally syncopating his left and right foot on the downbeat of each bar, "turning the time around," while several of the children march in quarter-note triplet hemiolas against the 4/4.

**Figure 8:** Harpo skips, *A Day at the Races* (1937).

Harpo leading, the crowd again dances in a circle, further inscribing the ritual space. A hold on the tempo, and a modulation of the key, herald a short tenor vocal solo from Allan Jones on the line, "Tomorrow is another day," to the accompaniment of a gospel choir. Another modulation and "Tomorrow" double-times into a climactic cadence, conducted with exaggerated gestures by Harpo, on " . . . is our wedding day." A cued decrescendo from Harpo, and Ivie Anderson steps forward to sing the opening line "I got a frown, you got a frown," Harpo miming akimbo "Jim Crow"–esque gestures to match her use of rubato.

Ivie initiates regular tempo with a vocal accelerando and moves into "All god's chillun got rhythm"; the camera frames her tightly, with the musicians in the background. Complex syncopation is present in the melody line, both as composed by Kaper / Jurmann and further manipulated in Ivie's vocal:

**Figure 9:** Ivie Anderson sings opening rubato of "All God's Chillun Got Rhythm," *A Day at the Races* (1937).

The syncopation is mirrored in her facial expressions and bodily motions: like the Lindy Hoppers who will take over and kick the scene into overdrive, on "Gonna push away those blues," with hips swinging and one hand over the pivot of her abdomen, Anderson literally "embodies" the sung hemiola:

At "When they start to go ho-ho, ho-de-ho," she and the musicians embody the 2 and 4 emphasis, stepping backward on 1 and 3, with the trailing foot moving—just as a dancer's would—on beats 2 and 4.

During the subsequent instrumental interlude and fanfare, which articulates the rhythm of the previous refrain's "All god's chillun got . . ." as an elongated 3–2 clave (ONE-and-two-AND-three-AND-four-and / one-AND . . . ), the crowd of child dancers advances across the screen, stepping in time with the polymetric accents. At the modulation and repeat of the refrain, the chorus takes up "All god's chillun got . . .," intercut with stop-time accents and Ivie's double-timed scat interjection, while

**Figure 10:** Ivie Anderson embodies the sung hemiola, *A Day at the Races* (1937).

the rhythm hits the accents as well. After the modulation, the bridge recurs in the new key and, at its closing line "Hold the push," Ivie dances a remarkable embodiment of the line: with her palms-down hands literally "pushing" down from sternum to pelvis and then out and away from her body (this "brushing away" move certainly borrowed from the Caribbean, where it occurs in the Afro-Cuban *son* among other dances) as her pelvis sways backward and forward at the end of a flexing spine.

The "hold the push" line and gesture is repeated, to the chorus and rhythm section's accompaniment, and then is double-timed with four repetitions on the words "push away their troubles"; as the chorus sings the upward modulation on the melisma'd "troubles," Ivie's body also rises.

The heightening energy, present in both pitch (the several upward modulations of key), rhythm (the call-and-response, the repetition and then double-timing of the "hold the push" line), and body vocabularies (the repetition and double-timing of the "hold the push" gesture, and the complex polyrhythmic quality of that gesture: hands moving downward and outward, pelvis swaying backward and forward) finds release in an instrumental "shout chorus" in the new key. The intensified energy is matched kinesthetically with a fantastic solo by Whitey's feature dancer John "Tiny" Bunch, who, at 6'4" and 350 pounds, is an overwhelming yet utterly fluid physical presence.[30]

**Figure 11:** Ivie Anderson, "Gonna push away those blues," *A Day at the Races* (1937).

**Figure 12:** John "Tiny" Bunch and Ivie Anderson, *A Day at the Races* (1937).

Interacting visually with Ivie, Bunch whirls through a series of virtuoso steps: one-footed kicking out or to the sides, his substantial belly moving contrarily to his feet and arms; one-footed 360-degree spins; advancing and retreating in mirror image to the petite Anderson; stepping in half-time to the 4/4 rhythm, his mobile facial expressions further syncopating the visual data; climaxing with an effortless, elongated sink to a full fore-and-aft split, his upper body still moving in time, and then an equally effortless rise to his feet; finishing with an advance in which he steps forward on "-AND / one" with the trailing foot dragging in time to beats 2, 3, and 4, as the chorus sings the repetitive "hey-hey, ho, hey-hey, ho" before the full band jumps into a double-timed Lindy Hop tempo as the partnered members of the Lindy Hoppers take the floor.

In their sequence, which was probably choreographed by (though uncredited to) troupe leader Frankie Manning, each couple runs through a series of expert partnering moves, emphasizing extensive overlap and "cutting-and-breaking" between and across pairs.[31] Wearing clothing fitted to enhance the choreography (ballooning high-waisted zoot-suit trousers and tight-fitting vests for the men, mid-calf skirts and tailored blouses for the women), they make akimbo splitting and breaking of vertical and horizontal planes and lines the center of their movement vocabulary. Facial expressions and eyes mirroring the akimbo language; rubber legs and elaborate spins, lifts, and carries (sometimes reversing gender expectations, with women lifting men

**Figure 13:** Whitey's Lindy Hoppers, *A Day at the Races* (1937).

and so forth): all manifest a wonderful sense of insouciant but commanding physical virtuosity. Though full of the improvisational facial and communicative interaction of people who dance together a lot, Manning's choreography likewise accommodates the band's musical arrangement, synchronizing percussive feet and momentum-breaking lifts and carries with musical unisons, syncopations, and percussive hits, most particularly during the trumpet soloist's bravura high-note passages.

It is also worth noting that the camera-work and editing during the Lindy Hoppers' sequence is quite different than that which precedes them: the earlier tracking and panning are largely abandoned in favor of a low-angle landscape frame that allows us to follow individual couples as they dance into, out of, and across the ritual circle, intercut with quick closeups on akimbo facial expressions and gestures. While this shift of editing style may be partly pragmatic—in order to capture a group sequence of this size and degree of complexity, choreographing more complex camera work would probably require Steadicam-style technology which did not yet exist—there are deeper interpretive reasons as well. The Lindy Hoppers' artistic practice almost certainly precluded complete and replicable consistency between takes. In this sense, the available technology and the group's improvisational practice (surely these partnered duets evolved over every take in a sequence that required long hours to film), combined to foreground the unpredictability and akimbo dynamics of street dance practice. Audio of the dancing was also recorded, even though the band "performance" is executed via recorded playback: on the soundtrack, we can hear the dancers' catcalling to one another and their call-and-response with the shouting, handclapping onlookers in the circle, heightening the vérité quality of the scene.

What is created here is a literal reenactment (that is, "another enactment") of the ritualized climax of a show at Roseland or the Cotton Club: all couples on the floor, dancing with one another and to the crowd, the crowd in the *bamboula* circle singing and clapping and egging them on. As with the theatricalizations of slave auctions, *Obi*, and John Canoe described in Chapter 2; the illustrations for Cable's "The Dances in Congo Square"; and Ira Aldridge's performances of "Possum Up a Gum Tree" at the African Grove or Bristol's National Theatre, so here on a Hollywood soundstage: the dance vocabularies of the street are transmuted to the theatrical frame, and "enact again" the transgressive, improvisational, participatory bodily rebellion which is subaltern communities' emblematic ritual of resistance.

At the end of the Lindy Hoppers' sequence, just as the competing couples exit the floor, the music modulates again, and slips into a brief up-tempo quotation of "Columbia, the Gem of the Ocean" ("Three cheers for the red, white and blue"). Harpo, like a cakewalking dandy, dancing *capoeira* player, or marching band drum major, grabs a pitchfork and leads a patriotic parade, twirling the pitchfork in akimbo fashion. Groucho and Harpo join in the dancing as part of the swaying, handclapping crowd.[32]

**Figure 14:** Harpo leads the "band," *A Day at the Races* (1937).

At precisely this moment, during the "patriotic" celebration, the fedora'd, dark-suited, fiercely scowling denizens of Caucasian authority stride into the barn. Spying their pursuers, the Brothers dive for concealment underneath a hay wagon, as the singing and dancing continue. Groucho notices grease on the wagon's axles, and all three Brothers hasten to apply this improvised disguise—which, as always in the case of blackface, is effective only against those denizens of authority whose racial prejudices are so rigid that even the barest simulacrum of "blackness" is sufficient for concealment.[33] Emerging from beneath the wagon, the Brothers, blackfaced except for Harpo, whose face is divided vertically half-black and half-white (a nice touch of the harlequinesque), wend their way through the crowd and join again in the loosely choreographed Lindy Hop of the ensemble, which culminates with a chorus-line final cadence directed to the two young lovers, as the musical sequence ends.[34]

Aside from the inevitable racial stereotyping, and beyond the sheer technical virtuosity of the music and the stupendous physical choreography, the complex signification within this performance provides rich opportunity for semiotic interpretation. In addition to the extensive troping of African American body vocabularies discussed earlier, a few meta-narrative observations are also in order. First is the idea that this street-style dance is engrossing across racial boundaries: the Brothers, led by Harpo, are willing and exuberant participants; indeed, until the

**Figure 15:** The Brothers join the band, in blackface, *A Day at the Races* (1937).

reappearance of pursuit, they appear completely and un-self-consciously engaged. Additionally, the infectious joy in the sequence connotes the idea that participation in such bodily expression is both liberating—specifically from the constraints of middle-class behavior or policing, just as blackface had been—but also creative, of participatory bodily pleasure: again, just as blackface had been.[35] At the same time, participation by whites in black expression is *risky*: the Brothers may be under pursuit for their interference in the racetrack's operation, but it is implicit that they are *also* at risk because of where they are, the company they are keeping, and the shared activity—akimbo dance—in which they are engaged.

Moreover, the scene is full of the rebellious "cutting-and-breaking," the "participatory discrepancies" of sound and body we have found in the African American traditions since first contact: bent arms and knees; distorted facial expressions; rolled or crossed eyes; syncopations of rhythm, bodily line, or appropriate public association.[36] In 1937, to "black up" and manifest such akimbo behaviors was still, provided the mask could be seen through or washed away, a paradoxical act of resistance and self-liberation. Just as it had done in the 1830s, even into the 1930s, "blacking up" permitted a degree of license that comic actors exploited to signify transgressive defiance of authority.

An additional, subtle, possibly unconscious but nevertheless powerful reference to creole transgression is Harpo's half-white, half-black face. In addition to literally signifying "racial halves" or in-between-ness, his vertically divided face paint simultaneously alludes to European harlequinade and to the Afro-Caribbean trickster tradition of the *orisha* variously called Elegua/Legba/Baron Samedi, who would wear a hat colored red in front and black in back, so that onlookers might argue, on the basis of having seen him either coming or going, about the color of that hat. The shape-shifting blurring of racial boundaries represented by the half-and-half nature of Harpo's face paint thus connects, in another medium beyond physical motion and sounding rhythm, with the Afro-Anglo creole synthesis.

Transgression is interpreted situationally: embodied and experienced differently in different contexts. Though abhorrent in (historical) Anglo-European aesthetics, akimbo body or sound vocabularies were, conversely, prized components of Afro-Caribbean expression. In the twenty-first century, as we will discover in Chapter 8, blackface and transvestism have, in a sense, swapped places: that is, in the modern West, the formerly common use of blackface as comic practice is generally condemned, while transgression of normative gender conduct evokes something of the liberating, liminal frisson blackface formerly carried.[37] Josephine Baker's extensive experiments with cross-dressing, for example, most notably in a series of tuxedo'd portraits that mimic Marlene Dietrich's similar series, invert the blackface "wench" role and spark transgressive sexual readings from viewers of both genders.[38]

Borshuk says, "The performance of drag does not entail an imitation of opposite gender identity; it reveals how gender itself is performative, a role played from an exterior script."[39] We might therefore comment in passing upon an additional trope subsequently overlaid upon *Races* post-1937: the denouement of the Whitey's Lindy Hoppers scene, when the Brothers "black up" with axle grease and rejoin the dance, prefigures and almost certainly influences a later, quite similar film climax: another riff on the same theme. At the end of the 1996 Nathan Lane / Robin Williams film, *The Birdcage*, a senatorial scion of intolerant right-wing American conservatism escapes discovery and scandal only by slipping through a crowd disguised as a pancake-made-up ("whitefaced") drag queen dancing to gay icons Sister Sledge.[40] As we will discover ahead, in the domestic social revolutions that followed World War II, analogous liberations of the dancing body became more possible than ever before.

CHAPTER 7

# Blackface Transformations II

## Voyeurism, Identity, and Double-Consciousness

Before Beatle-mania or Elvis, before the screaming and dancing teens iconicized in *A Hard Day's Night* (1964) or *Jailhouse Rock* (1957), equally massive crowds of bobby-soxers turned out in the pre-World War II era to listen and dance to, and make media stars of, 1920s crooners like Rudy Vallée (1901–1986) and late 1930s singers like Frank Sinatra (1915–1998), of whose opening at the Paramount Theatre in New York in 1942 Jack Benny is alleged to have said: "I thought the goddamned building was going to cave in. I never heard such a commotion."[1] The Swing era (ca. 1935–1946) was the first time that the music known as jazz (originating in Mississippi River contexts and ports, most notably New Orleans, Chicago, and St Louis, in the Teens and Twenties) made the transition from a niche music associated primarily with the black community—and with white collegians like Bix Beiderbecke who were the prototypical "hipsters"—to a mass market popular music widely consumed across diverse racial and economic demographics. In a parallel to the later semantic code-switch between black-targeted "rhythm & blues" and white-targeted "rock & roll," jazz in essence "became" swing when the small-group styles associated with King Oliver, Jelly Roll Morton, Louis Armstrong, and Beiderbecke transitioned to larger, more formalized ensembles playing for more diverse and integrated dancing audiences.

Yet there is surprisingly little hard data about the demographics of attendance at swing-dance events in the 1930s, the period of the music's first mass-market apotheosis. It cut across class and race lines—there were working-class and middle-class fans, black and white fans—and certainly the music had a particular appeal to young listeners, who would be called (by the 1950s) "teenagers"; yet the evidence for who attended what dances and how social arbiters felt about this attendance, prior to the 1950s, is mostly inferential and surprisingly indirect.[2] Conventional histories of jazz, rhythm and blues, and early rock 'n' roll dance have presumed that segregated audiences were the norm, and that the "risk" of miscegenation is precisely what drew the ire of cultural arbiters.[3] And certainly, with the expansion of the Civil Rights movement during and after World War II, there was a greatly heightened sensitivity regarding the possible deleterious influence of minority—especially black—popular culture upon the nation's middle-class white youth.[4] Dance, precisely because it was a public embodiment of physical exchange, was therefore a particular focus of critique. Kevin J. Mumford says of the period: "Of all the forms of public, interracial contact, black/white dance elicited the sharpest, most impassioned responses from authorities."[5]

But there is a corollary substratum to that race-challenging history that bears closer examination—a parallel thread suggesting that, even before Civil Rights and the Second World War, dance floors were accepted as liminal spaces in which transgressive contact between and across gender, race, and class frequently occurred.[6] In the antebellum period, for example, black-white working-class contact was a common factor in both blackface theaters and also in race-mixing dance halls.[7] The historian John Gennari emphasizes the degree to which music and dance provided temporarily liminal spaces in which "integrationist sympathies could be expressed, saying, "As an artistic practice that challenged the boundaries between performers and audiences, intellectuals (or patricians) and the 'masses,' and blacks and whites, *swing embodied a welcome symbol of social integration—a universal language and cultural practice that cut across lines of race, class, nation, and cultural hierarchy*."[8] These hierarchies, and specific historical examples of dance as a challenge to them, are the focus of the present chapter. I will suggest that the wildly inventive, physically (and socially) challenging street- and nightclub-dance captured in 1930s and early '40s films and eyewitness reports represents an ongoing tradition of cultural exchange, operative from first contact between African and European movement vocabularies. I argue that, for example, Malcolm X's *Autobiography* and Spike Lee's film *Bamboozled*, two works that centralize African American vernacular dance (partly as seen through white eyes), may be understood as metaphorical explorations of North Americans' conflicted cultural identities, and that each provides uniquely penetrating and usefully paradoxical interpretations of what street dance "means," specifically in the project of black nationalism. Throughout, I suggest that, though post–WWII cultural conservatives sought to limit the access of middle-class whites to African American music, dance, and experience, fears of "musical miscegenation" were implicit acknowledgments that dance-based cross-racial attraction and exchange had been going on in the Republic for two centuries.[9]

This chronology and trajectory can be traced directly from the live-music-and-dance venues that immediately preceded the swing ballrooms; these include the post–Civil War "concert saloons" where Tin Pan Alley pluggers tested new songs, to the underground speakeasies and "black-and-tan" clubs of the Roaring Twenties, and to opulent post-Prohibition 1930s nightclubs like the Savoy, Small's, and the Cotton Club where the acrobatic swing dance called the Lindy Hop was born.[10] For example, when the Savoy opened in 1926 Harlem, Howard Spring says it attracted large crowds "consisting of a wide variety of people: African Americans and European Americans, the social and economic elite, the middle class, blue-collar workers, Harlemites, and tourists." Spring suggests that it was precisely the inclusiveness of the Savoy that "made it easy for people from different social classes, geographic regions, and ethno-cultural backgrounds to experience the Lindy Hop and its music first-hand."[11] The following discussion situates transgressive movement in such "interzones," to use Mumford's evocative term (indebted to William Burroughs): liminal spaces in which many different kinds of rule-bending behavior could take place.[12] It was precisely the freedom to bend and blur boundaries around and strictures upon behavior that drew such a wide diversity of social groups to interzonal spaces (as we will see again in the discussion of New York's Stonewall Uprising, ahead).[13]

These nightspots, which were situated "Uptown" or "across the tracks," often in primarily black neighborhoods, which were staffed by black kitchen and floor workers and whose entertainers were the cream of African American talent, but whose clienteles were typically white, were places for the performance of identity—particularly of transracial or transgressive identity. This is part of the conventional historiography of the "slumming" associated, in the early twentieth century, with middle- and upper-class whites (particularly the Progressives of lower Manhattan and Greenwich Village) who made the Harlem clubs popular sites for voyeuristic entertainment. At the same time, the intensity, immediacy, and music and movement characteristics of African American performing arts at the end of the Harlem Renaissance found their way—and were appropriated—into white artists' novels, paintings, posters, films, and even operas: from the thinly veiled voyeurism of Carl van Vechten's (1880–1964) notorious 1926 *Nigger Heaven* and the near-ethnographic observation of his *Parties, Scenes from Contemporary New York Life* (1930), to the transracial experimentalism of the Gertrude Stein / Virgil Thomson opera *Four Saints in Three Acts* (completed 1927; staged 1934).[14] The crucial realization here is that this racial blurring was *not* a new phenomenon—that in fact there had been spaces for the performance of transracial identity as long as there had been a white middle class and a black underclass.[15]

That dancers like Vernon (1887–1918) and Irene (1893–1969) Castle, composers like Thomson, *litterateurs* like Stein and Van Vechten should have perceived Uptown entertainments as sites for appropriation is no surprise: the Harlem nightclubs, and others like them in cities across the country, were themselves theatricalized spaces that placed moving bodies on central display. As Vogel points out, the clubs were typically laid out with open-tiered seating, a centralized dance-floor, and raised entrances and stages, precisely in order that they could "allow performers to circulate among the spectators and . . . spectators to take a turn" at "performing" for the rest of the room.[16] Participation in nightclub dancing, in person or via film, thus enabled the theatricalized performance of (race- or gender-mixing) identity.[17]

Recognizing this performativity, for both resident blacks and slumming whites, in turn allows us to draw links from street dance to the nightclub, from the dance floor to the theatrical stage, and from the stage to the movie screen. Although shows like *Hellzapoppin'* (stage: 1938, screen: 1941) and *A Day at the Races* (1937) are fictionalized narratives churned out by Broadway and Hollywood screenwriters, composers, and producers, without pretensions to documentary verisimilitude, in their dance sequences these films *do* capture a particular historical moment—that moment in the 1930s when African American dance styles, born in the pressurized, improvisational setting of "Uptown" nightclubs, entered the entertainment experience and thereby the wider consciousness of middle-class white North America. For the purposes of this chapter, then, I emphasize the *continuity* and *cultural exchange* which was carried over from the masked ball to the concert saloon to the vaudeville theater to the dance hall, and thence to Hollywood films. I particularly emphasize the degree to which, regardless of the suspended-disbelief, gauzy fantasy, or "chin-up, pal!" anti-Depression optimism of these shows, what is captured in their dance sequences is near-documentary evidence of how the transracial kinesthetic exchange occurred.[18]

In the new medium of the motion picture, and especially the "talkies" whose sound capacities had first been widely popularized by the 1927 Al Jolson vehicle *The Jazz Singer* (with Jolson playing a Jewish cantor's son who "blacks up" as a minstrel, a treasure trove of semiotic data on 1920s middle-class attitudes about race and class), there had been little standardized control over content or expression until the enactment of the 1930 Motion Picture Production Code (popularly, "the Hays Code").[19] While the Code widely proscribed portrayal of crime, vulgarity, obscenity, profanity, revealing costume, religious critique, sexuality, excessive nationalism, and any other "Repellent Subjects," it did not neglect to constrain dance, singling out "dancing or costumes intended to permit undue exposure or indecent movements in the dance . . . suggesting or representing sexual actions or indecent passions . . . which emphasize indecent movements," and so forth.[20] In short, after the brief halcyon period between 1927–1930 when sound film provided a space for relatively frank portrayals of sex, race, class, and gender, the Hays Code quickly moved to restrict any such portrayals of behavior, including any dance, that challenged social norms. In the few years immediately prior to *The Jazz Singer*, companies like Phonofilm and Vitaphone had developed technology to capture vaudeville and theatrical performances, using cumbersome synched audio machinery shortly to be replaced by the sound-on-film Movietone approach, which became Hollywood's standard technology after 1927.[21]

However, we are speaking not of the capacity of new technology to shift the aesthetics and strategies of a performing idiom to match that new technology's strengths (as certainly occurred with elements of both live-action and animated film style) but rather the capacity of an existing cluster of performance idioms—namely African American improvisational and participatory couples dancing—to challenge the frame imposed by the new technology.[22] We will not argue that this dancing "became" the Lindy Hop because of its having been framed by the camera as spectacular performance, but rather that the dance idioms' own capacities to create the liminal zones of transracial exchange were capable of adapting to—and indeed of transforming the expectations of—the new idiom, at a highly fluid moment in the history of film.

Katrina Hazzard-Gordon has suggested that African American performance can be seen as constitutive of physical and semiotic "arenas": spaces within which, at least temporarily, heightened and liminal symbolic conduct is enabled to occur.[23] Throughout the history of the creolization process in the New World—and throughout this book—we have enumerated the adaptation of physical and cognitive spaces to fit creole-American movement aesthetics.[24] Moving forward in history to the post–World War II era addressed in this chapter, both the Roseland Ballroom's dance floor and the filmed television soundstage of *Bamboozled*, by the very acts of performance occurring within them, become *creolized* spaces.[25]

The black nationalist leader Malcolm X, born Malcolm Little in 1925, wrote about the experiences that shaped his political consciousness in the posthumously published 1965 *Autobiography*, a meditation upon race, identity, religion, and politics.[26] But Malcolm also includes descriptions of life in the black communities of Detroit, Boston, and the Brotherhood of Sleeping Car Porters, interweaving the early story of his experiences as an upwardly mobile burglar with that of his growth as a Lindy-Hop dancer. His evocations of Boston's Roseland Ballroom on contest nights, when the great bands of Ellington, Hampton, and Basie were playing, are remarkable, both for the vivid detail and sensitivity with which he portrays African American movement celebrations, and also for his capacity to recognize such celebration as inherently political. In this early period, prior to his imprisonment and political awakening, as "Detroit Red" (a reference to his hair's red tint after the painful straightening treatment called "conking"), Malcolm Little develops a reputation as a burglar and a champion Lindy Hopper, sought out by black and white women, "good girls" and "bad," and speaks of the exhilaration of the dance competitions.

> A third of the way or so through the evening the main vocalizing and instrumental stylings would come—and then showtime, when only the greatest lindy-hoppers would stay on the floor, to try and eliminate each other. All the other dancers would form a big "U" with the band at the open end.

The "U" he describes at Boston's Roseland Ballroom is the same shared perceptual and behavioral space as the "Corner" cited by dancers at the Savoy, as the ring-shout and the *calinda*, the "circ" or "cipher" of hip hop dance, and the circles and rings found throughout New World Anglo-African syncretic religion and dance.[27]

In the *Autobiography*, Malcolm uses his own recalled experiences of dancing as a lens through which to understand and seek to liberate African American experience, and to challenge expectations of race and class: dancing with Caucasian girlfriend Laura, he says, "As always, the crowd clapped and shouted in time with the blasting band. 'Go, Red, go!' Partly it was my reputation, and partly Laura's ballet style of dancing that helped to turn the spotlight—and the crowd's attention—to us."[28] Driven by inherited traditions of movement behavior, the rituals of transformation which Malcolm and his dance partners experienced were communal, contextual, and experimental: these factors were precisely the source of their social power. Malcolm was a remarkable speaker and storyteller and, after years on the streets and incarcerated in a Massachusetts state prison,

**Figure 16:** Lindy, Savoy Ballroom, circa 1950. AP Images.

**Figure 17:** Bamboula in Congo Square, E. W. Kemble after G. W. Cable, *Harper's*, ca. 1880.

followed by joining and then leaving Elijah Muhammed's Nation of Islam, he had become extremely adept at using the narrative of his own life as a metaphorical lens through which to describe, illuminate, and liberate African American experience. It is no coincidence that, in what is essentially a political autobiography, he includes detailed instructions on how to straighten hair, how to burgle an apartment, and how to dance; Malcolm saw all these as political and politicized acts. He says that it was in dancing that his "long-suppressed African instincts broke through, and loose."[29] Whether this (rather dated and essentialized) statement completely explains how dancing works, he quite specifically chose to frame it as a *political* explanation. Rituals of transformation are contextual, experimental, and admit the possibility of both failure and error. The shock of laughter, tears, or anger at the climax of a ritual is precisely a reflection of expectation and the completion or confounding of expectation. For Malcolm—and he was not alone in this among 1960s Civil Rights activists—the liminal arenas of African American dance held the possibility of transformation precisely because what happened within them was nonnormative, potentially transgressive, and contained at least the possibility of liberation.

In the rolling akimbo languages of African American expression, generations of blacks, whites, and creoles, willing or unwilling, welcoming or resisting, have recognized the possibility of previously unimagined renewal. These heightened experiential spaces have also—ever since the first parodies by blacks of whites in seventeenth-century Jamaica—permitted the possibility for subaltern communities (blacks, slaves, immigrants, mechanics and apprentices, women, gays, and lesbians), or other populations taking on the temporary mask, to critique, contest, or at the very least complicate dominant paradigms. Spike Lee's fictional film

*Bamboozled* (2000) situates the same liminal power within the television soundstage that Malcolm's *Autobiography* recognized in the ballroom and the political memoir.[30] It tells the story of two young performers, played by the singer/comedian Tommy Davidson and the dancer Savion Glover, whose characters are recruited literally off the street by a black TV executive, played by Damon Wayans. Wayans's "Pierre Delacroix" is plotting to escape his network contract through production of a wildly offensive pilot for a "New Millennium Minstrel Show," whose blackface antics, noxious stereotypes, caricatured dialog and costume, and openness to white appropriation are sure to cause its cancelation. In Mel Brooks's iconic 1967 film comedy, *The Producers*, the guaranteed-to-fail offensive show-within-a-show is *Springtime for Hitler*. In *Bamboozled*, it is Delacroix's *Mantan: A New Millennium Minstrel Show*, whose excruciating evocation of racist caricatures brings to the surface—in its production staff, cast, and especially its studio and viewing audiences—the collision of racist derogation and reluctant admiration (and appropriation) that had fired blackface minstrelsy.[31]

It is the paradoxical, conflicted nature of audience responses to *Bamboozled*'s show-within-a-show blackface performances, the staging and lead-in to which are fraught with elegiac mourning, that put on display—under the spotlights and within the heightened liminal space of the stage—both toxic racism and exhilarating virtuosity. This paradox—the double consciousness that can both mourn the racist caricatures and celebrate the artistry that transcends them—is at the heart of the film and of the "love and theft" that Eric Lott has famously described.[32] What makes *Bamboozled* great—beyond its rather manipulative discourse, its critique of North American media culture (made more powerfully and effectively in Sidney Lumet's 1976 *Network*, whose influence Lee acknowledges), and the unfortunately bizarre acting style Lee imposes on some of his actors—is the sheer power of the blackface performance set-pieces that form its performative core.[33] Though some previous scholarship has addressed those set-pieces, and the intentionally complex and conflicted viewer responses they elicit, there is still space for discussion of their paradoxical attraction/repulsion. Consisting of either dialect wordplay, slapstick comedy (chases and pratfalls), or music and dance—or all at the same time—these performances are powerful and *beautiful*: the sheer physical, comic, and gestural virtuosity with which Davidson and Glover execute them is undeniable. We cannot resist taking artistic pleasure in them—at the same time that we (like the TV audience) are also appalled at our own pleasure.

The performances are framed variously as rehearsals, a test/pilot, and an opening-night sequence, all set on the TV soundstage. They are preceded, in the film's narrative, by a sequence of short snippets portraying various talent auditioning for the planned show. These short auditions are played sometimes for comedy, with comically inept performances; sometimes to problematize models of "blackness," as various auditioning performers struggle to anticipate and cater to the particular models of the "negro" which the producers themselves cannot quite articulate; sometimes, I suspect, simply in order that director Lee can provide brief exposure—brief shout-outs—to talented artists working in various black vernacular forms; and also occasionally to further the narrative. The inept yet rage-filled hip hop crew, who will eventually assassinate a defenseless Manray live on the TV feed, completely overwhelm the frame of the TV audition; producer Delacroix recoils, exclaiming, "this is frightening!" in reply to which Jada Pinkett Smith's production assistant, "Sloan Hopkins," who at least initially serves as Delacroix's racial conscience, snaps out "*It should be*."

Each of the three *Mantan* performance set-pieces is prefaced by a long solo scene detailing the process through which Tommy Davidson's "Womack" and Savion Glover's "Manray" black-up. Using a classic reverse shot of each actor staring into his dressing-room mirror and employing Pinkett Smith's voice-over to describe the technical procedures of cooking, then crushing, then applying the burnt cork, and the fire-engine red lipstick, with the accompaniment of Terence Blanchard's haunting and mournful music, each blacking-up sequence captures the sorrow and shame that the minstrel mask has imposed—on the blacks caricatured by it, by the whites who appropriated it, and by we moderns who are the ambivalent inheritors of that long history.[34] Each time, at the end of the sequence, as the pain in Davidson's and Glover's faces is obscured by the blackface makeup, as they become "Sleep 'n' Eat" and "Man-Tan," there is a moment when the actor's face freezes, in the mirror's reversed image, into the rubbery immobility of the visual caricatures, as the mask of double-consciousness is completed.[35]

Each of the blackface performance sequences fulfills a pivotal narrative role: the first, at a prebroadcast pilot taping, captures the shock of the "New Millennium Minstrel Show's" overtly racist properties, costume, and staging, and the bewilderment of the mixed-race in-studio audience's ambivalent response. The second, which is taped after the show has unexpectedly been approved by network brass and begun to draw increased audiences, spins out the Tambo-and-Bones–style minstrel-show comic dialog, as well as the slapstick comedy, which blackface bequeathed to vaudeville and to early sound-film.[36] The third sequence further explores the tradition of blackface performance and—perhaps not coincidentally, considering its broadest assumption of the grossest racist caricatures of speech, movement, and character associated with minstrelsy—is portrayed as most popular with the TV audience and as heralding Delacroix's arrival as a "genius" TV producer. Just as Womack's and Manray's repulsion and resentment peaks, Delacroix attains success and completes the process of selling out, in voice-over and in particularly hyperbolized network awards presentations, to the most obsequious "house Negro" stereotypes. A last aborted sequence, which follows the final rupture of the artistic partnership between Womack and Manray (unable to stomach any further performance of the racist caricatures, Womack quits the show), intends to introduce Womack's onstage replacement, "Honeycutt" (Thomas Jefferson Byrd) gotten up as a blackface Honest Abe Lincoln. But the taping is cut short when Manray breaks the minstrel show's fourth wall, appearing unexpectedly without costume or blackface, confronting the audience directly, until he is fired by Dunwhittie and removed from the theater.

A more detailed explication of each performance uncovers the complexity of the semiotic messages that Lee intends music and dance to carry. The first sequence introduces the show's stars and its premise, a "New Millennium Minstrel Show." The small television soundstage is dressed with vaudeville-style stage properties, including a painted backdrop depicting a plantation house on a hill; cotton fields; and, for the band, "The Alabama Porch Monkeys" (portrayed by new-funk band The Roots) dressed in prison stripes; the front porch of a slave cabin in a watermelon patch. Glover's "Man-Tan" is dressed in blackface Interlocutor-style in an ill-fitted tuxedo and dented stovepipe hat, and Womack's "Sleep 'n' Eat" in a bellhop's short jacket and pillbox hat, reminiscent of a lawn ornament or cigarette packet.[37] The dialog, in blackface dialect, especially in Davidson's beautifully musical and richly timbred voice, introduces the dance, language, and racist nostalgia that will be central to the program, promising to take the audience "back to a simpler time" when "Neegras knew they place." This establishing sequence also introduces a riff upon the apocalyptic 1976 television fantasy *Network* and Peter Finch's rabble-rousing news anchor "Howard Beale," but neatly inverts *Network*'s anticorporate rant, transforming it into a roar of racist rage:

**MANTAN**: Cousins, I want you all to go to your windows . . .
**SLEEP 'N' EAT**: Open 'em up.
**MANTAN**: Go to your windows and yell out . . .
I'm tired of the drugs.
I'm tired of the crack babies born out of wedlock . . .
To crackhead AlD-infested parents.
I'm tired of the inflated welfare rolls . . .
While good wholesome Americans . . .
Bring less and less of their paycheck home . . .
Every two weeks.
**SLEEP 'N' EAT**: And that's a long time, too.
**MANTAN**: I'm tired. You're tired.
We're all tired . . .
Of all these so-called, uh, Bible-thumpin' . . .
**SLEEP 'N' EAT**: [Singing] Swing down, sweet low
**MANTAN**: God-fearin' . . .
**SLEEP 'N' EAT**: G. P., are you with me?

**MANTAN**: Whore-mongling professional athletes.
**SLEEP 'N' EAT**: You's a fine motherfucker, baby, back that ass up. Uh!
**MANTAN**: Cousins, I want you to go to your windows . . .
Yell out, scream with all the life you can muster up . . .
Inside your bruised and battered, assaulted bodies . . .
"I'm sick and tired of niggers . . .
"And I'm not gonna take it anymore!"
[collapses]

After Man-Tan has collapsed in emotional exhaustion, Sleep 'n' Eat resurrects him with the aroma of fresh watermelon before inquiring "Are there any pickan-ninies inna house?" The Roots' funk-soul groove brings on the dancers, who are costumed, like Man-Tan and Sleep 'n' Eat, in a range of racist archetypes: as Aunt Jemima (originating in 1893 as a trademark of the Quaker Oats company); the Chef "Rastus" from the Cream of Wheat porridge company (also debuted in 1893, by Nabisco, at the World Columbian Exposition in Chicago); ragged children loosely costumed after Allen "Farina" Hoskins and Billie "Buckwheat" Thomas (members of the *Our Gang* movie serials cast from, respectively, 1921 and 1934); a leopard-skinned shock-wigged "tribesman" reminiscent of the extras in *King Kong* (1933); Topsy (from Harriet Beecher Stowe's 1852 *Uncle Tom's Cabin*; see Chapter 3, Note 43)—all costumed with the burnt-cork faces, exaggerated red lips, and white gloves iconic of both blackface minstrelsy and early animated cartoons.[38]

There is an interesting internal contradiction in the dance sequence that follows. Though the visual cues are entirely those of racist caricature, and will recur throughout the film in the form of banks, toys, advertisements, and other objects of American material culture, both the music—the funk-soul of the Roots—and the dance vocabulary—Savion Glover's personal interpretation of elements of hip hop within the overall frame of jazz dance and tap dance—are entirely and unabashedly modern: until the very end of the sequence, Glover eschews obvious elements of blackface dance style. Though this was probably an essentially unexamined production decision on the part of Glover and director Lee—that is, the team simply had Glover do what he does, without attempting to replicate period dance style—it also makes a subtle but powerful statement about the double consciousness that W. E. B. DuBois first articulated and which has since been much cited by theorists of the African American experience, from Frantz Fanon and Paul Gilroy to Henry Louis Gates Jr. and Duke Ellington.[39] The first three are literary and cultural theorists, while Ellington was a bandleader and composer; Ellington's strategies for coping with the painful paradox of derogated subaltern status and artistic excellence—the need to show one face inside one's own community and another, simultaneous guarded and submissive, to the dominant culture—are particularly closely aligned to Glover's own. Just as Ellington accepted the term (and the programmatic obligations) of "jungle music" to accompany the grass-skirted light-skinned chorus girls and colonialist floor shows of the 1930s Cotton Club, while developing within that racist frame a compositional style that made him one of the greatest composers of the twentieth century, Glover's "Man-Tan" accepts the blackface and costume of the American racist imagination, while creating, behind that burnt-cork mask, a choreographic art of ferocious, defiant beauty.

This physical embodiment of double consciousness may or may not be intentional, but the end of the sequence confirms the transition away from the inner expression of Glover's own artistry and back outward to resume the "negro" mask that is the surface of the onstage characters: the music concludes with a series of stop-time riffs that belatedly evoke older jazz styles, which bring forth some classic akimbo steps from the dancers. At the end, there is a group freeze, all dancers framing their grinning faces with white gloves, another visual reference to blackface caricature and its translations into animated cartoons.

Throughout this sequence, Lee exploits the reflexivity of the show-within-a-show conceit (a la *The Producers*) to display not only the unvarnished racism and comic/kinesthetic beauty of the blackface dance idiom but also the conflicted responses of the TV audience and, by extension, of his film's viewers. Initially shocked and uncertain of appropriate responses, the white sophisticates, in the house for the taping, gradually take cues from those African Americans in the audience who laugh and cheer. But Lee eschews the didacticism to which he is otherwise prone throughout the film—in a single pan, we see whites and blacks, in both the audience and the studio's control room, manifesting every reaction from disgust to ambivalence to delight.

Not coincidentally, the narrative next transitions to Delacroix making a brief return to his own family's tradition within black entertainment by attending his stand-up comedian father Junebug's gig in an all-black nightclub. This scene is pivotal, because (in a rather ham-fisted way) it reconfirms Delacroix's estrangement from the "black experience": he is visibly uncomfortable around his father and in the backstage context of black theater. But more significant is the way the scene demonstrates that the impact of "offensive" language, both racist labels and X-rated terminology, is contextual and contingent: the use of "nigger" in the *Mantan* TV studio—outside the black community—is derogatory in a way that it is not in Junebug's all-black context. Realms of shared experience and communicative vocabulary, dance, and music are available to subaltern communities—people of color, women, gays and lesbians—which are or should be unavailable to members of the dominant culture. No matter how "down" Michael Rapaport's "Dunwhittie" may be, with his black trophy wife and etchings of black athletes, he is unentitled to claim minority experience and he remains a villain among Lee's dramatis personae: the complicity of white privilege within American history is inescapable.

The second performance sequence, again on the TV soundstage of *Mantan*, is again preceded by the emotionally fraught process of Davidson and Glover blacking-up in their respective dressing rooms, this time accompanied only by Blanchard's mournful instrumental music. Meanwhile, new M.C. "Honeycutt" (Byrd), gotten up as a blackface Uncle Sam, inaugurates new catchphrases and physical jokes (including a particularly brutal soccer-style chant "LET's go NIG-gers"), which will become part of the show's folklore as he warms up the pretaping audience. This sequence focuses much more upon the physical slapstick comedy associated with both blackface and its stepchild vaudeville and with the Tambo-and-Bones–style dialogue, which were the older style's bequest to vaudeville and film comedy. Set inside a three-sided chicken house whose lighting, plank walls, and floor recall the classic proscenium of theater and of vaudeville advertisements of the same, the dialogue is purposefully hilarious, impeccable, accessible, and appalling. By now, the audience responds with much more unalloyed delight. Discovered by a Panama-hatted white overseer armed with a shotgun, Sleep 'n' Eat provides the iconic, "Ain't nobody here but us chickens!" defense, before the pair engage in a beautifully choreographed slapstick chase and the arms-akimbo physical comedy whose descendants—more or less whitewashed—can be found in vaudeville, film comedy, and animation down to the present day.

The third of the three complete performance sequences presents the taping that follows the show's wildly and unexpectedly popular premiere; it thus involves a public audience primed and prepared for the transgressive content to come. The taping immediately follows a major artistic quarrel between Womack and Manray. Womack, disgusted by their culpability in the show's racism, is ready to walk away, while Manray is convinced that he can still "handle his business." Blacked-up and in costume, they enter through the mouth of a gigantic laughing animated burnt-cork face to discover that the entire audience is dressed in *Man-Tan* T-shirts, and that all—black, white, Asian, and other—are likewise wearing blackface.[40] Perhaps seeking to convey the way in which blackface self-caricature, when successful and rewarded, becomes an insidious temptation, Lee makes the caricature in this sequence even broader: if a little "N-word" humor works, more will work better? Opening with Davidson's virtuoso dialect riff on the ancient "I'm my own grandpa" vaudeville joke, the sequence moves (via "Feets, do yo' stuff") into a two-beat jazz-accompanied solo by Glover. Both the music and the choreographic language evoke the tradition of blackface performance more literally and extensively than in the previous tapings and feature banjo, a modified 16-bar blues progression rhythmic stop-time from the band, and the akimbo-armed "raggedy" body language of "Jump Jim Crow" and classic minstrelsy; similarly, Manray is shortly joined by the corps. Then the sequence segues to a double-time song from Davidson whose catchy refrain is the repeated line, "You ain't never seen no niggers like this."

The studio audience is roaring with delight, while both black and white crew members and production staff are laughing hysterically in the control room (Dunwhittie embraces Delacroix, exclaiming "You couldn't hold out any more, could ya?")—and then we cut to the rundown apartment of the spurned Mau-Mau hip hop collective, who watch the program stony-faced (except for one member who snickers involuntarily and is roundly castigated). This is precisely the moment when Mos Def's "Julius Hopkins" aka "Big Blak Afrika," black-sheep brother to Pinkett Smith's executive, decides that the collective's members have no choice but to kill the show's stars.

Delacroix's voice-over confirms that not only audiences, production staff, and year-end awards ceremonies, but also critics, roundly applaud the program: it is "ground-breaking, earth-shaking"; Delacroix becomes "Hollywood's favorite Negro." Shortly after, Womack quits the program in a fury ("It's the same bullshit! Just done over!") when Manray suggests that Womack had always been a drag on their act. The partners' last conversation ends chillingly, with Womack literally passing a hand across his face, assuming the cross-eyed minstrel mask, to draw the veil of double consciousness between himself and his erstwhile partner, and saying "Yassuh, whatchoo want me do fo' ya, Massah? Anything yo' want. I sang for ya, I tap-dance fo' ya." It is easily the most powerful and most heartbreaking piece of acting in the film, and it is the moment that most effectively—rather than didactically—shows the human cost *to its practitioners* of the blackface archetype.

**Figure 18:** Tommy Davidson, Womack's "minstrel mask," *Bamboozled* (2000).

The final, abortive performance sequence begins with the whole audience in blackface and Honeycutt as a blacked-up "Honest Abe" (Lincoln), who are interrupted when Manray, late for the taping, crashes Honeycutt's opening without costume or blackface. The M.C. further elaborates the opening catchphrases and physical comedy, passing the microphone from one audience member to another with the repeated phrase "Is you a nigger?" to which each (black, white, Asian, Hispanic, male, female) responds in the gleeful affirmative. "Do you know why?" "Why?!?" "Do you know why?" "WHY?!?" "'Cause niggers is a BEAUTIFUL thing." Manray enters through the backdrop's Bakhtinian carnivalesque mouth and addresses the audience directly, in an explicit echo of the speech with which he had opened the first taping: "Cousins, I want you all to go to your windows. Go to your windows, and yell out, scream with all the life that you can muster up inside of your bruised, assaulted, and battered bodies, 'I am sick and tired of being a nigger and I am not going to take it anymore!'" Again, he collapses to the stage in a red light, but this time, there is no "Sleep 'n' Eat" to revive him with the aroma of watermelon.

Suddenly, Manray leaps up and begins a frenetic a cappella tap dance, until Dunwhittie storms the stage, screaming, "Stop dancing, stop dancing"; he stutters to the audience that "Man-Tan" has "come down with a severe case of Coon-itis." Backstage, Dunwhittie fires Manray, sending Honeycutt back to the stage to take over while Manray is ejected from the building, only to be confronted, kidnapped, and eventually executed—on live television feed—by the Mau Maus. The film concludes with a SWAT team's assault upon the collective's stronghold, when all are shot down, with the exception of one black-identifying white member, who screams "Yo, why didn't you kill *me*?!?" No one, not even Pinkett Smith's and Wayans's upwardly mobile bourgeois characters, escapes consequences.

However, the real denouement of the film is not the apocalyptic violence, which Lee substitutes for any actual narrative resolution, but the long postnarrative closing sequence (almost 4:00 minutes), beautifully edited without dialog or voice-over, accompanied only by Blanchard's music, of blackface-themed cartoons, period films, white and black performers, Griffiths's *Birth of a Nation*, toys, and advertisements, which play out and play through the blackface trope. It is the moment when Lee most effectively declines the didacticism that otherwise shapes his narrative: when he simply presents the evidence of the nation's culpability before the bar of history. Conversely, it is in the performance sequences, in the African American rhyme and dance that were literally born on the streets (and which, in the personae of Womack and Manray, are literally borne to the TV stage), that he shows the shared painful hold that blackface still places upon that history.

Were it possible to watch the performances by Davidson, Glover, and the Roots absent any racist or historical connotations, they would still be of great affective power. But it is precisely because, as Americans, we *cannot* thus strip blackface performance of its connotations and our own culpability, that these set-pieces are so important. Lee forces us directly to confront the attraction and repulsion that racist comedy, indeed the North American legacy of racial prejudice, embodies and the expressive power and virtuosity that pushes back and makes these constraints ironic. The blackface performances can even be read as an embodiment of the dilemma of African American performance virtuosity: sophisticated, complex, grounded in a challenging movement tradition, executed with meticulous solidarity and artistry—and yet still subsumed within the surface caricatures of racist stereotype.[41] As Greg Tate, one of the most acute and subtle scholars working on the situation of African American performance within contexts of American popular culture, puts it, "The best parts of the film are, of course, the performance scenes. . . . In these skits, Spike shows himself to be a master coonologist—a high-flying scholar of the varied forms of black performance style."[42]

However, I would go further and grant Lee credit for his recognition that it is precisely in the "classicism" of the blackface routines, on the floorboards of the minstrel stage—whether in an 1830s Bowery theater or a Hollywood sound studio—that the "love and theft," which has always characterized the fraught dynamics of class and race in American entertainment meet in complex, vital paradox. In *Bamboozled*'s virtuosic performance sequences, Lee weaves together the defiant beauty and vile caricature of the idiom, creating a meta-discourse upon race and racism, comedy and ethnic caricature.[43] Though he cannot resist climactic didacticism or apocalyptic violence, within those sequences Lee refrains from dictating our responses.[44] Instead, he shows us *both* the horrific racial hatred that drives the pickaninny/coon stereotypes and the sheer vertiginous beauty of the art forms—the dancing, singing, wordplay, and physical comedy—that arose within, and in response to, that noxious world.

*Bamboozled*'s soundstage sequences capture, more self-consciously, what we have previously seen in blackface, Josephine Baker, and the Marx Brothers: like those others, it forces us to confront the joy and discomfort, hatred and admiration that racially coded performance arts have always elicited in American popular culture. And, whether Lee intended this or not, it also evokes—over 300 years after Hans Sloane's Jamaican field reports on creole dance—the sheer trickster vitality, and the coded mockery W. E. B. DuBois called "double-consciousness," that for centuries have allowed African-based, European-appropriated, "creolized" music-and-dance to roll with the punches, to side-slip the frame, to "wheel about and turn about and do just so," and thus, to revive us again.

## CHAPTER 8

# Body and Spirit in a Post-1960s World

## Hippies, Queens, Punks, and B-Boys

Somewhere in the existential depths of that brawl of screaming transvestites were all the antiwar marches, the sit-ins, the smoke-ins, the freedom rides, the bra-burnings, the levitation of the Pentagon, the endless meetings and broken hearts.

—Martin Duberman and Andrew Kopkind, on the Stonewall Uprising, June 27, 1969

The Dionysian movement vocabularies of 1960s youth culture—in this context, iconicized in the obviously tripping free-form dancers beloved of rock concert-film editors—are so well-documented as to be virtually a cliché.[1] Certainly dance was perceived, during both celebratory and confrontational moments in the 1960s, as a kind of embodied freedom.[2] A more nuanced understanding of the meaning of dance within the decade's social culture, however, entails situating it within political landscapes of liberation: not only the liberation of middle-class white youth—the prototypical baby-boomer hippies—but also that of ethnic minorities, of same-sex gender orientations, and, most relevantly, of public spaces. The interplay of hippie and Civil Rights Movement culture, and the role of dance within their respective political aesthetics, leads directly to the dynamics of dance as resistance in 1970s social revolutions: for our study, those of Women's Rights, Gay Rights, (predominantly white) punk rock, and the (predominantly black and brown) hip-hop nation.[3] To understand and map these progressions and trajectories is to recover 1960s hippie dance as a precursor to communal rebellion, not just self-absorbed individual catharsis in a post–Civil Rights world, and to link 1960s dance revolutions with those previously addressed in this book.[4]

The 1954 *Brown v. Board of Education* Supreme Court ruling is rightly seen as a watershed in the quest for African American civil rights: the moment when the highest court in the land finally passed a decision making institutionalized segregated education a federal offense.[5] Attempts to subvert *Brown*, most notoriously in Arkansas Governor Orval Faubus's attempt to bar black students' entry into Little Rock Central High School (1957), had the paradoxical impact of raising the national media visibility, and thereby—arguably—of accelerating or expanding the impact of school integration.[6]

The pursuit of African American civil rights activity in the United States, more widely defined, reaches back to the 1863 Emancipation Proclamation and, indeed, to the first public discourse questioning black chattel slavery—for example, Thomas Jefferson's draft paragraphs in the Declaration of Independence, which were tellingly excised from the final version.[7] A whole series of subsequent historical and legal watersheds mark civil rights' pre-*Brown* history: all contributed to the radical reorganization of United States economics, living patterns, world politics, self-perceptions, and race relations, in the wake of the Allied victory in World War II, that shaped the 1960s.[8]

The postwar landscape of the nation was permanently changed, and these changes flowed across boundaries of class, race, geography, income, education, and experience. It is no coincidence that the early 1950s saw the simultaneous expansion of prosperity, global militarism (most notably, the "domino" theory, which led to the police action in Korea and then to postcolonial intervention in Southeast Asia) and domestic repression (most notoriously, the activities of the House Un-American Affairs Committee), and the rise of oppositional social movements.[9] The flamboyant foliage of the 1960s Cultural Revolution may thus be understood as rooted in largely underground 1950s movements arising from subaltern "hidden" communities.[10] To understand dance as rebellion in black, gay, and working-class white consciousnesses since the 1960s, it is therefore necessary to understand the wider origins of these dance communities and their impact upon, and influence from, the decade's cultural revolutions.

## Hippies

The stereotypes of 1960s culture—stereotypes later promulgated precisely in order to delegitimize the decade's political agendas—include the accusation that hippies were spoiled, entitled, materialist, impractical, and/or self-centered bourgeois children of privilege.[11] There is no question that the postwar boom in middle-class economics and youth opportunity on one side, and the vast expansion of the draft driven by Vietnam War escalation on the other, were primary motivating factors for the linkup between hippie culture and antiwar activism.[12] But it has been a vast oversimplification to presume that bourgeois entitlement or fear of the draft was the sole impetus, or that hippie culture collapsed "after Altamont," the catastrophic

December 1969 rock concert at Altamont Speedway in California at which several died. Though revisionist histories attempted to paint 1960s activism as having "sold out" to an intervening 1970s "Me Decade," many hippie veterans remained highly active, if less visible, in the burgeoning Women's Rights, Gay Rights, antinuclear, indigenous peoples', and environmental movements.[13] In reality, threads of activism and, more specifically, the activist street tactics of theater and dance, flow directly from 1960s actions into 1970s cultural politics, often carried by individuals who were to experience both.[14]

Dance was a central component to 1960s culture, not least because it was an essential and visible component of hippie dance halls' multimedia sensory immersion. The Avalon Ballroom and Fillmore Auditorium in San Francisco and the Fillmore East and Beacon Theater in New York, specialized in presenting a wide variety of musics—often including the introduction of relatively unknown artists, from Ravi Shankar to Albert King, to hippie audiences—in an environment that combined music, dancing, and light shows (a new art form, involving the real-time improvised projection of lights and images). The prototype of these events was the series of Acid Tests run by novelist Ken Kesey's Merry Pranksters, a loose extended family also heavily involved in Bay Area street theater and new media, which culminated in January 1966 with the Trips Festivals in San Francisco, which were early launch pads for Bay Area rock bands like the Grateful Dead, Jefferson Airplane, and Janis Joplin's Big Brother and the Holding Company.

Dancing, sometimes under the influence of hallucinogens, was a central component of these immersive experiences; the comparative mythologist, Joseph Campbell, who became a friend of Dead drummer, Mickey Hart, commenting in 1986 about large rock shows, made a historical comparison to pre-Christian festivals: "The first thing I thought of was the Dionysian festivals, of course. This energy and these terrific instruments with electric things that zoom in. . . . This is more than music. It turns something on in here (the heart?). And what it turns on is life energy. This is Dionysus talking through these kids. . . . This is a wonderful fervent loss of self in the larger self of a homogeneous community. This is what it is all about!"[15]

However, the archetypal acid-fired freestyle dancing associated with the Trips Festivals, rock ballrooms, and later outdoor festivals like Monterey Pop and Woodstock, is not our primary focus. As an embodiment of the politics of personal rather than communal liberation, hippie free-form dancing was more revolutionary in terms of its implicit, indirect, and (often) unintentional contradiction of middle-class body vocabularies—not unlike the implicit challenge posed by the akimbo theatrics of blackface dance 100 years before.[16] But precisely because it occurred in the liminal (if temporary) environments of individuals' transformed consciousness, hippie dancing less commonly or communally confronted the normalizing body politics of 1960s public urban spaces.[17]

When hippie body liberation *did* appear in contested public spaces, it was—as in later manifestations during the Stonewall Riots, punk-rock political actions, and hip hop street dancing—perceived as profoundly revolutionary. As Craig Calhoun says, *"for ordinary citizens to claim public spaces in protest is among other things to upset the usual symbolic control of those spaces by government and 'forces of order.'"*[18] The power of the subaltern to act in "tactical" ways (see discussion of de Certeau, earlier), to "upset the usual symbolic control," is manifested in public dance, defined both narrowly and more broadly, and was widely recognized throughout hippie political culture. In the 1970s, activists' symbolic occupations of contested spaces themselves took powerful cues from direct street actions pioneered by the Civil Rights movement's use of sit-ins, especially those that sought to desegregate public spaces like restaurants and protest marches and before that by similar tactics employed by Mohandas Gandhi in the cause of Indian independence.[19]

This book suggests that defiant occupation of contested public spaces by opposing bodies, and those defiant bodies' concerted motion to music, has often constituted conscious and intentional political action. Within this broader definition of "dance"—that is, "bodies moving in concert in physical spaces"—everything from the chanting and dancing of James Davenport's apostates in the First Great Awakening to the chanting and dancing of Ghost Dancers in Wyoming can be analyzed as oppositional and intentional. Even the 1960s "dance" of protesting crowds breaking up and fleeing, only to coalesce at a different location within the urban grid—a policing challenge that ran from the Watts Uprising in 1965 to Newark in 1967 to the Los Angeles Uprising of 1992—can be so understood.

But dance, more literally defined, also played a much more explicitly revolutionary role in 1960s protest as well. During the summer of 1968, for example, street confrontations between politicians, activists, police, and media at the Democratic National Convention in Chicago mirrored the apocalyptic domestic and worldwide chaos of that year.[20] The principle organizers of the protests, the "MOBE" (National Mobilization to End the War in Vietnam) political action group and the Yippies (street theater pranksters influenced by the Diggers), taught self-defense techniques in anticipation of the police violence that had been essentially promised by Chicago's authoritarian mayor (and Democratic kingmaker) Richard M. Daley. As part of their improvised physical training, participants learned the linked-arm "snake-dancing" called *washoi*, which Japanese Shinto parades had traditionally employed to resist policing.[21]

During the convention, most of the Yippie sympathizers in Chicago's Lincoln Park, shocked by the extent, brutality, and openness of the CPD's "riot"—a retaliatory violence mirrored very widely at street protests throughout the decade by other police and paramilitary, most notoriously at the Kent State (May 4) and Jackson State (May 13) 1970 massacres—did not find *washoi* dance an adequate response.[22] However, the lessons learned by activists during 1960s street actions, and about

**Figure 19:** *Washoi* dancers at Grant Park 1968; production still from *Medium Cool* (1969).

the capacity of dance to embody contestation of public space, were not forgotten; nor did radical dance strategies disappear. On the contrary: those lessons, sometimes carried by hippie and civil rights veterans, played out in the foundation of multiple liberation movements of the subsequent decade.

## Gays

Civil rights direct-action philosophies recurred, for example, in the early roots of the Gay Liberation movement. While advocacy for gay rights had expanded in the post-WWII period, with the foundation of the first public advocacy organizations (most notably, the West Coast–based Daughters of Bilitis and the Mattachine Society), the movement—like the Women's Rights movement, which was catalyzed in the same period—received an enormous influx of strategic and tactical energy as a result of lessons learned by participants in the Sixties antiwar and civil rights cohorts.[23] In the newly reimagined world of Gay Liberation, dance was employed not only for as community reinforcement and solidarity, but also as a tool of direct street confrontation and protest.[24]

Establishing environments in which to safely dance together had been a crucial community-building exercise in North American gay culture since, at latest, the 1890s mixed-orientation bars of bohemian Greenwich Village—and, in all likelihood, in earlier mixed-race urban spaces (taverns, concert saloons, brothels, and so forth), which had always been places for behavior crossing the boundaries of race or gender identification.[25] San Francisco's first major lesbian-identified community organization, for example, the Daughters of Bilitis, was founded by eight women who "initially came together to be able to have a safe place to dance."[26] As we have seen in other historical contexts, spaces in which gender- and race-crossing liaisons could be embodied in dance were often located in socially- and/or geographically marginal places: the alley "back houses" of New York, New Orleans, and Washington, D.C.; "black-and-tan" clubs in African American neighborhoods, which specifically catered to a white clientele; the waterfront bars of New Orleans and Cincinnati reported by Lafcadio Hearn; and so forth.[27] The location of these sites and the marginality of their legal and economic status made them vulnerable to exploitation or persecution but also rendered them receptive to liminal conduct.

In the post–World War II period, however, just as returning African Americans veterans were far more prepared to publicly confront institutionalized discrimination, gay service people discovered the same sense of a community, particularly in those cities that had seen a large influx of civilian workers and enlisted service members.[28] The general strategic philosophy of the first postwar organizations like the Daughters of Bilitis and the Mattachine Society was to "normalize" gay identity—that is, to emphasize the degree to which, with the exception of sexual orientation, gays and lesbians were otherwise like "normal" other middle-class 1950s Americans. Shifts in postwar public discourse meant that these 1950s normalizing strategies were gradually supplemented or even supplanted, in the mid- to late-1960s, by more direct, confrontational, and (often) theatrical methods.[29] The watershed event commonly described as the birth of this post–Civil Rights Gay Liberation movement—whose shift of tactics is indicated in the shift of terminology from intentionally obscure references to "Bilitis" or "Mattachine" to ready acceptance of the label "gay"—is the June 1969 street confrontation precipitated by an NYPD raid on the Stonewall Inn, a gay/lesbian bar on Christopher Street in lower Manhattan. Situated in a Greenwich Village neighborhood that had been friendly to bohemian social and sexual minorities since the nineteenth century, the Stonewall, like other gay establishments across urban North America, was a marginalized space, not only because of its clientele but also because of the opportunism of its investors: like the Cotton Club in 1930s Harlem, the Tijuana Club in 1950s New Orleans, and Almack's Cellar in 1840s New York (where Dickens saw Master Juba dance), the Stonewall's openness to boundary-crossing sexual liaisons resulted from its economic function as a money-laundering operation for organized crime.[30] The criminal affiliations of the Stonewall's owners and their willingness to bribe members of the NYPD to turn a blind eye to violations not only of vice laws but also health codes and zoning laws, meant that the club was an atypically wide open space. The Stonewall employed a system of door security, private "drag" rooms, and warning-light signals to minimize the impact of the frequent pro forma police raids.[31] The predictability of these raids extended to their typically early hour (so that activity could resume after the cops had left) and the expected exchange of bribes of cash or booze.

In this same period, there was among gays and lesbians growing awareness of more aggressive resistance tactics, fueled by the high visibility of actions like the Chicago Democratic National Convention in 1968 and the student occupation of Columbia University buildings in the same year. More specifically to the issue of gay and lesbian activity, several West Coast confrontations prefigure the seemingly spontaneous mass resistance at Stonewall in June 1969: for example, the August 1966 antipolice resistance by transgendered customers at Compton's Cafeteria in San Francisco's Tenderloin and the series of public actions by the newly organized PRIDE (Personal Rights in Defense and Education) advocacy group precipitated by a violent raid on the Black Cat Tavern in December 1967. Taking into account the accelerating pace and visibility of massed crowd resistance to authoritarian police actions in various contexts, it is therefore not surprising that eventually similar resistance would arise in New York.

Stonewall itself, as an iconic moment of resistance to violent authoritarianism, has entered the canonic history of U.S. gay rights, and both its details and its semiotic meaning have been well-documented.[32] A raid on June 27, 1969, by a small force of New York police—its abusive authoritarian dynamic probably precipitated by increasing tensions between the Inn's organized crime-affiliated owners, corrupt NYPD officers, and the state Alcoholic Beverage Commission—quickly spun out of control. The patrons' seemingly spontaneous resistance, perhaps intensified by the cops' particularly aggressive conduct, began when several of the drag queens and possibly others struck back at the police; at the same time, also atypically, those who escaped arrest did not flee the area but gathered in a rapidly expanding crowd outside the Inn. Logistical problems—most notably a delay in the arrival of patrol wagons to carry the arrestees to detention—provided time for the crowd to grow larger; when one of the drag queens was hit, she struck back and, to quote an eyewitness, "the crowd went berserk." They chanted, began to sing "We Shall Overcome," threw garbage barrels and beer cans, and eventually drove the small force of police to barricade themselves inside the Inn. More recent historiography has suggested that in fact some of the crowd's most aggressive resistance came from "street kids"—very young runaways, some of them gay, who made a living hustling and as prostitutes; the implication is that these youngsters, like the drag queens who were most vulnerable to arrest under the city's vice laws, simply had much less to lose.[33] Carter quotes participant Michael Fader's own thoughtful, retrospective account, which explicitly links the night's action to wider liberation issues:

> We all had a collective feeling like we'd had enough of this kind of shit. It wasn't anything tangible anybody said to anyone else, it was just kind of like everything

> over the years had come to a head on that one particular night in the one particular place, and it was not an organized demonstration . . . All kinds of people, all different reasons, but mostly it was total outrage, anger, sorrow, everything combined, and everything just kind of ran its course. It was the police who were doing most of the destruction. We were really trying to get back in and break free. And we felt that we had freedom at last, or freedom to at least show that we demanded freedom.[34]

The rioters displayed unprecedented physical resistance: the small force of cops was besieged inside the bar, while the crowd outside surged back and forth chanting and throwing missiles and, by now numbering "500–600," literally used battering rams to try to drive in the barricaded doors and free the few remaining arrestees. Other protesters recalled lessons learned at previous demonstrations: Craig Rodwell, for example, a Stonewall patron who understood the importance of shining public light on police brutality, ran to a pay phone and called the press rooms of the *New York Times*, the *New York Post*, and the *Daily News*—though the *Village Voice*, which was located almost literally across the street, declined to send a reporter or photographer.[35] Testimony of participants confirms that, while the event was terrifying for all parties (arrestees, crowd members, and the members of the small police team all subsequently described it so), there was also among the protesters a tremendous sense of both liberation and familiarity. This was one more upswelling, one more example of activists "putting their bodies on the line," as the Freedom Riders and sitters-in; SNCC and CORE members; MOBE members and Yippies; and Free Speech advocates had all done before, culminating with the assassinations and police riots of '68.

But in this same moment—sometime between 2:30–3:00 a.m. on the morning of June 28, as the crowd swelled and screamed and hurled bricks and battered at the barricaded door of the Stonewall with garbage cans and uprooted parking meters—the uprising took on certain characteristics that could have been undertaken only by this particular revolutionary subcommunity, and *only* in the wake and awareness of earlier antiauthoritarian protests, and *only* through the medium of dance: those drag queens who had either escaped arrest, or been released, formed up in the street, and, as the paramilitary Tactical Police Force finally arrived to rescue the barricaded cops—they *danced*:

> When the police whirled around to reverse direction at one point, they found themselves face to face with their worst nightmare: a chorus line of mocking queens, their arms clasped around each other kicking their heels in the air Rockettes-style and singing at the tops of their sardonic voices:
>
> *We are the Stonewall girls*
> *We wear our hair in curls*
> *We wear no underwear*

*We show our pubic hair..*
*We wear our dungarees*
*Above our nelly knees!*[36]

This improvised parodic street dancing—this playing out in heightened public fashion precisely those cross-dressed body anxieties that middle-class white authority sought to contain or criminalize—of course has resonances in earlier U.S. resistance movements addressed throughout this book.[37] This is the mockery of rustic "Jim Crow," urban "Zip Coon," and cross-dressed "wench" characters who "wheeled about and turned about" in blackface minstrelsy, the cakewalk's mockery of 1890s white "swells" and Josephine Baker's stirred rump mocking 1920s voyeurism, the cartoonish sneers and safety-pinned noses of the 1970s U.K. punks (discussed ahead). It is the theatricalized "signifyin(g)" that, as Henry Louis Gates Jr. has argued, forms a fundamental, embodied resistance strategy for subaltern communities.[38]

The riot, and the "fearless chorus line of queens [who] insisted on yet another refrain," did more than just provoke the NYPD to fury: in the weeks after the uprising, they also signaled a sea change in gay activists' strategic palette. Gays and lesbians in the early Seventies more and more borrowed and implemented political insights, rhetorical strategies, and street tactics they had learned in earlier movements, and a number of new gay advocacy societies were founded, especially on college campuses, in the next several years.[39]

Gay political activism would play out with even greater urgency in response to the AIDS crisis, which initially appeared most widely among populations of urban gay men; Act Up! (founded in 1987) and like organizations would battle to increase medical awareness and counter government indifference to the scope of the epidemic. The gains made by political activity in the area of gay rights in the early 1970s provided a fertile environment for the enhanced visibility of a nexus of social / racial / sexual boundary-crossing and exchange between black and white, gay and straight communities which had been part of underground integrated urban settings for literally over a century.[40]

The raising of consciousness and visibility, which was catalyzed by the social factors that erupted at the Stonewall in the summer of 1969, was matched by the presence of gays and lesbians (especially white males) in the small bars and private parties where, in the early '70s, funk and R&B gave birth to both disco-style dancing (when moved to purpose-built nightclubs), the primacy of the DJ, and the roots of hip hop culture.[41] In these semiprivate dance spaces (David Mancuso's "The Loft," in Manhattan, was permitted to continue operation only after a landmark zoning hearing in which he confirmed that, because he was not selling alcohol or food, he could not be required to hold a nightclub license), the immersive experience of the

1960s hippie dance hall was transmuted into an environment in which nonstop dancing, and dancers, became the locus of the performance.[42] Gillian Frank comments, "Disco placed the bodies of its audience on display"—it likewise placed on display, and permitted the questioning of, the entire construct of masculine versus feminine identities.[43]

Because of the long-standing affinity between homophilic and racially integrated dance musics and spaces, discos became a common site for gay (especially male) celebration of community. While some scholarship on the gay presence in disco has focused upon the homophobic backlash against it, I am more interested in situating disco's "performance" of bodily liberation as another manifestation of post-Sixties dance revolution.[44] Following Frank, we can better understand disco as both an idealized group experience evoking "Victor Turner's notion of communitas," and recognize the central role of *dancing together*, in defiance of heteronormative control, as a performance and celebration of gay public identity.[45] Disco, and the rave culture that grew out of its revival in the 1990s, became, like so many boundary-blurring dance spaces in the history of the nation, sites for the creation of "temporary autonomous zones" of freedom, acceptance, equality, and love.[46]

## Punks

Punk rock's political agendas originated in early 1970s reactions to trends in both pop music and the wider culture. The commercialization of the late '60s rock industry and concomitant impulses toward virtuosity, complexity, and sheer bigness (of artistic conceptions, events, and profits) led in turn to a fan-driven grassroots push back.[47] With inspirations in early 1970s U.S. groups like the Velvet Underground, the Stooges, and the New York Dolls, New York–based punks like Television, Patti Smith, and the Ramones in 1974–1975 developed an aesthetic melding musical primitivism, onstage intensity, and—often—lyrical or topical erudition.[48] In the wake of personal contacts and a brief overseas tour by the Ramones, the movement took root very swiftly as well across the Atlantic, particularly among unemployed black and white youth in London, by the summer of 1975 spawning the Sex Pistols, the Clash, and the Damned.[49]

Early punk-rock discourse tended to be much more politicized in the U.K. than in the United States. While the North Americans focused upon musical experimentation (Television), poetic complexity (Patti Smith), and/or the social dynamics of three-chord dance songs (Ramones), the sociological situation of Britain under Prime Ministers Edward Heath (1970–1974) and Harold Wilson (1974–1976), which included very extensive youth unemployment, government assaults on labor unions, and the presence of a large and aggressive neo-Nazi National Front, led U.K. punks to a much more explicit engagement with political action.[50] Particularly, the class warfare promulgated by the Sex Pistols ("God Save the Queen," "Anarchy in the U.K.," and "Holidays in the Sun") and the address to racial injustice and corporate corruption by the Clash ("White Riot" and "Complete Control") lent British punk a strong progressive political aura, which was iconicized in the antifascist Rock Against Racism, founded in 1976.[51]

Comparable levels of overt political rhetoric surface in the United States with the early 1980s hardcore punk movement, its formative bands largely coming from southern California, Washington, D.C., and various regional underground scenes.[52] The Southern California and D.C. bands were typically the most explicitly political, not only in terms of lyrics but also in their anticorporate practices. Black Flag founder Greg Ginn's SST Records pioneered the hardcore scene's "DIY" ("Do It Yourself") rejection of 1960s structures for recording and touring in favor of an ethos of self-determination: developing venues and touring networks, pressing records, and controlling publicity strategies on their own.[53] Following Ginn's example, D.C.-based bands like Minor Threat and Fugazi, both fronted by Ian MacKaye (himself the offspring of 1960s activists), extended this politics of self-sufficiency: sharing group homes, working and partnering very widely with a range of activist organizations, insisting on all-ages access, releasing their own recordings, and rigorously controlling prices and business practices.

It is also with the '80s hardcore movement that *dance* becomes an overt and central political act. In the 1970s, U.S. and U.K. punk had certainly embodied a radically democratized approach to music-making, and some bands had erased the stage-versus-dance-floor boundaries between musicians and fans: for example, the 1980s quasi-documentary *Rude Boy*, which borrows from reggae a Jamaican outlaw term, captures members of the Clash sneaking the title character into their shows.[54] But the '80s hardcore bands made dancing a much more explicit expression of group solidarity and collective identity. Though the mostly male "mosh pit" (the space immediately in front of and/or below the stage—typically hardcore bands played in small or improvised performance venues) garnered a great deal of horrified press, "slam-dancing" was understood by participants as a "ritual of trust:"[55]

> Even analysts who portray the pit as involving actual violence recognize that rules limit or control behavior in the pit. . . . The fundamental rules of this Etiquette insist that people look out for one another and react instantly when they see something going wrong. . . . The idea of these etiquettes is that people should intervene communally when they see something they don't like.[56]

Punk dance's communal ethos and mutually supportive intentions were significantly misunderstood by outsiders and nonparticipants.[57] In reality, hardcore bands—none more than MacKaye's politically sophisticated Fugazi—made an onstage point of seeking to defuse bad conduct:

> At one early gig . . . a handful of merciless slam dancers were ruining the show for everybody else. "Put your hands in the air if these guys are bugging you," [Fugazi guitarist Guy] Picciotto told the crowd. Immediately the place was a forest of hands. So the band told everybody but the slam dancers to get up onstage, while [bassist Joe] Lally, [guitarist] MacKaye, and Picciotto came down to the floor and played as the slammers did a circle dance around them. "It was great," Picciotti said afterward, "the whole thing was like a celebration of life."[58]

Key architects of the American hardcore scene (MacKaye; Mike Watt, and D Boon of the Minutemen; Henry Rollins of Black Flag), understanding punk dancing as a mostly metaphorical expression of resistance to anomie and disengagement, took steps to safeguard the mosh pit. MacKaye in fact found in the dancing a metaphor for the punk community's joyful sharing:

> At a festival [in Brazil], five or six hundred people circle—would develop. And Guy and I were watching this. We were incredulous. This seemed impossible that this many people were dancing. It was a huge, huge circle pit thing and Guy said, "I'll give you a buck if you go for that" [joined the "circle pit thing"]. I just did the whole, one circulation. It was incredible, actually. I was laughing so hard. It was totally enjoyable. Those kids were not slamming, per se. there were no punches being thrown. Just dancing in a giant circle.[59]

Likewise "stage-diving," which intentionally violated the clear-cut audience versus artist divisions reified by 1970s stadium-rock shows. Dancers would jump onstage, look outward to the mosh pit to make eye contact, and then somersault or dive forward, typically rolling onto their backs to minimize the chance of dangerous elbows or facial injuries. Most commonly, the crowd would catch stage-divers without significant injury; this is the origin of the later, more widely practiced rock concert behavior of "crowd-surfing." What might seem to have been an aggressive or self-destructive act in fact became a performance of group trust.[60]

American punk's willingness to speak truth to power could take quite direct paths to the street, not limited only to lyrical content or to the creation of communal dance spaces like those described earlier. On January 12, 1991, five days before the start of the aerial bombing campaign that opened Operation Desert Storm, the campaign intended by a U.S.-led military coalition seeking to knock out Iraqi military capacities, Ian MacKaye's Fugazi played an open-air show in Lafayette Park, with the White House as backdrop. At least a portion of the show (12 songs) is documented in a many-times-duplicated video that captures the frigid conditions, the youth and intensity of the tightly packed crowd, the band's explicit political address (especially in MacKaye's onstage raps), and the centrality of irruptive noise and movement in that address.[61] At one point, MacKaye says to the crowd, "I thought 'There's no way this country's going to go to fucking war, again,'" before the band starts the song "Keep Your Eyes Open"—at which the bundled-against-the-cold crowd explodes into mosh-pit dancing and crowd-surfing.

Punk rock, like hip hop, was a metaphorical "fantasy of subversion"—or, more generously, a performance of an oppositional model personal and communal liberation.[62] The conventional historical trope is that, by the late 1970s, this idealism had been co-opted by the rock music business and rapidly mutated to less confrontational and more palatable "New Wave." In fact, this is a vast oversimplification: 1980s hardcore punk continued to exert influence extending beyond the borrowing of its musical style characteristics, most notably in its outreach and receptivity to hip hop (see the Beastie Boys, Rage Against the Machine) and in the lasting influence of its DIY ethos.[63] In addition to the stamina and longevity demonstrated by the foundational 1980s artists, their "Book Your Own Fucking Life" ethos took over much of the processes of music touring, recording, and sales, via the radical democratization made possible by digital technology and the Internet.[64] Hip hop artists learned from, borrowed, and inspired these self-reliant paradigm shifts, and the parallels between the DIY and dance aesthetics of punk rock and hip hop, though sometimes neglected by scholarship, are too essential for the present study to be ignored.[65]

## B-Boys (and -Girls)

"Hip hop audiences do not . . . merely listen—passive reception is no longer possible. Layer upon layer—one to dance to, one to think on, one to *add to the din*. Hip hop itself is not merely music (though it is certainly that); it is a cultural recycling center, a social heterolect, a field of contest, even a form of psychological warfare."[66]

As Russell Potter makes clear in this quotation, hip hop culture, understood as an aesthetic that encompasses dance, texts, technology, music, and visual art (especially graffiti writing), can also be understood as—among other things—a *heterolect*: that is, a set of sophisticated, overlapping symbolic strategies. As with the other post-Sixties dance undergrounds discussed earlier, hip hop is deeply rooted in historical processes and in participants' conscious and intentional responses to those processes. Roughly coinciding with the rise of disco in the early 1970s—and sharing many of the same musical influences in the late-Sixties R&B and funk of Sly Stone, Parliament/Funkadelic and, most especially, James Brown—it represents the confluence of musical, oral-literary, political, and technological traditions rooted in urban experience. Its "heterolect" originates in black and brown communities' ongoing capacity, specifically in the South Bronx in the mid-1970s, to assimilate and indigenize a wide variety of expressive resources.[67]

The completion of the Cross-Bronx Expressway in 1963, and the resultant demographic and geographic shifts that resulted, left New York's South Bronx literally as well as sociologically cut off from the rest of the five boroughs. At the same time, a general trend toward urban renewal via the construction of gigantic vertical housing projects further eroded street life and the tax base.[68] Working-class "white flight" from these neighborhoods, and the difficulty of finding new tenants, fueled a mid-1970s spate of vacancies and sometimes arson by landlords seeking to empty decrepit or rent-controlled buildings for insurance settlements.[69] The tax base dwindled. Mid-decade citywide spending cuts further eroded social services, code enforcement, and police presence; homelessness, poverty, drug addiction, and gang activity flourished.[70] By 1980, over 40 percent of the Bronx's buildings had been burned or abandoned.[71]

Hip hop thus originated inside a black and brown population largely cut off from middle-class awareness or infrastructure and with comparatively limited financial and political resources.[72] As with other subaltern musics emerging from urban ghettos (in Harlem, Watts, Kingston, the South Side, Havana, Tremé, and so forth), hip hop's roots reflect the collision of diverse peoples' cultural and musical experience: along with New York Latino/a street culture, the influence of immigrant Jamaican musical practice is especially significant.[73] That island nation's small record-production industry, itself confined largely to the Trenchtown ghetto of Kingston, had, by the 1950s, developed a rich complex of musical practices out of the influence of earlier Caribbean musics (especially calypso and mento) and, very significantly, American R&B, heard on imported 45s and via the powerful signals of radio stations in Memphis, Nashville, New Orleans, Miami, and Brownsville, Texas. Because Kingston's urban population did not represent a sufficient market for record sales, powerful producers/record-store owners (the terms were often synonymous) developed mobile stores called *sound systems*, carried on the chassis of small trucks with powerful public address systems built in. Sound systems could haul product up into the forested hills to find the small villages already reached by Kingston and Stateside radio signals, where drivers would park and blast the latest sides, often hosting impromptu dance parties to boost sales. Eventually, competing sellers began using anonymized "dub plates"—acetates of bass-heavy rhythm tracks, with the labels scratched off to keep other producers from pirating new talent—and then to speak and rhyme over the "riddims"; this "toasting" made stars out of the DJs who practiced it and the "selectors" who chose and sequenced the tracks.[74]

The ambience of this Kingston record business is captured in the watershed quasi-documentary film *The Harder They Come* (1972), which borrowed details from the career of a legendary Trenchtown gunman, Vincent "Ivanhoe" Martin (1924–1948), whose prison escapes, robberies, murders, and mocking letters to police earned the nickname *Rhyging* (Jamaican patois: "raging").[75] The soundtrack features musician Jimmy Cliff in performances of "You Can Get It if You Really Want," and of the title track, whose ferocity mirrors the intensity of his lead character; it likewise introduced reggae stars, Toots and the Maytals, the Melodians, Desmond Dekker, and the Slickers, and Cliff himself, to international pop audiences. Bob Marley (1945–1981), who later became reggae's most influential ambassador and a figure of liberation on behalf of "sufferahs" worldwide, with his band, The Wailers, released his first Island Records LP, *Catch a Fire*, an explicit paean to social revolution, in April 1973.[76] Early 1970s economic uncertainty and political turmoil in Jamaica would lead many to emigrate overseas to the United States or to England (Bob himself had spent time in the midsixties in Delaware, and left for England after 1976).[77]

Jamaican immigrants came to the Bronx as well and brought both music and musical practices with them. In what might appear a romantic foundation myth were it not factually accurate, around 1972 a Kingston-born teen, Clive Campbell (born 1955), who had immigrated with his family in 1967, began to host and DJ for dance parties in the recreation center of his high-rise apartment building at 1520 Sedgwick, which literally overlooked the Cross-Bronx Expressway. Campbell (who became known as "DJ Kool Herc" for his size, strength, and commanding skills on the basketball court) imported the Jamaican art of the sound system and of "toasting" over R&B, salsa, and funk records.[78] Spinning at parties, Herc also pioneered the art of "the break"—the sequential repetition, on two turntables, of the hottest section from two copies of the same vinyl record, an extension of the studio sound manipulations of the Kingston "dub" producers. The break—a literal interruption and usurpation of a corporate recording's rhythmic language, and its spontaneous recomposition—made it possible to find the most danceable section of a record, and then to extend that break, either by switching between two copies or by switching and cuing between different records with compatible tempi and instrumental sounds. Herc's disciples, most notably Grandmaster Flash (born Barbados, 1958) and Afrika Bambaataa (born in the Bronx, 1957), further extended these techniques, pioneering a whole series of physical manipulations of the turntables and amplifier, turning needle scratching, abrupt cross-fades, manual ritardando or accelerando, into a complex and potent sonic palette. DJs essentially invented a new set of sonic possibilities, one (because based in part upon recutting quoted material, playing with the dynamics of familiarity versus unfamiliarity) uniquely reflecting the "Signifyin(g)" semiotics identified by Henry Louis Gates Jr. Herc, Flash, Bambaataa, and their disciples were legendary, not only for their physical virtuosity but also for encyclopedic knowledge of recorded music of many genres and for a sophisticated ability to read a crowd and spin so as to maximize the desire to dance.[79]

MCs, the masters of ceremonies whose adaptations of Jamaican toasting and North American radio jocks' vocalizing gave hip hop its lyrical core, likewise built a rhetorical vocabulary out of the communities' own street patois and traditions of verbal art (see, for example, the venerable rhythming poetry of "The Dozens").[80] But it was not until 1982's "The Message," by Grandmaster Flash and the Furious Five, that hip hop was seen as widely and directly addressing considerations of inner-city history and social dynamics, as had R&B singers like Sam Cooke ("A Change Is Gonna Come") and Marvin Gaye ("What's Goin' On") before them.[81] In the 1970s, hip hop's political address was therefore not originally textual—not based in words spoken explicitly to power—but rather sonic and spatial. Nevertheless, as Tricia Rose says, "To dismiss rappers who do not choose 'political' subjects as having no politically resistive roles ignores the complex web of institutional policing to which all rappers are subjected, especially in large public-space contexts."[82] For early hip hop sound, speech, and movement to occupy physical, sonic, and cognitive space as an oppositional heterolect was therefore to resist; resistance could take many forms, some more explicitly political and others less.[83]

As is often true of syncretic urban musics, a complex interplay also exists between hip hop's musical roots, its sociocultural contextual specifics, and its movement languages. Like jazz in New Orleans and Kansas City; reggae in Kingston; calypso in Port of Spain; electric blues in Chicago, and in many other settings, the stark realities of urban working-class existence (including variously unemployment, crime, drug addiction, and youth gang activity) influenced hip hop aesthetics politics as much as its musical inspirations did. Long before the rise of West Coast "gangsta" rap, whose explosive topics, texts, and visual rhetoric modernized the Rhyging / Staggerlee "legendary bad man" trope to target late capitalism, hip hop DJs found audiences, dancers, converts, and crews among the rank of Black and Latino youth gangs.[84] Just as stylistic exchange between Black and Latino musics yielded the disco and funk that Herc and his followers spun, interplay between gangs fueled the hip hop movement revolution. Several gang leaders, most notably Bambaataa (born Kevin Donovan in the Bronx River Projects in 1957), recognized the expressive and community-building capacities of nascent hip hop culture; a noted DJ in the Herc mold, by 1973 Bambaataa had transformed his Black Spades street gang into a loose creative collective called "The Universal Zulu Nation."[85]

Hip hop was crucial to the burgeoning sense of this subaltern community's dance identity: Chang, for example, provides a powerful description of particular gangs' identification with particular songs: "At the climax of a Plaza Tunnel night, when DJ John Brown put on [James Brown's funk anthem] 'Soul Power,' . . . Black Spades would overrun the floor, hollering 'Spade Power!'"[86] That empowered communal identity, tied directly to the performance of group unity via music and movement, is at the core of hip hop's spatial strategies. Along with certain iconic Latin recordings (most notably the Incredible Bongo Band's "Apache"), the work of James Brown was a particularly potent influence—1969's "Funky Drummer," featuring a drum break by Clyde Stubblefield, was only one of dozens of JB tunes at the center of the DJ's arsenal. But Brown was influential also as an icon of black self-sufficiency. In addition to managing his own recordings and tours, he released a series of musically innovative singles at the end of the decade whose titles themselves are a paean to post-Civil Rights community identity: "Say It Loud—I'm Black and I'm Proud, Pt.1" (1968); "I Don't Want Nobody to Give Me Nothing (Open Up the Door, I'll Get It Myself" (1969); "Brother Rapp" and "Get Up, Get Into It, Get Involved, Pt. 1" (1970); "Hey America" (1971); "King Heroin" (1972); and so forth.[87]

An additional factor shaping certain elements of nascent hip hop consciousness, one which has been somewhat under-theorized, is the continuity between elements of hip hop's political perspectives and longer threads of historical awareness inherited from the 1960s. The Black Panther Party, for example, founded in Oakland in 1966 as a community-based empowerment movement, had built on the archetypes of earlier self-help organizations—most notably Elijah Muhammad's Black Muslims and Marcus Garvey's United Negro Improvement Association—yoked to a sophisticated understanding of television-age semiotics. By mid-1968, their paramilitary uniforms, dark glasses, legal display of firearms, and combative rhetoric had made them iconic in both black working-class and white liberal consciousness, and a principal target for the FBI's notorious COINTELPRO program of intimidation, entrapment, and propaganda. Though less widely reported, their activities within the black community, emphasizing neighborhood self-help, work with prison inmates, and drug and alcohol programs, provided ongoing models for African American young people's developing political consciousness.[88] The Panthers' linkup with Latino/a and working-class white groups—their modernization of the community-based self-help programs modeled by Garvey and before that, by social organizations like the Rara groups and Mardi Gras Indians—provided a further model for hip hop artists' shift from street crime to creative politics.[89]

Finally, just as Hollywood gangster films and Westerns had been a favorite of Kingston "rude bwais," and had played a role in creating the myth of Rhyging and the filmic language of *The Harder They Come*, early '70s "American New Wave" cinema provided theatricalized models for the urban antiheroes who helped shape nationalist consciousness in the early hip hop world.[90] In this era, African American filmmakers, many of them actors previously denied the opportunity to direct or produce, developed their own properties and funding; most influentially, in 1971 the actor Melvin Van Peebles shot *Sweet Sweetback's Baadasssss Song*, a "chase" movie, in only 19 days, as an independent production, both directing and playing the title character.[91] Featuring a score by the then-unknown Earth, Wind, and Fire, the soundtrack was actually released for fund-raising purposes in advance of the film's premiere in April 1971. Though highly controversial (it includes several un-simulated sex scenes and the antihero title character, having assaulted a pair of brutal cops, eventually escapes to Mexico), *Sweet Sweetback* was extremely popular in the black community.[92] Partly because *Sweetback* depicts one sympathetic character as a Black Panther, it was also regarded as essential viewing for members of the BPP—indeed, Minister Huey P. Newton dedicated an entire essay to it, while Stephen Holden identifies an explicitly "political anger that boils through . . . the entire blaxploitation genre."[93]

All these archetypes—youth gangs and James Brown, Jamaican toasting and Latin dance grooves, the Black Panthers and Blaxploitation—became grist to hip hop's syncretic reimagination of Black Nationalism. Hip hop's oppositional stance was already politically transgressive before it was ever politically explicit. As with the Mardi Gras Indians and the social clubs of New Orleans, the *escolas do samba* of Rio, and many other urban neighborhood self-help groups, that stance literally *embodied* resistance by virtue of its contestation of dominant culture's control of the street. Tricia Rose sees these tactics as "a blueprint for social resistance," as a way of learning to exploit, "social rupture," the "cracks," which de Certeau describes, that "open in the surveillance of the proprietary powers."[94] And, out of that opposition and a few borrowed tracks, a couple of turntables, and the human body on the street corner, it became possible to forge a uniquely syncretic subaltern artistry.

## Hip Hop Moves

Where does street dance fit into these cultural landscapes? Scholars of the hip hop complex have provided clues, which can inform our understanding not only of hip hop but of all the dance rebellions discussed in this chapter—and, indeed, throughout this book; Frazier and Koslow, for example, suggest that "Street dancers *embody* space—they give expression to their identities and make visible counter-arguments about how space should be used and who can use it."[95] Historically, these arguments were sounded and embodied—"made visible"—rather than articulated in prose, but they were no less eloquent for the absence of expository prose. And here perhaps a personal anecdote becomes relevant and resonant:

> In 1977, I was a student in the inaugural Freshman Year Program (undergraduate) offered by the New School for Social Research. Housing its small initial cadre in NYU dorms on East 10th Street, the FYP held its seminars at the New School's main campus at 66 West 12th. As part of my activities that year, I assisted a Program colleague as a volunteer teaching literacy at a school in East Harlem two days a week after my own classes. We'd ride the Number 6 Line north from 14th Street, and walk from 125th Street east to the primary school. I thus first heard hip hop—which at that time was still several years away from LP recordings, much less visibility on television—on East Harlem playgrounds: MCs toasting, DJs wiring their salvaged turntables

> and amplifiers into the light posts on basketball courts. Though my musical tastes and experience were both narrow and directed elsewhere, as an instrumentalist I was immediately and lastingly struck by the sheer digital mastery of the DJs.[96]

This autobiographical experience, which long predates my scholarly engagement with street dance and hip hop culture (in 1977, the term was "barely employed") suggests the immediacy with which this form of expression could "occupy"—and thus temporarily claim—public spaces. In a society and physical geography (New York's five boroughs and more specifically the South Bronx), in which working-class black and brown youth were largely isolated from wider cultural currents and economic opportunity, the continued capacity to create art was an essential identity tool. Guthrie Ramsay theorizes the urban landscape as a series of "community theaters . . . public and private spaces [that] provide audiences with a place to negotiate with others—in a highly social way—what cultural expressions such as music mean."[97] The use of sonic and visual noise—the archetypal oversized cassette-playing boom boxes that B-boys ("break boys") shouldered on the New York subways and the dances that took over playgrounds, sidewalks, and vacant lots—were equally essential and theatrical strategies of resistance.[98] Motion itself—especially improvisational motion—resisted authoritarian constructs of space.[99]

*B-boying*—the complex of dance vocabularies that developed as part of hip hop culture parallel with and complementary to its lyrical, sonic, and technological innovations—is understood to be an essential component of the community's expressive arsenal.[100] Like MC'ing (rhyming poetry), DJ'ing (creating beats for dancers and MCs), and graffiti writing, B-boying is a competitive, improvisational, and deeply personalized oral-tradition art form that depends upon both individual choice, awareness of traditional practices and watershed innovators, and community recognition and approval. Its archetypal venue is the *cipher*—a circle of participant-observers reminiscent of the ring-shout, the *calinda*, the *capoeira* players' circle (another possible influence on hip hop), Mardi Gras Indian practice rings, and a range of other Afro-Caribbean performance sites.[101] B-boys are eloquent and articulate about what goes on within this sacred space: "It happens in an exchange. He's giving me something I can relate to and I have to answer with something that he can relate to so we can continue this battle."[102] Improvisation fuels innovation, as dancers constantly seek and develop new moves and responses to different music and competition.

This innovation and personalization of dance style is accelerated because B-boying places such a high premium on live performance: dancers may develop and fine-tune new moves in practice, but the selection, combination, and sequencing of that vocabulary in the real-time act of performance represents—just like bebop or the blues—spontaneous kinesthetic conversation. That performance occurs and is assessed in the midst of an audience of actively engaged peers:

> At the core of hip hop is the notion of something called the "cipher." Partly for competition and partly for community, the cipher is the circle of participants and onlookers that closes around battling rappers or dancers as they improvise for each other. If you have the guts to step into the cipher and tell your story and, above all, demonstrate your uniqueness, you might be accepted into the community.[103]

It is important to add here that the cipher—like the ring-shout, the calinda, and the many other circular dances mentioned previously—is *portable:* it can be created within seconds anywhere within public or private space. Given the particularly light footprint of early hip hop, whose rhyming and dancing could happen in the absence of *any* technology and whose supporting technology (a boom box, with perhaps a couple of salvaged turntables) was likewise portable, it seems essential to understand dance as an essential part of hip hop's reclamation of public space. The precision and integration of Sally Banes's description of B-boying's politics and aesthetics, and the clarity of her linkage of graffiti, dance, and speech as mutually reinforcing strategies for resistance, merits quotation:

> The intensity of the dancer's physicality gives breaking a power and energy even beyond the vitality of graffiti and rapping. If graffiti is a way of "publishing," of winning fame by spreading your tag all over the city, breaking is a way of claiming the *streets with physical presence,* using your body to publicly inscribe your identity on the surfaces of the city.[104]

The B-boys built their dance vocabularies out of the long and rich traditions of African American dance, ransacking old videos and parallel dance styles (especially New York Puerto Rican or "Nuyorican"), just as the DJs ransacked the vinyl racks.[105] James Brown's explosive onstage dancing was a particular touchstone, as it was to the 1970s-1980s R&B stars Michael Jackson and Prince, but so were the acrobatics of swing and mambo, the footwork of salsa and disco, the flow of Sixties R&B choreographies, and the athletics of kung fu films and *capoeira* (martial arts movies eventually became as strong a source of urban mythography for hip hop groups like Wu-Tang Clan as was the Nation of Islam).[106]

Overwhelmingly, though, it was the intensified white-heat spontaneous creativity of the cipher/circle, particularly at the "battles" of DJs, MCs, and B-boys, everywhere from the street to Madison Square Garden, that made hip hop dance a tsunami of bodily creativity. Even a cursory survey of the sprawling history and cultural geography of B-boying style and the interplay of its circumstances and dancers are beyond the scope of the present study, yet a larger salient point holds: B-boying, like the "visual noise" of graffiti writing, the "sonic noise" of scratching, and the "textual noise" of MCs on the mic, provides a way to claim, contest, and refigure urban space.

Scholarship has tended to focus upon hip hop's texts (not only raps, but also interviews, where MCs' prosodic skills are unsurprisingly very effective, and also the "visual texts" of videos) and its DJs' musical *bricolage*.[107] While discussions of B-boying's meanings for its participants are wide and rich, only a few studies have specifically linked dancing and public space, though as Schloss says, "To dance well to the chosen songs is to live in hip hop history."[108] Thomas DeFrantz calls this "'a performative oratory,' a complex rhetorical vocabulary which demands and rewards 'readers' expertise.[109] Sound—the sound of beats via battery-powered boom boxes—also enabled claims to public space, and made possible the demarcation of territory, in what Murray Forman calls "the overlapping influences of personae and turf."[110]

Discussions of hip hop dance have tended to focus on individual style and source influences, not its role in urban geography (unlike, say, the example of the New Orleans Second Line, for which there is a rich analytical literature).[111] A happy exception to that sparsity is Ronni Armstead's exploration of female hip hop dancers in Havana, which is solidly grounded in social theory, including Foucalt, Gilroy, and R. Murray Schafer.[112] A second happy exception further enriches our understanding of hip hop dance in public space: Robeson Taj Frazier and Jessica Koslow's investigation of West Coast krumpin'.[113] Though krumpin' as a dance style should be distinguished from the foundations of B-boying, Frazier and Koslow's framing of its fraught relationship with Los Angeles' geographic, demographic, and political landscapes is so effective that it effectively illuminates our East Coast discussion.[114] In situating krumpin' as resistance, Frazier and Koslow describe LA's "general culture of domination and regulation . . . where black and brown working class youth's mobility and use of public space is increasingly curtailed."[115] In this fashion, they supply a much-needed contextualization of the "spatial ecology," the physical and cognitive spaces, of the "session" (the krumpin' version of the cipher). Paraphrasing George Lipsitz, in order to speak specifically about dancing, they argue that dance performance can be a way for subaltern groups "to create and exercise more liberating modes of existence," and to push back against dominant constraints upon space, sound, and movement.[116]

As we have seen, dominant hierarchies' response to irruptive subaltern noise indexes its impact. Revolutionary noise, in aural and visual realms, pushes back against authoritarian control of space.[117] Public noise was restricted precisely because of the middle-class anxiety it evoked, especially when that anxiety was exacerbated by racial concerns.[118] In the hip hop heterolect, the line-, level-, boundary- and rule-"breaking" associated with B-boying represents another cycle of bodily resistance, what Michael Hanson calls "a meta-narrative of the shifting terrain of political self-consciousness and resistance."[119] This oppositional meta-narrative is particularly essential, and particularly powerful, in the context of African American embodiment: both the history of its racist exploitation, and of dance's capacity for resistance.[120] In an electronically mediated nation-state in which hegemonic cultural representations are particularly pervasive, the danced embodiment of "cutting" and "breaking"—African American strategies of resistance that Charles Keil has identified in music as "participatory discrepancies"—has political power.[121]

It is for this reason that hip hop, like reggae before it, has become an empowering symbolic system, not only in its originating communities, but to other disenfranchised communities worldwide.[122] Participatory dance was, is, and will continue to be an intentional, strategic, and efficacious tool employed by subaltern communities to contest dominant-culture and authoritarian control of physical, sonic, and cognitive spaces. The ethnomusicologist and educator Christopher Small used the term *musicking* to convey the interaction of players and audience in African American concerts, and he articulated that interaction as embodying participants' own ideal, if temporary, networks of relationships:

> The act of musicking establishes in the place where it is happening a set of relationships, and it is in those relationships that the meaning of the act lies. They are to be found not only between those organized sounds which are conventionally thought of as being the stuff of musical meaning *but also between the people who are taking part, in whatever capacity, in the performance*; and they model, or stand as metaphor for, ideal relationships as the participants in the performance imagine them to be.[123]

We might add, furthering Small's thesis, that musicking together—dancing together—likewise establishes the ideal relationships that in turn collectively shape meaning. In all four historical cases cited here—1960s hippie culture, punk rock, drag, and hip hop—dance was experienced as a literal, if temporary, revisioning of community. In all four cases, the capacity of movement to "bring into existence the ideal society," at least for the duration of a performance, provided a fundamental means by which humans embodied the shared physical experience of freedom.

# CHAPTER 9

# Street Dance and the Dream of Freedom

## "It's an invitation across the nation . . ."

> The body . . . is at once the most personal, intimate thing that people possess and the most public. The body, then, provides a "basic political resource" in struggles between dominant and subordinate classes.
>
> —Dorinda Outram, *The Body and the French Revolution: Sex, Class, and Political Culture*, 1989

As this epigraph intimates, this book began with the suggestion that multiple incidents of participatory street dance over the course of North American history might reveal consistent patterns of communication, experience, and revolutionary meaning.[1] We have investigated a range of case studies, stretching across time periods, geographical locations, individuals, and groups, and have found that, despite the complex and unique circumstances that shaped each of these instances, consistent patterns of rebellious intention or reception are in fact revealed. This chapter opens outward, again, to situate participatory dance as part of wider dynamics of culture and community, and to suggest avenues and applications for further investigation.

### Why Dance?

Dance has been a powerful part of human communicative, symbolic, and experiential culture for at least 40,000 years, since the Aurignacion Age of the Upper Paleolithic.[2] In an enormous diversity of locations, eras, and human societies, dance has been employed for its contribution to spiritual, psychological, physiological, and expressive energy. It has been understood as an embodied expression of freedom, whether individual or communal, whether bounded by an aesthetic vocabulary or unbounded except by the body's human (or momentarily superhuman) capacities; that it plays a role in subaltern resistance is therefore logical and explicable. From the ballets, which closed French Baroque political operas by reading the dancing figure of Louis XIV as the literal "Sun" of the planets in their course, to the frenzied "acid dancing" of 1960s '60s rock festivals, freedom enjoyed by or constraint imposed upon dancing has served as a metaphor for freedom or constraint upon the human experience.[3]

Yet dance, like musical hearing—the question, for example, "what is a beautiful sound?"—is also a unique product of individual enculturation: like music, it is implicated at a deep level in individual cultures' value systems and aesthetics. These modes of expression are so deeply embedded, within specific cultural experiences, that encounters with unfamiliar movement or music systems' aesthetic priorities can be literally inexplicable; for example, missionaries, first witnessing the polyrhythms of West African percussion music or the timbral specifics of Native American music, completely misheard those musics as "random noise." In the history of the United States, such context- and experience-specific hearing and seeing has been further and significantly complicated by issues of race and class: cultural elites have frequently sought to devalue underclass music and movement, derogating it as noisy, ugly, or immoral.

Dance aesthetics are, if anything, even more specific to individualized culture groups than are movement vocabularies; simple comparison reveals this. Movement aesthetics vary so widely, not only across global zones or language groups, but even within a given society's contrasting age, ethnicity, or affinity groups, that we can literally if unusually speak of a region's or group's "movement accent" or dialect the way we might the vocables of spoken language, or, more metaphorically, details of sounding musical performance practice.

Moreover, hierarchized social dynamics recur in dance as they do in other embodied symbolic systems: New World movement "accents," the specific subtle details of culture groups' body vocabularies, therefore reflect colonial history. In the specific cases we have examined, we identified movement accents expected of or assigned to dominant and subaltern social groups; from the winking double-consciousness of the 1890s cakewalk (whites mocking blacks whom they failed to realize were mocking whites) to the changes of stance, expression, and eye contact that Jim Crow–era blacks were taught, literally as a means of self-preservation.[4] This imposition of social hierarchy, of dominant control seeking to control subaltern bodies, and, in response, that control's manipulation and parody by subaltern groups for purposes of resistance, have been a central topic of much of this book.

A parallel and complementary topic has been the exploitation of nonverbal systems like instrumental music and, especially, movement as uniquely and strategically elusive means of symbolic expression. We have found this multivalent quality to be present even in the largely un-notated, improvisational, and unpredictable New World vernacular traditions, whose symbolic meaning has often been ignored, misunderstood, or devalued. Dominant culture's intuition (or presumption) that the implications of vernacular dance are either uncontrollable, or possibly subversive, has led to repeated cycles of fulmination, castigation, legislation, or repression—only to have revolutionary dance pop up again, in other streets, venues, social classes, guises, or eras. The very fact, for example, that antebellum race laws, 1890s and 1930s Jim Crow laws, 1950s broadcast laws, and 1970s vice laws all sought unsuccessfully to prevent the "integration," through dance, of diverse races, gender orientations, or economic classes—the sheer redundancy of such legislation—confirms the threat that participatory vernacular dance was perceived to represent, as well as its elusive vitality. Thus, to neglect consideration of dance as data within the analysis of political history, musicology, historiography, or cultural anthropology would be to ignore one of North American human communities'—especially subaltern communities—richest and most powerful strategies for symbolic resistance.

In addition: dancing together, like singing together and playing together, has always been a crucial tool for socialization, cultural empowerment, and community revitalization.[5] Just as with a cradle tongue, social etiquette, or musical style, participatory dance—especially dance which is inculcated as part of family, tribe, or society life-cycle events—has been in many situations an especially immediate, lasting, and integrative channel for experiencing one's body's place in space, time, and human context. Like the work song, for example—another participatory vernacular form that integrates sound and movement in service of communal goals—dance accomplishes crucial social and functional business. It can therefore be understood as, not only subaltern rebellion or individual aesthetic but also a sophisticated, body-integrative tool for rebuilding and teaching community—connection, communication, negotiation, compromise, and achievement. Thus, as scholars and pedagogues of human culture, were we to ignore or underplay the historical resonance and contemporary relevance of participatory dance, then the stories we tell would be fundamentally incomplete.

Participatory street dance is likewise a literal, if fluid, embodiment of cultural geography: specifically, of how and where communities have experienced their bodies within landscapes. As we have seen in multiple instances throughout this book, North American street dance and its relatives have often been a way for subaltern communities to temporarily, but very powerfully, claim and hold specific urban spaces. As with the whistles, bucket drums, and "human megaphone" of 2012 Occupy protests in New York City, which both inspired, and were inspired by, other protests around the world (see discussion later), resistant sound and movement are subaltern tactics.[6] Like Small's "musicking," the hip hop cypher, the *washoi* dance in Grant Park, the mosh pit at a Fugazi show, the can-can line outside the Stonewall Inn, occupation via group motion and noise provided both "a medium of action, and at the same time a desired state of being."[7]

## Occupying the Future

The case studies I have investigated, the methodologies I have sought to integrate in service of that investigation, and the range of conclusions I have proposed, together suggest that similar approaches might be effectively employed to understand analogous historical situations elsewhere. Such examinations might originate from the fields of cultural anthropology and geography, for example, and focus upon the impact of internal and external landscapes and perceptions of landscapes as they shape human communities. Likewise, articulating the dancing body as a site of subaltern-culture resistance and dominant-culture repression has relevance for the fields of political, historical, gender, and Queer studies. The siting of my investigation within the geographical and historical context of North America and related zones means that my topics and methods have potential relevance for colonial and postcolonial studies. Finally—circling back to my own root disciplines—this book's topics, methods, and conclusions demonstrate what I believe is a useful and original synthesis of music and dance historiography, fields which have too often operated beyond one another's horizons. These interdisciplinary examinations are important precisely because they aid in the process of recovering voices that have been lost and silenced in the history of human culture. As Robert C. Allen puts it:

> Because society is ordered in terms of power relations and structured in terms of registers of dominance and subordination, cultural production expresses these relations and these structures. All groups within society produce culture, but not all groups are in a position to disseminate "their" cultural products widely within a society and export them to others, to legitimate and naturalize their tastes in cultural products via social institutions (education, chief among them).[8]

Two more short anecdotes of recent dance-as-resistance should help to illustrate the contemporary relevance of this book's revisionist understandings and the potential for their application in other historical or cultural situations. During a series of nonviolent public demonstrations defending Istanbul's Gezi Park, a small leafy oasis in Taksim Square (a historically resonant site), in the late spring and summer of 2013, the authoritarian and socially conservative Turkish Prime Minister Recep Tayyip Erdogan ordered the use of tear gas to disperse the protesters, a decision for which he was criticized worldwide.[9] As had been the case in the Occupy NYC actions of 2012, themselves inspired by the so-called "Arab Spring" of political activism that swept across the Near East from 2010 onward, the Gezi Park protesters developed a succession of nonviolent, symbolically resonant tactics to oppose the Erdogan government's repressive edicts. These included physical encampment (a tent city and improvised community infrastructure), the massive internet circulation of images of abuse, exploitation of worldwide social media (especially Twitter, with the hashtag #OccupyGezi making the Occupy NYC connection explicit), satirical graffiti and other visual noise, the manufacture and distribution of penguin-logo T-shirts (mocking Turkish television's substitution of a penguin documentary for CNN coverage of the protests), the "Standing Man" silent protest (protestors, silenced by edict, stood motionless for hours, staring at the flags above the Ataturk Cultural Center), boycotts, and a range of other non-violent resistance tactics.

By June 1, 2013, government repression had escalated to the extensive use of military police to intimidate protesters, most notably through the use of water cannon and tear gas, illegal detention, and physical mistreatment. Amnesty International documented these allegations widely, yet the Erdogan government responded defiantly, accusing Western governments of a double standard, and citing the NYPD's use of similar tactics at Zuccotti Park.[10] The situation escalated throughout summer 2013, and not only protestors but also medical volunteers, journalists, and movement lawyers were all targeted; there were multiple deaths and over 3000 arrests across the country. The authoritarian government was the subject of international condemnation, the Turkish stock market and Istanbul tourist industry plummeted, and the European Union tabled Turkey's application for member nation status.[11]

Especially pertinent to our discussion is one other resistance tactic employed by the Gezi Park protestors, consistent with the encampment's twenty-first-century transnational awareness, and especially resonant considering the neoconservative economic and social policies of the Erdogan government. In June 2013, in the midst of another police assault using tear gas, members of the encampment donned gas masks and particle masks and *danced a tango*. This represented not only a protest against physical intimidation, a resistance to dominant enclosure of urban space (there had been various outbreaks of diverse dance types during the occupation), but, even more precisely, the use of this particular New World syncretic dance—notable for its intimate sharing of proximate bodily experience, for its brooding affect and grave, meticulous pace—at this particular moment of crisis precisely, courageously, and concretely "embodied" Gezi Park's ethos of subaltern community. The June 8 issue of London's *Daily Mail* carried the headline: "Turks Tango in Their Gas Masks as They Defy Orders of Prime Minister and Carry On with Protests," and accompanied its report with a series of remarkable photographs credited to Getty Images, which, in their beauty, emotional resonance, and literal embrace of physical connection, amid the clouds of gas, made an indelible visual and symbolic statement.[12]

At the ground-zero point of dominant-versus-subaltern contestation of public space, and in the face of authoritarian bans, censorship, and violent repression of free speech and assembly, these eloquent images of tango as defiant, communal, bodily liberation were received with sympathy around the globe: subaltern dance

**Figure 20:** Tango dancers, Taksim Gezi Park, Istanbul 2013. Getty Images.

stood, quite literally, in defiance of authoritarian clubs, tanks, and tear gas. Eventually, as at lower Manhattan's Zuccotti Park, the encampment at Gezi Park was dismantled and the protesters dispersed, leaving the authoritarian government in place. But the terms of the debate nevertheless shifted in this period, and group movement had played a central role.[13]

I will close with one final example of the power and mutability of dance as revolutionary tactic, of the ubiquity of that tactic across a wide range of cultural contexts, and an example perhaps slightly more optimistic, presenting a faint glimpse of a North American dream of multicultural freedom.[14] The Seattle-based rapper, producer, and sound engineer Sir Mix-a-Lot (born Anthony Ray 1963) has distinguished himself as a recording and performing artist, talent scout, and technology entrepreneur. As with many 1980s–1990s hip hop artists, he built this diversified career out of early success in the niche market of a regional rap scene, followed by several chart hit singles: first 1987's "Posse on Broadway" (whose title is a reference to his hometown, not New York City), and then the massive double platinum "Baby Got Back" from 1992's *Mack Daddy* (on the seminal producer Rick Rubin's Def American label).[15]

"Baby Got Back" became a cross-market anthem, especially in the wake of its accompanying music video, which was briefly banned by MTV before being re-released though restricted to late-night programming. Specifically, this restriction was imposed because "Baby Got Back" is a paean to a specific part of the female anatomy. In 1992, in a stratified commercial music world in which New Orleans "bounce" and Janet Jackson's booty were the object of censorship, not celebration, and in which Kim Kardashian, Miley Cyrus, and the dance called "twerking" were unimagined by white music fans, a song and video that celebrated the buttocks of curvaceous women (of any ethnicity) were regarded as both salacious by the industry and inherently exploitative by a wide range of critical and scholarly commentators.[16] From a contemporary perspective looking back two decades, "Baby" may be understood, with perhaps greater nuance, as both a great "novelty record" (in the venerable R&B tradition of "under the counter" or "blue" records like 1954's "Work with Me, Annie" and "Annie's Aunt Fannie") and more substantively as a sly and sophisticated parody of 1980s dominant culture's beauty norms. In a decade when women's beauty magazines like *Vogue* and *Cosmopolitan* and music videos by Whitesnake, Ratt, and Bon Jovi objectified big-haired, thin-hipped teenaged female Caucasian models, the idea of celebrating contrasting female body types represented more than simple sexual opportunism.[17]

No doubt "Baby" *is* salacious and was so intended and received—just as the performances of Josephine Baker and pre–Hays Code actresses were—but it also intended and achieved a subtle subversion of dominant norms. The dancers in the original MTV video, the video that was first banned and then restricted to late-night broadcast, represent a celebration of the female body—specifically the black and brown female body—and of music that celebrates that body's motion. The pelvis and rear end have been a central part of African and Afro-Caribbean dance aesthetics for 500 years, and for the entire historical span addressed in this book, and a subject of dominant/white culture voyeurism and critique for nearly as long.[18] Thankfully, some commenters on "Baby Got Back," particularly those benefiting from a few years' historical hindsight and/or a feminist perspective, provide a more nuanced and culturally sophisticated reading.[19] Janell Hobson, for example, precisely articulates the racist implications of the body types idealized by 1980s media culture:

> Both the song and video uphold and celebrate the black body precisely because it differs from the standard models of beauty in white culture. The white female body, a "legitimate" emblem of beauty in white dominant culture, Sir Mixalot exposes for its inauthentic beauty, a product of a mechanized world that disables white men, making it impossible for them to "shout." Sir Mixalot castigates the beautiful white body as a "silicone toy," an unreal and unnatural Barbie doll.[20]

But there is more to be understood about the interplay of racial, sexual, and gender dance politics in "Baby," so a fresh analysis of the original video document is worthwhile. It begins, in the classic tradition of the comic "race" or "hillbilly" record (or for that matter South African *kwela* or West African highlife records), with a bit of parodic dialog, a framing device borrowed from vaudeville and, before that, blackface minstrelsy: two teenaged Caucasian actresses, dressed in stereotypical late-'80s pastels and with the moussed hair typical of the type, observe an African American model in a tight knit dress through a stylized keyhole. Their "Valley Girl" dialog voice-over is actually provided by Mix's then-companion, Amylia Dorsey-Rivas, a mixed-race actress and model whose own body experience in part had inspired the song: "[Mix would] say 'I don't understand why you can't get modeling work,' and I'd say 'Look behind me'":[21]

Oh, my, God Becky, look at her butt
It is so big, she looks like
One of those rap guys' girlfriends.
But, ya know, who understands those rap guys?
They only talk to her, because,
She looks like a total prostitute, 'kay?[22]

The rhythm track, rooted in the electro-house originally pioneered by Afrika Bambaata but which became dominant on the West Coast in the mid-1980s (see Chapter 8), begins, dominated by synth-bass, as the Valley Girl continues:

I mean, her butt, is just so big
I can't believe it's just so round, it's like out there

The camera zeroes in on the African American model's outthrust hind end, as the monolog continues:

I mean gross, look
She's just . . . so . . . *black*

In an abrupt cut, Mix's baritone roar—its guttural range and pounding staccato consonants a powerful musical counterpoint to the Valley Girls' drawling, elongated vowels—enters:

I like *big* BUTTS and I cannot lie
You other Brothers can't deny

And the camera pulls back on Mix, in his iconic Mack-Daddy (street pimp) leather coat and fedora, perched atop a giant abstract peach-shaped pair of honey-colored hills, surrounded by his crew, and a group of African American female dancers in tight workout shorts.[23] These dancers are an especially important part of the video, which, we must remember, was the "MTV-Music TV" medium via which Mix, along with a number of other hip hop artists, crossed over to white audiences in the '80s and early '90s. In contrast to the dancers and models appearing in most rock videos of the period, the women in "Baby Got Back" are not disposed seminude around the frame like appliances or jewelry. Rather—as was common in both hip hop videos of the period, and more importantly, throughout the West Coast live-dance krunking scene (see Chapter 8), which was the basis for Mix's own Seattle style—the female dancers provide a powerfully physical, visible, and independent expression of the rhythm track. Yes, they interact verbally with one another and the rapper (when Mix yells, "Ladies!" they respond, in unison, "YEAH!"—"Ladies!" "YEAH!"), while the camera angles and edits leave no mistake about the video's focus on the female posterior. But here, just as with B-boying and krunking, and in eloquent polyrhythmic counterpoint to the musical track, the dancers are powerful, individual agents (one climactic moment in the rhythm track, a whiplash electronic *crack* over a stop-time pause, is mirrored in the video by one dancer's flawlessly executed martial arts sidekick).[24] The video explicitly includes visual references to contrasting female body ideals: for example, a short but very rich sequence, shot in sepia tones, references Josephine Baker's iconic banana skirt and contrasts it with the brassy metallic Aryan bustier designed by Gaultier for Madonna's *Blonde Ambition* tour.[25]

This description should, one hopes, induce the reader to seek out and view in its entirety the original MTV video for "Baby Got Back." In light of the arguments about bodies, movement, and resistance made throughout this book, it is richly rewarding—but here are a few short snippets of Mix's rhymes that locate the song's political critique of body aesthetics in text as well as movement and visual imagery:

> I'm tired of magazines
> Sayin' flat butts are the thing . . .
>
> So I'm lookin' at rock videos
> Knock-kneed bimbos walkin' like hoes . . .
> So *Cosmo* says you're fat
> Well I ain't down with that . . .
>
> To the beanpole dames in the magazines
> You ain't it, Miss Thing

Mix and its other producers were explicit about the *political* nature of the message of "Baby Got Back." Patti Galluzzi, at the time senior vice president of music and talent for MTV, comments:

> Mix told me that he felt that the message of the song is that all women are constantly bombarded with images of superthin models on TV and in magazines, and he thought that women and young girls need to hear that not everyone feels that way, as well as defending a more African American body image. He was also speaking directly to me: I had back and front, then and now. So I said, "You know what? I'll go back to NYC and bring this to the top."[26]

When it did finally air as part of MTV's late-night rotation, "Baby Got Back" exploded; beyond its novelty status and phenomenally hooky beats, perhaps the most trenchant and explicit argument *against* simplistic interpretation of "Baby Got Back" as sexist objectification comes from Dorsey-Rivas, the song's original inspiration and voice-over artist, who said, "Even if I'd never contributed to it, I would still have appreciated what it did. When people said it was degrading, I would say there's not one thing degrading about that song to anyone who felt like me."[27] As Mix commented: "Girls who didn't have big butts thought the song was cute, but girls who did have butts thought it was a revolution."[28]

"Baby Got Back" literally embodied subaltern resistance, and its cultural resonance continued. In 2013—literally twenty years after the song dropped and MTV belatedly got on board—Sir Mix-a-Lot returned to his hometown to guest with the Seattle Symphony in their "Sonic Encounters" series, concerts being undertaken precisely with the intention of drawing in new and more diverse audiences to this regional symphony's performances. What transpired was a concrete explication of twenty years of change in movement paradigms, partly as a result of "Baby Got Back" and its impact; likewise, of twenty years' infiltration of dominant-culture sensibilities by hip hop's subaltern aesthetics; and of mass communications' democratization via the Internet and viral video (a nonfactor in 1992, but—as we have seen—a maker of both careers, and revolutions, in 2013). Most significantly, and most relevantly for the narrative of this book, the Sonic Encounters performances were a demonstration, via participatory dance (and, subsequently, the worldwide audience of YouTube), of the ongoing and unstoppable processes of bodily creolization—of the exchange of body knowledge as a site for resistance, rebellion, and liberation—which have obtained in the Americas for 500 years.

The clip, uploaded June 7, 2014, to the symphony's own YouTube channel, is shot in high definition from an angle above and house-left, looking down and across the stage. Most of the small, chamber-sized orchestra is visible, as is conductor Ludovic Morlot, along with a substantial expanse of unoccupied stage apron, bounded by the hall's modest drop to the front rows. We begin *in media res*, with Mix—20 years on but still wearing his iconic Mack Daddy leather car coat and brim-up fedora—and one posse member striding into frame from stage left; he chants, out of cadence, on the wireless microphone:

> So what I wanna do now is something you really should not do . . .
> But since tonight is 'Orchestral Movements from the Hood' night,
> I'm going to leave some of this open
> If a couple of ladies would like to get up on the stage . . .

Though the audience is not in frame, we can infer an immediate and positive response to Mix's truncated invitation, based on the off-camera laughter and applause, as Mix says, "all right, there we go, we got a few comin.'" What becomes immediately apparent is that the audience response is very strong indeed—perhaps even greater than had been anticipated—when almost two dozen women, of all shapes, sizes, and markers of ethnicity, in every manner of dress from workout clothes to evening gowns and cocktail dresses, stream to the stage, while Mix points the way to the stairs.[29]

> My conductor is like . . ."Oh my God!"
> Okay, there we go . . .
> Okay, we got enough [laughs] . . .
> Okay, okay, you guys spread out, and we're gonna keep . . .

He interrupts himself, as even more women come up the staircase:

> Lord have mercy!
> Wow
> All right, um . . . I learned this from Ellen DeGeneres [as he takes a moment for a panoramic self portrait with the volunteers] It's the Selfie from Hell!
> Okay, we're going to try a little something you may never have heard before
> And [indicating conductor Morlot] this genius back here . . .
> By the way: this man is the shiznitt, trust me!
> Go ahead

Conductor Morlot leads the orchestra into the electro-bop groove of "Baby." There is a roar of recognition and approval from the audience, and—almost instantly—the invited crowd of women begin spontaneously to dance. So far, this has been a charming, lighthearted bit of entertaining chaos in an orchestral domain that would stereotypically be considered a bastion of Anglo-European dominant-culture aesthetics.

What kicks the performance into the stratosphere, however, out of the world of dominant culture privilege, and into the subaltern, liminal realm of syncretic movement expression, is the diversity and abandon of the dance vocabularies on display. The women dancing make it clear that, in the United States in the year 2013, it is no longer necessary, nor indeed possible, to presume that Anglo-European versus Afro-Caribbean body vocabularies should automatically map onto Anglo-European versus Afro-Caribbean bodies. The dancers are, again, of every body type, size, and skin tone, and there is little or no parity between visible markers of ethnicity and body vocabularies. Indeed, the most accomplished dancing of all in this performance, that which shows the most familiarity with both the movement vocabulary of the original video *and* of the gladiatorial world of West Coast African American krunk in which that vocabulary is based, comes from a tall, curvaceous Anglo woman, later identified by friends as Shawn Bounds, a real estate agent.[30] Ms. Bounds wears horn-rimmed eyeglasses and a black cocktail dress, in keeping with the wardrobe that might be expected at a semiformal symphony concert.

What sets her apart, what draws Mix's attention, and what kicked the YouTube video into the viral category (145,486 views as of 1/11/2016), is the expertise and abandon with which Ms. Bounds throws herself into the performance.[31] Her dancing becomes a touchstone for the other women onstage, as it would become for YouTube viewers worldwide.[32]

But the more profound takeaway point here, the point that is consistent with Mix's own original 1992 testimony about the song's intentions, with Gilman's and Hobson's feminist and Black Studies–based analyses and with the evidence of our own eyes as we watch the YouTube video, is the *joy* and sense of limitless possibilities that emanates from this performance. In this improvised moment, Sir Mix-a-Lot, the symphony, conductor Morlot, and the ladies of the audience, led by Shawn Bounds, once again discover together a touchstone for the abandon, bodily community, and physical joy that street dance has made available in the Americas for the past 500 years to *all* who would participate.

In contrast to the widespread condemnations of the original 1992 release "Baby Got Back," I suggest that both the MTV video and this 2013 performance place upon display profoundly feminist and racially empowering semiotics. A group of *women*, from the audience, of all colors and body types (including a full range of body types ignored or erased by popular culture, both in 1992 and in 2013), together stormed the stage and, like the working-class mechanics and apprentices who jumped up at the Bowery Theater in 1833 to help Thomas Dartmouth Rice sing 57 verses of "Jump Jim Crow," the drag queens who stormed *out* of the Stonewall Inn in 1969 and the tango dancers who took over Taksim Gezi Park in Istanbul in 2013, just a few weeks before the Sonic Encounters concert, employed communal subaltern dance as a powerful antidote to the dominant paradigm of control, regulation, standardization, and obedience. This is the message of bodies dancing in the street—or of dancing street-style on film, the vaudeville stage, at protest actions, at evangelical forest revivals, and on the streets of the South Bronx. To dance together, to dance a community into existence—if only, as Christopher Small put it, "for the duration of the performance"—is itself to participate in the invention and reinvention of human liberation.[33]

## Postlude

This book is written with a revolutionary agenda, and proceeds from a radical precept: for my entire professional career as a musicologist, and in a preceding career as a working musician, I have operated from the observed and intuited conviction—formerly a minority opinion, but now more widely supported by scholarship, experience, perspective, and a noticeable, though belated, shift in my field's own goalposts—that vernacular culture represents an enormously valuable, enlightening, and rewarding field of activity: as scholarly subject, artistic inspiration, and philosophical resource. Yet, leaving aside the enduring contest between cultivated versus vernacular, and dominant versus subaltern, cultural forces, which conflict has obtained at least since the aural/oral tradition of the Homeric recitations was codified into written literature, the politics of the propertied have historically inclined toward hierarchized control. For 500 years, since the enclosure of public "commons" that began, in the English-speaking world, with Henry VIII's confiscation of monastic lands, and continued with the drive toward private ownership fueled by the Industrial Revolution, capital has sought to claim, enclose, and control public space. The enclosure of public land was largely completed by the end of the eighteenth century but its ethos continued, with the shift to a wage-based Protestant work economy that sought to enclose not only workers' available spaces but even their available hours, and to circumscribe their freedom of time and of movement.[34] This is the motivation behind the transition in payment models, from artisanal piecework to hourly wage labor: in piecework, the artisan was selling individualized items whose value was market-driven, not dictated by requisite hours of activity. In contrast, wage-labor meant that the worker was selling his or her *hours*, hence experiencing enclosure of both space and time. The fullest expression of this control in the New World came in the slavery era, when it was considered essential for the survival of white minority dominant populations that the time, movements, and even expressive arts of chattel slaves should be controlled, lest freedom of movement or thought lead to plans for rebellion.[35]

During the early stages of North American industrialization and urbanization in the antebellum period, the blackface minstrel show had acted out the pressures felt by working-class whites from above—from the bourgeois middle class who were rapidly privatizing public space and "colonizing" the national discourse—and from below—from the blacks and immigrants whom they saw as economic and social competitors.[36] In the postbellum period, increased immigration of non-Protestant populations heightened further dominant culture's concerns about retaining a mythic white Anglo-Saxon national identity and motivated semiotic contestation using as weapons everything from Thomas Nast cartoons to Tin Pan Alley "coon songs" to urban noise ordinances.[37] By the late twentieth century, despite gains for human rights and minority self-determination after World War II, push back from oligarchic multinational corporations was even enclosing intellectual property, seeking to copyright knowledge and resources (musical forms, DNA strands, national parks, indigenous peoples' reservations, biomedical compounds) formerly held in common. This hegemonic enclosure was repeatedly contested from the grass roots—through street demonstrations, "back to the land" and "Occupy" movements worldwide, Creative Commons licensing, and net neutrality activism—but was not, ultimately, defeated.

Too often implicated in the corporate/government project that seeks to control the spaces of public life and experience have been universities, which have served as loci for information and discourse. Historically, the academy's hands have not been clean: from chemical and biological warfare research in its science labs, to the hierarchizing canons promulgated by too many of its arts and humanities departments, to the classist and racist elements of its admissions policies, to militarized policing of public-space student protest against policies, the university has too often functioned as the intellectual rationale for dominant culture's enclosure of resources: physical, intellectual, psychological, spatial, and experiential.[38] Anti-hegemonic actions from without and push back from within, which have sought to interrogate and "unhook" the symbiosis between the academy and the dominant elite, are significantly out-gunned, and the battle never ends.

But, as the saying goes in the world of inclusive education, the first step that the democratizing impulse should take is to interrogate its own privilege. I hope that this book, investigating the street arts of music and dance as a form of subaltern resistance, may be seen this way: as an interrogation of privilege, and as another expression of an ethos of the Commons: as an attempt to "re-Occupy" a neglected story of working-class North American vernacular culture. I seek to honestly and ethically serve the wisdom of the 99 Per Cent: that wisdom which the singer and labor activist Bruce "Utah" Phillips described as "the Long Memory."[39] This book thus represents an attempt to open the gates of the Ivory Tower from within; or, as John Lennon put it, "to break *out* of the palace."[40] That is, out of the palace, and into the wider world.

Or, to put it another way:

*They'll be laughing and singing, music swinging, and dancing in the street*

*. . .*

—9/4/2011–1/12/2016, the night of the first African American POTUS's final State of the Union Address.

# Notes

## Preface

1. I am acutely aware that some of the greatest dance musicians have also been some of the great dancers. But, with apologies to the majestic shades of Baby Dodds and Papa Jo Jones, Michael Coleman and Bill Monroe, I've had to content myself, as a responsible dance musician, with *learning* the steps—even without relishing them.

2. For the useful distinction between "cultivated" (e.g., literate, notation- and repertoire-driven) as opposed to "vernacular" (oral/aural, improvisation- and memory-driven) traditions, see Wiley Hitchcock, *Music in the United States: A Historical Introduction* (Englewood, N.J.: Prentice-Hall, 1988), 53–63.

3. Another version of the same quote is, "You could listen to Woody Guthrie songs and actually learn how to live." Bob Dylan, quoted in Robert Santelli and Emily Davidson, *Hard Travelin': The Life and Legacy of Woody Guthrie* (Middletown, Conn.: Wesleyan University Press, 1999), 49.

4. See Eric Lott, *Love & Theft: Blackface Minstrelsy and the American Working Class* (New York: Oxford University Press, 1993); Annemarie Bean, James V. Hatch, Brooks McNamara, and Mel Watkins, eds., *Inside the Minstrel Mask: Readings in Nineteenth-Century Blackface Minstrelsy* (Middletown, Conn.: Wesleyan University Press, 1996); William J. Mahar, *Behind the Burnt Cork Mask: Early Blackface Minstrelsy and Antebellum American Popular Culture* (Urbana: University of Illinois Press, 1998); Robert C. Allen, *Horrible Prettiness: Burlesque and American Culture* (Chapel Hill: University of North Carolina Press, 1991). Anthony Shay describes North Americans "seeking new identities, attempting to be someone else through dancing the dances and playing and singing the music of the 'Exotic Other,'" a "potent medium of exchange" we will see replicated elsewhere. Shay suggests that "Cul-

tural artifacts such as dance, with its promise of the sexual and forbidden, also became a by-product of the uneven exchange between the metropolitan centers of the powerful West and its more primitive Other. Belly dance, tango, samba, and a host of other dances on display at the [nineteenth century] world exhibitions were 'tamed' for the consumption of white middle-class bodies through the process of 'slumming' and the search for the exotic and erotic and became a potent medium of exchange." Anthony Shay, *Dancing across Borders: The American Fascination with Exotic Dance Forms* (Jefferson, N.C.: McFarland, 2008), 6, 18, 19. In the same vein, Averill describes a kind of "musical transvestism"; Filewood discusses a rejection of contemporary technological/materialist/bourgeois culture in favor of a more "authentic" experience; Gubar explores "racial camp"; and Baxendale describes a classist hierarchy in folk-song collection, and so forth. For "musical transvestism," see Gage Averill, 2008, quoted in Shay, 21. For the complex problematics of "authenticity," see Alan Filewood, "Receiving Aboriginality: Tomson Highway and the Crisis of Cultural Authenticity," *Theatre Journal* 45/3, Colonial/Postcolonial Theatre (October 1994), 365. For "racial camp," see Susan Gubar, "Racial Camp in *The Producers* and *Bamboozled*," *Film Quarterly* 60/2 (Winter 2006), 26–37. For the "authenticity" trope in Progressive-era folk-song collecting, see John Baxendale, "'Into Another Kind of Life in Which Anything Might Happen': Popular Music and Late Modernity, 1910–1930," *Popular Music* 14/2 (May 1995), 149.

5. Ted Solis, ed., *Performing Ethnomusicology: Teaching and Representation in World Music Ensembles* (Berkeley: University of California Press, 2004), 94. Emphasis original.

## Introduction

1. Jane C. Desmond, "Embodying Differences: Issues in Dance and Cultural Studies," In *Meaning in Motion: New Cultural Studies of Dance*, ed. Jane C. Desmond (Durham: Duke University Press, 1997), 29.

2. A good description of this Afro-Caribbean "akimbo" body vocabulary is Joann W. Kealiinohomoku, "A Comparative Study of Dance as a Constellation of Motor Behaviors among African and United States Negroes," in Adrienne L. Kaeppler, *Reflections and Perspectives on Two Anthropological Studies of Dance*, CORD Dance Research Annual (New York: CORD Inc., 1976), 15–180: "The head, hands, and feet are especially relaxed, while the torso, arms and legs are not as relaxed. The head is 'hung' . . . or used for swaying movements; the torso is flexed forward and exhibits some form of swayback; hip and shoulder movements are common; the arms are flexed with the upper arms close to the body; hands are flexed and limp; the legs are flexed or alternately flexed and overextended; the whole foot carries the body and thus appears flat, and foot gestures are performed with flexion" (122). See also Katrina Hazzard-Gordon, "African-American Vernacular Dance: Core Culture and Meaning Operatives," *Journal of Black Studies* 15/4, African and African-American Dance, Music, and Theatre (June 1985), 432.

3. Wendy James, "Reforming the Circle: Fragments of the Social History of a Vernacular African Dance Form," *Journal of African Cultural Studies* 23/1 (June 2000), 144. Rose says, "Powerful groups maintain and affirm their power by attempting to dictate the staging of public celebrations, . . . by strategically concealing subversive or challenging discourses,

[and] by preventing access to the public stage . . . [while] resistive hidden transcripts that attempt to undermine this power block . . . create alternative codes that invert stigmas, direct our attention to offstage cultures of the class or group within which they originated, and validate the perceptions of the less powerful." Tricia Rose, *Black Noise: Rap Music and Black Culture in Contemporary America* (Middletown, Conn.: Wesleyan University Press, 1994), 100. Regarding orthography, the constructions "hip-hop" and "hip hop" appear variously in the literature cited throughout this book.

4. James," Reforming the Circle," 144.

5. A useful and unusual scholarly work on a topic related to my own is Ann Wagner, *Adversaries of Dance: From the Puritans to the Present* (Urbana: University of Illinois Press, 1997). Wagner's book is primarily a chronicle of Protestant theological opposition to dance. It impinges upon the current study, particularly Chapter 2 of this book, as a good summation of the doctrinal response to both the hellfire-and-brimstone evangelism of Edwards and Whitefield and—at least by inference—the bodily ecstasy of Davenport and the Cane Ridge Revival. It is based in primary sources: dance manuals, courtesy and etiquette manuals, religious tracts, and so on and finds that "the American tradition of dance opposition has emanated from white, male, Protest clergy and evangelists who argued from a narrow and selective interpretation of biblical passages and who persisted in seeing dancing only within a moral and spiritual frame of reference" (xiv–xv). A crucial difference, however, between Wagner's focus and my own, is that I am more interested in discovering what was done, what it intended, and how it worked, rather than focusing upon the doctrinal and theological bases upon which dance was opposed.

6. See, for example, Alexandra Kolb, ed., *Dance and Politics* (Bern: Peter Lang AG, 2010), which includes chapters on radical choreographers, works inspired by the Red Army Faction and the Weather Underground, "patriotic" dance in Nazi Germany and the 1940s United States, and postwar political and politicized concert dance. Typically, dance histories of "the political" echo this theatrical and choreographic focus. Similarly, when vernacular art forms have entered or engaged with university contexts, their meanings or ownership have shifted and mutated, because the Academy itself has sought to appropriate and depoliticize their functional meanings: to treat them as symbolic reinforcements of the dominant status quo. A study of the recurrent strategies and rhetoric through which vernacular music genres have been adapted and reframed in order to render them acceptable for appropriation into the academy is Austin B. Caswell and Christopher Smith, "Into the Ivory Tower: Vernacular Music and the American Academy," *Contemporary Music Review* 19/1, Traditions, Institutions and American Popular Music (2000), 89–111.

7. It should be mentioned that two topic areas within the existing dance scholarship provide major exceptions to this general statement: there is a small but growing literature consisting of ethnographic investigations of dance and identity, especially in Latin American and Caribbean culture; these might include Cindy García, *Salsa Crossings: Dancing Latinidad in Los Angeles* (Durham: Duke University Press, 2013); Christopher Washburne, *Sounding Salsa: Performing Latin Music in New York City* (Philadelphia: Temple University Press, 2008); Barbara Browning, *Samba: Resistance in Motion* (Bloomington: Indiana University Press, 1995); Elizabeth A. McAlister, *Rara!: Vodou, Power, and Performance*

*in Haiti and Its Diaspora* (Berkeley: University of California Press, 2002); Gage Averill, *A Day for the Hunter, a Day for the Prey: Popular Music and Power in Haiti* (Chicago: University of Chicago Press, 2008); and Yvonne Daniel's *Rumba: Dance and Social Change in Contemporary Cuba* (Bloomington: Indiana University Press, 1995). The present volume is indebted to interpretive studies like these, but in contrast is primarily *historiographic* and comparative, rather than ethnographic, in orientation. Similarly, there is a significant body of scholarship on dance as an anti-hegemonic expression of subaltern identity, whether African American, Latino/a, female, or Lesbian-Gay-Bisexual-Transsexual-Queer (LGBTQ), as, for example, the Desmond-edited collection, *Meaning in Motion*. But this scholarship—which informs the chapter on Josephine Baker and the Marx Brothers, especially—tends to focus on the body politics of iconic solo or concert performers, *not* upon either group or participatory dancing, which are precisely the focus of my book.

8. Blackface minstrelsy's wheeling and turning, and hip hop's popping, locking, and breaking, are only two especially vibrant historical examples of a syncopated, akimbo aesthetic, which both conveyed and sometimes intended resistance. An exciting addition to the literature on dance as a platform for cultural meetings is Paul A. Scolieri, *Dancing the New World: Aztecs, Spaniards, and the Choreography of Conquest* (Austin: University of Texas, 2013), which builds on his dissertation ("Choreographing Empires: Aztec Performance and Colonial Discourse," New York University, Graduate School of Arts and Science, 2003); however, this book primarily examines "dance" as a literary trope in period writings about the colonial encounter—it is not an examination of movement vocabularies or what they mean about cultural exchange.

9. A note about time-bound language and perspectives: in citing primary sources on popular, vernacular, and working-class art forms in American historical contexts, and especially in addressing art forms originating in subaltern communities, problems of racist, sexist, classist, and homophobic portraiture, caricature, and appropriation inevitably arise. Because exploitation and injustice, specifically as contested within street dance, are part of the focus of this book, my text necessitates encounters with visual imagery and written language that display historical racism, sexism, classism, misogyny, and homophobia. Of course, I make every effort to avoid reinscribing these perspectives, while always acknowledging their existence and impact. Any reproduction of offensive period language or imagery is therefore undertaken consciously, with intent, awareness, and (I hope) sensitivity to its impact. My goal, in writing this "history from below," is to empower these subaltern voices (for "history from below," see E. P. Thompson, "History from Below," *Times Literary Supplement*, April 7, 1966, 279–280; and Marcus Rediker, "The Poetics of History from Below," *Perspectives on History: The Newsmagazine of the American Historical Association* (September 2010). https://www.historians.org/publications-and-directories/perspectives-on-history/september-2010/the-poetics-of-history-from-below. Accessed September 29, 2018.

10. Eric Lott says, "the black dandy literally embodied the amalgamationist threat of abolitionism, and allegorically represented the class threat of those who were advocating it." Eric Lott, *Love & Theft: Blackface Minstrelsy and the American Working Class* (New York: Oxford University Press, 1993), 134.

11. W. E. B. Du Bois, *The Souls of Black Folk: The Oxford W. E. B. Du Bois* (Cambridge: Oxford University Press, 2007), 3.

12. Robert C. Allen, *Horrible Prettiness: Burlesque and American Culture* (Chapel Hill: University of North Carolina Press, 1991), 173. On the "assurance and achievement" of free men of color in New York City, see also W. T. Lhamon, "Every Time I Wheel About I Jump Jim Crow: Cycles of Minstrel Transgression from Cool White to Vanilla Ice," in Annemarie Bean and James V. Hatch, eds., *Inside the Minstrel Mask: Readings in Nineteenth-Century Blackface Minstrelsy* (New Haven: Wesleyan University Press, 1996), 259–260.

13. The jazz specialist Danielle Robinson says, "Within imposing structures of social power and systems of subordination lie crevices and crannies within which marginalized people express localized resistance and lay claim to empowerment in creative and courageous ways." Danielle Robinson, "'Oh, You Black Bottom!' Appropriation, Authenticity, and Opportunity in the Jazz Dance Teaching of 1920s New York," *Dance Research Journal* 38/1–2 (Summer–Winter 2006), 37.

14. See, for example, Gary A. Donaldson, "A Window on Slave Culture: Dances at Congo Square in New Orleans, 1800–1862," *Journal of Negro History* 69/2 (Spring 1984), 65.

15. Similarly, in lieu of blanket prohibitions that had proved unenforceable, the 1984 urban renewal of Rio's downtown to include a purpose-built "Samba-drome" along the Ave. Marquês de Sapucaí intended precisely the same channeled containment. See Scolieri on "The Mystery of Movement," 127–149.

16. One thinks, for example, of the horror of moral arbiters at the sight of 1940s "teens" dancing to swing music, or of attempts to control public whistling in postbellum Chicago and street busking in contemporary New Orleans. On the integrationist dynamics of the Swing era, see John Gennari, *Blowin' Hot and Cool: Jazz and Its Critics* (Chicago: University of Chicago Press, 2010), 94–99. For whistling as a West African symbol of resistance, see Joan Wescott, "The Sculpture and Myths of Eshu-Elegba, the Yoruba Trickster. Definition and Interpretation of Yoruba Iconography," *Africa: Journal of the International African Institute* 32/4 (October 1962), 336–354. For anti-whistling noise ordinances, see (among many others) Derek Vaillant, "Peddling Noise: Contesting the Civic Soundscape of Chicago, 1890–1913," *Journal of the Illinois State Historical Society (1998-)* 96/3 (Autumn 2003), 258.

17. While I do not approach this topic as a dance specialist, my perspective, grounded more widely in the history of American popular and vernacular expressive culture, may provide fresh insights. In addition—and particularly in light of the indirect nature of dance data in the preelectronic-recording record—the cultural historian's methods of evidence analysis take on refreshed relevance.

18. See, for example, Kevin M. Scott, "The 'Negro Touch' and the 'Yankee Trick': William Sidney Mount and the Art of Race and Ethnicity," *Visual Resources* 24/3, 233–252; Barbara S. Glass, *African American Dance: An Illustrated History* (Jefferson, N.C.: McFarland and Company, 2007); Anthony Shay, *Dancing across Borders: The American Fascination with Exotic Dance Forms* (Jefferson N.C.: McFarland, 2008).

19. A good summary of primary sources and some exegesis on the flash press is Patricia Cline Cohen, with Timothy J. Gilfoyle and Helen Lefkowitz Horowitz, *The Flash Press: Sporting Male Weeklies in 1840s New York* (Chicago: University of Chicago Press, 2008).

20. A good source on the recurrence of these Anglo-European versus Afro-Caribbean body aesthetics is Kealiinohomoku, "A Comparative Study of Dance," 142–160.

21. Brenda Dixon Gottschild, "Digging the Africanist Presence in American Performance: Dance and Other Contexts," *Contributions in Afro-American and African Studies* 179 (Westport, Conn.: Greenwood Press, 1996), 8–9. Emphasis added. For more on "angularity" and "asymmetry" as prominent and important parts of Afro-Caribbean movement aesthetics, see Jacqui Malone, *Steppin' on the Blues: The Visible Rhythms of African American Dance* (Urbana: University of Illinois Press, 1996), 34–35.

22. For more on European dance aesthetics, and dance as "embodiment" of cultural values, see Loren Monte Ludwig, "'Equal to All Alike: A Cultural History of the Viol Consort in England, c.1550–1675," PhD dissertation, University of Virginia, 2011. On African and Afro-Caribbean body aesthetics, in contrast, see Carvalehaes: "The ability to get down does not mean surrender or subservience but rather, an assurance that the body had strength to move, to twist, to shake, to hold an energy that was like a belief. . . . The knee bent was a certainty that final death was not close by, and that even the rigidity of the social system demonstrated through exploitation, violence and death could not hold back the aliveness of those bending knees. Moreover, these bending joints, these fighting knees that, along with the movements of hands, arms, hips, torso, head, and foot, would bring about changes in culture and would write and change history." Claudio Carvalhaes, "'Gimme de kneebone bent': Liturgics, Dance, Resistance and a Hermenenutics of the Knees," *Studies in World Christianity* 14/1 (2008), 215.

23. William J. Mahar, *Behind the Burnt Cork Mask: Early Blackface Minstrelsy and Antebellum American Popular Culture* (Urbana: University of Illinois Press, 1998), 1–2. For useful counterbalance on the more street-based and African American sources of blackface theatrics, see specifically W. T. Lhamon, *Raising Cain: Blackface Performance from Jim Crow to Hip Hop* (Cambridge: Harvard University Press, 1998); and Lott, *Love & Theft*.

24. Texts deploying ethnomusicology's classic complex of history, fieldwork, and interpretation include Averill, *A Day for the Hunter*; Laura Clawson, *I Belong to This Band, Hallelujah! Community, Spirituality, and Tradition among Sacred Harp Singers* (Chicago: University of Chicago Press, 2011); Steven Feld, "Sound Structure as Social Structure," *Ethnomusicology* 28/3 (1984), 383–409; Timothy Rice, *May It Fill Your Soul: Experiencing Bulgarian Music* (Chicago: University of Chicago Press, 1994); Jeff Todd Titon, *Powerhouse for God: Speech, Chant, and Song in an Appalachian Baptist Church* (Austin: University of Texas Press, 1988); Thomas Turino, *Nationalists, Cosmopolitans, and Popular Music in Zimbabwe* (Chicago: University of Chicago Press, 2008). A watershed 1997 collection problematizing fieldwork's range of ethical and perspectival challenges is Timothy J. Cooley and Gregory Barz, eds., *Shadows in the Field: New Perspectives for Fieldwork in Ethnomusicology* 2nd edition (New York: Oxford University Press, 2008). A good example of a more contemporary critique of ethnographic privilege is George Lipsitz, "Cruising around the Historical Bloc: Postmodernism and Popular Music in East Los Angeles," *Cultural Critique* 5 (Winter 1986–1987), 157–177; the more activist discipline of "activist" or "outreach" ethnomusicology is well-represented by Angela Impey, "Culture, Conservation and Community Reconstruction: Explorations in Advocacy: Ethnomusicology and Participatory Action Research in Northern Kwazulu Natal," *Yearbook for Traditional Music* 34 (2002), 9–24.

25. A collection by Jonathan McCollum and David G. Hebert, eds., *Theory and Method in Historical Ethnomusicology* (Los Angeles: University of California Press, 2014), is only a more recent recognition of this challenge, likewise confirmed by the Society for Ethnomusicology's "Special Interest Group for Historical Ethnomusicology" (see http://www.ethnomusicology.org/?Groups_SIGsHE, accessed December 24, 2014) of an awareness that history presents to the discipline that reaches back over a decade: see Benjamin Brinner, *Hearing the Past: Essays in Historical Ethnomusicology and the Archaeology of Sound* (New York: W. W. Norton, 1995); and Bruno Nettl, *The Study of Ethnomusicology: Thirty-one Issues and Concepts* 2nd edition (Urbana: University of Illinois Press, 2005), 284–286.

26. See Christopher J. Smith, "Chapter Four: Long Island and the Lower East Side," *The Creolization of American Culture* (Urbana: University of Illinois Press, 2013). However, a clarification is in order: though the foundation texts of HIP pertaining to "reconstruction," "recovery," or "recomposition" of old music mostly emerged from the work of musicologists and composers, I develop my methodology for recovering past sounds not so much from the written texts by those pioneers, but from their actual played results—concerts, recordings, and direct apprenticeship. For works that have influenced my own thinking on historically informed performance's potential contributions to historical musicology, see Paul Badura-Skoda, *Interpreting Bach at the Keyboard*, translated by Alfred Clayton (New York: Oxford University Press, 1993); Thurston Dart, *The Interpretation of Music* (London: Hutchinson and Co., 1954); Nicholas Kenyon, *Authenticity and Early Music* (New York: Oxford University Press, 1988); and Richard Taruskin's notoriously acute critique, *Text & Act: Essays on Music and Performance* (Oxford: Oxford University Press, 1995). Practical works include books by Ross Duffin, *A Performer's Guide to Medieval Music* (Bloomington: Indiana University Press, 2000); Jeffery Kite-Powell, *A Performer's Guide to Renaissance Music* 2nd edition (Bloomington: Indiana University Press, 2007); and especially Timothy J. McGee, *Medieval and Renaissance Music: A Performer's Guide* (Toronto: University of Toronto Press, 1985).

27. See, most significantly and characteristically, Thomas M. Binkley, "The Work Is *Not* the Performance," in *Companion to Medieval and Renaissance Music* (New York: Schirmer Books, 1992), 36–43.

28. See, for example, Richard Leppert, *The Sight of Sound: Music, Representation, and the History of the Body* (London: Diane Publications, 1993).

29. See, for example, Christopher J. Smith, "Papa Legba and the Liminal Spaces of the Blues: Roots Music in Deep South Film," in *American Cinema and the Southern Imaginary*, ed. Deborah Baker and Kathryn B. McKee (Macon: University of Georgia Press, 2011), 317–335.

30. See Ruth Finnegan, *The Hidden Musicians: Music-Making in an English Town* (reprint edition; Middletown, Conn.: Wesleyan University Press, 2007).

31. See Henry Glassie, *Passing the Time in Ballymenone: Culture and Folklore in an Ulster Community* (Bloomington: Indiana University Press, 1997); see also Daithí Kearney, "Crossing the River: Exploring the Geography of Irish Traditional Music," *Journal of the Society for Musicology in Ireland* 3 (2007–2008), 127–139; and Mel Mercier, "The Mescher Bones Playing Tradition: Syncopations on the American Landscape," PhD dissertation, University of Limerick, 2011.

32. The reference is to Christopher Alexander et al., *A Pattern Language: Towns, Buildings, Construction* (New York: Oxford University Press, 1977).

33. Examples informing the current study would include Ian Cook, David Crouch, Simon Naylor, and James R. Ryan, eds., *Cultural Turns/Geographical Turns: Perspectives on Cultural Geography* (London: Prentice Hall, 2000); Finnegan, *The Hidden Musicians*; Glassie, *Passing the Time in Ballymenone*; Daithí Kearney, "Crossing the River: Exploring the Geography of Irish Traditional Music," *Journal of the Society for Musicology in Ireland* 3 (2007–2008), 127–139; Mercier, "The Mescher Bones Playing Tradition; Susan J Smith, "Beyond Geography's Visible Worlds: A Cultural Politics of Music," *Progress in Human Geography* 21/4 (1997), 502–529. See also Wolfgang and Lutz Musner Maderthaner, "Outcast Vienna 1900: The Politics of Transgression," *International Labor and Working-Class History* 64, Workers, Suburbs, and Labor Geography (Fall 2003), 29, which identifies the semiotic as well as practical implications in portrayals of workers' suburbs as "fringe" to the imperial capital. This reading of workers' ghettos as not only geographically but also cognitively marginal is consistent with the case of other urban-historical population zones out of which new urban musics have arisen, before being co-opted, mercantilized, and moved to the bourgeois center.

34. In my own work, for example, an analysis of patterns of occupancy on the antebellum Cincinnati waterfront, as revealed by census data, provided rich insights into cultural, musical, occupational, and genealogical contact between immigrant Irish and Germans and free blacks. See Smith, *The Creolization of American Culture*. Similarly, in the current study, recognizing the geographical significance of Fort Duquesne (site of present-day Pittsburgh) at the confluence of two west-flowing Appalachian rivers, the Allegheny and the Monongahela, with the Ohio, helps us understand the movement and influence of river-borne entertainers like New Orleans's "Old Corn Meal" and the acting troupes of Thomas Dartmouth Rice and George Washington Dixon, while the presence of both Afro-Caribbean and Anglo-Appalachian musicians on the Ohio River ports of Louisville and Cincinnati likewise informs our understanding of migration, dance synthesis, and religious syncretism in the Cumberland Plateau.

35. Dance scholar Judith Lynne Hanna has defined *kinesics*, in a dance-studies context, as "the systematic study of learned body motion which has communicative value." See Hanna, "Movements toward Understanding Humans through the Anthropological Study of Dance [and Comments and Reply]," *Current Anthropology* 20/2 (June 1979), 316.

36. Katrina Hazzard-Gordon, "Dance in Hip Hop Culture," in William Eric Perkins, ed., *Droppin' Science: Critical Essays on Rap Music and Hip Hop Culture* (Philadelphia: Temple University Press, 1996), 220–237.

37. "The rhythm, vigorous movements, their coordination and synchronization, tend to induce some degree of catharsis. . . . The essential psychological function of the dance, in fact, is the prevention of depression and accumulation of psychic stresses." Judith Lynne Hanna, *To Dance Is Human: A Theory of Nonverbal Communication* (Austin: University of Texas Press, 1979), 68. See also Chapter 2 of this book.

38. Rebecca Sachs Norris, "Embodiment and Community," *Western Folklore* 60/2–3, Communities of Practice: Traditional Music and Dance (Spring–Summer, 2001), 116.

39. "Performers specialize in putting themselves in disequilibrium and then displaying how they regain their balance psychophysically, narratively, and socially—only to lose their balance, and regain it, again and again." Richard Schechner, *Performance Theory* (New York: Routledge, 1988), xiv.

40. The iconic articulation of this semiotic theory within African American culture is Henry Louis Gates Jr., *The Signifying Monkey: A Theory of African-American Literary Criticism* (Oxford: Oxford University Press, 1988). Though originating as a literary construct, Gates's method has been effectively utilized in the analysis of music semiotics as well; see Robert Walser, "Out of Notes: Signification, Interpretation, and the Problem of Miles Davis," *The Musical Quarterly* 77/2 (Summer 1993), 343–365; also Walser, "Rhythm, Rhyme and Rhetoric in the Music of Public Enemy," *Ethnomusicology* 39/2 (Spring–Summer), 193–217; Christopher Smith, "A Sense of the Possible: Miles Davis and the Semiotics of Improvised Performance," *TDR The Drama Review* 39/3 (1995), 41–55. In reference to the current volume, see Michael Borshuk: "An Intelligence of the Body: Disruptive Parody through Dance in the Early Performances of Josephine Baker, in *Embodying Liberation: The Black Body in American Dance*, ed. Dorothea Fischer-Hornung and Alison D. Goeller (Berlin: LIT Verlag, 2001).

41. See, for example, Chapter 7 on Josephine Baker and the Marx Brothers. For more on the semiotics of popular performance, see Maria-Elena Buszek, "Representing 'Awarishness': Burlesque, Feminist Transgressions, and the 19th-Century Pin-Up," *TDR (1988-)* 43/4; German Brecht, *European Readings* (Winter 1999), 151–152, on Marlene Dietrich, Madonna, and similar "gender-transgressive" icons, who notes that most of these are disempowered people (women, gay men) using transgression to open up semiotic space; Amy Koritz, "Moving Violations: Dance in the London Music Hall, 1890–1910," *Theatre Journal* 42/4, Disciplines of Theater: Fin De Siècle Studies (December 1990), 421, provides a lengthy discussion of the context, content, impact, and semiotics of "Ta-ra-ra-boom-de-ay"; Lorraine Leu, "'Raise Yuh Hand, Jump Up and Get on Bad!': New Developments in Soca Music in Trinidad," *Latin American Music Review / REvista de Músic Latinoamericana* 21/1 (Spring–Summer 2000), 47–48, reads the move to perform calypso outdoors at fetes as paralleling an enhanced visibility and respectful treatment for soul/calypso song; Ken McLeod, "Space Oddities: Aliens, Futurism and Meaning in Popular Music," *Popular Music* 22/3 (October 2003), 348, reads hip hop and dance-club icons for their capacity to "signify upon" pop music stylistic and gender norms. See also Daniel A. Segal and Richard Handler, "Serious Play: Creative Dance and Dramatic Sensibility in Jane Austen, Ethnographer," which provides an effective reading of the amateur theatricals in *Mansfield Park* as "a complex, semiotically constructed and negotiated series of experiences that always allow and call for creative interpretation and reinterpretation." *Man*, New Series 24/2 (June 1989), 338.

42. Borshuk, "An Intelligence of the Body," 41.

43. Barbara E. Lacey, "The World of Hannah Heaton: The Autobiography of an Eighteenth-Century Connecticut Farm Woman," *William and Mary Quarterly* (1988), 280–304.

44. The communities associated with the "Second Great Awakening" in the Northeast during the period between the Revolution and the Civil War share demographic particulars with a range of other "progressive" social ideas also implicating body behaviors—not

only temperance and slavery abolition, but also women's rights—and lead in turn to the movement vocabularies of the mid-nineteenth-century utopian and free love communities, discussed later.

45. The term *communitas* is employed by Turner in his highly influential analyses of the anthropology (and psychology and ethnography) of performance: "*Communitas* represents behavior characteristic of marginal or transitional social situations where immediacy, equality, and spontaneity prevail. . . . *Communitas* takes place in events that permit and encourage its expression in 'the vita'lizing moment'": Victor Turner, quoted in Catherine A. Shoup, "Scottish Social Dancing and the Formation of Community" *Western Folklore* 60/2–3, Communities of Practice: Traditional Music and Dance (Spring–Summer, 2001), 142. Turner calls *communitas* "a strong, total communal experience of oneness in which an individual senses . . . a merging of awareness [though which] each performer can become acutely aware of everything happening around him/her, while s/he automatically performs her/his part. Victor Turner, *The Ritual Process: Structure and Anti-Structure* (Ithaca, N.Y.: Cornell University Press, 1969), 182–183.

46. In Rio, parades of the *Escolas do samba* (costumed and masked neighborhood samba associations) followed the bleachers-lined Ave. Presidente Vargas; after 1984, a permanent "Samba-drome" was constructed along Ave. Marquês de Sapucaí. In Trinidad and Tobago, the banning of stick-fighting after the 1881 Canboulay Riots led, eventually, to the development of the steel-pan orchestra; in Haiti, "Kanaval"s transgressive music, dancing, and lyrics (associated with vodou) brought Protestant condemnation. It is worth noting that such controls are still very much part of twenty-first-century culture in the same contexts as, for example, the Summer 2014 noise ordinances imposed on Bourbon Street. See Richard Rainey, "Bourbon Street Noise Ordinance Heads to New Orleans City Council," *New Orleans Times-Picayune*, April 21, 2014. http://www.nola.com/politics/index.ssf/2014/04/bourbon_street_noise_ordinance.html. Accessed January 2, 2015.

47. https://southernspaces.org/2012/unhappy-trails-big-easy-public-spaces-and-square-called-congo. Accessed August 1, 2013.

48. There are obvious parallels here to the European traditions of Carnival, on the one hand, and the sacred connotations of drumming and dancing in West African religion, on the other.

49. Anne Elise Thomas describes the "networks of responsibility and responsiveness, in a present exchange of embodied knowledge," which are enacted by group dance: "The sociability of the dance, even as a stage genre, contributes to its potential to invite transcendence and a feeling of group cohesion in all who are present in the performative moment." Thomas, "Practicing Tradition: History and Community in an Appalachian Dance Style," *Western Folklore* 60/2–3, Communities of Practice: Traditional Music and Dance (Spring–Summer, 2001), 176, 177.

50. For Shulman, see her oral-history interview in *Women's Review of Books* 9/33 (December 1991). http://ucblibrary3.berkeley.edu/Goldman/Features/dances_shulman.html. Accessed August 22, 2014. The second reference is to the iconic Motown song by Martha and the Vandellas (1964; composed by Mickey Stevenson, Ivory Joe Hunter, and Marvin Gaye).

## Chapter 1. Sacred Bodies in the Great Awakenings

1. Sachs Norris explicitly links folk dance, "religious feeling," and the experience of community: "Just as one element of religious feeling is that of belonging to something larger than oneself, so, too, participation in folk dance, with its social and gestural history, entails the experience of belonging to something larger than oneself." Rebecca Sachs Norris, "Embodiment and Community," *Western Folklore* 60/2–3, Communities of Practice: Traditional Music and Dance (Spring–Summer 2001), 118. Emphasis added.

2. Ibid., 119.

3. Eliot D. Chapple and Martha Davis, "Expressive Movement and Performance: Toward a Unifying Theory," *TDR (1988-)* 32/4 (Winter 1988), 67. See also: "The instrument of dance is the human body, remarkable in its expressiveness, but always carrying with it, however implicitly, the undertones of musical rhythm" (61).

4. See Wilson H. Kimnach, *Jonathan Edwards's Sinners in the Hands of an Angry God: A Casebook* (New Haven: Yale University Press, 2010).

5. Whitefield believed that "dancing and like entertainments" tended to "divert [the mind and soul from God and lull] it asleep as much as drunkenness and debauchery." Ann Wagner, *Adversaries of Dance: From the Puritans to the Present* (Urbana: University of Illinois Press, 1997), 83.

6. "Reverend James Davenport of Long Island," Rev. Joseph Fish, 1767. Quoted in William S. Simmons, "Red Yankees: Narragansett Conversion in the Great Awakening," *American Ethnologist* 10/2 (May 1983), 116–117.

7. For their critique of Davenport, see David C. Harlan, "The Travail of Religious Moderation: Jonathan Dickinson and the Great Awakening," *Journal of Presbyterian History (1962–1985)* 61/4 (Winter 1983), 421–422. For the brevity and extremism of Davenport's mission, see ibid.; Harry S. Stout and Peter Onuf, "James Davenport and the Great Awakening in New London," *Journal of American History* 70/3 (December 1983), 556–578; Reverend Joseph Fish (1767), quoted in Simmons, "Red Yankees," 254–255; Sarah Valkenburgh, "Jonathan Edwards and the Great Awakening," The Society of Colonial Wars in the State of Connecticut, https://www.colonialwarsct.org/1740_s.htm. Accessed November 24, 2014.

8. Christine Heyrman likewise draws a connection between the democratizing impulses of the Awakening and of maritime culture: "The awakening also threatened the social order in the maritime town of Marblehead, Massachusetts where 'women and even Common Negroes [took] upon them to extort their Betters in the pulpit before large assemblies.' Hence some blacks took the message of the new birth far beyond what many whites considered reasonable bounds and threatened, especially, cherished social boundaries." Heyrman, *Commerce and Culture: The Maritime Communities of Colonial Massachusetts, 1690–1750* (New York: Norton, 1984), 377; quoted in Frank Lambert, "'I Saw the Book Talk': Slave Readings of the First Great Awakening," *Journal of African American History* 87, The Past before Us (Winter 2002), 17. An anecdote that warmed the heart of this hometown boy from Marblehead!

9. Barbara E. Lacey, "The World of Hannah Heaton: The Autobiography of an Eighteenth-Century Connecticut Farm Woman," *William and Mary Quarterly* 45.2 (1988), 280–304.

10. Benjamin Franklin likewise was an early supporter of evangelical preaching, and women were also involved. See ibid.

11. Douglas L. Winiarski, "Jonathan Edwards, Enthusiast? Radical Revivalism and the Great Awakening in the Connecticut Valley," *Church History* 74/4 (2005), 683–739.

12. The communities associated with the Second Great Awakening in the Northeast in the period between the Revolution and the Civil War overlap a range of other "progressive" social ideas also implicating the liberation of body behaviors—not only temperance and slavery abolition, but also women's rights—and lead in turn to the movement vocabularies of the nineteenth-century utopian and free love communities, discussed ahead.

13. See David T. Morgan Jr., "George Whitefield and the Great Awakening in the Carolinas and Georgia, 1739–1740," *Georgia Historical Quarterly* 54/4 (Winter 1970), 517, 524–525.

14. "Of all the disorderly practices of Davenport's followers, singing in the streets, at the top of their lungs often at night was most disturbing to public order." Stout and Onuf, "James Davenport," 568.

15. For a good summary of the European carnivalesque roots of charivari, see Natalie Zemon Davis, "The Reasons of Misrule," in *Society and Culture in Early Modern France*, ed. Natalie Zemon Davis (Stanford: Stanford University Press, 1975). See also William Beik, "The Violence of the French Crowd from Charivari to Revolution," *Past & Present* 197 (November 2007), 75–110.

16. Stout and Onuf, "James Davenport," 557; in light of riverine and maritime zones' capacity to foster liminal cultural exchange (especially music and dance), it is interesting to note that Davenport's bonfire of books in 1743 took place on Christopher's Wharf at New London's harbor.

17. For much more on Dixon, and his oppositional stance via the theatrical stage and the street newspaper, see Dale Cockrell, "Zip Coon," in *Demons of Disorder: Early Blackface Minstrels and Their World* (Cambridge: Cambridge University Press, 1997), 92–139.

18. For more on dance in early Charleston (which was settled by relocating planters from Jamaica and Barbados), see Wagner, *Adversaries of Dance*, 75–77.

19. See also Christopher J. Smith, *The Creolization of American Culture: William Sidney Mount and the Roots of Blackface Minstrelsy* (Urbana: University of Illinois Press, 2013), on "Haytian" elements in Nathaniel Hawthorne, the paintings of W. S. Mount, and the body percussion of Northeastern street dance, also discussed ahead.

20. The full quotation, though quite technical in its language, provides a concrete physiological model for the cognitive impact of group dance: "The communicative efficacy of dance lies in its capacity to fully engage the human being; it is a multidimensional phenomenon codifying sensory experience. . . . Dance may be used as a driving technique to facilitate right hemisphere dominance, resulting in gestalt, timeless, nonverbal experiences. . . . The prolonged activation of ergotropic (energy-expending or stress) response ultimately leads to trophotropic (rest reactivity) response, including a shift to right hemisphere cognition, easing distress and providing pleasure. . . . Altered states of consciousness may be induced by socialized responses to the contextual situation; by autosuggestion; and by physical behavior, such as energetic dancing, which may change brain wave frequencies, adrenalin, and blood-sugar content. These changes include gid-

diness through high speed or sensory rhythmic stimulation in more than one sensory mode." Judith Lynne Hanna, *To Dance Is Human: A Theory of Nonverbal Communication* (Austin: University of Texas Press, 1979), 66, 69. We may here also cite Charlotte Wolff on "Kinaesthetic Consciousness," in Wolff, *A Psychology of Gesture* (New York: Arno Press, 1948/1972), 25. Lawrence Grossberg draws an explicit connection between bodily pleasure and dance in the African American tradition; see Grossberg, "Another Boring Day in Paradise: Rock and Roll and the Empowerment of Everyday Life," *Popular Music* 4, Performers and Audiences (1984), 238.

21. Smyth argues that watching, as well as participating, is a kinesthetic experience: "The perceptual input [vision] links to the motor command system, which becomes active and somehow gives rise to sensations which actually are from the observer's body, and another is that the input links to stored memory representations of what movements feel like without involving the motor commands. . . . [Hence] the sight and possibly the sound of others dancing is able to create activity in the neuromuscular system. . . . [Thus] Kinesthetic experience of someone else's movement could arise if the sight of the movement triggered memories of what it felt like to perform that movement, or movements of that type." Mary M. Smyth, "Kinesthetic Communication in Dance," *Dance Research Journal* 16/2 (Autumn 1984), 19–21.

22. "A fundamental dynamic of the tension/release type is of great value in coalescing communal feeling. The drama of tension and release, or problem and solution, mirrors the performative action on the [contra] dance floor . . . as well as the dynamics of the dance itself. . . . Crisis, schism, and conflict are all expressed by the bodily actions of drama. . . . The overall result of the tension/release dynamic is *cathexis*, a raising of energy that occurs not only physically, but emotionally and mentally. The demand that raises physical energy need not be aerobic, but it is often 'merely' a matter of coordination and timing. The mental demand occurs in the need to remember the sequence of figures. The demand that raises emotional energy has much to do with feelings of self-enjoyment, the spirit of play, and the satisfaction of belonging to a community. It has been speculated that the cathectic contour of a dance event involves the production of endorphins, chemical messages resulting in 'the dancer's high,' an experience of self that leaves dancers in a state of euphoria. This may be the case, *but the point is moot*. For dancers, the rationale for dancing is enjoyment, which depends largely on cathexis, which in turn depends on a reiterated dynamic of tension and release." Paul Jordan-Smith, "About That Swing: 'Sleaze' Dancing and Community Norms at River Falls Lodge," *Western Folklore* 60/2–3, Communities of Practice: Traditional Music and Dance (Spring–Summer 2001), 197–198. Emphasis added.

23. It had taken over, in Presbyterian thought, some of the religious calendar and theological functions of Catholic Corpus Christi; there are also some parallels with harvest festivals influenced by the pre-Christian calendar.

24. The musicologist Samuel R. Floyd describes the ring-shout thus: "The participants stood in a ring and began to walk around it in a shuffle, with the feet keeping in contact with or close proximity to the floor, and that there were 'jerking,' 'hitching' motions, particularly in the shoulders. These movements were usually accompanied by a

spiritual, sung by lead singers, 'based' by others in the group (probably with some kind of responsorial device and by hand-clapping and knee-slapping)." Samuel A. Floyd Jr. "Ring Shout! Literary Studies, Historical Studies, and Black Music Inquiry," *Black Music Research Journal,* 22 Supplement: Best of BMRJ (2002), 50. The ring-shout is explicitly identified in the 1840s (see Robert Palmer, *Deep Blues* (London: Penguin Books, 1981), 38; however, related circle dances are known throughout the Caribbean, and their roots lie in West Africa (Courland, cited in Floyd, "Ring Shout!," 52). See also J. Lorand Matory, "The Illusion of Isolation: The Gullah/Geechees and the Political Economy of African Culture in the Americas," *Comparative Studies in Society and History* 50/4 (October 2008), 955, and Anne Grimes, "Possible Relationship between 'Jump Jim Crow' and Shaker Songs," *Midwest Folklore* 3/1 (Spring 1953), 54. This phenomenon of the circle of participants as the center of expressive power recurs repeatedly, most notably in the secular *calinda* depicted widely (see George Washington Cable, "The Dance in Place Congo," in *The Negro and His Folklore.* Bruce Jackson, ed. [Austin, Tex.: The American Folklore Society, 1967], 207.), the hip hop "cipher," and so forth. For the cipher, see Jeff Chang, "It's a Hip hop World," *Foreign Policy* 163 (November–December 2007), 60. See Matt Sakakeeny, "New Orleans Music as a Circulatory System," *Black Music Research Journal* 31/2 (Fall 2011), 295. Shoup employs the term *centripetal* to capture the psychological intensification which occurs in such circular group dance; see Catherine A. Shoup, "Scottish Social Dancing and the Formation of Community," *Western Folklore* 60/2–3, Communities of Practice: Traditional Music and Dance (Spring–Summer 2001), 140.

25. The full quote is also relevant: "Nowhere was this more evident than in the leveling effect created by camping at the meetinghouse site. . . . It had the effect of reducing the contrast between rich and poor and creating a special, if temporary, community. Second, . . . participation in the sacrament on Sunday as not restricted to church members but rather open to all. Third, in sharp contrast . . . the event strived to embrace all society, regardless of denomination or spiritual status. That the people of Cane Ridge would be receptive to these controversial innovations—which soon led to a break with Calvinism—seems in keeping with the egalitarianism evident in the congregation's early history." Ellen Eslinger, "Some Notes on the History of Cane Ridge Prior to the Great Revival," *Register of Kentucky State Historical Society* 91/1 (Winter 1993), 22. Such leveling was already a feature of the Scottish sacrament season, before it ever came to North America. See Leigh Eric Schmidt, *Holy Fairs: Scotland and the Making of American Revivalism* (Grand Rapids, Mich.: William Eerdmans, 1989), 64–65, although Schmidt admits that the Cumberland revivals displayed considerably more "heterogeneity."

26. This frontier-based "usual way" of singing, including "lining-out," spontaneous reharmonization, and significant improvisation, was seen as "un-scientific" in light of the rationalized, standardized, and by-note hymnody espoused by Northeastern choristers.

27. See Ivan E. McDougle, "The Social Status of the Slave," *Journal of Negro History* 3/3 (July 1918), 295–296.

28. Alan Jabbour has suggested that, for example, the Appalachian banjo "came originally from black musicians in the Virginia and North Carolina Piedmont, whence it spread southwestward into the Appalachians and beyond." In *The Hammons Family: A Study of a*

*West Virginia Family's Traditions*, Library of Congress AFS, 165–166, album and booklet (Washington, D.C., 1973), 28. Quoted in Cecelia Conway, "Mountain Echoes of the African Banjo," *Appalachian Journal* 20/2 (Winter 1993), 158.

29. See, for example, Melanie Lou Sovine, "The Mysterious Melungeons: A Critique of the Mythical Image," PhD dissertation, University of Kentucky, 1982.

30. The word is thus best understood as a loose umbrella term referring to peoples of widely disparate origins whose shared characteristic is precisely their diverse ethnic origins: European, Native American, and African American.

31. Ann Toplovich, "Melungeons," *Tennessee Encyclopedia of History and Culture*, December 25, 2009, updated January 1, 2010, accessed February 18, 2013. See also Roberta J. Estes, Jack H. Goins, Penny Ferguson, and Janet Lewis Crain, "Melungeons, A Multi-Ethnic Population," *Journal of Genetic Genealogy* (April 2012).

32. Paul Heinegg, "Church and Cotanch Families," Free African Americans. http://www.freeafricanamericans.com/Church_Cotanch.html. Accessed August 30, 2015. The exchange shaped both Native American and African American syncretic cultural systems; for black influence upon the Creek, see Kathryn E. Holland Braund, "The Creek Indians, Blacks, and Slavery," *Journal of Southern History* 57/4 (November 1991), 608–609.

33. These mixed-race persons were the result of unions between Irish indentured sugar workers "Barbadozed" by Cromwell's Irish campaigns of the 1650s and of Native and African slaves who gradually supplanted them. See L. E. Salazar, "Barbados and the Melungeons of Appalachia." http://multiracial.com/site/content/view/441/27. Accessed September 14, 2015. See also C. S. Everett, "Melungeon History and Myth," *Appalachian Journal* 26/4 (Summer 1999), 363. Their Caribbean-to-Continent migration would be mirrored in reverse by the journeys of black preachers from the Cumberland to evangelize in Jamaica and elsewhere in the Caribbean. See, for example, Butler on Haitian Pentecostal movement behaviors: Melvin L. Butler, "The Weapons of Our Warfare: Music, Positionality, and Transcendence among Haitian Pentecostals," *Caribbean Studies* 36/2 (July–December 2008), 25.

34. Everett, "Melungeon History and Myth," 68.

35. Anecdotally, this French and Spanish Caribbean influence is evident in the ubiquity of the Spanish Caribbean's silver peso, which provided the basic rationale for adoption of the Yankee dollar. The ethnic diversity of the frontiers was established very early, well before the Cumberland was settled: "Charles Woodmason, an Anglican itinerant, noted the unusual degree of racial intermixture in churches of the Carolina backcountry in the 1760s . . . Woodmason remarked: 'Here I found a vast Body of People assembled—Such a Medley! such a mixed Multitude of all Classes and Complexions I never saw.'" Richard J. Hooker, ed., *The Carolina Backcountry on the Eve of the Revolution: The Journal and Other Writings of Charles Woodmason, Anglican Itinerant* (Chapel Hill: University of North Carolina Press, 1953), 56; quoted in Lambert, "I Saw the Book Talk," 20–21. On the influence of the *peso*, see Ned Sublette, *The World That Made New Orleans: From Spanish Silver to Congo Square* (Chicago: Chicago Review Press, 2008), 21.

36. http://nancy-melungeonresearch.blogspot.com/2010/10/barbados-link-may-provide-smoking-gun.html. Accessed August 30, 2015.

37. See, among other sources, Smith, *The Creolization of American Culture*.

38. Significant cities are Newport/Covington/Cincinnati, located on different sites at the confluence of the Licking and the big river; Paducah, where the Tennessee and Ohio meet; and Louisville (at the Falls of the Ohio, the most significant portage site between the upper river and the Mississippi). For more on flatboat chronology, technology, and demographics, see Sublette, *The World That Made New Orleans*, 162–164.

39. See Julie Nicoletta, "The Architecture of Control: Shaker Dwelling Houses and the Reform Movement in Early Nineteenth-Century America," *Journal of the Society of Architectural Historians* 62/3 (September 2003), 358.

40. Formally, "The United Society of Believers in Christ's Second Appearing."

41. National Park Service: Shaker Historic Trail, "The Shakers." http://www.nps.gov/nr/travel/shaker/shakers.htm. Accessed January 27, 2015.

42. "Pinkster," an Afro-Dutch spring festival, originated in upstate New York celebrations of Pentecost (*Pfingster*), and from the early eighteenth century had been an occasion for leisure, celebration, display, and black-white expressive exchange. By the first decade of the nineteenth century, approximations of Pinkster were being presented on New York theatrical stages and thus form another influence upon the eventual development of the blackface minstrel troupe. See Shane White, "Pinkster: Afro-Dutch Syncretization in New York City and the Hudson Valley," *Journal of American Folklore* 102/403 (January–March 1989), 68–75. "Negro 'Lection Day" also began in New England, in the 1740s, as a parodic imitation of the (very loosely organized) elections for colonial governments. See Shane White, "'It Was a Proud Day': African American Festivals and Parades in the North, 1741–1834," *Journal of American History* 81/1 (June 1994), 13–50. There were many other similar festive events in the early colonies and the Republic: militia muster days, seasonal holidays, and political campaigns all provided opportunity for transgressive behavior and the evocation of (temporarily) liminal spaces. For the direct quote, see Melvin Wade, "'Shining in Borrowed Plumage': Affirmation of Community in the Black Coronation Festivals of New England (ca. 1750–ca. 1850)," *Western Folklore* 40/3 (July 1981), 216.

43. Wade says, flatly, "There was much free and open exchange of cultural traits within the festivals by both blacks and whites." Wade, "Shining in Borrowed Plumage," 218.

44. Fink (ca. 1770/1780–ca. 1823) was born in Pennsylvania, had been an Indian scout before taking to the rivers, and was a legendary fount of frontier tall tales. Whether truthful or (more likely) not, Cartwright's story of besting Fink itself takes on the dimensions of another "stretcher." See Robert Bray, "Beating the Devil: Life and Art in Peter Cartwright's Autobiography," *Illinois Historical Journal* 78/3 (Autumn 1985), 180–181.

45. See Estella T. Weeks and Ernest W. Baughman, "Shakerism: Shakerism in Indiana: Notes on Shaker Life, Customs, and Music," *Hoosier Folklore Bulletin* 4/4 (December 1945), 59–60.

46. Grimes, "Possible Relationship," 52.

47. Andrew Lee Feight, "James Blyth and the Slavery Controversy in the Presbyterian Churches of Kentucky, 1791–1802," *Register of Kentucky State Historical Society* 102/1 (Winter 2004), 16–17.

48. Black revivalists had been participants in the Awakening of the 1740s, and some Virginia owners supported evangelism among slaves because it theologized further enclosing

their conduct, and of the Sabbath free time which, in the slave populations of the Catholic Caribbean, was a day of significant relaxation, social interaction, and cultural exchange (see Place Congo, later). On the other hand, some white owners opposed evangelizing slaves as disruptive of hierarchical discipline. And their paranoia may have been well-founded: certainly the apocalyptic rhetoric of evangelism played a role in the slave revolts of Gabriel Prosser (ca. 1800) and, later, Nat Turner (1831). See Lambert, "'I Saw the Book Talk."

49. Robert Stuart, "Reminiscences, Respecting the Establishment and Progress of the Presbyterian Church in Kentucky," *Journal of the Presbyterian Historical Society (1943–1961)*, 23/3 (September 1945), 172–173. Emphasis added.

50. Ibid.: "*The running exercise.*—The individual under this excitement would suddenly start, as in a race, and run, leaping over obstacles that chanced to be in his way with preternatural agility. . . . *The barking exercise.*—The subject of this exercise, would, with undistinguished exactness, imitate this *sagacious animal.*"

51. Ibid. "*The dancing exercise.*—Under this exercise the subject would *dance to a lively tune*, often very gracefully, but often ludicrously enough to excite, at least, a smile."

52. The hyperbolic itinerant preacher and memoirist Peter Cartwright (1785–1872) provides a long and rather lurid account of inflicting the jerks upon two young women and of facing down their brothers when they threatened to horsewhip him for doing so. See Bray, "Beating the Devil," 88.

53. Richard McNemar saw the phenomenon as evidence of holiness; he interpreted the jerks as "the privilege of exhibiting by a bold faith, what others were moved to by blind impulse." McNemar, *History of the Kentucky Revival.* http://bit.ly/1rG6IMz. Accessed February 3, 2015. Still later, dancing was seen among the Shaker congregations as a way of "shaking . . . into a state of relaxation" called "the Whirl." Estella T. Weeks and Ernest W. Baughman, "Shakerism: Shakerism in Indiana: Notes on Shaker Life, Customs, and Music," *Hoosier Folklore Bulletin* 4/4 (December 1945), 65–66.

54. Simpson, reporting in the 1940s, says, "Suddenly a dancer will whirl herself about, leaping and going through a series of violent contortions. Her behavior stimulates the dancers and the drummers as she reels, cries, and throws herself on the ground." George Eaton Simpson, "The Vodun Service in Northern Haiti," *American Anthropologist*, New Series, 42/2, I (April–June 1940), 243; also "One might describe it as a sort of collective hysteria. Only ten to twenty per cent of the faithful ever become possessed at a *service*, but all of them enjoy the drumming, dancing, singing, drinking, and the mysterious rites (247)." For multiweek durations, see ibid., 237. Likewise, the 1970s fieldwork of Ira P. Lowenthal confirms the durable retentions of practice in the vodou complex: "There is an essential and integral connection between the aesthetic and performative features of the sèvis [Haitian *Kriyo*: "service"] and its devotional ends. This connection goes beyond the simple fact that the *lwa* ["pantheist gods"] are said to desire song and dance; its precise nature has to do with the folk theory of possession and its ritual importance. Ira P. Lowenthal, "Ritual Performance and Religious Experience: A Service for the Gods in Southern Haiti," *Journal of Anthropological Research* 34/3 (Autumn 1978), 402. It should be noted here that there is very little period description of vodou or similar ceremony in Haiti, though there *was* a strong awareness—and fear—of its transgressive implications; see the parallels with *obi* in Jamaica.

55. The full title is *Description topographique, physique, civile, politique et historique de la partie française de l'isle Saint-Domingue*. New ed. by Blanche Maurel and Étienne Taillemite (Paris: Librairie Larose for the Société de l'histoire des colonies françaises), 1958.

56. Sublette calls it "the most extended description of eighteenth-century slave dancing that we have anywhere." See Sublette, *The World That Made New Orleans*, 179; 180–181.

57. Moreau de St.-Méry, *Danse* (Philadelphia, 1796), 64–68; quoted in Sublette, *The World That Made New Orleans*, 184. Emphasis added.

58. We may note in passing that, while certain festival behaviors are consistent between the Haitian *sèvis* and the ca. 1800 Kentucky frontier "revival"—namely public song, dance, prayer, glossolalia, drink, and social interaction—on the other hand, drums, a frequent marker of Africanism throughout the New World from the 16th century, and central to Haitian worship, are notably absent in descriptions of the Cumberland. We know that the *Codes Noir* of the French Caribbean and the standard practices of slaveowners, especially in the Protestant Southern United States, tended to rigidly restrict blacks' access to and employment of drums, but we may wonder whether such legalisms are sufficient to account for the marked absence of drumming in the revivals. In light of my suggestion of Afro-Caribbean and specifically Haitian influence, I propose that this marked contrast—that is, the *absence* of drums in Cumberland worship—is actually consistent with the "creolization" of Afro-Haitian worship practices through intermingling with Presbyterian and Methodist Pentecostalism. Drums and drumming were so closely associated with black solidarity, so tightly circumscribed by slavery's strategies for inculcating docility and self-abnegation, and so strongly evoked fears of black rebellion, that their marked absence does not disprove the influence of Afro-Caribbean sacred practices. Certainly there is circumstantial evidence in the Cane Ridge revivals for the presence of percussive "noise" as part of the soundscape: the sound of hand-clapping and of feet on resonant post-and-beam or puncheon floors—as in the case of the extended wooden "Slave Gallery," which was expanded to handle overflow crowds—were fully present in the creole sound-and-movement practices of the revivals. For this usage of the term *creolization*, originating in linguistics, see Smith, *Creolization of American Culture*, and Roger D. Abrahams, *The Man-of-Words in the West Indies: Performance and the Emergence of Creole Culture* (Baltimore: Johns Hopkins University Press, 1983).

59. The full quote is sufficiently trenchant as to merit more complete reproduction here: "The song and dance of voodoo ritual, and the nature of people's involvement in it, are clearly instrumental to the induction of trance or dissociative states. The *cultural* significance of . . . the act of calling the *lwa*, however, is not simply that they are objectively effective in bringing on trance. Rather, this effectiveness helps to create a subjective reality . . . in which the *essence* of worship comes to be participation in the collective creation of song and dance. Religious experience in the context of the sèvis is, above all, kinetic and aural, sensual and aesthetic. Fervent devotion is virtually defined in terms of activities which are felt to be pleasurable and satisfying in and of themselves. . . . The pervasive dichotomization of experience in the Judeo-Christian tradition, which associates secular/religious with sensual/spiritual distinctions, is of little analytic value here. Beyond this merging of the satisfying and the sacred in voodoo ritual, possession belief has further

implications for those who, through it, are brought into a direct social relationship with their gods." Ira P. Lowenthal, "Ritual Performance and Religious Experience: A Service for the Gods in Southern Haiti," *Journal of Anthropological Research* 34/3 (Autumn 1978), 405. Lowenthal's description of vodou's bodily experience likewise closely parallels the physical descriptions from the ca. 1800 revivals we have previously described: "I would suggest that possession involves, at the very least, an increased precision and fluidity of body movement, coupled with an apparent loss of self-consciousness and the *sense* of control over the body itself . . . The body seems endowed with an energy and endurance which counteract the effects of fatigue and allow the *lwa* to dance for hours on end without pause. The possessed appear to achieve a total, single-minded concentration on whatever they are doing, particularly in dance. Their bodies merge completely with the sound of drums and singing and appear to respond immediately and effortlessly to this aural stimulus (407, n9).

60. The contemporary ethnomusicologist Bobby C. Alexander, working with black Pentecostal communities in Brooklyn and interpreting their ritual behavior through the lens of Victor Turner's concept of liminality, describes the "psychokinetic experience" of sacred dance as "ethnographic confirmation of Pentecostal worship's classic ritual function." See, for example, Victor Turner, *The Ritual Process: Structure and Anti-Structure* (Ithaca, N.Y.: Cornell University Press, 1969).

61. Alexander critiques what he calls the "misinterpretation" of Turner's structure-antistructure dyad to argue that ritual liminality *can* actually support social and cultural critique; that it is not, as mistakenly presumed, solely reinscriptive of societal norms. Bobby C. Alexander, "Correcting Misinterpretations of Turner's Theory: An African-American Pentecostal Illustration," *Journal for the Scientific Study of Religion* 30/1 (March 1991), 26–34. Alexander also, for example, argues that ritual possession-à la contemporary black Brooklyn Pentecostals or early-nineteenth-century Kentucky revivalists may be read as "a form of concrete protest against the dominant social structure in American society and its oppressive consequences"—and, by implication, suggests that such a function for ritual possession was potentially *always* available to those who experienced themselves as "outsiders," "others," or otherwise disenfranchised (27). For the concept's application in contemporary ethnography, see ibid., 27–34. Alexander makes explicit the Afro-Caribbean roots of the "ritual communitas," which yields speaking in tongues and dancing in the spirit.

62. See Gunter Lenz: "In literate societies a liminal phase can be the result of a serious crisis that produces the experience of communitas as a revolt against the dominating social structure. . . . What is possible during the liminal phase, at a liminal place, is the subversion of the governing notion of reality, a projection of *alternative* . . . 'models for living,' the spontaneous experience of communitas in 'social dramas, fields, and metaphors,' in symbolic action, kinds of *open*, non-teleological rituals." Lenz, "Symbolic Space, Communal Rituals, and the Surreality of the Urban Ghetto: Harlem in Black Literature from the 1920s to the 1960s," *Callaloo* 35 (Spring 1988), 310. For African American sacred performance, see Ray Allen, Conclusion, "Gospel Quartet Performance and *Communitas*": "singers must first overcome the physical and social space separating them from their

listeners. . . . Singers and listeners come together as the performance accelerates toward a moment of spiritual communion, a state of 'spontaneous communitas.'" Allen, "Shouting the Church: Narrative and Vocal Improvisation in African-American Gospel Quartet Performance," *Journal of American Folklore* 104/413 (Summer 1991), 313–314.

63. See, for example, the Online Etymology Dictionary, which includes the following: *Merry-bout*, "an incident of sexual intercourse" was low slang from 1780. *Merry-begot* "illegitimate" (adj.), "bastard" (n.) is from 1785. *Merrie England* (now frequently satirical or ironic) is 14c. *meri ingland*, originally in a broader sense of "bountiful, prosperous." *Merry Monday* was a 16c. term for "the Monday before Shrove Tuesday" (Mardi Gras). http://www.etymonline.com/index.php?term=merry. Accessed February 3, 2015.

64. Jeroen DeWulf, "Pinkster: An Atlantic Creole Festival in a Dutch-American Context," *Journal of American Folklore* 126/501 (Summer 2013), 266.

65. From McNemar's *History of the Kentucky Revival*, (60).

66. Ibid., 104–105.

67. At Union Village, Ohio; South Union, Logan County, Kentucky; and Mercer County, Kentucky.

68. Emmett later in life returned to collect tunes and songs from his neighbors, the free black musicians of the Snowden family, in Mount Vernon. See—despite its optimistic interpretations of influence—the archival reporting in Howard L. Sacks and Judith R. Sacks, "Way Up North in Dixie: Black-White Musical Interaction in Knox County, Ohio," *American Music* 6/4 (Winter 1988), 410.

69. By 1846, the twenty-year-old aspiring songwriter Stephen Foster was working as a steamship company's bookkeeper on the Cincinnati waterfront, within sound of the boats' whistles.

70. Baklanoff, for example, cites the role of dance and possession in African American Primitive Baptist communities further south and west. See Joy Driskell Baklanoff, "The Celebration of a Feast: Music, Dance, and Possession Trance in the Black Primitive Baptist Footwashing Ritual," *Ethnomusicology* 31/3 (Autumn 1987), 381–394. See Samantha Erin Futrell, "They Came Up Out of the Water: Evangelicalism and Ethiopian Baptists in the Southern Lowcountry and Jamaica, 1737–1806," MM Thesis, Liberty University, 2013, 46. Similarly, the *Runnin Sperchils* and "Prayer Bands" of the Sea Islands; the Kumina cults of Jamaica, Pentecostals of Haiti, and the Spiritual Baptists of St. Vincent; the "trembling" in the Chamba dances of Carriacou: all provide further and parallel evidence for the synthesis and ongoing influence of Afro-Caribbean and Pentecostal Anglo-Scots worship, later in the Antebellum period. See Walter Pitts, "Keep the Fire Burnin': Language and Ritual in the Afro-Baptist Church," *Journal of the American Academy of Religion* 56/1 (Spring 1988), 85. For Haitian Pentecostalism, see Melvin L. Butler, "The Weapons of Our Warfare: Music, Positionality, and Transcendence among Haitian Pentecostals," *Caribbean Studies* 36/2 (July–December 2008), 25. For Spiritual Baptists, see Erika Bourguignon, "Ritual Dissociation and Possession Belief in Caribbean Negro Religion," in *Afro-American Anthropology*, Norman E. Whitten Jr., and John F. Szwed, eds. (New York: The Free Press, 1970). For the Chamba dances of Carriacou, see Donald R Hill, "West African and Haitian Influences on the Ritual and Popular Music of Carriacou, Trinidad, and Cuba," *Black Music Research Journal* 18/1–2 (Spring–Autumn 1998), 186.

## Chapter 2. A Tale of Two Cities I

1. Karen E. Bond and Susan W. Stinson, "'I Feel like I'm Going to Take off!': Young People's Experiences of the Superordinary in Dance," *Dance Research Journal* 32/2 (Winter 2000–2001), 53.

2. See Christopher J. Smith, *The Creolization of American Culture: William Sidney Mount and the Roots of Blackface Minstrelsy* (Urbana: University of Illinois Press, 2013). See likewise Ira Berlin on the role of Atlantic creoles "in the historic meeting of Europeans and Africans on the west coast of Africa" and the impact of "their linguistic skills and their familiarity with the Atlantic's diverse commercial practices, cultural conventions, and diplomatic etiquette." Berlin, "From Creole to African: Atlantic Creoles and the Origin of African-American Society in Mainland North America," *William and Mary Quarterly* 53, no. 2 (April 1996): 254–255.

3. Dale Cockrell, *Demons of Disorder: Early Blackface Minstrels and Their World* (Cambridge: Cambridge University Press, 1997), 8–11.

4. Smith, *The Creolization of American Culture*, 28–78.

5. "Musicians during this time necessarily sought work in a more legitimate public sphere and played the noisy, formerly underground music they knew best, a music that the nation and the world came to love." Dale Cockrell, "Blood on Fire: Sex and Music in America, 1840–1917." Unpublished paper delivered at Columbia University. May 2, 2014.

6. Melvin Wade, "'Shining in Borrowed Plumage': Affirmation of Community in the Black Coronation Festivals of New England (ca. 1750–ca. 1850)," *Western Folklore* 40, no. 3 (July 1981): 223.

7. Shane White, "'It Was a Proud Day': African Americans, Festivals, and Parades in the North, 1741–1834," *Journal of American History* 81 no. 1 (June 1994), 18. Similar celebrations are recorded in Maryland and North Carolina (John Canoe); the coastal Carolinas (Pinkster); and, in New England, 'Lection Day (Norwich, Hartford, Derby, and New Haven, Conn.: Newport and Kingsport, R.I.; Salem Mass.; Portsmouth, N.H.). See Katrina Hazzard-Gordon, *Jookin': The Rise of Social Dance Formations in African-American Culture* (Philadelphia: Temple University Press, 1990), 39ff.

8. White describes the location of slave festivals like Pinkster and Negro 'Lection Day as existing "in small pockets along the coast and up the valleys of the major rivers." White, "It Was a Proud Day." See also Andrew Adgate, *A PINKSTER ODE for the Year 1803. Most Respectfully Dedicated to CAROLUS AFRICANUS, REX: Thus Rendered in English: KING CHARLES, Capital-General and Commander in Chief of the PINKSTER BOYS. By His Majesty's Obedient Servant, ABSALOM AIMWELL, Esq.* (Albany: Printed Solely for the Purchasers and Others, 1803).

9. White, "It Was a Proud Day," 19. Gottschild adds: "These influences have existed in European American life and culture since Africans and Europeans together set foot on American shores. Plantation-era contacts between the two groups forged and shaped a unique, Creolized, Afro-Euro-American culture." See Brenda Dixon Gottschild, *Digging the Africanist Presence in American Performance: Dance and Other Contexts*, Contributions in Afro-American and African Studies 179 (Westport Conn.: Greenwood Press, 1996), 3.

10. From Thomas De Voe's *Market Book*: "The first introduction in this city of public 'negro dancing' no doubt took place at this market. The negroes who visited here were

principally slaves from Long Island who have leave of their master for certain holidays, among which 'Pinkster' was the principal one; . . . then, as they usually had three days holiday, they were ever ready, by their 'negro sayings and doing,' to make a few shillings more. So they would be hired by some joking butcher or individual to engage in a jig or breakdown, as that was one of their favorite pastimes at home on the barn-floor, or in a frolic." Scott cites De Voe's description of "Ned (Francis), a little wiry negro slave . . . another named Bob Rowley . . . and Jack, belonging to Frederick De Voo, all farmers on Long Island." Thomas De Voe, *The Market Book; A History of the Public Markets of the City of New York* (Thomas F. De Voe, 1862), quoted in Kevin M. Scott, "Rituals of Race: Mount, Melville, and Antebellum America," PhD dissertation, Purdue University, 2004, 51–52.

11. Pierce Egan and Charles Hindley, *The True History of Tom and Jerry, Or, The Day and Night Scenes of Life in London, from the Start to the Finish! With a Key to the Persons and Places, Together with a Vocabulary and Glossary of the Flash and Slang Terms Occuring in the Course of the Work* (London: Reeves and Turner, 1890). http://books.google.com/books?id=8l3iku13i-oC&printsec=frontcover&dq=The+True+History+of+Tom+and+Jerry+1890. Accessed August 30, 2014.

12. 'Lection Day is reported in Norwich, Hartford, Derby, and New Haven, Conn.; Newport and Kingsport, R.I.; Salem Mass.; and Portsmouth, N.H. See Hazzard-Gordon, *Jookin'*, 39ff; see also White, "It Was a Proud Day," 13–50.

13. Describing 'Lection Day, William D. Piersen finds "an interesting parallel in the *chaluska* Mardi Gras dance in Haiti where the participants dressed as nineteenth-century generals to achieve the effect of comic mimicry." Pierson, "Puttin' down Ole Massa: African Satire in the New World." *Research in African Literatures* 7, no. 2 (Autumn 1976): 166–180.

14. Judith Bettelheim provides extended excerpts of detailed primary sources that confirm the syncretic nature of nineteenth-century Kingston Christmas celebrations. See Bettelheim, "Women in Masquerade and Performance," *African Arts* 31/2, Special Issue: Women's Masquerades in Africa and the Diaspora (Spring 1998), 70.

15. For Spain, see public protests against Aznar's politicization of terrorist bombings "with the noise of tin cans banging on the street." Jack Santino, "The Ritualesque: Festivals, Politics, and Popular Culture," *Western Folklore* 68/1 (Winter 2009), 25. In Rio, parades of the *Escolas do samba* (costumed and masked neighborhood samba associations) followed the bleachers-lined Ave. Presidente Vargas; after 1984, a permanent "Sambadrome" was constructed along Ave. Marquês de Sapucaí. In Trinidad and Tobago, the banning of stick-fighting after the 1881 Canboulay Riots led, eventually, to the development of the steel-pan orchestra; in Haiti, Kanaval's massed music, dancing, and lyrics (associated with vodou) brought Protestant condemnation. It is worth noting that such controls are still very much part of twenty-first-century culture in the same contexts, as, for example, the Summer 2014 noise ordinances imposed on Bourbon Street. See Richard Rainey, "Bourbon Street Noise Ordinance Heads to New Orleans City Council," New Orleans *Times-Picayune*, April 21, 2014. http://www.nola.com/politics/index.ssf/2014/04/bourbon_street_noise_ordinance.html. Accessed February 28, 2015.

16. For multiple examples of this creole synthesis in the interaction of working-class blacks and whites on the rivers, harbors, and ship decks of the Atlantic and Caribbean,

and in the paintings and sketches of vernacular artists like William Sidney Mount (1807–1867), see Smith, *The Creolization of American Culture,* especially Chapter 4, "Minstrelsy's Material Culture," 122–147.

17. Jane C. Desmond says, "Dancing bodies are performative in every sense of the word. They enact a conception of self and social community mediated by the particular historical aesthetic dimensions of the dance forms and their precise conditions of reception. They engage every sense of the body and do so in socially meaningful ways, which emphasize certain sensations over others. Such an analysis of nonverbal symbolic systems that are not only embedded in social context but also are formative of those contexts of lived experience can expand our understandings of ideologies and their discursive mobilization in realms that are often so overlooked as to be naturalized." Desmond, Introduction, in Jane C. Desmond, ed., *Meaning in Motion: New Cultural Studies of Dance* (Durham: Duke University Press, 1997), 16–17.

18. See Anna Beatrice Scott, "Spectacle and Dancing Bodies That Matter: Or, if It Don't Fit, Don't Force It," in Desmond, *Meaning in Motion,* 265–265.

19. See Micah J. Hawkins and Oscar Wegelin, "The Saw-Mill or, a Yankee Trick. A Comic Opera in Two Acts," *Magazine of History* (1927); act I, scene 4. Similarly, see also White's quotation of a 1744 traveler's tale, describing a request for directions while traveling with his black servant Dromo on Long Island: "Dis de way to York?" asks Dromo. "Yaw, dat is Yarikee," said the wench, pointing to the steeples. "What devil you say?" replies Dromo. "Yaw, mynheer," said the wench. "Damne you, what you say?" said Dromo again. "Yaw, yaw," said the girl. "You a damn black bitch," said Dromo, and so rid on. Quoted in Shane White, "A Question of Style: Blacks in and around New York City in the Late Eighteenth Century," *Journal of American Folklore* 102, no. 403 (January–March 1989), 23–25.

20. The specific reference is to the character "Raccoon," whose name and dialect were anachronistically presumed, by later scholars, to be racist caricature. In fact, the "Raccoon" character (whose name acquired racist connotations only in the late nineteenth century—not the early eighteenth) is, like "Norchee," Pennsylvania Dutch, not African American. Carolyn Rabson, acknowledging the dialect's racist association, uneasily argues for Raccoon's Dutch, rather than African American, identity; yet quotes a WPA-era review, which reads: "Raccoon . . . although not a Negro, nevertheless indulges in a dialect which shows Negro influence." Margaret G. Mayorga, *A Short History of the American Drama until the Revolutionary War* (New York: Dodd, Mead and Co., 1932), 29–30; quoted in Carolyn Rabson, "Disappointment Revisited: Unweaving the Tangled Web. Part I," *American Music* 1, no. 1 (Spring 1983): 15ff and n25.

21. Hawkins, *The Saw-Mill,* act 1, scene 3. It is also worth noting that these details, especially hair "queued" with an eel-skin wrapping, are entirely consistent with the *Market Book*'s depictions of African Americans "dancing for eels" on the Lower East Side in the 1840s.

22. Cockrell, "Blood on Fire."

23. Dominique Cyrille reminds us that dance behaviors were creolized simply by the daily contact between African and European movement vocabularies in the context of slavery, especially in shared dancing; she says, "Domestic slaves learned altered versions of European dances especially designed by seventeenth-century missionaries who

wanted to suppress the 'outrageous' postures of African dancing." Dominique Cyrille, "Sa Ki Ta Nou (This Belongs to Us): Creole Dances of the French Caribbean," in Susanna Sloat, ed., *Caribbean Dance, from Abakua to Zouk: How Movement Shapes Identity* (Gainesville: University Press of Florida, 2002), 225. Similarly, in the 1730s, the *Virginia Gazette* advertised dance schools in Hampton and Yorktown, whose dance master was listed as "one Stephen Tenoe, who was an African American slave." Ralph G. Giordano, *Social Dancing in America, a History and Reference I: Fair Terpsichore to the Ghost Dance, 1607–1900* (Westport Conn.: Greenwood, 2007), 66ff.

24. Ibid., 56.

25. On challenges in and strategies for recovering three-dimensional movement from two-dimensional static images, see Don Herbison-Evans on "Suspended Moments": "Some moments in a dance—when a dancer changes from rising to falling, from compressing to expanding, from reaching to contracting or from stretching to contracting—have in common a moment of zero velocity with a nonzero acceleration. *This gives the visual appearance of both stillness and motion at the same time.* . . . These moments linger visually because of the zero velocity and linger mentally because of the paradoxical perception. These are moments of maximum and minum [*sic*] breath, the peak of a rise, the moment of recovery." Herbison-Evans, "The Perception of the Fleeting Moment in Dance," *Leonardo* 26/1 (1993), 46.

26. Whistling, like dancing and singing in public, was closely associated with minstrelsy's transgressive impact; see "Bobolink Bob" Rowley, cited by W. T. Lhamon, *Raising Cain: Blackface Performance from Jim Crow to Hip Hop* (Cambridge: Harvard University Press, 1998), 4. "Tucky Squash" was a comic archetype a la "Zip Coon" or "Jim Crow," though the name "Quashee" is Akan in origin; "double trouble" and "hoe corn" are syncretic dance steps; the reference to a "Long Island negro" as emblematic of creole dance reminds us of the Anglo-Dutch creole spoken in the traveler's tale cited previously. Irving's description of a "Haytian" creole ball is likewise worth remembering for our discussion of the watercolor *A Grand Jamaica Ball*, later. See Washington Irving, James Kirk Paulding, and Washington Irving, *Salmagundi or, The Whim-whams and Opinions of Launcelot Langstaff, Esq., and Others* (New York: Thomas Longworth and Company, 1820), 115–116. http://books.google.com/books?id=f_oqAAAAMAAJ&dq=Salmagundi+Or,+The+Whim-whams+and+Opinions+of+Launcelot+Langstaff,+Esq.,+and+Others&source=gbs_navlinks_s. Accessed February 2, 2015.

27. Washington Irving, "The Legend of Sleepy Hollow" (first published 1820) (New York: Sterling Children's Books, 2013). It may be coincidence or intent that Irving's theatricalized text description of the scene matches, remarkably, W. S. Mount's early painting *Rustic Dance after a Sleigh Ride* (1830), which includes parallels to Irving's setting, focal dance character, and "negro" fiddler.

28. Cláudio Carvalhaes, "'Gimme de Kneebone Bent': Liturgics, Dance, Resistance and a Hermeneutics of the Knees," *Studies in World Christianity* 14/1 (2008), 15. See also Jennifer Thorp, "Eloquent Bodies: Humanist and Grotesque Dance," review of Jennifer Nevile, *The Eloquent Body: Dance and Humanist Culture in 15th-century Italy*, in *Early Music* 33, no. 4 (November 2005), 702–704. We might likewise mention here, as an anecdotal parallel case

of "akimbo" body vocabularies, Szwed and Farris Thompson's fascinating "substratist exegesis of the origins of baton twirling"; identifying such practices in northern Kongolese festive behaviors, thereafter recurring in Haitian Rara, New Orleans Mardi Gras Indian culture, and up the Mississippi to the first postbellum African American free universities. Cited in David Buisseret and Steven G. Reinhardt, eds., *Creolization in the Americas* (College Station: Texas A & M University Press, 2000), 104.

29. Buckley comments only in passing on the diverse ethnicities and body vocabularies depicted: "James reserved his broadsides for the local [that is, Jamaican] white inhabitants, whom he found laughable and absurd. Women are buxom, mostly youngish, frivolous, mindless children. The men are older, a few wizened, and all lecherous and shifty. All are indulgent, coarse, and blithesomely ignorant in their peripheral existence on the frontier. And drink is the addiction of all." Roger N. Buckley, "The Frontier in the Jamaican Caricatures of Abraham James," *The Yale University Library Gazette* 58, nos. 3–4 (April 1984), 156. Of James's treatment of ethnicity, he says only "the blacks in his cartoons were the so-called privileged house slaves" (152).

30. Edward A. Chappell and Louis P. Nelson describe James's disdain for colonials and see *A Grand Jamaica Ball!* and *Segar Smoking Society in Jamaica* as emblematic of this disdain. Edward A. Chappell and Louis P. Nelson, "Falmouth, Jamaica: Early Housing in a Caribbean Town." *Falmouth, Jamaica Field Guide*. Vernacular Architecture Forum, 2011 Annual Conference, May 31–June 5, 2011, 6. Regarding body vocabularies, Chappell and Nelson merely comment in passing on James's "lampooning [of] the behavior of Jamaican elites, including cigar-smoking, hard-drinking, and publicly sprawling white women." The lampooning is no doubt intentional, but we should also recall the discussion of the New Orleans "tricolor" balls, cited in Chapter 4; see Emily Clark, "Elite Designs and Popular Uprisings: Building and Rebuilding New Orleans, 1721, 1788, 2005," *Historical Reflections / Réflexions HIstoriques* 33/2, French Colonial Urbanism (Summer 2007), 174–175.

31. *The Creolization of American Culture*, for example, touches on works by a generation of American vernacular painters: George Caleb Bingham (1811–1879), James Henry Beard (1812–1893), and James Goodwyn Clonney (1812–1867), as well as Mount and the anonymous "Dancing for Eels 1820 Catharine Wharf." The author discovers degrees of useful visual reportage in their works about period music and dance practices.

32. That is, *Mustee*, which is a period term describing the racial classification of a person of seven-eighths Caucasian and one-eighth African ethnicity; hence, a "Creolean" identity. "Spanish Town" was the English settlement on the site of the Spanish-era capital, from 1534–1655; it was rebuilt after an earthquake and served as the seat of colonial administration until the 1870s. "Mama" bidding "sad Red Coats shift" implies a protective mother, escorting her daughter's debut in society, shooing away army officers who represent insufficiently prestigious marital prizes.

33. Black musicians had been an essential part of colonial armies: for example, the 1723 Virginia Militia Act allowed that "Such free Negroes, Mulattos or Indians, as are capable, may be listed and emploied as Drummers or Trumpeters." See Peter H. Wood, *Strange New Land: Africans in Colonial America* (Oxford: Oxford University Press, 1996/2003), 63. Wood likewise mentions the account of black drummer Mat Anderson playing and

teaching younger slave musicians at Thomas Jefferson's home (64). Bolster confirms black presence in maritime recruiting as well, citing black drummers playing for rendezvous ("rondy") at taverns. W. Jeffrey Bolster, *Black Jacks: African American Seamen in the Age of Sail* (Cambridge: Harvard University Press, 1998), 33–34. For drummers marking gatherings, see Charles Rappleye, *Sons of Providence: The Brown Brothers, the Slave Trade, and the American Revolution* (New York: Simon and Schuster, 2006), 108.

34. On colonial planters moving up the social scale by marrying their offspring—some the result of mixed-race liaisons—to European spouses, see Thomas Fiehrer, "Saint-Domingue/Haiti: Louisiana's Caribbean Connection," *Louisiana History: The Journal of the Louisiana Historical Association* 30/4 (Autumn 1989), 423–424. Sublette points out that, though nearly all planters in Saint-Domingue, for example, desired to retire in France, comparatively few were successful: the sugar fortunes were made by British and French merchants more often than by Caribbean planters. This made the effectuation of upwardly mobile matches for planters' offspring even more important. See Ned Sublette, *The World That Made New Orleans: From Spanish Silver to Congo Square* (Chicago: Chicago Review Press, 2008), 136–137.

35. Bond and Stinson describe the result of dance within such rituals as "superordinary states in which bodily feeling is heightened with a corresponding emotional and cognitive awareness or transformation," and point out that "bodily resonance"—that is, measurable physical and cognitive responses—can "occur in a range from high intensity excitement to feelings of relaxation and tranquility." Bond and Stinson, "I Feel like I'm Going to Take Off!" 56.

36. Gilbert, for example, cites "the historical role played by theatre in negotiating the suppressed fears and fantasies of colonizing nations." Helen Gilbert, "Black and White and Re(a) All Over Again: Indigenous Minstrelsy in Contemporary Canadian and Australian Theatre," *Theatre Journal* 55/4, Theatre and Activism (December 2003), 680.

37. Jeffrey D. Mason comments: "If social space itself is a field of contention, then social performance becomes a means of urging that contention, of expressing difference, asserting ownership and displaying relationship. Any action from concerted effort to choosing to attend an event can constitute a performative strategy." Jeffrey D. Mason, "Street Fairs: Social Space, Social Performance," *Theatre Journal* 48/3, Enacting America(n)s (October 1996), 307.

38. See James Maher, "Ethiopian Skits and Sketches: Contents and Contexts of Blackface Minstrelsy, 1840–1890," in Annemarie Bean, James V. Hatch, and Brooks McNamara, eds., *Inside the Minstrel Mask: Readings in Nineteenth-Century Blackface Minstrelsy* (Middletown, Conn.: Wesleyan University Press, 1996), 179–222. Rachel Sussman says, of the remarkable longevity and durability of minstrel tropes in American popular culture, "Minstrelsy was a way for white Americans to ignore the pressing issues of race, believing that the reality of slavery was as it was portrayed on the minstrel stage." Rachel Sussman, "The Carnavalizing of Race," *Etnofoor* 14/2 MASQUERADES (2001), 79.

39. See Smith, "The Creole Synthesis in the New World: Cultures in Contact," in *The Creolization of American Culture*, 28.

40. See, for example, Paul Gilroy, *The Black Atlantic: Modernity and Double-Consciousness* (Cambridge: Harvard University Press, 1995).

41. However, Sublette points out that "it was not primarily planters who got rich from sugar, but rather the merchants and bankers who made the trade possible. Almost all planters wanted to retire in France but few did." Sublette, *The World That Made New Orleans*, 136–137.

42. See, for example, Mordecai Noah's period account "High Life among the Coloured Folks," *New-York National Advocate,* March 18, 1825, quoted in Peter Buckley, "*Obi* in New York: Aldridge and the African Grove," *Romantic Circles,* Praxis Series. http://www.rc.umd.edu/praxis/obi/buckley/buckley.html. Accessed April 13, 2015.

43. See Marvin Edward McAllister, *White People Do Not Know How to Behave at Entertainments Designed for Ladies & Gentlemen of Colour: William Brown's African & American Theater* (Chapel Hill: University of North Carolina Press, 2013), 158.

44. "While the segregation system prevented Negroes from crossing the color line and participating in white activities and using white facilities, it was virtually powerless to prevent whites who so desired from mixing freely with Negroes in colored taverns, bawdyhouses, and dance halls. In these clandestine pursuits, the color line broke down completely. . . . It was quite common for white men and boys to frequent these Negro saloons 'to revel and dance . . . for whole nights with a lot of men and women of saffron color, or quite black, either slave or free.'" Roger A. Fischer, "Racial Segregation in Ante Bellum New Orleans," *American Historical Review* 74/3 (February 1969), 933.

45. Jonathan Dewberry, "The African Grove Theatre and Company," *Black American Literature Forum* 16 (1982), 129.

46. McAllister, "'White people do not know how to behave at entertainments designed for ladies and gentlemen of colour': A History of New York's African Grove/African Theatre," PhD dissertation, Northwestern University, 1997.

47. Of the conduct of whites attending the African Grove, Jonathan Dewberry says "The African Grove Theatre and Company had to be mobile when they started doing plays because the police were constantly raiding their performances, and pressuring them to stop performing, due to the rowdiness of the white members of the audience. William Over states that the whites had initially found it curious and amusing that a black company of actors was attempting to do Shakespeare, but that they later became very hostile." "New York's African Theatre: The Vicissitudes of the Black Actor," *Afro-Americans in New York Live and History* 3/2 (1979); quoted in Dewberry, "The African Grove Theatre and Company," *Black American Literature Forum* 6/4, Black Theatre Issue (Winter 1982), 129. For information on the assault upon Aldridge, see "Ira Aldridge," The New York African Free School Collection, New-York Historical Society. http://www.nyhistory.org/web/africanfreeschool/bios/ira-aldridge.html. Accessed April 13, 2015.

48. *Memoir and Theatrical Career of Ira Aldridge, the African Roscius*, in Bernth Lindfors, *Ira Aldridge, the African Roscius* (Rochester: University of Rochester Press, 2007), 23.

49. Lindfors says, "He was consistently praised for the manly vigor with which he played Othello," and for his "vigor, sensuality, and ardent passion as authentic markers of his race," while reviews alluded to his "polished professionalism, for here was a versatile actor who could play a variety of parts with equal skill." Bernth Lindfors, *Ira Aldridge: Performing Shakespeare in Europe 1852–1855* (London: Boydell and Brewer, 2013), 39, 71, 249.

50. A London paper, noting that he was "the first to make English theatricals popular in Berlin," reported that his earnings for the four nights his troupe appeared at the Royal Courter Theater . . . came to £364. 11s. 8d., equivalent to about £28,800 in the United Kingdom in 2010. Unspecified London newspaper, quoted in Lindfors, *Ira Aldridge Performing Shakespeare*, 79, n61. Lindfors notes further: "When Aldridge toured Europe, he proved a powerful audience attraction. Admiring crowds greeted him in Berlin, Vienna, and St. Petersburg. Students at Moscow University, hailing his Othello, unhitched his horse from his carriage and pulled him triumphantly through the streets. The king of Prussia bestowed upon him the Gold Medal of the First Class for Arts and Sciences, a distinction shared by only three others (Alexander von Humboldt, Gasparo Luigi Spontini, and Franz Liszt)." Lindfors, *Ira Aldridge, the African Roscius*, 74.

51. See Frances R. Botkin, "Revising the Colonial Caribbean: 'Three-Fingered Jack' and the Jamaican Pantomime," *Callaloo* 35, no. 2 (2012): 494–508.

52. Benjamin Moseley, *A Treatise on Sugar: With Miscellaneous Medical Observations* (1799; reprint Cambridge: Cambridge University Press, 2012). Caliban in *The Tempest* (inspired by descriptions of a shipwreck on the coast of Elizabethan Virginia) is only the most famous example of a number of "noble savages" in English language theater. See Rob Nixon, "Appropriations of *The Tempest*," for an example of a creole translation that makes Caliban's resistance explicit. Nixon, *Critical Inquiry* 13, no. 3, Caribbean and Africa (Spring 1987), 572–573.

53. Toussaint's Saint-Domingues revolutionaries were commonly described as "Black Jacobins," an explicit reference to Revolutionary France, and emigration from the island was tightly controlled due to fears that this Jacobin revolutionary fervor might spread to other slave populations around the Caribbean.

54. As Alan Richardson comments, "literary exoticism cannot easily be disentangled from political and economic developments," and *Obi* evoked similarly threatening allure in British colonies as did *vodou* in French." Richardson, "Romantic Voodoo: Obeah and British Culture, 1797–1807," *Studies in Romanticism* 32, no. 1 (Spring 1993), 4. De Quincey, Coleridge, Maria Edgeworth, and Wordsworth all authored poems or essays on Caribbean topics, especially including portrayals of creole characters (Edgeworth even makes an African American "Juba" a central figure in the first editions of her 1801 *Belinda*) and of *Obi* rituals. Ironically, Bristol, because its connections to the Caribbean involved investing in and shipping sugar, rather than Liverpool's more direct involvement in shipping slaves, became a center for abolitionism—so much so, that by 1800 there was literature that explicitly linked sugar to the traffic in human chattel. Moseley's 1799 *Treatise* in fact was a convoluted, pseudoscientific attempt to justify sugar as a source of physical health and well-being.

55. The parallels to both English and North European mumming traditions, and their theatricalized performance of various folk rituals, and more widely to European and Caribbean costuming and carnivalesque behaviors, are obvious. Syncretic Mumming traditions are found throughout the English-speaking Caribbean; see for example the "nation dances" employed in Christmas house-visiting rituals in the nineteenth century. Donald R. Hill, "West African and Haitian Influences on the Ritual and Popular Music

of Carriacou, Trinidad, and Cuba," *Black Music Research Journal* 18/1–2 (Spring–Autumn 1998), 185.

56. White makes this hierarchical distinction drawn between colonials and "European metropoles" explicit: "Elites also reestablished their belonging to French social structures and practices by echoing the material culture of their peers and kin in France, by asserting their privileged status through etiquette practices taught to the few, and by advertising their rank visually and materially through their food, posture, deportment, cleanliness, and dress. . . . Those in European metropoles obsessed about the progressive seasoning and degeneracy that might result from the presence of Europeans in the New World . . . [while] colonists themselves elaborated a more nuanced understanding of the differences between permanent and temporary transformations." See Sophie White, "Massacre, Mardi Gras, and Torture in Early New Orleans," *The William and Mary Quarterly* 70/3 (July 2013), 537.

57. Bernth Lindfors, *Ira Aldridge: The Early Years, 1807–1833* (Rochester: University of Rochester Press, 2011), 132.

58. W. T. Lhamon Jr., *Jump Jim Crow: Lost Plays, Lyrics, and Street Prose of the First Atlantic Popular Culture* (Cambridge: Harvard University Press, 2003).

## Chapter 3. Spaces, Whistles, Tags, and Drums

1. Ronni Armstead, "Las Krudas, Spatia Practice, and the Performance of Diaspora," *Meridians* 8/1, Representin': Women, Hip-Hop, and Popular Music (2008), 131.

2. Also in contrast to the more detailed individual case studies, this chapter spans a particularly wide historical range, demonstrating the recurrence and longevity of dominant culture's attempts to contain noise ever since the seventeenth century.

3. "Sound-as-communication-as-negotiation materializes in public space." Matt Sakakeeny, "'Under the Bridge': An Orientation to Soundscapes in New Orleans," *Ethnomusicology* 54/1 (Winter 2010), 19.

4. Michel de Certeau, *The Practice of Everyday Life*, Steven Randall, trans. (Berkeley: University of California Press, 1984), 106. Emphasis added.

5. For useful commentary on Western elite music's "clear bias toward the discrete, measurable pitch, and clean, clear production value," see Mary Russo and Daniel Warner, "Rough Music, Futurism, and Postpunk Industrial Noise Bands," *Discourse* 10/1 (Fall–Winter 1987–1988), 60–61.

6. "Slaves . . . were forced to rely upon orality and performance—and thus on ephemerality and subtlety—rather than on permanent material displays." Susan A. Phillips, "Crip Walk, Villain Dance, Pueblo Stroll: The Embodiment of Writing in African American Gang Dance," *Anthropological Quarterly* 82/1 (Winter 2009), 76. "In the broader colonial Caribbean, the control of sounds, noise, and rhythm was a similarly important condition for the definition and demarcation of space, and thus of identity." Martin Munro, "Music, Vodou, and Rhythm in Nineteenth-Century Haiti," *Journal of Haitian Studies* 14/2 (Fall 2008), 67.

7. Helen A. Regis, "Second Lines, Minstrelsy, and the Contested Landscapes of New Orleans Afro-Creole Festivals," *Cultural Anthropology* 14/4 (November 1999), 486–487. We will further unpack this and other examples in Chapter 4 on the French Caribbean.

8. The classic texts include Attali's *Noise: The Political Economy of Music* and Bakhtin's study of the carnivalesque in his seminal *Rabelais and his World*. On Attali, see Russo and Warner, "Rough Music, Futurism, and Postpunk," 59. On the Rabelaisian elements of U.K. punk rock (cited in Chapter 8), see Peter Jones, "Anarchy in the UK: '70s British Punk as Bakhtinian Carnival," *Studies in Popular Culture* 24/3 (April 2002), 26.

9. "Shocks, crackling, and atmospherics are noises in a radio transmission. A white or black spot on a transmission screen, a gray fog, some dashes not belonging to the transmitted message, a colored spot of ink on a newspaper, a tear in page of a book, a colored spot on a picture are 'noises' in visual messages. A rumor without foundation is a 'noise' in a sociological message." All Moles quotes from Abraham Moles, *Information Theory and Esthetic Perception*, Joel E. Cohen, trans. (Urbana: University of Illinois Press, 1968), 78; quoted in Russo and Warner, "Rough Music, Futurism, and Postpunk," 60.

10. Ibid.

11. As Robert Allen puts it, "insubordination is resistance contained by discourse: the temporary and circumscribed upsetting of another group's symbolic ordering—graffiti, rude noises at the back of the classroom, the hiss, the boo." Allen, *Horrible Prettiness: Burlesque and American Culture* (Chapel Hill: University of North Carolina Press, 1991), 33.

12. See Dale A. Cockrell, *Demons of Disorder: Blackface Minstrels and Their World* (Cambridge: Cambridge University Press, 1997).

13. Dale Cockrell, "Jim Crow, Demon of Disorder," *American Music* 14/2 (Summer 1996), 174.

14. Robert Allen comments, "The very low otherness of the blackface minstrel allowed him to serve as a vehicle for a displaced, bottom-up critique of the social order." Allen, *Horrible Prettiness*, 170. See also Cockrell, *Demons of Disorders*; Lott, *Love & Theft: Blackface Minstrelsy and the American Working Class* (New York: Oxford University Press, 1993); William J. Mahar, *Behind the Burnt Cork Mask: Early Blackface Minstrelsy and Antebellum American Popular Culture* (Urbana: University of Illinois Press, 1998).

15. Paraphrasing Bakhtin, for example, Halnon cites musical bodies' carnivalesque "spasms, tensions, popping eyes, convulsions of arms and legs, or hanging tongues" as examples. Karen Bettez Halnon, "Heavy Metal Carnival and Dis-alienation: The Politics of Grotesque Realism," *Symbolic Interaction* 29/1 (Winter 2006), 37. This "spasmodic" physical language of the carnivalesque will be especially relevant in the discussion of Josephine Baker, ahead.

16. See also Violet Alford, "Rough Music, or Charivari," *Folklore* 70/4 (1959): 505–506; and Jack Santino, "The Ritualesque: Festivals, Politics, and Popular Culture," *Western Folklore* 68/1 (Winter 2009), 17.

17. Stout and Onuf quote a period source asserting that "of all the disorderly practices of [his] followers, singing in the streets, at the top of their lungs, often at night, was most disturbing to public order," while a July 1741 account of public worship at New London, Connecticut, describes Davenport and his followers screaming, singing, and praying, in the throes of massed public fervor. Harry S. Stout and Peter Onuf, "James Davenport and the Great Awakening in New London," *Journal of American History* 70/3 (December 1983),

568. "Diverse women were terrified and cried out exceedingly. When Mr. Davenport had dis-missed the congregation some went out and others stayed; he then went out into the broad alley, which was much crowded, and there he screamed out, 'Come to Christ! come to Christ! come away! come away!' Then he went into the third pew on the women's side, and kept there, sometimes singing, sometimes praying; he and his companions all taking their turns, and the women fainting and in hysterics. This confusion continued till ten o'clock at night, and then he went off singing through the streets" (569).

18. Peter Smith, "Cane Ridge Meeting House 1801: Revival Reverberates Today: Seminal Event's Bicentennial Celebrated," *Courier-Journal*, July 30, 2001. https://www.aarweb.org/sites/default/files/pdfs/Programs_Services/Journalism_Award_Winners/2002Smith.pdf. Accessed August 9, 2015.

19. Tricia Rose, *Black Noise: Rap Music and Black Culture in Contemporary America* (Middletown, Conn.: Wesleyan University Press, 1994).

20. "The Spy," *New-York Weekly Journal*, March 7, 1736. Quoted in Jeroen DeWulf, "Pinkster: An Atlantic Creole Festival in a Dutch-American Context," *Journal of American Folklore* 126/501 (Summer 2013), 262.

21. Wall says, "That carnivalesque symbolic formations center around anxious constructions of class and race is made nowhere more explicit than in official responses to the popularity of Negro Election Days and Pinkster celebrations. . . . In the symbolic realm of bourgeois consciousness, carnivalesque images of the distorted and exaggerated grotesque body always appear as the terrifying racial and social Other." David Wall, "'A Chaos of Sin and Folly': Art, Culture, and Carnival in Antebellum America," *Journal of American Studies* 42/3, Film and Popular Culture (December 2008), 525–526. Period account quoted by Cockrell, *Demons of Disorder*, 33. Mark McKnight, "Charivaris, Cowbellions, and Sheet Iron Bands: Nineteenth-Century Rough Music in New Orleans." *American Music* 23/4 (Winter 2005), 412.

22. See Raymond W. Smilor, "Personal Boundaries in the Urban Environment," *Environmental Review* 3 (Spring 1979), 26: "Responding to public pressure, cities began to pass ordinances to eliminate din." In a particularly sophisticated examination of antinoise ordinances in Gilded Age Chicago, Derek Vaillant shows that such regulation "encouraged insidious forms of cultural bias to gain purchase on certain persons and soundscapes [and] permitted biased cultural preferences to creep into the law and the idealized body politic that the law constructed and listened for." Vaillant adds, "Aural scrutiny and policing would remain a powerful mechanism in future determinations of permissible attributes of public culture so important in shaping the character of the nation." Vaillant, "Peddling Noise: Contesting the Civic Soundscape of Chicago, 1890–1913," *Journal of the Illinois State Historical Society (1998-)* 96/3 (Autumn 2003), 275.

23. Yablon says, "In particular, it was the mobile quality of these various urban sounds, more than any quantifiable increase in their volume, that finally prompted civic elites to search for various measures that would act as auditory bulwarks protecting residential spaces." Nick Yablon, "Echoes of the City: Spacing Sound, Sounding Space, 1888–1916," *American Literary History* 19/3 (Autumn 2007), 632. Yablon finds additional persuasive

evidence of progressives' desire to control urban noise in Bellamy's utopian novel *Looking Backward* (1888) and Norris's *The Pit: A Story of Chicago* (New York: Doubleday, Page and Co., 1903), 630–631.

24. Raymond W. Smilor, "Cacophony at 34th and 6th: The Noise Problem in America, 1900–1930," *American Studies* 18/1 (1977), 30–31. For additional consideration of the class issues implicit in Rice's campaign, see also Peter Andrey Smith, "The Society for the Suppression of Unnecessary Noise," *The New Yorker*, January 11, 2013: "Rice argued that the city's poor, particularly the insane and the sick, confined in public hospitals along the East River, on Randall's and Blackwell's islands, suffered miserably on account of tugboat noise." https://www.newyorker.com/culture/culture-desk/the-society-for-the-suppression-of-unnecessary-noise. Accessed April 1, 2018.

25. Emily Thompson, *The Soundscape of Modernity* (Cambridge: MIT Press, 2002), 124.

26. Vaillant, "Peddling Noise," 259.

27. Founded in 1905, the IWW was a power in labor organizing until 1919, when post-WWI paranoia and government repression led to widespread crackdowns, police violence, assassinations, and deportations. However, their ethos of Solidarity ("an injury to one is an injury to all") was a powerful influence upon later, non–craft-specific union organizers like Cesar Chavez and Lech Walesa.

28. "You will eat, bye and bye / In that glorious land above the sky / Work and pray, live on hay / You'll get pie in the sky when you die." Joe Hill, *Songs of the Workers to Fan the Flames of Discontent: The Little Red Songbook* (Philadelphia: Industrial Workers of the World, 2005).

29. Ray Stannard Baker, *American Magazine*, 1912, quoted in Aaron Brenner, Benjamin Day, and Immanuel Ness, *The Encyclopedia of Strikes in American History* (New York: Routledge, 2015), 109.

30. Robin D. G. Kelley, "'We Are Not What We Seem': Rethinking Black Working-Class Opposition in the Jim Crow South," *Journal of American History* 80/1 (June 1993), 76.

31. Ibid., 75, on singing as a safer, metaphor-driven version of passive resistance.

32. *Grayned v. City of Rockford*, 408 U.S. 104 (SCOTUS 1972); No. 705106; argued January 19, 1972. http://law.justia.com/lawsearch?query=noise%20ordinance%20%22new%20orleans%22. Accessed August 30, 2014.

33. Raymond W. Smilor, "Personal Boundariesin the Urban Environment," 30. Mimesis in sound and movement is a very significant part of the inheritance of West Africa into the Caribbean and North America. As with the Gullah children's dance (imitating a "jancrow"), which became "Jump Jim Crow" in the performances by the blackface minstrel George Washington Dixon (1801?–1861), antebellum theatrical sources describe the mimetic whistling of multiple blackface performers; see George C. D. Odell, *Annals of the New York Stage* (New York: Columbia University Press, 1927–1949), IV, 426–427; quoted in Delmer D. Rogers and E. T. S., "Public Music Performances in New York City from 1800 to 1850," *Anuario Interamericano de Investigacion Musical* 6 (1970), 35.

34. However, there is a rich history to be written about use of the subversive whistle by other subaltern cultures, precisely because of its elusive, nearly invisible dynamics. See for example Allison Hoffman's comments on the European Yiddish tradition; she mentions

Lauren Bacall's "Put your lips together, and blow," in *To Have and Have Not* (1944), Sophie Tucker whistling along with her band's instrumental breaks, and Pesakh'ke Burstein (1896–1986), scion of an American theater dynasty, and "a Plish performer nicknamed *der Pfeifer*—or the Whistler, in Yiddish—who delighted audiences with his rakish Jack Nicholson grin and jaunty whistling choruses." Allison Hoffman, "Whew! The Unsung Art of Whistling Returns," *Forward,* March 11, 2005. http://forward.com/articles/3086/whew-the-unsung-art-of-whistling-returns/. Accessed August 7, 2015. The whistle appears as interruptive or transgressive in classical history as well; see the discussion of whistling in the Homeric hymns in T. L. Agar, "The (Homeric) Hymn to Hermes," *Classical Quarterly* 20/2 (April 1926), 84; but even Agar recognizes the North American association with minstrelsy archetypes.

35. Joan Wescott, "The Sculpture and Myths of Eshu-Elegba, the Yoruba Trickster. Definition and Interpretation of Yoruba Iconography," *Africa: Journal of the International African Institute* 32/4 (October 1962), 347, 352.

36. There is a particularly direct transfer of interruptive festival behaviors (both sound and motion in space) between Haiti and New Orleans, discussed in Chapter 4. On the use of whistles as part of Rara and Mardi Gras Indian processions, see Helen A. Regis, "Second Lines, Minstrelsy, and the Contested Landscapes of New Orleans Afro-Creole Festivals," *Cultural Anthropology* 14/4 (November 1999), 385. On whistles as part of syncretic Caribbean/Quebecois Carnival, see Marcia Gaudet, "'Mardi Gras, Chic-a-la-Pie': Reasserting Creole Identity through Festive Play," *Journal of American Folklore* 114/452, Southwestern Louisiana Mardi Gras Traditions (Spring 2001), 165, 166, 170. It should also be noted that, although this chapter primarily engages with the physical act of whistling, the physical object called the whistle is likewise distributed throughout both European and Afro-Caribbean festival traditions. In addition to those mentioned in the text, other iconic uses of mechanical whistles in Afro-Caribbean traditions include the samba whistles of Brazilian *Carnivale,* and the presence of tin whistles in Jamaican mumming and the New Orleans–based Mardi Gras Indians tradition. See Michael P. Smith, "Behind the Lines: The Black Mardi Gras Indians and the New Orleans Second Line," *Black Music Research Journal* 14/1, Selected Papers from the 1993 National Conference on Black Music Research (Spring 1994), 48.

37. Dena J. Epstein provides period sources that describe slaves who "without teaching, whistle, and sing, and play on the Jews' harp and banjo and with a little practice master that difficult instrument, the violin." Epstein, "Slave Music in the United States before 1860: A Survey of Sources (Part 2)," *Notes* Second Series 20/3 (Summer 1963), 381.

38. Ronald Radano, "On Ownership and Value," *Black Music Research Journal* 30/2 (Fall 2010), 365. Emphasis added. Radano quotes an advertisement that describes one runaway as being "'fond of whistling, which he performs in a peculiar manner with his tongue."

39. Kristina Wirtz says "That 'strange whistle' . . . became a staple trope of blackface . . . authenticity up to [Al] Jolson." Wirtz, "A 'Brutology' of Bozal: Tracing a Discourse Genealogy from Nineteenth-Century Blackface Theater to Twenty-First-Century Spirit Possession in Cuba," *Comparative Studies in Society and History* /4 (2013), 827. Shane White, "'It Was a Proud Day': African Americans, Festivals, and Parades in the North, 1741–1834," *Journal*

*of American History* 81, no. 1 (June 1994), 23. "Bobolink Bob" Rowley, an antebellum street musician from Long Island, was recognized as a champion whistler; White confirms that, in New York, "whistling was called 'Negro Pinckster Music' long after the (Afro-Dutch Pentecost) festival itself had died." For Bob Rowley, see W. T. Lhamon Jr., *Raising Cain: Blackface Performance from Jim Crow to Hip Hop* (Cambridge: Harvard University Press, 1998), 4; and Christopher J. Smith, *The Creolization of American Culture* (Urbana: University of Illinois Press, 2013), 87. Seeley Simpkins, one of Dan Emmett's major influences, could play fiddle and banjo, call dances, and "outwhistle all creation": Norton (1862) says of Simpkins that, in an underpopulated Ohio where it "took four counties to make a [militia] regiment," he "gave a challenge to outwhistle any man within them" and was undefeated." On Simpkins, see Norton (1862), 16–17, quoted in Howard L. Sacks, "From the Barn to the Bowery and Back Again: Musical Routes in Rural Ohio, 1800–1929," Phillips Barry Lecture, *Journal of American Folklore* 116/461 (Summer 2003), 317. It should also be noted that whistling's mimetic birdsong imitations were rooted deeply in African American expressive culture, as is implied in "Bobolink," Bob Rawley's nickname; even Thomas Dartmouth Rice's iconic song, "Jump Jim Crow," may have been rooted in observations of the Afro-Caribbean "jancrow" dance and song. See Smith, *The Creolization of America Culture*, 141.

40. "Tucky Squash" is an archetypal slave-era name, often used for comic theatrical characters, and based upon the West African word *Quashee* (Akan) or "Sunday," from the habit of naming a child after the day of the week upon which she or he was born. See "Quashee," dictionary.com. http://bit.ly/1JODQZI. Accessed August 30, 2014. See Washington Irving, *Salmagundi and Voyages and Discoveries of the Companions of Columbus*; from *The Works of Washington Irving* V (New York: The Co-operative Publication Society, Inc., n.d.), quoted in Smith, *Creolization of American Culture*, 36.

41. Mark Twain, *The Adventures of Tom Sawyer*. Project Gutenberg. http://www.gutenberg.org/files/74/74-h/74-h.htm. Accessed September 26, 2018. Emphasis added. The archetypal Twain citation of the minstrel show is his nostalgic panegyric to the form in Charles Neider, ed., *The Autobiography of Mark Twain* (New York: Harper Collins, 1959), 58–59.

42. See, for example, Anthony J. Beret, "Huckleberry Finn and the Minstrel Show, *American Studies* 27/2 (Fall 1986), 37–49.

43. The derogatory *pickaninny* (for an African American child) probably derives from the Spanish *pequeño* ("little, small") or Portuguese *pequenino* ("small one, young one"). http://bit.ly/1ISJrok. Accessed August 8, 2015. Apropos later influence, Autumn Rhea Lauzon calls Topsy an "archetypal character"; see Rhea Lauzon, "Just Another 'Poke in the Ribs': Calvinist Humor in Uncle Tom's Cabin," *Studies in American Humor* New Series 3/24, Special Issue: Funny Girls: Humor and American Women Writers (2011), 20.

44. Harriet Beecher Stowe and Hollis Robbins (annotations), *The Annotated Uncle Tom's Cabin*. (New York: W. W. Norton and Company, 2007), 250. Topsy's whistle also recurs at moments of emotional intensity: "'No; she can't bar me, 'cause I'm a nigger!—she'd 's soon have a toad touch her! There can't nobody love niggers, and niggers can't do nothin'! *I* don't care,' said Topsy, beginning to whistle" (295). For Du Bois's classic formulation of African American "double consciousness," see W. E. B. Du Bois, *The Souls of Black Folk* (New York: Arc Manor, 2008), 12.

45. Johnson subsequently developed a secondary specialization, even more popular, in recording one-off cylinders of his "Laughing Song."

46. "Brooks and Spottswood claim that he could even whistle the new 'Washington Post March' recently introduced by Sousa's U.S. Marine Band." See Joshua Gunn, "Canned Laughter," *Philosophy & Rhetoric* 47/4, EXTRAHUMAN RHETORICAL RELATIONS: Addressing the Animal, the Object, the Dead, and the Divine (2014), 434; Tim Brooks and Richard Keith Spottswood, *Lost Sounds: Blacks and the Birth of the Recording Industry, 1890–1919* (Urbana: University of Illinois Press, 2004), 27.

47. For example, Stephen Nunn provides an excellent and detailed exegesis of whistling in the career of Billy Golden (1858–1926), who recorded a whistled version of the pop song, "Listen to the Mocking Bird," and, with Joe Hughes, "Whistling Pete" (1911), a "vaudeville sketch." See Nunn, "'Rabbit Hash': Billy Golden, a Critical Biography," *Musical Quarterly* 79/4 (Winter 1995), 595–600 and n47.

48. See John Kenrick, *Al Jolson: A Biography* (2003). http://bit.ly/1Tbo6AG. Accessed August 7, 2015. In the mythologizing *Jolson Story*, a 1946 biopic for which Jolson himself provided the soundtrack's sung and whistled vocals, his character "charm[s] a cabaret crowd by peppering his breakthrough performance with birdcalls." Hoffman quotes the bio-pic's dialog: "'Wait a minute, I tell ya, you ain't heard nothin'! Do you wanna hear 'Toot, Toot, Tootsie'? All right, hold on, hold on . . . Lou, Listen. Play 'Toot, Toot, Tootsie!' Three choruses, you understand. In the third chorus I whistle. Now give it to 'em hard and heavy. Go right ahead!" Allison Hoffman, "Whew! The Unsung Art of Whistling Returns." http://forward.com/articles/3086/whew-the-unsung-art-of-whistling-returns/. Accessed August 7, 2015. See Lott, *Love & Theft*, for more on the paradoxical empowerment to "say the unsayable" which the minstrel mask conferred upon working-class white performers.

49. A grand jury declined to indict Bryant and Milam; protected by the law against double jeopardy, they later gave interviews confirming that they had murdered Emmett Till. See Hugh Stephen Whitaker, "A Case Study in Southern Justice: The Murder and Trial of Emmett Till," *Rhetoric and Public Affairs* 8/2, Special Issue: 50 Years Later: Emmett Till, Rosa Parks, and Martin Luther King Jr. (Summer 2005), 201.

50. Tricia Rose, "'Fear of a Black Planet': Rap Music and Cultural Politics in the 1990s," *Journal of Negro Education* 60/3, Socialization Forces Affecting the Education of African American Youth in the 1990s (Summer 1991), 277.

51. On hobo symbols, used to communicate essential information regarding safety, food, and housing, see https://www.nsa.gov/about/cryptologic-heritage/museum/exhibits/#history_of_hobos. Accessed April 1, 2018. For "Kilroy," see Jerold E. Brown, *Historical Dictionary of the U.S. Army* (New York: Greenwood, 2001), 264.

52. In the 1980s, there were widespread attempts to ban the sale of markers and aerosol cans to persons under 18, precisely because of their association with graffiti writing.

53. As a Manhattan resident in the 1970s, I remember the very wide prevalence of tags all over the exterior and interior of the subway cars.

54. Rose's *Black Noise*, invaluable here as on a number of other aspects of hip hop aesthetics, provides an excellent discussion and analysis of graffiti writers' origins, aesthetics, and battles with hegemonic forces. Rose, *Black Noise*, 44–47.

55. Susan Phillips calls graffiti writing a "counterliteracy," while Sally Banes points out that the graffiti writers created "networks for socializing, writing graffiti, and rapping, as well as dancing, [which were] held together by a strict code of ethics and loyalty." Phillips, "Crip Walk, Villain Dance, Pueblo Stroll: The Embodiment of Writing in African American Gang Dance," *Anthropological Quarterly* 82/1 (Winter 2009), 75. Sally Banes, ed., *Writing Dancing in the Age of Postmodernism* (Middletown, Conn.: Wesleyan University Press, 2011), 148.

56. Derek Conrad Murray, "Hip-Hop vs. High Art: Notes on Race as Spectacle," *Art Journal* 63/2 (Summer 2004), 19.

57. Richard Faulk, *The Next Big Thing: A History of the Boom-or-Bust Moments That Shaped the Modern World* (New York: Houghton Mifflin Harcourt, 2015), 167.

58. Karen McCarthy Brown, "Art and Resistance: Haiti's Political Murals, October 1994," *African Arts* 29/2, Special Issue: Arts of Vodou (Spring 1996), 56.

59. Certeau, *Practice of Everyday Life*. Emphasis added.

60. Ibid.

## Chapter 4. A Tale of Two Cities II

1. Tremé, "All on a Mardi Gras Day" (dir. David Simon, HBO, 2010). The reference is to the Mardi Gras Indian tribes of New Orleans street festivals; see discussion later.

2. This chapter is also heavily informed by the remarkably detailed, rigorous, yet empathetic writing of Matt Sakakeeny (cited later) on New Orleans street music and culture.

3. Alternate candidates to anchor the North American node of this analysis (see earlier and Chapter 2) might be French Mobile or Natchez, both very early settlements, which like New Orleans were intended to link French Quebec and the Gulf; or Charleston, a British town but with a long history of hosting French refugees from Huguenots to Haitian planters; or even Pensacola, an early Spanish outpost. However, by the 1780s, New Orleans was the most significant *port* south of New York and by the postbellum period would surpass its volume of shipping.

4. For the argument that the Spanish occupation shaped New Orleans expressive culture particularly strongly, especially in the wake of French neglect and several catastrophic fires, see Ned Sublette, *Cuba and Its Music* (Chicago: Chicago Review Press, 2004). For information on the impact of Kongo-born Cuban slaves in New Orleans during this period, see Sublette, and Gwendolyn Midlo Hall, *Africans in Colonial Louisiana: The Development of Afro-Creole Culture in the Eighteenth Century* (Baton Rouge: LSU Press, 1992), 119–155. Fiehrer says that between May 1809 and January 1810, "shiploads of Saint-Dominguais began arriving from eastern Cuba at New Orleans. . . . The total influx doubled the city's population." Thomas Fiehrer, "Saint-Domingue/Haiti: Louisiana's Caribbean Connection," *Louisiana History: The Journal of the Louisiana Historical Association* 30/4 (Autumn 1989), 431.

5. Sublette, *Cuba and Its Music*, 107.

6. Ibid., 165–167.

7. The earlier principle port city, Cap-Haïtien, on the north coast, was highly significant in the earlier colonial period, but from the mid–eighteenth century, Port-au-Prince was the locus of colonial government and the target of revolutionary military campaigns.

8. Richard Brent Turner, for example, describes two waves of Haitian immigration: one in the 1790s, most of whose population went to the English-speaking colonies of Charleston, Philadelphia or Baltimore because the Spanish government in New Orleans was worried about importing Haitian slaves, precisely because of their potential for "revolutionary infection"; the second, in 1809–1810, arriving after a relatively brief sojourn in Santiago de Cuba (which sojourn strongly impacted Afro-Caribbean culture in the eastern end of that island). See Turner, "The Gede in New Orleans: Vodou Ritual in Big Chief Allison Tootie Montana's Jazz Funeral," *Journal of Haitian Studies* 12/1 (Spring 2006), 98.

9. See Sublette, *Cuba and Its Music*, 174.

10. Thompson describes *placage* as resulting from "liaisons between white men and women of color, [which placed] the women in roles that ranged the gamut from the temporary concubine to the lifelong common law wife." Shirley Thompson, "'Ah Toucoutou, ye conin vous': History and Memory in Creole New Orleans," *American Quarterly* 53/2 (June 2001), 242.

11. There is considerable literature on the recent street culture of the Mardi Gras Indians and the parallel-but-separate city traditions of brass bands and Second Line parades, but the historical, sociological, political, cultural, and geographical dynamics specifically of street *dance* in NOLA have not been so extensively theorized. See, for example, in addition to those elsewhere cited: Ned Sublette, *The World That Made New Orleans: From Spanish Silver to Congo Square* (Chicago: Chicago Review Press, 2008); Jason Berry, "African Cultural Memory in New Orleans Music," *Black Music Research Journal* 8/1 (1988), 3–12; Jason Berry, with Jonathan Foose and Tad Jones, *Up from the Cradle of Jazz: New Orleans Music since World War II* (Lafayette: University of Louisiana at Lafayette Press, 2009); Joseph Roach, "Carnival and the Law in New Orleans," *TDR (1988-)* 37/3 (Autumn 1993), 42–75; Helen A. Regis, "Second Lines, Minstrelsy, and the Contested Landscapes of New Orleans Afro-Creole Festivals," *Cultural Anthropology* 14/4 (November 1999), 472–504; Michael P. Smith, "Behind the Lines: The Black Mardi Gras Indians and the New Orleans Second Line," *Black Music Research Journal* 14/1, Selected Papers from the 1993 National Conference on Black Music Research (Spring 1994), 43–73; Richard Brent Turner, "Mardi Gras Indians and Second Lines/Sequin Artists and Rara Bands: Street Festivals and Performances in New Orleans and Haiti," *Journal of Haitian Studies* 9/1 (Spring 2003), 124–156; Turner, "The Gede in New Orleans" ; and George Lipsitz, "Mardi Gras Indians: Carnival and Counter-Narrative in Black New Orleans," *Cultural Critique* 10, Popular Narrative, Popular Images (Autumn 1988), 99–121.

12. See Roach on the French Caribbean's "racially transgressive behaviors," in addition to festivals, which included also *placage* (the generally accepted business arrangements between white men and mixed-race mistresses) and "the attractions of the Quadroon Balls," at which Creole women regularly initiated such contracts with likely patrons. Roach, "Carnival and the Law," 57. On the Quadroon balls, see also Alan C. Turley, "The Ecological and Social Determinants of the Production of Dixieland Jazz in New Orleans," *International Review of the Aesthetics and Sociology of Music* 26/1 (June 1995), 112; and Arnold R. Hirsch and Joseph Logsdon, eds., *Creole New Orleans: Race and Americanization* (Baton Rouge: LSU Press, 1992), 146.

13. Emily Clark, "Elite Designs and Popular Uprisings: Building and Rebuilding New Orleans, 1721, 1788, 2005," *Historical Reflections / Réflexions HIstoriques* 33/2, French Colonial Urbanism (Summer 2007), 174–175.

14. Ibid. Emphasis added.

15. R. Randall Couch mentions the 1817 foundation of the Orleans Theater and Ballroom, managed by "an enterprising *émigré*," Edward Bertus, who was also a dance instructor "from the French island of Saint-Domingue," which Latrobe visited. Couch provides an excellent, detailed, and lengthy description of its attendees in the 1820s, as class boundaries were steadily eroded in the same period; Couch, "The Public Masked Balls of Antebellum New Orleans: A Custom of Masque outside the Mardi Gras Tradition," *Louisiana History: The Journal of the Louisiana Historical Association* 35/4 (Autumn 1994), 413, 416, 418. He also describes, by the late 1820s, the attendance of some high-society women who came disguised as courtesans precisely in order to seek anonymized sex (418).

16. Hirsch and Logsdon, *Creole New Orleans*, 144.

17. Pierre Clément de Laussat, *Memoires of My Life to My Son during the Years 1803 and After*, Sister Agnes-Josephine Pastwa, trans., Robert D. Bush, ed. (Baton Rouge: LSU Press, 1978), 92–93.

18. Moreover, Jerde confirms that events occurring on saloon stages reflected, and were reflected in, dance events in the street: he cites a growth in black music activity in the "last decade of the eighteenth century [which] began primarily in connection with dance activity . . . had strong association with the growth of a pervasive street and saloon ambiance." See Curtis D. Jerde, "Black Music in New Orleans: A Historical Overview," *Black Music Research Journal* 10/1 (Spring 1990), 18. For more on the early attempts to contain black street dance expression, see also Smith, "Behind the Lines," 47.

19. Sublette mentions the flight of white colonials after the 1770 earthquake in Port-au-Prince, and Lachance cites Saint-Dominguais migrations to the east coast of North America by 1793, to Jamaica by 1798, and to Cuba by 1805. Sublette, *Cuba and Its Music*, 108.

20. Paul F. Lachance, "The 1809 Immigration of Saint-Domingue Refugees to New Orleans: Reception, Integration and Impact," *Louisiana History: The Journal of the Louisiana Historical Association* 29/2 (Spring 1988), 110.

21. Thomas Fiehrer, "Saint-Domingue/Haiti," 431–432. Lachance says that 10,000 "displaced colonials" came from Saint-Domingue via Cuba to New Orleans in 1809. Lachance, "The 1809 Immigration," 109–110.

22. Both Sublette and Jerde confirm that open-air dancing experienced explosive growth in popularity during the years of the Spanish occupation 1763–1801; Jerde suggests that this growth was in part due to the expansion of the slave population during this period: "Open-air dancing, [which was] permitted pragmatically . . . as a measure of control, probably did not necessitate the imposition of statutory proscription until the slave population had increased as significantly as it did in the 1780s." Sublette, *The World That Made New Orleans*, 74. Jerde further cites a 1786 law that "forbade slaves to dance in public squares on Sundays and holy days until the close of the evening service" and thus tended to confirm that efforts at containment were already well in place two decades

before Latrobe's visit. Jerde, "Black Music in New Orleans," 19. Panetta points out that "hogface" (erotic) dancing was accepted in African American New Orleans nightclubs but not in the street, in the late nineteenth century. See Vincent J. Panetta, "'For Godsake Stop!': Improvised Music in the Streets of New Orleans, ca. 1890," *Musical Quarterly* 84/1 (Spring 2000), 20.

23. In fact, Latrobe's widely cited descriptions from 1807 may not have been made at Congo Square's current location (on the north side of the Vieux Carre, between the Quarter and Fauborg Tremé) at all, but rather at the regular weekly "market of the Congolese" held in present-day Jackson Square—a much more logical location, convenient to the levee, and at the heart of the Quarter's nineteenth-century cultural life. By the 1750s, *La Place des Negres* was already well-established, and Tremé (on the north side of the Quarter, the later site of Place Congo) was already known as a neighborhood of Haitian expatriates. See Turner, "The Gede in New Orleans," 98, 133. Donaldson cites the pre–*Place Congo* history of the city's attempts to control public mixed-race dance gatherers, including sources that indicated that by 1786 dancing throughout the city was already viewed as a problem, and describing examples from 1799 of "vast numbers of negro [*sic*] slaves, men, women, and children assembled together on the levee, drumming, fifing and dancing in large rings," and from 1808 of dancing at various locations throughout the City. See Gary A. Donaldson, "A Window on Slave Culture: Dances at Congo Square in New Orleans, 1800–1862," *Journal of Negro History* 69/2 (Spring 1984), 64. As Roach puts it: "Law . . . tends eventually to annex the ludic space at its margins simply by *legalizing the offenses it declines to prosecute.* Carnival becomes law." Roach, "Carnival and the Law," 45. Emphasis added.

24. Matt Sakakeeny, "New Orleans Music as a Circulatory System," *Black Music Research Journal* 31/2 (Fall 2011), 295.

25. Richard Brent Turner says, "The concept of the Kongo crossroads was transported across the Atlantic Ocean to Haiti and New Orleans where it was recreated in music, dance and material art performances that consecrated special locations." Turner, "Mardi Gras Indians," 129.

26. Rachel Breunlin and Helen A. Regis, "Putting the Ninth Ward on the Map: Race, Place, and Transformation in Desire, New Orleans," *American Anthropologist,* New Series 108/4 (December 2006), 746.

27. See Berry, Foose, and Jones, "In Search of the Mardi Gras Indians," in *Up from the Cradle of Jazz.*

28. Roach, in fact, points out that the reality of African American and Native American cultural exchange in the Mississippi Valley "sets up a potentially subversive alternative to an uncontested narrative of exclusive Anglo/European expansion as world-historical inevitability." Roach, "Carnival and the Law," 58. Michael P. Smith connects the Indians to "the independent, self-protected marches of the Maroons, or Afro-Creole people, who, on Sundays during the eighteenth and early-nineteenth centuries, emerged from their various sanctuaries and workplaces in and around the city to gather in the central marketplace." Smith, "Behind the Lines," 55. A persuasive argument for the roots of the Indians' masking and marching in vodoistes ceremonial processions through alien neighborhoods is

Turner, "Mardi Gras Indians," 133–136. Sublette also confirms this in *The World That Made New Orleans*, 174. Turner provides a sophisticated summary of the complex strains of cultural influence that shaped Indian identity: "When people started masking Indian on carnival days in the late nineteenth century, Black New Orleanians were continuing a rich heritage of slave resistance [including]: a complex African maroon culture involving traditional and cultural exchanges with local Native American tribes; the cross-fertilization of Haitian and New Orleanian vodou that happened in Congo Square; the reinterpretation of African ceremonial music and dance in new jazz performance cultures; and the survival of a beautiful Creole 'gumbo people' caught up in a vicious color caste system." Turner, "Mardi Gras Indians," 140. Sakakeeny likewise points out that "between 1860 and 1910, the black population of New Orleans quadrupled and the number of black musicians and music teachers more than doubled," and has described the pre-jazz street musics that emerged as "less of a specialized art form than an everyday activity based on performance practices that were antithetical to the rigidity of European American performance, including collective improvisation, audience participation, rhythmic syncopation and repetition, and the use of pentatonic scales and blue notes." Sakakeeny, "New Orleans Music," 309.

29. Hirsch and Logsdon, for example, explicitly link the intermarriage of slaves and Native Americans to resistance movements and make a concrete historical argument that dominant-culture attempts to curb the rebellious capacities of subaltern communities *and* their carnivalesque mixed-race expressive cultures emerged from well-founded paranoia. Hirsch and Logsdon state, "A number of African slaves had been involved in key ways with the [1729] Natchez revolt. For a decade the slave population and the Indian population had increasingly intermarried. African slaves, mostly males, had taken wives from among the female Indian slave population, and runaway African slaves had often moved into Indian communities or formed mixed Indian-African maroon settlements." Hirsch and Logsdon, *Creole New Orleans*, 38. They also cite the impact of Bambara slaves on rebellions through the 1730s (76).

30. Averill and Wilcken date the earliest documentation of Rara-style songs to the Taino, the now-extinct indigenous people of the island. See Gage Averill and Lois Wilcken, "Haiti." In *The Garland Encyclopedia of World Music, Vol. 2: South America, Mexico, Central America, and the Caribbean*, ed. Dale A. Olsen and Daniel E. Sheehy (New York: Garland Publishing, 1998), 881–895. Likewise, Nesin provides useful and succinct information about Taíno influence on Haitian culture; see Barbara Nesin, "The Influence of Native American and African Encounters in Haitian Art," *Journal of Haitian Studies* 11/1 (Spring 2005), 77–78.

31. Cited in Ned Sublette, "The Art of Prayer," 9. https://bombmagazine.org/articles/the-art-of-prayer/. Accessed November 9, 2018.

32. Michael Largey, "Politics on the Pavement: Haitian Rara as a Traditionalizing Process," *Journal of American Folklore* 113/449 (Summer 2000), 243. An excellent survey of the idiom, which significantly informs the present discussion, is Elizabeth A. McAlister, *Rara! Vodou, Power, and Performance in Haiti and Its Diaspora, Volume 1* (Berkeley: University of California Press, 2002), 6.

33. McAlister describes Rara as "large groups of poor people going down the roads making noise," and calls it "a potential weapon in the peasants' ongoing power struggle

against the elite." See Elizabeth McAlister, "New York, Lavalas, and the Emergence of Rara," *Journal of Haitian Studies* 2/2 (Autumn 1996), 133. In addition to the fearful reaction described in Moreau de St. Méry's account from the 1780s at the height of anti-Jacobin paranoia, Rara was also suppressed during the economic Depression of the 1920s and '30s, and again under the authoritarian regimes of the Duvaliers, Lafontant, and Cédras.

34. McAlister, *Rara! Vodou, Power, and Performance*, 4.

35. Gaudet provides a good summary of the close connections between both urban and rural Mardi Gras costuming in Louisiana and that which obtains in Rara. See Marcia Gaudet, "'Mardi Gras, Chic-a-la-Pie': Reasserting Creole Identity through Festive Play," *Journal of American Folklore* 114/452, Southwestern Louisiana Mardi Gras Traditions (Spring 2001), 165–166. Roach points out that, in addition to the appropriateness of celebrations in the liminal period between the license of Carnivale and the abstention of Lent, in these cities that were built in part on the Sugar Trade, Mardi Gras/Carnivale falls just at the close of the sugar harvest. Roach, "Carnival and the Law," 56.

36. Susan Elizabeth Tselos, "Threads of Reflection: Costumes of Haitian Rara," *African Arts* 29/2 Special Issue: Arts of Vodou (Spring 1996), 61. On the other hand, the dance vocabularies of Rara and the Indians differ, with the former emphasizing footwork and pelvic motion, while the latter uses the expansion/contraction of the torso and the akimbo motions of elbows, knees, feet, and head associated with African American mimesis and the roots of blackface dance: the archetype is the crooked "wheeling and turning" of "Jump Jim Crow." See discussion of blackface body vocabulary, Christopher J. Smith, *The Creolization of American Culture* (Urbana: University of Illinois Press, 2013), 177–178.

37. See Tselos, "Threads of Reflection," 58. Averill and Wilcken cite, in the presence of *Majò jòn* (stick twirler), an "exuberant and sensual celebratory ethos." Averill and Wilcken, "Haiti." As we have seen, whistling, whether by employing mechanical aids or through simple manipulation of the tongue, lips, and larynx, has been a common feature in transgressive creole idioms throughout the hemisphere, from Rara and the Mardi Gras Indians to blackface minstrelsy to early vaudeville and the subversive physical comedy of the "mute" Harpo Marx.

38. R. B. Turner, "Mardi Gras Indians and Second Lines," 132.

39. Berry, for example, cites an 1823 report from St. Martinville, Louisiana (founded by voyageurs around 1700 on Bayou Teche near present-day Lafayette), which describes "fantastic dances" by mixed-race participants outside the church on Sundays. Bettleheim even points out the consistency of color coding in Caribbean contexts, demonstrating the consistency with which New World *lwas* and *orishas* are costumed in colors associated with their West and Central African antecedents: "combined with specific performative codes, or standardized choreographic moves, [these] may have developed initially as a form of covert communication." Judith Bettelheim, "Women in Masquerade and Performance," *African Arts* 31/2, Special Issue: Women's Masquerades in Africa and the Diaspora (Spring 1998), 70; Berry, "African Cultural Memory," 6.

40. On this point, Jeffrey Anderson's summation merits citation at length, precisely because of its close parallels with New Orleans Indian behavior: "Rara performances are produced primarily by the rural class and comprise numerous throngs that cover the roads and snarl traffic with boisterous music and animated dance maneuvers. Motorists

who dance in their seats are waved through the crowds, while other motorists unmoved by the music must pay a small toll to drive through the streets. The Rara bands are not haphazardly structured, but rather are organized by several key members. The concept behind Rara is generally a sacred promise to a *lwa* or group of *lwa*. . . . Rara bands perform consecratory ceremonies and extensive rehearsals in the weeks leading up to Easter Sunday. . . . While performing, the band leader directs his group with a whistle or whip to cajole the street marchers or dancers along. . . . The rather rigid organization of musical discipline and coarse language serves both a sacred and profane purpose. In fact, Rara songs tend to venerate obscene situations and/or contain references to political topics and historic events. Rara's association with lower-class roots, vodou congregations, and secret societies has won for it a poor reputation among Christian elites and the secular middle classes of Haiti." Jeffrey E. Anderson, *The Voodoo Encyclopedia: Magic, Ritual, and Religion* (New York: ABC-CLIO, 2015), 195–196.

41. As Roach says, "carnival and the law both offer themselves as surrogates for more overt forms of violence." Roach, "Carnival and the Law," 53. In all likelihood, this results from the two traditions' shared origins in street tactics employed by subaltern peoples in antagonistic urban geographies; as Sakakeeny points out, there is a political strategy at work in such paraded sound, which "draws attention to . . . the durability of shared cultural traditions." Matt Sakakeeny, "'Under the Bridge': An Orientation to Soundscapes in New Orleans," *Ethnomusicology* 54/1 (Winter 2010), 21.

42. Echoing a statement made by music educator and ethnomusicologist Christopher Small (see Chapter 8), Rebecca D. Sager has argued, in the specific case of vodou and its secular sibling Rara, "During vodou festivals, aesthetically engaging performance forms a way to control and create a properly ordered time and social space that lasts for the duration of the performance." Rebecca D. Sager, "My Song Is My Bond: Haitian Vodou Singing and the Transformation of Being," *The World of Music*, 51/2, Music for Being (2009), 93.

43. McAlister, *Rara! Vodou, Power, and Performance*, 7. Emphasis added. Hunt says that "Many of the dances that Moreau de Saint Méry saw in St. Domingue just prior to the revolution were also performed by free blacks and slaves in Congo Square some ten years later." The calinda, for example, was a dance of African origin. Another dance brought to New Orleans by black St. Dominigans is the bamboula. Alfred N. Hunt, *Haiti's Influence on Antebellum America: Slumbering Volcano in the Caribbean* (Baton Rouge: LSU Press, 2006), 78.

44. "Embodied practice": Jess McAllister, "Listening for Geographies," 35. http://soundcloud.com/jess_mcallister/. Accessed November 9, 2018. George Lipsitz, "Mardi Gras Indians: Carnival and Counter-Narrative in Black New Orleans," *Cultural Critique* 10, Popular Narrative, Popular Images (Autumn 1988), 115.

45. Lipsitz, "Mardi Gras Indians," 102–103.

46. "The openness of New Orleans society was greatly enhanced by the ecology of the city and its surrounding cypress swamps and luxuriant waterways. The maroon communities of escaped African and Indian slaves that began during the first half of the eighteenth century evolved into permanent settlements under Spanish rule. By the 1780s, a stable community almost entirely made up of creole slaves had created maroon

villages in the swamps surrounding the city." Hirsch and Logsdon, *Creole New Orleans*, 76. Conventionally, this maroon connection is cited as origin of the appellation "Mardi Gras *Indian*" and of the elaborate "Indian suits," though the likelier factual explanation is the influence of late-nineteenth-century theatrical entertainments like Bill Cody's Wild West Show (which toured to NOLA in 1884 and 1885). See Willam E. Deahl, "Buffalo Bill's Wild West Show in New Orleans," *Louisiana History: The Journal of the Louisiana Historical Association* 1975, 289–298. However, a significant percentage of distinguished New Orleans music families attribute Native American ethnicity to themselves (for example, the Neville Brothers), and certainly Choctaw, Black Creeks, and Seminoles are as much a part of the city's ethnic mythography as are Creoles and *gens de coloeur*; see Jim Faber, "'Buried History': Unearthing the Influence of Native Americans on Rock'n'roll," *The Guardian* (July 19, 2017). Retrieved September 28, 2018. Roach also cites historical examples of Africans "masking Indian" during the Seminole Wars (1816–1819; 1835–1842, and 1855–1858), the 1790s Haitian revolutions, and the 1811 Louisiana uprising, though it would be more accurate to recognize that escaped slaves and mixed-race persons might well have fought on the anticolonists' side simply because of their own reinvented ethnic self-identification. See Roach, "Carnival and the Law," 59. Michael Smith provides a persuasive and nuanced understanding of the "maroon rites of passage" shared in common between working-class social and fraternal organizations like the Indians, the Cuban *cabildos*, the Brazilian *Escolas do samba*, and the Haitian *Raraistes*. "In today's New Orleans, in each club or location where the gangs practice, a complicated cultural ritual unfolds, empowered by traditional drumming, tribal dance, and oral poetry in which the various participants, including women and children, interact according to maroon rites of passage." Smith, "Behind the Lines," 62. Emphasis added.

47. In writing on New Orleans, Matt Sakakeeny suggests situating such "research on African continuities . . . 'on the ground,' . . . by expanding the field of inquiry to accommodate the exceptional levels of diversity, interaction, racial mixing, and cultural creolization," which obtained throughout the city and indeed throughout the French and Spanish Caribbean. Sakakeeny, "New Orleans Music," 293.

48. As Regis puts it: "The collective ownership of the streets, that is experienced by participants of the second line, has important political implications. It works against the numerous forces that create atomization in urban neighborhoods and increase the difficulty of building civil society across physical and social distance." Helen A. Regis, "Blackness and the Politics of Memory in the New Orleans Second Line," *American Ethnologist* 28/4 (November 2001), 756. In another article on New Orleans, Regis describes the "lived landscape [that] is produced through both the quotidian practices of spatial apartheid and the transformative practices of the second line which subverts and transcends those patterns." Regis, "Second Lines, Minstrelsy," 475–476.

49. As Lorraine Leu says of contemporaneous *soca* (soul-calypso) parades in Trinidad, "the space opened up by the crowd gathering to share the experience of [soca] poses a threat to the order police are trying to restore." Lorraine Leu, "'Raise Yuh Hand, Jump Up and Get on Bad!': New Developments in Soca Music in Trinidad," *Latin American Music Review / Revista de Músic Latinoamericana* 21/1 (Spring–Summer 2000), 48. Other parallels

that resonate throughout the case studies discussed in this book include the crackdowns on gang dances in the South Bronx in the early 1980s; see Jeff Chang, *Can't Stop Won't Stop: A History of the Hip Hop Generation*, 62; see also Yippie use of Japanese snake-dancing to resist crowd containment by police (cited in Chapter 8).

50. As Roach puts it, in the case of New Orleans, "carnival and the law obviously still provide antagonistic sites for the playing out of the cultural politics of racial identity and difference. Both . . . have operated as agents of cultural transmission . . . yet both have also served as instruments of contestation and change." Roach, "Carnival and the Law," 44.

51. Jess McAllister says of *Rara* that it "shaped the space into a pulsating, vibrating, energized place," while Helen A. Regis says that the Second Line (the impromptu dancers who follow Indians and brass bands) "through the transformative experience of the parade . . . *become owners of the streets*." McAllister, "Listening for Geographies," 25; Regis, "Second Lines, Minstrelsy," 478. Breunlin and Regis provide a particularly elegant interpretation of the marching bands' use of retaining ropes—like the velvet rope at an exclusive nightclub—as portable means of delineating the mobile "insider"/liminal versus "outsider"/spectator spaces of the band in the road versus the spectators on the sidewalk. See Breunlin and Regis, "Putting the Ninth Ward on the Map," 754.

52. McAlister says "The distinction between audience and performer is erased as soon as it is constructed." McAlister, *Rara! Vodou, Power, and Performance*, 6. Emphasis added. And Regis says, of New Orleans: "The second line takes people in. it incorporates all those who will move to its music, who become a single flowing movement of people unified by the rhythm. . . . In incorporating [all of] them, it recasts them into different roles, creating relationships that would not otherwise be possible in everyday life, which is dominated by the moral economy of the postindustrial city." Regis, "Second Lines, Minstrelsy," 480.

53. Ibid., 484.

## Chapter 5. Utopian Movements and Moments

1. Randy Martin, *Critical Moves: Dance Studies in Theory and Practice* (Durham: Duke University Press, 1998), 1.

2. Ames, for example, an early historian of the Ghost Dance, explicitly links under "crowd movements": "the Indian ghost-dance, the religion of the American negro, [and] the Scotch-Irish revival in Kentucky in 1800." Edward S. Ames, "The Psychology of Religion II," *The Biblical World* 49/4 (1917), 256.

3. A number of North American utopian communities—particularly those that espoused nontraditional gender roles and sexual prescriptions—have made dance and other pleasurable bodily activities such as team sports, swimming, physical exercise, and/or nudity, central media for their rejection of mainstream restrictions. See, for example, Wagner on the Oneida community (1840s), but also the Northampton Association of Education and Industry (also 1840s), and more recent scholarship than Wagner's on the Shakers (from the 1770s onward). Ann Wagner, *Adversaries of Dance: From the Puritans to the Present* (Urbana: University of Illinois Press, 1997), 181–182; Christopher Clark, "A Mother

and Her Daughters at the Northampton Community: New Evidence on Women in Utopia," *New England Quarterly* 75/4 (December 2002), 596, 619; Janet Sarbanes, "The Shaker 'Gift' Economy: Charisma, Aesthetic Practice, and Utopian Communalism," *Utopian Studies* 20/1 (2009), 123–124; James Isaac, Irwin Altman, and Jamie Isaac, "Interpersonal Processes in Nineteenth Century Utopian Communities: Shaker and Oneida Perfectionists," *Utopian Studies* 9/1 (1998), 26–49.

4. It is, of course, important to recognize that these were not the only subaltern groups in North American history who engaged in utopian dance—implicit rebellion against bourgeois sexual and economic politics was at least as strong in the 1920s Jazz Age and 1960s hippy-era dance cultures, for example. However, it is fair to say that Protestant Shakers and animist Ghost Dancers are among the best known, explicitly *religious* (and utopian) dance communities in U.S. history, and to suggest that they thus serve as a reasonable template for our analysis.

5. Bourguignon speaks in detail about brain function in such states and about "ecstatic dance . . . as a psychokinetic experience of the dancer and as an aesthetic-religious experience of the spectators." See Erika Bourguignon, *A Cross-cultural Study of Dissociational States* (Columbus: The Ohio State University Foundation, Ohio State University, 1968), 57.

6. See Julie Nicoletta, "The Gendering of Order and Disorder: Mother Ann Lee and Shaker Architecture," *New England Quarterly* 74/2 (June 2001), 303.

7. "Treatise Concerning the Religious Affections." "It is plain the Scripture often makes use of bodily effects to express the strength of holy and spiritual affections; such as trembling, groaning, being sick, crying out, panting and fainting (*Works of President Edwards Vol. III*, (New York, [no publisher indicated] 1869), 27. Quoted in Peter Oliver, "'Probationers for Eternity': Notes on Religion in the United States in the Year 1800," *Harvard Theological Review* 37/3 (July 1944), 229, n46.

8. See Edward D. Andrews, "Shaker Songs," *The Musical Quarterly* 23/4 (October 1937), 507: "For introducing the dance into their worship, the Shakers suffered severe criticism and persecution. They were charged with indulgence in the wildest orgies; with fiddling, telling fortunes, playing cards, drunkenness, and most often, dancing naked."

9. There is actually very little primary source documentation of historical events in the Shakers' early history. Because they were opposed to dogma and prioritized personal and "revealed" experience, most of the factual history of the sect and of Mother Ann herself was written much later—in the Era of Manifestations. So it is difficult to separate factual biographical data from hagiographic revisionism in her story. See Martha Ellen Stortz, "Ritual Power, Ritual Authority: Configurations and Reconfigurations in the Era of Manifestations," in *Religious and Social Ritual: Interdisciplinary Explorations*, Michael B. Aune, and Valerie DeMarinis, eds. (Albany: SUNY Press, 1996), 115. See also Stephen J. Stein, *The Shaker Experience in America: A History of the United Society of Believers* (New Haven: Yale University Press, 1994), 3–4.

10. See Christopher J. Smith, "The Creole Synthesis in the New World: Cultures in Contact," in *The Creolization of American Culture*, (Urbana: University of Illinois Press, 2013), 28–78.

11. Stortz, "Ritual Power, Ritual Authority," 116.

12. Later in the 1830s, for example, Emerson and other cultured literati visited and commented disparagingly upon the communities' subversion of bourgeois behavior and bodily politics; these commentators include James Fenimore Cooper, Nathaniel Hawthorne, Herman Melville, and Horace Greeley among others. See Flo Morse, *The Shakers and the World's People* (Lebanon, N.H.: University Press of New England, 1987), xvi. Stein, *The Shaker Experience in America*, 101, quotes the account of a traveler in South Union, Kentucky (1810), who saw "'42 women formed in a Solid Column ranging each way, but facing toward a body of about the Same number of Men formed in like manner all Singing & Jumping with Very exact time & Step, or rather Jump and with much to the tune and words Sung . . . at the end of about a Minute every person on the floor Jumped quite round but without Moving out of Spot, & this exercise Continued at least 14 or 20 Minutes when they all Clapped hands for about half a minute & then all Stood Still." Other observers reported seeing sect members being "seized with a mighty trembling . . . a mighty shaking . . . occasionally exercised in singing, shouting, or walking the floor . . . shoving each other about—or swiftly passing and repassing each other," and similarly transgressive movement behaviors. Stortz, "Ritual Power, Ritual Authority," 116.

13. As architecture scholar Arthur McLendon puts it: "Both the Shakers and their meetinghouse embodied belief in a unique rhythmic convergence of the built and human geometries of celestial order." McLendon, "Leap and Shout, Ye Living Building! Ritual Performance and Architectural Collaboration in Early Shaker Meetinghouses," *Buildings & Landscapes: Journal of the Vernacular Architecture Forum* 20/2 (Fall 2013), 51.

14. McLendon contrasts the Shaker architecture with earlier Congregationalist and Anglican designs: "Where columns, boxed pews of fixed seating, and upper galleries [had] focused static audience attention on an elevated pulpit, the Shakers instead created an unobstructed horizontal space for freedom of movement during dance worship that could be easily adaptable to movable seating as needed." McLendon, "Leap and Shout, Ye Living Building!" 50.

15. See Leigh Eric Schmidt, *Holy Fairs: Scotland and the Making of American Revivalism* (Grand Rapids, Mich.: William Eerdmans, 2001), 24.

16. They also built churches as they came: for example, Ambrose Maulding (1755–1833, a Revolutionary War veteran, built first a fort (1780) and then a church (after 1789) at Red River, near present-day Adairville. http://bit.ly/1LAn3Ki. Accessed June 30, 2015.

17. At Cane Ridge, "[The meeting house's] capacity depended, in large part, on a gallery or balcony that extended toward the raised side-wall pulpit from three sides. . . . *Although often referred to as a slave gallery* and reached by a steep outside staircase or ladder, this space was too large, and too much needed, to be restricted to blacks." See Paul Keith Conkin, *Cane Ridge: America's Pentecost*. http://bit.ly/13TIq6p,78. August 30, 2014. Emphasis added. The integrated—or at least socially fluid—environment of the "slave gallery" thus parallels that of the third and fourth tiers in nineteenth-century working-class theaters previously discussed.

18. In Randolph County in western North Carolina, minister Samuel E. McCorkle observed participants to be all manner of people, including as many blacks as whites."

Letters by Samuel M'Corkle, quoted in Paul Keith Conkin, *Cane Ridge: America's Pentecost* (Madison: University of Wisconsin Press, 1990), 110. On the impact of Cane Ridge upon later Shakerism in Free-State Ohio, see Anne Grimes, "Possible Relationship between 'Jump Jim Crow' and Shaker Songs," *Midwest Folklore* 3/1 (Spring 1953), 52. Also Stortz, "Ritual Power, Ritual Authority," 118: "The earliest converts to Shakerism . . . were often people from other revival movements." Nancy Kirkland Klein, "Music and Music Education in the Shaker Societies of America," *Bulletin of Historical Research in Music Education* 11/1 (January 1990), 37.

19. Frontier Shakers also claimed to receive songs and dances as visions from various informants (including "Indian" ones). See Grimes, "Possible Relationship between 'Jump Jim Crow,'" 51, 53. Grimes cites "shuffling" dance steps in slave-worship as "another Shaker clue," but we should recall here the very old and virtually ubiquitous Afro-Christian dance ceremony of the ring-shout and its secular cousin, the *calinda*, recognizing the equivalent possibility that the movement influence went also in the opposite direction (54). Sublette finds citations of the calinda/calenda as early as 1654, and groups it with dances that tended to travel from port to port in the Caribbean, including Saint-Domingue, Havana, and New Orleans. See Ned Sublette, *The World That Made New Orleans: From Spanish Silver to Congo Square* (Chicago: Lawrence Hill Books, 2008), 74.

20. See, for example, William Bartram describing Cherokee dance in 1791: "They have an endless variety of steps, but the most common . . . and indeed the most admired and practiced among themselves, is a slow, shuffling alternate step; both feet move forward one after the other, first the right foot foremost, and next the left, moving one after the other, in opposite circles . . . the men with the course of the sun, and the females contrary to it." William Bartram, *Travels through North & South Carolina, Georgia, East & West Florida . . . Containing an Account of the Soil and Natural Productions of Those Regions, Together with Observations on the Manners of the Indians* (Philadelphia: James and Johnson, 1791), 505; reproduced at UNC-CH digitization project *Documenting the American South*. http://docsouth.unc.edu/nc/bartram/bartram.html. Accessed July 7, 2015.

21. Martin describes a series of [Native American] "prophetic resistance movements from before 1616." Martin, *Critical Moves*, 683.

22. Ibid., 693. As Martin observes: "in several significant Native American religious revolts, the prophets and the initiated attached crucial importance to learning new bodily gestures, especially new sacred dances."

23. Kathryn E. Holland Braund, "The Creek Indians, Blacks, and Slavery," *Journal of Southern History* 57/4 (November 1991), 602–603.

24. Ibid., 606. This is the other end of the slave trade that established Melungeons from Barbados in the southwestern Appalachians by the mid–eighteenth century (see Chapter 1, "Sacred Bodies in the Great Awakenings"). Among the peoples of African ethnicity in the western slope, some were Afro-Caribbeans, while others were escaped slaves arrived only recently directly from Africa. Braund, "The Creek Indians," 612.

25. Ibid., 606–607. As Braund points out, the vast majority of black slaves working for Europeans were of necessity bilingual; this would have facilitated their escape and assimilation into Native communities (623).

26. Ibid., 617. Braund summarizes aptly, saying, "Blacks were a common sight to all Muscogulges by the middle of the eighteenth century." Braund, "The Creek Indians."

27. See Emisteseguo ("The Big Fellow"); see also Coushatta chief Alexander McGillivray, Nanyehi ("Nancy Ward"), William Weatherford, Peter McQueen, Mico William McIntosh, many others. Braund, "The Creek Indians," 609–619.

28. Gwendolyn Midlo Hall makes the point that many intra-Native conflicts were a result of white settlement, pointing out that, in this period, Choctaw and Chickasaw were allies to opposite sides in the Seven Years' War. Hall, *Africans in Colonial Louisiana* (Baton Rouge: LSU Press, 2018), 14–16.

29. Lawrence E. Sullivan, "Song and Dance: Native American Religions and American History," *Religion and American Culture: A Journal of Interpretation* 4/2 (Summer 1994), 271. See also Reginald Laubin and Gladys Laubin, *Indian Dances of North America: Their Importance to Indian Life* (Norman: University of Oklahoma Press, 1989), 52ff, which likewise situates the late-nineteenth-century Ghost Dance within a longer history of revivals and revolutionary dance.

30. McLoughlin points out that these tensions were sometimes as fierce between indigenous and mixed-race persons as they were between indigenous people and whites and notes the complex role of mixed-race people, most of whom were better equipped to adopt, adapt, and assimilate to white encroachment. William G. McLoughlin, "New Angles of Vision on the Cherokee Ghost Dance Movement of 1811–1812," *American Indian Quarterly* 5/4 (November 1979), 327. Braund comments, "In many ways the Creek War was a reaction to the new materialism of the mixed-blood elite by non-slaveholding traditionalists who hoped to oppose American expansion by revitalizing Indian culture and driving out those who practiced commercial agriculture." Braund, "The Creek Indians," 631.

31. Martin, *Critical Moves*, 678, 681.

32. Steven A. Littleton, *Voices of the American Indian Experience* (New York: ABC-CLIO, 2013), 196.

33. Sullivan, "Song and Dance," 268, 270. Emphasis added. See also Sugden, who quotes period descriptions of Creek who would "shake their bodies in the ritualistic manner of other supporters of the Shawnee Prophet." John Sugden, "Early Pan-Indianism: Tecumseh's Tour of the Indian Country, 1811–12," *American Indian Quarterly* 10/4 (Autumn 1986), 287. Emphasis added.

34. "Some of the [Creek] females are mutilating fine muslin dresses and are told they must o their dancing reels and country dances which have become very common amongst the young people." McLoughlin, "New Angles of Vision," 119, 127. The revivalist rejection of European semiotics was explicit: "Kill the old chiefs, friends to peace; kill the cattle, the hogs and fowls; do not work, destroy the wheels and looms, throw away your ploughs and everything used by the Americans. Sing 'the song of the Indians of the northern lakes and dance their dance.'" Benjamin Hawkins, *American State Papers: Documents, Legislative and Executive of the Congress of the United States, Part 2, Volume 1*, Walter Lowrie and Matthew St. Clair Clark, eds. (Washington, D.C., 1831), 4/845.

35. Martin, *Critical Moves*, 684–685, 688. Sullivan describes the Muskogee revolts as "the cauldrons where preexisting worldviews clash and fuse and where views of a New World emerge for parties on all sides of the confrontation."

36. Sullivan, "Song and Dance," 270.

37. The aftermath of the Creek War, which ended in their defeat at the hands of Andrew Jackson and the 1814 Treaty of Fort Jackson, ceded millions of acres to the U.S. government. Tribe members who declined to surrender escaped to Florida and were part of the Seminole coalition, continuing resistance until the 1819 Adams-Otis Treaty forced Spain to cede Florida to the U.S. government as well. By 1829, with the inauguration of Andrew Jackson, harsher government policy culminated with the forced removal of southeastern tribes to Oklahoma—the infamous Trail of Tears.

38. This kind of paradoxical "revival" or "rediscovery," exactly coincident with the eradication of indigenous communities, is replicated throughout the nation's colonial history: as only one example, the first extensive ethnographic fieldwork among Native American peoples (Alice Fletcher, born 1838) actually predated the massacre at Wounded Knee (1890), and followed within three years of the Sioux victory over Custer's Seventh Cavalry at Greasy Grass (1876). Jacob Gruber has called this impulse, which recurs in many late-colonial situations, "salvage ethnomusicology"; he suggests the same was already in operation in the case of Native Americans by the late 1840s. Gruber, "Ethnographic Salvage and the Shaping of Anthropology," *American Anthropologist* New Series 72/6 (December 1970), 1295.

39. Of course, it is axiomatic that the exchange of sacred constructs was not mono- but unidirectional—the evidence is clear that Shakers borrowed aspects of Native American practice but that Creek and Cherokee millenarianism, for example—like the later Western Ghost Dance—were strongly influenced by Christian Pentecostalism as well. In the Creek War, the prediction that if the nation were to sufficiently purify itself, the "souls of the dead [would] come back to life" concurs with Shaker belief. Michelene E. Pesantubbee, "When the Earth Shakes: The Cherokee Prophecies of 1811–12," *American Indian Quarterly* 17/3 (Summer 1993), 303. In addition to resurrectionism, Shakers and Native Americans shared beliefs in: sacred gifts from the dead, dance as numinous experience, and sacred baths for purification. See McLoughlin, "New Angles of Vision," 328, and compare to sacred ablutions in the late Ghost Dance (Laubin and Laubin, *Indian Dances of North America*, 58).

40. George Eaton Simpson, "Afro-American Religions and Religious Behavior," *Caribbean Studies* 12/2 (July 1972), 5–30. Moreover—and perhaps not coincidentally—the Shaker repertoire of dances and songs is immensely enriched in this period with a much wider rhythmic vocabulary, most notably in the much extended use of meters of 6/8 and 3/4. This may reflect the influence of Afro-Caribbean polymetric practices. See Klein, "Music and Music Education," 39.

41. Stortz, "Ritual Power, Ritual Authority," 118.

42. Ibid., 119.

43. Ibid., 123–127. Stortz cites the tension present in charismatic communities when they seek to evolve past the leadership of the Founders: in the Era of Manifestations, this pattern of consolidation, censure, and regularization led Shaker authorities to prioritize "scientific" and rhetorical discourse over experiential bias. See also Clark, "A Mother and Her Daughters," 619.

44. Estella T. Weeks and Ernest W. Baughman, "Shakerism in Indiana: Notes on Shaker Life, Customs, and Music," *Hoosier Folklore Bulletin* 4/4 (December 1945), 72.

45. Nicolas de la Salle's 1682 expedition down the Mississippi Valley recorded similar dancing. At the other end of the historical continuum, Silvia King, interviewed as part of the WPA's Texas Slave Narratives ca. 1930, provides a richly-detailed recollection: "De black folks gits off down in de bottom and shouts and sings and prays. Dey gits in de ring dance. It am jes' a kind of shuffle, den it git faster and faster and dey gits warmed up and moans end shouts and claps and dances. Some gits 'xhausted and drops out and de ring gits closer. Sometimes dey sings and shouts all night, but come break of day, de nigger got to git to he cabin. Old Marse got to tell dem de tasks of de day." http://bit.ly/1H4GIi9. Accessed July 3, 2015. See also Gary A. Donaldson, "A Window on Slave Culture: Dances at Congo Square in New Orleans, 1800–1862," *Journal of Negro History* 69/2 (Spring 1984), 68. On Native American circle dances, see Laubin and Laubin, *Indian Dances of North America*, 62. See also the 1791 epigraph that opens this chapter. Both Key and Rosenbaum explicitly link the Afro-Caribbean ring-shout and Native American circle dances in the southeast. "The slavery time 'shout' consisted of moving about in a ring, shuffling the feet along inch by inch, sometimes dancing silently, but more frequently singing spirituals. 'The foot is hardly taken from the floor, and the progression is mainly due to a jerking, hitching motion, which agitates the entire shouter, and soon brings out streams of perspiration.'" Joseph Patrick Key, "The Calumet and the Cross: Religions Encounters in the Lower Mississippi Valley," *Arkansas Historical Quarterly* 61/2 (Summer 2002), 157; Margo M. Rosenbaum, *Shout because You're Free* (Athens: University of Georgia Press, 1998), 18–19. See also discussion of the hip-hop "cipher," Chapter 7.

46. Weeks and Baughman say that "either one shook out of oneself all latent evil . . . or one shook to invite the operations of the Spiritual Force, the Power of the Almighty." The passage, at greater length, further nuances the statement: "The Shakers taught that one . . . should 'shake' one's whole body, or some particularly tense parts of it, into a state of relaxation, even unto a trance-like state . . . in order to being one into communion with the supernatural—the spiritual world—and so into a condition receptive to wisdom, to song, to admonishment and guidance by way of messages. . . . Either one shook out of oneself all latent evil . . . or one shook to invite the operations of the Spiritual Force, the Power of the Almighty." Weeks and Baughman, "Shakerism in Indiana,"65–66, 71. Stortz links these convictions to Turner's theory of liminality, mapping ritual's capacity to dislodge as well as to reinscribe social structures: "What if chaos, plurality, and polyphony could be entertained as values as well? What if ritual were seen both to present and to resolve chaos? What if ritual were to begin and end, not only in structure, but in indeterminacy as well?" Stortz, "Ritual Power, Ritual Authority," 122.

47. Regarding dance-as-opposition, Stortz quotes Catherine Bell to the effect that "ritualization is a strategic play of power, *of domination and resistance*, within the arena of the social body," and suggests that "only such a broadly dialectical understanding of ritual and ritualizations will enable us to understand the ritual practices in the Shaker Era of Manifestations." Stortz, "Ritual Power, Ritual Authority," 123.

48. Weeks and Baughman, "Shakerism in Indiana," 69.

49. In Northampton, Massachusetts, for example, Carter provides a remarkable image of the African American activist Sojourner Truth's (1797–1893) daughters dancing

a secular waltz at a summer picnic attended by Shakers in 1844. Clark, "A Mother and Her Daughters," 618.

50. African American converts from the Cumberland, for example, brought variants of Shaker trance and dance back to the Caribbean islands, where Shaker doctrine blended again with a complex network of syncretic Afro-Protestant belief systems. Simpson cites the "Spiritual Baptists (Shakers) of St Vincent. In this group, the trancer 'jerks, rocks, trembles, but there is no patterned choreography and he does not move far." Simpson, "Afro-American Religions," 5–30. See M. G. Smith; see also Pitts on the ring-shout, "praying bands," and "*runnin sperchils*." Smith describes these sects: "occupying a position at one extreme of sectarian Protestantism are the Shouters, Shakers, or Spiritual Baptists, who combine spirit-possession, divination, the use of cabalistic signs and other ritual differentiae with a liturgy and ethic of 'Protestant' character. At the other, Catholic extreme of this dimension of folk religion are Shango or the African Dance, and its forerunner the Big Drum or Nation Dance cult." M. G. Smith, "Dark Puritan: The Life and Work of Norman Paul," *Caribbean Quarterly* 5/1 (June 1957), 34. As William Suttles puts it, "the connections between some kind of secretive or "occult" religious exercises and violent rebellion seem fundamental to understanding the progressive history of exploited groups in the Americas. The connection was evidenced in some of the fateful struggles between the Spanish and Amerindians in the sixteenth century, and it *was still operative in the Ghost Dance Religion that initiated the North American Sioux Outbreak in 1890*." William C. Suttles Jr., "African Religious Survivals in American Slave Revolts," *Journal of Negro History* 56/2 (April 1971), 98. Emphasis added.

51. "Gullah Jack, one of [Denmark] Vesey's lieutenants in the insurrection in South Carolina in 1822, was regarded as a sorcerer. Like the sorcerers during the Haitian revolution, he convinced his followers that his charms would make them invulnerable. In addition, it was believed that Jack would provide all the arms needed for the revolt." N. N. Puckett, *Folk Beliefs of the Southern Negro* (Chapel Hill: University of North Carolina Press, 1926), 284. Quoted in Simpson, "Afro-American Religions," 19–20.

52. Little Wound at Pine Ridge, 1890, immediately prior to the massacre at Wounded Knee. *New York Times*, November 23, 1890. Quoted in in Rani-Henrik Andersson, *The Lakota Ghost Dance of 1890* (Lincoln: University of Nebraska Press, 2008), 207. He continued, with great poignancy in light of the subsequent massacre, "I have also understood that I was not to be recognized as a chief any longer. All that I have to say to that is neither you nor the white people made me a chief and you can throw me away as you please, but let me tell you, Dr. Royer, that the Indians made me a chief, and by them I shall be so recognized so long as I live. . . . We do not intend to stop dancing."

53. Wovoka a/k/a "Jack Wilson" (1856–1932) "in Washington and Oregon . . . had contact with Shakers and Dreamers. Their doctrines, coupled with the Christian teachings he had received . . . fired him dreams of glory and achievement." Laubin and Laubin, *Indian Dances of North America*. His rough contemporary, the Lakota chieftain Kicking Bear, for example, described a Ghost Dance vision in which he journeyed by railroad to consult with the Great Spirit. See also Scott L. Pratt, "Wounded Knee and the Prospect of Pluralism," *Journal of Speculative Philosophy*. New Series 19/2 (2005), 151.

54. Laubin and Laubin, *Indian Dances of North America*, 63.

55. Joel W. Martin, *Sacred Revolt: the Muskogees' Struggle for a New World* (Boston: Beacon Press, 1991), 693.

56. Typical of the white perspective was the anonymous *New York Times* reporter who responded to Little Wound's open letter (cited earlier) by writing: "This letter is an open defiance to the troops [now stationed at Pine Ridge]. The ghost dancers have been warned to stop their revolting orgies and this is their answer." Anonymous, "It Looks More like War; The Northwestern Indians Becoming Very Aggressive. A Letter of Defiance Sent Yesterday—The Ghost Dances Continue—The Probable Battle Ground," *New York Times*, November 23, 1890. Quoted in Pratt, "Wounded Knee and the Prospect of Pluralism," xi. Pratt observes that even sympathetic whites "struggle[d] to understand the meaning of the religion," and suggests further that the flames of white hysteria were fanned by the period's "massive influx of immigrants from Europe and Asia and the migration of southern blacks to Northern cities" (150, 160).

57. Laubin and Laubin, *Indian Dances of North America*, 65–66.

58. As one indicator, over twenty Medals of Honor were handed out to troopers participating in this campaign. A reassessment of the massacre and of the culpability of Colonel James Forsyth and the Seventh Cavalry did not become part of the public discourse until Dee Brown's 1970 *Bury My Heart at Wounded Knee: An Indian History of the American West* (New York: Henry Holt, 2007).

59. Stortz, "Ritual Power, Ritual Authority," 123. Slagle says the dancing that arises in such challenging circumstances is a kind of *weltzschmerz* that is "always and everywhere characteristic of threatened or disintegrating societies." See Al Logan Slagle, "Tolowa Indian Shakers and the Role of Prophecy at Smith River, California," *American Indian Quarterly* 93, American Indian Prophets: Religious Leaders and Revitalization Movements (Summer 1985), 367.

60. Stortz, "Ritual Power, Ritual Authority," 123.

61. Among the Tolowa of northern California, for example, traditional dances "cast in the mold of the old Indian Shamanistic god-man and culture heroes" were incorporated into the Indian Shaker church and—as in the Ghost Dance and the Shaker Era of Manifestations—featured magical garments, dancing, apparitions, and exorcisms; see Slagle, "Tolowa Indian Shakers," 368, for borrowings from the old Tolowa religion into Indian Shaker practice.

## Chapter 6. Blackface Transformations I

1. Mark Hellinger, "Bill Robinson Gets 'Em Told," *Chicago Defender*, September 29, 1928 (reprinted from *New York Daily News*), quoted in Kimberley Monteyne, *Hip Hop on Film: Performance Culture, Urban Space, and Genre Transformation* (Jackson: University Press of Mississippi, 2013), 19–20.

2. See Dale Cockrell, "Blood on Fire: Prostitution, Music, and Dance in Victorian America" (unpublished paper read at national meetings of the Society for American Music, March 2011, Cincinnati). Though the cakewalk, whose subversive intentions are well-

documented, is possibly the best known of these postbellum cross-cultural idioms, it is by no means the only instance in which the body vocabularies of this transracial creole synthesis show through. Similar cases can be made for their appearance in a variety of other period social dances; see, for example, Robert B. Winans, "Black Instrumental Music Traditions in the Ex-Slave Narratives," *Black Music Research Journal* 10/1 (Spring 1990), 43–53, 55. See also Michael Borshuk, "An Intelligence of the Body: Disruptive Parody through Dance in the Early Performances of Josephine Baker," in *Embodying Liberation: The Black Body in American Dance*, Dorothea Fischer-Hornung and Alison D. Goeller, eds. (Berlin: LIT Verlag, 2001), on the meaning of the cakewalk. See Karen Blackstein on the parodic strategies of the Charleston, which "mocked the prancing of the white masters who dances those quadrilles." Quoted in Borshuk, "An Intelligence of the Body," 48. See likewise, in Chapter 7, discussion of the extended descriptions of 1940s. Lindy Hop steps that included the "flapping eagle," "the kangaroo," and the "split," in Malcolm X, *The Autobiography of Malcolm X*, Chapter 4. http://autobiography-of-malcolm-x.wikispaces.com/4_laura. Accessed August 30, 2014.

3. Borshuk, "An Intelligence of the Body," 42.

4. A good biography and career summary is Bennetta Jules-Rosette, *Josephine Baker in Art and Life: The Icon and the Image* (Urbana: University of Illinois Press, 2007).

5. "By mixing American musical theater with blues and jazz phrasings and French music hall aesthetics, Baker was able to create dissonant humor. This dissonance, one might argue, emerged out of that end space." Daphne Ann Brooks, "The End of the Line: Josephine Baker and the Politics of Black Women's Corporeal Comedy," *S&F Online* 6.1–6.2 (Fall 2007/Spring 2008), 4. Accessed September 30, 2016.

6. Karen C. C. Dalton and Henry Louis Gates Jr., "Josephine Baker and Paul Colin: African American Dance Seen through Parisian Eyes," *Critical Inquiry* 24/4 (Summer 1998), 911. For descriptions of Master Juba, see Charles Dickens, *American Notes for General Circulation* (New York: Penguin, 2001), 48–49.

7. See Charles Keil, "Participatory Discrepancies and the Power of Music," *Cultural Anthropology* 2/3 (August 1987), 275–283.

8. Brooks, "The End of the Line," 4.

9. For discussions of Baker's reception in Europe as compared to the United States, see Borshuk, "An Intelligence of the Body," 42–43. *Shuffle Along*, the watershed 1921 Broadway hit by Noble Sissle and Eubie Blake (music and lyrics) and Flournoy Miller and Aubrey Lyles (book), ran 504 performances, played to integrated audiences, and launched the careers of Adelaide Hall and Paul Robeson as well as Baker herself. It had first been conceived at an NAACP benefit in Philadelphia the year before.

10. Baker employed this cross-eyed comic expression in many photographic portraits and performance stills, as a means of subverting and parodying the conventions of studio portraiture. Brooks, "The End of the Line."

11. Quoted in Dalton and Gates, "Josephine Baker and Paul Colin," 911, from Bryan Hammond and Patrick O'Connor, *Josephine Baker* (London: Cape, 1988), 9–10. It is worth noting that, in addition to the crossed eyes, the "knees folding under her, eccentric wise," is precisely the lower-body gesture that connoted Jim Crow aesthetics; see the numerous crossed-legs

illustrations of Jim Crow dance and the use of that same crossed-legs "creole" stance in *A Grand Jamaica Ball!* (discussed in Chapter 2).

12. Paul Colin, *La Croûte (Souvenirs)* (Paris: Le Table Ronde, 1957), 81.

13. There is a 1927 series of hand-colored lithographs of Baker by Colin, for which Dalton and Gates suggest she modeled by dancing; one of these portraits is discussed later. See *Le Tumulte noir*, reproduced in Dalton and Gates, "Josephine Baker and Paul Colin," 903–904.

14. Anthea Kraut, "Between Primitivism and Diaspora: The Dance Performances of Josephine Baker, Zora Neale Hurston, and Katherine Dunham," *Theatre Journal* 55/3, Dance (October 2003), 437: "These same dances and gestures . . . read very differently in a French setting, where since the turn of the twentieth century, the Parisian avant-garde had been gripped by 'negrophilia.'"

15. Borshuk says "her shows seemed to confirm stereotypes so they could tear them apart." Borshuk, "An Intelligence of the Body," 43. See, in this context, Robert Allen's citation of Bakhtin on the "classical" and "grotesque body": "The classical body is closed, finished, smooth, symmetrically proportioned, separated from other bodies and from connections with the outside world, and separated from its connections with procreation, birth, and death. The grotesque body, on the other hand, is 'a body in the act of becoming.' It seems to outgrow its own limits." Robert C. Allen, *Horrible Prettiness: Burlesque and American Culture* (Chapel Hill: University of North Carolina, 1991), 174.

16. Judith Bettelheim, "Women in Masquerade and Performance," *African Arts* 31/2, Special Issue: Women's Masquerades in Africa and the Diaspora (Spring 1998), 69.

17. Paul Colin, *Le Tumulte/Josephine Baker, Palm Skirt*, 1927, lithograph, National Portrait Gallery, Simthsonian Institution.

18. Walery was extremely active, particularly in Paris, ca. 1883–1930, particularly as an erotic photographer. His selection as portraitist for Baker's 1926–1927 shots surely results in part from this reputation.

19. "Just as there can be explicitly subordinate discourse, there can also be insubordinate discourse: discourse that transgresses or inverts existing orderings, discourse that challenges the nation of fixed orders or the ordinative authority of another discourse." See Allen, *Horrible Prettiness*, 34.

20. For more on the Brothers as subversive immigrant outsiders in *A Day at the Races*, see Daniel Lieberfeld and Judith Sanders, "Here under False Pretenses: The Marx Brothers Crash the Gates." *American Scholar* 64/1 (Winter 1995), 103–105. For a long discussion of the "All God's Chillun" sequence's role in the history of swing dancing, see Tamara Stevens and Erin Stevens, *Swing Dancing* (New York: ABC-CLIO, 2011), 71.

21. There is a parallel here with some of the first "talkies" made ca. 1925–1927 using the Vita-Graph technology for synchronizing silent film and audio recording; in these early pre–*Jazz Singer* shorts, the mostly vaudeville-based performers betray considerable unself-consciousness regarding the camera: never having seen vaudeville *shtick* on screen, they have no expectations or presumptions about how it "should" look.

22. Stevens and Stevens, *Swing Dancing*, 84. On Rheingold and Rosenberg (the latter "a Bronx 'tough guy,' [who] came from a family so poor that he had spent two years in an orphanage when they were unable to raise him at home"), see Carrie Stern, "Savoy Ballroom," *Dance Heritage Coalition* (March 3, 2012), 3–5.

23. See Stevens and Stevens, *Swing Dancing*, 84.

24. Brian Harker, "Louis Armstrong, Eccentric Dance, and the Evolution of Jazz on the Eve of Swing," *Journal of the American Musicological Society* 61/1 (Spring 2008), 87.

25. The release was "All God's Chillun Got Rhythm" (credit to Ivie Anderson and Her Boys from Dixie) (Variety VA-591) June 8, 1937.

26. The use of danced rings and circles to delineate ritual space is an element of West African movement vocabularies found widely throughout both sacred and secular genres in the Caribbean and southwest Atlantic. See Ayesha Morris, "The Power of Dance: Bamboula Has Deep and Strong Ties to African Heritage, Island History and Freedom Fight," *Virgin Islands Daily News*, February 25, 2006. Also of interest here is the degree to which Harpo's (dubbed) tin whistle and the accompanying tom-toms evoke the sound of North Mississippi fife and drum music, a syncretic African American style with particular strong roots connecting to Afro-Caribbean and West African dance music.

27. Both ring-shout and *bamboula* are Afro-Caribbean dances, one sacred and the other secular, which are based upon the creation of danced circles in order to delineate performance spaces. For Afro Caribbean dance spaces as antiauthoritarian, see Lorraine Leu, "'Raise Yuh Hand, Jump Up and Get on Bad!': New Developments in Soca Music in Trinidad," *LatinAmerican Music Review / REvista de Músic Latinoamericana* 21/1 (Spring–Summer 2000), 48.

28. See Barbara S. Glass, *African American Dance: An Illustrated History* (Jefferson, N.C.: McFarland and Company, 2007), 55.

29. No more specific credits than "Crinoline Choir" are available for this group.

30. Bunch had previously appeared in the iconic Aaron Siskind 1935 photo, *At the Savoy*, with partner Dot Moses; *Harlem Document: Photographs 1932–40*. See Frankie Manning, with Cynthia R. Millman, *Frankie Manning: Ambassador of Lindy Hop* (Philadelphia: Temple University Press, 2008), 246. "Despite being 6'4" tall and weighing 350 pounds, he was a graceful light-footed dancer." Stevens and Stevens, *Swing Dancing*, 74.

31. The sequence won the 1937 Academy Award for Best Dance Direction. "Dave Gould" is credited with staging the musical numbers, but the nature of the Lindy Hoppers' choreography, and the degree to which their sequence is self-contained and based upon their own existing dance vocabulary, argue that the credit should go to Manning. A detailed breakdown and identification of the various couples' dances can be found at http://lindyloowho.tumblr.com/post/56455393905/oh-mah-god-its-time-for-another-shorty-georges. Accessed September 30, 2016.

32. *Capoeira*, a dance/martial arts style whose practitioners are called "players," originated in Brazilian slave populations for whom it was essential to conceal combat practices within a surface veneer of "harmless" dance. It is highly likely that stick-fighting techniques from West Africa were transmitted to the Caribbean and eventually, via riverine culture, into historically black populations and historically black colleges in North America.

33. "Antagonists are the only ones fooled by the disguise. The blackface mask does not hide the 'performer'; instead the mask highlights and draws the audience's attention to the irrepressible nature of the protagonists. The transparency of the disguise is made particularly notable in *Round Up* and *Races* by having the principal characters perform in blackface alongside African Americans. There is no attempt on the part of the white

characters to strive for an authenticity in their performance of blackness; the goal is, in fact, the reverse." Peter Stanfield, *Body and Soul: Jazz and Blues in American Film, 1927–63* (Urbana: University of Illinois Press, 2005), 12.

34. It will shortly devolve into a slapstick yet rather frighteningly chaotic physical climax in which the villains are variously knocked about, tied up, or trampled by the escaped horse, whose character and narrative function is fundamentally differentiated from the dance sequence that precedes it.

35. For "liberation from the constraints of middle-class behavior," see Eric Lott, *Love & Theft: Blackface Minstrelsy and the American Working Class* (New York: Oxford University Press, 1993), 134. For "participatory bodily joy," Paul Spencer observes "A dance performance may be endowed with a similar ["charismatic"] elusive quality capable of generating an infectious excitement." Spencer, "Introduction," in *Society and the Dance: The Social Anthropology of Process and Performance* (Cambridge: Cambridge University Press, 1986), 17.

36. Keil, "Participatory Discrepancies."

37. For more on theatrical transvestism as intentionally transgressive, see Anthony Shay, *Dancing across Borders: The American Fascination with Exotic Dance Forms* (Jefferson, N.C.: McFarland & Company, 2008), 186–187. For more on the long history of theatrical transgression, see Mark Franko, "Double Bodies: Androgyny and Power in the Performances of Louis XIV," *TDR (1988-)* 38/4 (Winter 1994), 71–73. See Borshuk on drag; citing Judith Butler, as "a challenge to received notions of essential gender traits, rather than a mere impersonation." Borshuk, "An Intelligence of the Body," 50.

38. "Dietrich's embodiment of the femme fatale is 'spectacularized' . . . as a 'new woman,' an excessively sexual yet sterile woman (*Berlinerisch*). This 'masculine woman,' who is known for her sexual aggressivity and her ability to cross-dress, appropriates the charge of the seducer. Her possession of agency, as opposed to passivity . . . destabilizes the traditional heterosexual romantic narrative and confounds another set of inculcated gender barriers." Kriss Ravelto, *The Unmaking of Fascist Aesthetics* (Minneapolis: University of Minnesota Press, 2001), 63. On Baker's use of transvestism: "Cross-dressing was the flip side of titillating nudity. . . . Both cross-dressing and nudity challenged conventional restrictions on the autonomy and comportment of women in bourgeois society. Removing clothing and dressing as a male were sources of feminine empowerment." Jules-Rosette, *Josephine Baker in Art and Life*, 66.

39. Borshuk, "An Intelligence of the Body."

40. Gene Hackman, in a masterful comic turn as "Sen. Kevin Keeley," in *Birdcage* dir. Mike Nichols (MGM/UA 1996). See also Allen, *Horrible Prettiness*, for the many practical and semiotic links between burlesque gender-bending and "wench" roles in blackface minstrelsy.

## Chapter 7. Blackface Transformations II

1. *A Hard Day's Night* (dir. Richard Lester; United Artists 1964); *Jailhouse Rock* (dir. Richard Thorpe; MGM, 1957); for the Jack Benny quote, see Nancy Sinatra, *Frank Sinatra, My Father* (New York: Simon and Schuster, 1986), 44.

2. See David Halberstam, *The Fifties* (New York: Ballantine, 1994), 73–74, for a good discussion of the demographic and economic changes that made "the teenager" a new and lucrative target for marketing and sales in a prosperous post–WWII United States. http://bit.ly/1JpPrec. Accessed September 26, 2018.

3. Opposition to transgressive lifestyles and behaviors came from all quarters: not only social conservatives, but also progressives (particularly those aligned demographically with Anglo-Protestant reformers espousing temperance and women's rights): Jane Addams, for example, had spoken out in 1912 against the immoral contexts of "cheap theaters and dance halls." Khalil Gibran Muhammad, *The Condemnation of Blackness* (Cambridge: Harvard University, 2010), 117.

4. See, for example, Glenn C. Altschuler, *All Shook Up: How Rock 'n' Roll Changed America* (Oxford: Oxford University Press, 2003); *New York Times*, April 15, 1957; *NYT*, May 5, 1958; "Jersey City Orders Rock-and-Roll Band," *NYT*, July 10, 1956; "Rock 'n' Roll Banned," *NYT*, September 20, 1956; "Rock-and-Roll Called Communicable Disease," *NYT*, March 28, 1956.

5. Kevin J. Mumford, *Interzones: Black/White Sex Districts in Chicago and New York in the Early Twentieth Century*. http://bit.ly/1mkT8wz, 30–31. Accessed June 1, 2013.

6. On critique of 1910s-1920s cabarets as "experimental" zones, see Julie Malnig, "Two-Stepping to Glory: Social Dance and the Rhetoric of Social Mobility." In Ann Dils and Ann Cooper Albright, eds., *Moving History / Dancing Cultures: A Dance History Reader* (Middletown, Conn.: Wesleyan University Press, 2001), 282–284.

7. Stevens and Stevens say, "Dance halls were prevalent in the ghetto neighborhoods and, as African Americans and Irish Americans co-mingled [*sic*] in these communities, dancing was a popular pastime." Tamara Stevens and Erin Stevens, *Swing Dancing* (New York: ABC-CLIO, 2011), 14.

8. John Gennari, *Blowin' Hot and Cool: Jazz and Its Critics* (Chicago: University of Chicago Press, 2010), 94. Emphasis added.

9. Malnig, for example, cites ongoing middle-class white borrowings of African American "rag" and related dances from 1908 onward, and describes cabarets in the period as places to perform dance rituals of upward mobility. Malnig, "Two-Stepping to Glory," 272–273. See also Christopher J. Smith, *The Creolization of American Culture* (Urbana: University of Illinois Press, 2013).

10. The Lindy Hop was nicknamed after Charles Lindbergh's 1927 trans-Atlantic solo flight, but its roots as an acrobatic couples dance go back at least to the 'teens, if not earlier. See Howard Spring's excellent chronology of the evolution of couples dancing in the first decades of the century: Spring, "Swing and the Lindy Hop: Dance, Venue, Media, and Tradition," *American Music* 15/2 (Summer 1997), 183, which traces the repeated patterns through which dances originating in the African American community enter the white mainstream. On the concert-saloons, see Peter Stanfield, "'An Octoroon in the Kindling': American Vernacular & Blackface Minstrelsy in 1930s Hollywood," *Journal of American Studies* 31/3, 1: Part I: Looking at America: The USA and Film (December 1997), 419. On New Orleans masked balls in various eras, see Joseph Roach, "Carnival and the Law in New Orleans," *TDR (1988-)* 37/3 (Autumn 1993), 56,

and Michael P. Smith, "Behind the Lines: The Black Mardi Gras Indians and the New Orleans Second Line," *Black Music Research Journal* 14/1, Selected Papers from the 1993 National Conference on Black Music Research (Spring 1994), 47. On speakeasies and black-and-tan clubs, see Mumford, *Interzones*, 29; and Brian Harker, "Louis Armstrong, Eccentric Dance, and the Evolution of Jazz on the Eve of Swing," *Journal of the American Musicological Society* 61/1 (Spring 2008), 87.

11. Spring, "Swing and the Lindy Hop," 184–185. Spring adds, "The Savoy Ballroom had strong ties to the local community, yet it was racially integrated; thus, it provided a line of transmission between the black and white communities" (189).

12. Mumford, *Interzones*, 30. The original reference is to William Burroughs and James Grauerholz, *Interzone* (New York: Penguin Books, 1990); as a place name, "Interzone" appears again in Burroughs's better-known *Naked Lunch* (Paris: Grove Press, 1959).

13. In venues like these, Shane Vogel says "the movements of everynight life and the tenor of mundaneness challenge[d] the reification of social relations, the positivism of social scientific knowledge, and the standardization of racial and sexual norms." Shane Vogel, *The Scene of Harlem Cabaret: Race, Sexuality, Performance* (Chicago: University of Chicago Press, 2009), 18.

14. "Slumming," a feature of New York middle-class and progressive white entertainment ever since the 1840s, is a focal theme in Carl van Vechten, *Nigger Heaven* (New York: Knopf, 1926), and *Parties, Scenes from Contemporary New York Life* (New York: Knopf, 1926). Leading lights of the 1920s Harlem Renaissance included the dancers Josephine Baker (1906–1975), cited elsewhere in this book, the Nicholas Brothers Fayard (1914–2006) and Harold (1921–2000), and Bill "Bojangles" Robinson (1878–1949); the authors Countee Cullen (1903–1946), Langston Hughes (1902–1967), and Zora Neale Hurston (1891–1960); and the poets James Weldon Johnson (1871–1938) and Claude McKay (1889–1948); as well as a host of musicians, especially the leaders of big bands.

15. For more on the history of black-white exchange in liminal working-class zones, see (among others), Smith, *The Creolization of American Culture*; see also Blair A. Ruble, "Seventh Street, Black D.C.'s Music Mecca," *Washington History* 26, Jazz in Washington (Spring 2014), 4–7.

16. Vogel, *The Scene of Harlem Cabaret*, 68. This aspect of nightclub design was borrowed for many of the "stage-door" musical films of the 1930s and '40s, for the same reasons. On the same topic, see David W. Stowe, *Swing Changes: Big Band Jazz in New Deal America* (Cambridge: Harvard University Press, 1996), 44.

17. The Savoy, which set up admissions policies precisely so that middle-class and female patrons could feel comfortable, actually encouraged white onlookers to join in on the participatory dancing by "establishing a dance floor on which the rich mixed with the working poor." Carrie Stern, "Savoy Ballroom," *Dance Heritage Coalition* (March 3, 2012), 3, 5.

18. That this exchange of movement vocabularies occurred first in the liminal zones of black-and-tan nightclubs, and later through the asynchronous medium of the middle-class movie screen, is consistent with patterns of white middle-class appropriation since the earliest days of blackface minstrelsy. Typically: new urban-based syncretic music styles (from blackface to vaudeville to ragtime to jazz) began on the subaltern working-class outskirts, and only when they had achieved a certain degree of synthesis, virtuosity,

and (for lack of a better word) expressive maturity did they become visible, and therefore subject to appropriation by middle-class white consumer culture and its organs.

19. Talkies made in that "pre-Code" era, ca. 1927–1930, tended to a degree of frankness in dialog and visual imagery which would be unimaginable only a few years later. Al Jolson, *The Jazz Singer* (film), directed by Alan Crosland (Hollywood, Calif.: Warner Brothers, 1927).

20. The more extended quote is (pun unintended) quite revealing: "VI. Costume [and] 4. Dancing or costumes intended to permit undue exposure or indecent movements in the dance are forbidden," as well as "VII. Dances . . . 1. Dances suggesting or representing sexual actions or indecent passions are forbidden; 2. Dances which emphasize indecent movements are to be regarded as obscene" and "VII. Dances . . . which suggest or represent sexual actions, whether performed solo or with two or more; dances intended to excite the emotional reaction of an audience; dances with movement of the breasts, excessive body movements while the feet are stationary, violate decency and are wrong." See http://www.artsreformation.com/a001/hays-code.html. Accessed February 1, 2016.

21. These 1923–1927 "soundies," though employing a technology that Movietone would quickly render obsolete, are important for a different reason than just chronology—because, in these few years, Phonofilm and Vitaphone captured a generation of theatrical performers for whom film was an unfamiliar and therefore un-self-conscious medium. By 1927's *The Jazz Singer*, and certainly in the period leading up to the Hays Code in 1930, actors and other performers were conscious of and able to play to the frame and expectations of sound film. But prior to '27, soundies captured an entire world of vaudeville and theatrical performance of a remarkably un-self-conscious character. They provide a kind of window into that brief period when new technology made it possible to capture and preserve live performance, but before live performers had become fully conscious and desirous of playing to the camera's frame and "listening ear." Soundies thus let us see and hear vaudeville "as if" from a prefilm age. Something analogous happened with the technology of audio recording, during the transition—also in the mid-1920s—from recordings employing acoustical horns to capture sound to those that used the electrical diaphragm microphone. The compressed dynamic range of the horn had restricted both what repertoires were recorded (brass bands and solo tenors were popular) and also what instrumentation was employed—for example, the string bass begins to replace tuba in recorded jazz bands because the horn could handle its dynamics better. So performers recording before the introduction of the electrical microphone (by Victor and Columbia) could have little idea of how their "live" sound might translate, whereas those who recorded later in the '20s and '30s had the advantage of cutting their teeth on predecessors' electrical records. Older African American musicians like Henry Thomas (born 1871) and Charlie Patton (born ca. 1891), who played in an essential pre–recording-era style, were much less self-conscious about recorded sound than were those of one generation later, like Robert Johnson (born 1911), whose small body of recordings betrays a keen and sophisticated understanding of the unique demands of the recording medium, and of earlier recordings by that older generation.

22. A useful summary of the transformations that the new media imposed upon existing performance styles is Nicholas Sammond, *Birth of an Industry: Blackface Minstrelsy and the Rise of American Animation* (Durham: Duke University Press, 2015).

23. Hazzard-Gordon, "Afro-American Core Culture Social Dance," 21–26. Hazzard-Gordon quotes extensively from Malcolm X's autobiography.

24. This would include the meetinghouse slave gallery and open-air preaching at Cane Ridge, the ballrooms of colonial Jamaica and theatrical stages of antebellum Manhattan, the streets of Portland and Chicago during political protests, the creole zones Congo Square and the wharves of Port au Prince, the utopian spaces of Shaker meetinghouses and Dakota Ghost-Dance circles, the nightclubs and theaters of Harlem and Paris, the ring-shouts of the Caribbean, E. W. Kemble's engravings of *bamboula* dances in Place Congo (fictions based upon George Washington Cable's indirect reminiscences), and the overhead shots in the "All God's Chillun" sequence in *A Day at the Races* (1937).

25. Brenda Dixon Gottschild, "Crossroads, Continuities, and Contradictions: The Afro-Euro-Caribbean Triangle," in Susanna Sloat, *Caribbean Dance from Abakuá to Zouk: How Movement Shapes Identity* (Gainesville: University Press of Florida, 2002), 9. Indeed, Spike Lee's staging of the Malcolm/Lindy scenes is a conscious and intentional homage to Whitey's Lindy Hoppers in *A Day at the Races* (which was, remarkably, choreographed by the venerable Frankie Manning—who had also done the earlier film).

26. See Malcolm X and Alex Haley, *The Autobiography of Malcolm X, as Told to Alex Haley* (New York: Ballantine, 1989).

27. See Stern, "Savoy Ballroom," 7. On "The Circle," see also Jacqui Malone, *Steppin' on the Blues: The Visible Rhythms of African American Dance* (Urbana: University of Illinois Press, 1996), 101.

28. Malcolm X and Haley, *Autobiography*, Chapter 4.

29. Ibid.

30. *Bamboozled* (dir. Spike Lee, New Line Cinema, 2001).

31. Mel Brooks, *The Producers* (Twentieth Century Fox, 1968). On the dynamic relationship between *The Producers* and *Bamboozled*, see Susan Gubar, "Racial Camp in *The Producers* and *Bamboozled*," *Film Quarterly* 60/2 (Winter 2006), 29.

32. Eric Lott, *Love & Theft: Blackface Minstrelsy and the American Working Class* (New York: Oxford University Press, 1993).

33. Paddy Chayefsky, *Network* (film), directed by Sidney Lumet (Hollywood, Calif.: United Artists, 1976) "most notably, the 'odd Grace-Kelly-meets-James-Earl-accent,' which Lee imposes upon Daman Wayans's protagonist Delacroix." See Cynthia Lucia et al., "Race, Media and Money: A Critical Symposium on Spike Lee's 'Bamboozled,'" *Cinéaste* 26/2 (2001), 10. For Lee's own acknowledgment of this influence, see "Spike Lee Talks about *Bamboozled* on Its 15th Anniversary," interview with Ashley Clark on the opening night of *Behind the Mask: Bamboozled in Focus*, uploaded to YouTube October 30, 2015. https://youtu.be/_Jxa83KgAy4. Accessed January 3, 2016.

34. The phrase is from Annemarie Bean, James V. Hatch, and Brooks McNamara, eds., *Inside the Minstrel Mask: Readings in Nineteenth-Century Blackface Minstrelsy* (Middletown, Conn.: Wesleyan University Press, 1996).

35. Lee reports that "every time we had to do a scene, and they had to blacken up, they were crying. It was painful." See Lee, "Spike Lee Talks."

36. "Tambo" and "Bones" were the stage names associated with tambourine- and bones-players in the classic blackface quartet: the "end-men" whose comic malapropisms

and other dialect humor played off the dignity of the "Interlocutor," the best-dressed and-spoken of the group. These comic exchanges become even more important—and more codified—in the postbellum period and are a direct influence on the dialect and dialog humor of groups like the Marx Brothers, the Three Stooges, and Abbott and Costello.

37. See, for example, Philip Morris cigarette packets and a very wide array of toys, jewelry, and lawn ornaments.

38. For more on blackface costume and iconography, see Lott, *Love & Theft*; for more on the carryover of blackface tropes into later art forms like animation, see Daniel Goldmark, *Tunes for 'Toons: Music and the Hollywood Cartoon* (Berkeley: University of California Press, 2005), 84–85. Also, Sammond, *Birth of an Industry*.

39. See Frantz Fanon, *Black Skin, White Masks*, Charles Lam Markmann, trans. (New York: Grove Press, 1967); Paul Gilroy, *The Black Atlantic: Modernity and Double Consciousness* (Cambridge: Harvard University Press, 1993); Henry Louis Gates Jr., *The Signifying Monkey* (New York: Oxford University Press, 1988).

40. The Bakhtinian carnivalesque oral symbolism of this sequence in *Bamboozled* has been discussed by Rachel Sussman but is not our primary focus here. See Sussman, "The Carnavalizing of Race," *Etnofoor* 14/2 MASQUERADES (2001), 79.

41. Inevitably, there is in fact a movement arguing for "historically informed performance" of blackface repertoire that has Civil War reenactors blacking-up in the interests of authenticity; for examples, see "The Free and Accepted Minstrels of Old New Orleans," (compact disc), *Gems of Minstrelsy* (self-published, 2003), http://www.cjdaley.com/newsletter/Oct04.htm. Accessed August 30, 2014, and Darren Keast, "Black Eye: Modern Minstrels—Historical Hootenanny or Racist Revival?" (October 23, 2003). https://www.thepitchkc.com/arts-entertainment/music/article/20610520/black-eye. Accessed August 30, 2014. However, the expressive intentions of these (Caucasian) reenactors are diametrically opposed to those Lee intends in *Bamboozled*. See John Strausbaugh, *Black like You: Blackface, Whiteface, Insult & Imitation in American Popular Music* (New York: Penguin, 2007), 245.

42. Greg Tate, in Lucia et al., "Race, Media and Money," 15–16.

43. As Susan Gubar puts it: "The charismas of Savion Glover and Tommy Davidson make [the TV show] more than a statement about the historical racism that infiltrates visual imagery from *The Birth of a Nation* (1915) and *The Jazz Singer* (1927) to contemporary sitcoms. Because of their magnetism, the television-show-within-the-movie illustrates the vertiginous ironies of racial camp." Gubar, "Racial Camp in *The Producers* and *Bamboozled*," 32.

44. As Greg Tate puts it, "It's obvious that Lee had written himself into a box and chose to shoot his way out of it." In Lucia, et al., "Race, Media and Money," 15.

## Chapter 8. Body and Spirit in a Post-1960s World

1. Martin Duberman and Andrew Kopkind, "The Night They Raided Stonewall," *Grand Street* 44 (1993), 146.

2. John Carlevale provides an effective and nuanced analysis of such elements in "Dionysus Now: Dionysian Myth-History in the Sixties," *Arion: A Journal of Humanities and the Classics*, Third Series, 13/2 (Fall 2005), 77–116. For stereotypical examples of "hippie

dancing," see concert sequences in films like *Woodstock* (1969), *Monterey Pop* (1967), and others.

3. While this chapter focuses upon four examples of 1960s-and-after dance consciousness—the hippie movement, punk rock, Gay Liberation, and the hip-hop nation—no evaluative hierarchy should be presumed: though they lie beyond the scope of the present study, the Women's Rights movement, the American Indian Movement, and Chicano / La Raza / Brown Power consciousness were equally vital extensions of post–Civil Rights activism (all cited at various points), and there is valuable work still to be done exploring street theater and dance as part of their tactics. For the role of same-sex dances as part of the women's music movement, see, for example, Kathy Rudy, "Radical Feminism, Lesbian Separatism, and Queer Theory," *Feminist Studies* 27/1 (Spring 2001), 196ff; see also leslie smith and toni white, "'ourstory/herstory': the washington, d.c. feminist community from 1968 to 1979," *Off Our Backs* 10/2, TEN YEARS GROWING! (February 1980), 12–13, 26–27. Though the lesbian-identified "Womyn's Music movement" tended to emphasize highly personal songwriting, more than the construction of dance music, creating spaces for same-sex dancing was as important in the movement as it was in the wider contexts and history of gay culture, addressed in this chapter. In addition to the sources cited extensively in Chapter 4, additional information on historical and symbolic connections between the Ghost Dance, Native American activism in the post-1960s (especially the occupation of Wounded Knee by members of the American Indian Movement in 1973), and connections between revivals of the traditional sun dance and modern phenomenon of festival pow-wow dancing, can be found in Philip D. Roos, Dowell H. Smith, Stephen Langley, and James McDonald, "The Impact of the American Indian Movement on the Pine Ridge Indian Reservation," *Phylon (1960-)* 41/1 (1st quarter 1980), 96ff; Gerald Vizenor, "Dennis [Banks] of Wounded Knee," *American Indian Quarterly* 7/2 (Spring 1983), 53; and Peter Matthiessen's magisterial history of Native American resistance, *In the Spirit of Crazy Horse: The Story of Leonard Peltier and the FBI's War on the American Indian Movement* (New York: Penguin, 1992). Likewise, the 1960s United States Civil Rights movement echoed worldwide; not only in the impact of liberation figures like Bob Marley (Jamaica) and Thomas Mapfumo (Zimbabwe) but also in Haiti's *Kilti libete* ("Freedom Culture") movement. See Gerdes Fleurant, "The Song of Freedom: Vodun, Conscientization and Popular Culture in Haiti," *Journal of Haitian Studies* 2/2 (Autumn 1996), 115–116.

4. In marked contrast to revisionist historians' dismissal of the hippie movement, serious scholarship even in the period recognized dance links to earlier ecstatic and utopian communities: "We would suggest that an antinomian stage, a stage of extreme disorganization that may include anything from solitude to drunken orgies to ecstatic dancing to drug-induced hallucinations, is the appropriate antecedent to virtually all the established countercultural movements with which we are familiar. In the case of early Christian monasticism, this antinomian stage expressed itself in the virtual autism of the desert hermits, an autism which was easily displaced in later years by the cenobitic monastery. . . . So staid a group as today's Quakers have public nudity in their early history . . ., and the rigoristic Shakers drew converts from the quite antinomian revivals of Kentucky in the nineteenth century. . . . Adler notes that the antinomian personality appeared

in many historical movements before hippiedom, Gnostic sects, the Manichaeans, the Anabaptists, and nineteenth-century Romanticism, among others." Kenneth Westhues, "Hippiedom 1970s: Some Tentative Hypotheses," *Sociological Quarterly* 13/1 (Winter 1972), 95.

5. A good summary of the political shifts in the Jim Crow South that were precipitated by the activism of black War veterans, and the wave of mob violence and lynchings that attempted to suppress this activism, is found in Taylor Branch, *Parting the Waters: America in the King Years 1954–63* (New York: Simon and Schuster, 1988), 63–64.

6. For Virginia's "massive resistance," the choice to close rather than integrate public schools (1956), see Robbins L. Gates, *The Making of Massive Resistance: Virginia's Politics of Public School Desegregation, 1954–1956* (Chapel Hill: University of North Carolina Press, 2014). For the Little Rock story, see Karen Anderson, *Little Rock: Race and Resistance at Central High School* (Princeton, N.J.: Princeton University Press, 2013)—and the version of Charles Mingus's "Original Faubus Fables," with lyrics," on *Charles Mingus Presents Charles Mingus* (Candid CCD-79005, 1960).

7. Jefferson's original "draught" had included the following accusation of George III, a subtle piece of rhetorical disavowal considering Jefferson's own status as a slave-owner: "He [King George] has waged cruel war against human nature itself, violating its most sacred rights of life & liberty in the persons of a distant people who never offended him, captivating & carrying them into slavery in another hemisphere, or to incur miserable death in their transportation thither. this piratical warfare, the opprobrium of infidel powers, is the warfare of the CHRISTIAN king of Great Britain determined to keep open a market where MEN should be bought & sold, he has prostituted his negative for suppressing every legislative attempt to prohibit or to restrain this execrable commerce: and that this assemblage of horrors might want no fact of distinguished die, he is now exciting those very people to rise in arms among us." http://www.loc.gov/exhibits/declara/ruffdrft.html. Accessed July 15, 2015.

8. An incomplete list of Civil Rights watersheds might span from the Emancipation Proclamation (1863) to the surrender at Appomattox (1865); the 15th Amendment (1870), the 1877 Compromise, which withdrew Northern troops and made possible the reinscription of racial and economic exploitation; the Gilded Age legal and economic actions, which further solidified disenfranchisement via state legislature and culminated in *Plessy v. Ferguson* (1896); the foundation of the NAACP (1909); the whitewashing of the prewar South epitomized in Griffith's *Birth of a Nation* (1915); and the interplay of repression (the Palmer Raids) and liberalization (especially in professional athletics) in the Roaring Twenties.

9. For example, the accelerating tide of the African American Civil Rights movement (especially after 1954's *Brown v. Education* Supreme Court decision), the literary and social liberation politics of the Beats, the first high-visibility same-sex advocacy groups, the demographic research that led Betty Friedan to write *The Feminine Mystique* (published in 1963), and the Community Service Organization (1947) that trained Cesar Chavez and birthed the United Farm Workers.

10. Peter Jones, speaking of punk rock, explicitly links an "anarchic semiotic and somatic realm" and to the transgressive and revolutionary implications to Bakhtinian carnival, but

his commentary is equally relevant to considerations of 1960s hippie movements and 1980s hip-hop: "The liberation and articulation of utopia or egalitarian ideals is accompanied by the subversion and demystification of the conventions, symbols, and values underpinning the established order by such devices as inversion and parody. It also involves the transgression of social norms and propriety by the avowed and frequent use of obscenities and stress on excess and corporeality. The carnival is thus an anarchic semiotic and somatic realm." Jones, "Anarchy in the UK: '70s British Punk as Bakhtinian Carnival," *Studies in Popular Culture* 24/3 (April 2002), 26.

11. A particularly poignant variant on this trope of missed opportunities appeared quite early, in Tom Wolfe's *Electric Kool-Aid Acid Test*, which chronicled the rise and fall of Ken Kesey's Merry Pranksters and their vision of social liberation via community living and psychedelics. Its sad coda is Wolfe's account of the "Acid Graduation" of Halloween 1966, when, during a long sacramental acid ritual, a member of Kesey's group repeatedly chants, "We blew it! We blew it! We blew it!" Wolfe, *The Electric Kool-Aid Acid Test* (New York: Farrar, Straus, and Giroux, 1968), 411–412.

12. Gitlin describes these stereotypical hippies as "middle-class kids comforting themselves with plans for the future while supporting themselves with checks from Mommy in their dull-eyed present." Todd Gitlin, *The Sixties: Years of Hope, Days of Rage* (New York: Random House, 2013), 225. A sensitive and articulate reflection upon this Sixties-versus-Seventies dynamic is Robert Fitch's "Remembering Jerry Rubin," *Solidarity*, April 1995. http://www.solidarity-us.org/site/node/2843. Accessed April 10, 2018.

13. See Tom Wolfe, "The 'Me' Decade and the Third Great Awakening," *New York Magazine*, August 23, 1976. http://nymag.com/news/features/45938/. Accessed July 15, 2015. Sixties veterans who maintained their activism in subsequent decades are exemplified by, for example, poet and Earth Day founder, Gary Snyder (environmentalism and the No Nukes movement); LSD activist and professional clown, Wavy Gravy (free and expanded medical care in underdeveloped nations); Stephen Gaskin (founder of "The Farm" intentional community in rural Tennessee); and Jim Fouratt, former Yippie and Stonewall veteran (gay rights). A solid and rigorous history of these movements and their transformation in the postsixties era is *The Sixties: Years of Hope, Days of Rage* (New York: Random House, 2013) by Todd Gitlin, a movement veteran. Patrick Conover comments: "The period since 1968 has been a period of major cultural creation and diffusion and of institutional innovation." Patrick W. Conover, "An Analysis of Communes and International Communities with Particular Attention to Sexual and Gendered Relations," *The Family Coordinator* 24/4 (October 1975), 454. On Stephen Gaskin's "The Farm" intentional-living community in Tennessee, see James Windolf, "Sex, Drugs, and Soybeans," *Vanity Fair* (May 2007). http://www.vanityfair.com/news/2007/05/thefarm200705. Accessed July 15, 2015.

14. Members of San Francisco's Diggers, for example, were subsequently involved in the postsixties "back to the land" movement, which established communal homesteads in rural settings, and were among the many Sixties veterans who maintained their activism, at lower visibility, into the next decades. The Diggers, probably the best known of the direct-action groups, were founded in 1966 by members of the San Francisco Mime

Troupe and specialized in street performance which "acted out" their vision of radical community activism. Inspired by the seventeenth-century English pastoral anarchists from whom they took their name, the Diggers ran free clinics, food stores, and housing collectives, and, in tandem with the Mime Troupe, engaged in spectacular put-ons ("The Death of Money," "The Death of Hippie") strongly influenced by Dada and the Marxist Situationist International. The Diggers' social and political consciousness is relatively well documented, as many of the founding members remained active and actively recorded their origins and radical aesthetic; SF Mime Troup / Digger leader Peter Berg became a leading advocate for bioregionalism and environmental causes. See "The Digger Papers," formerly archived at http://www.diggers.org/ (offline as of 8/6/2015). Berg said "Well, the Digger group members were more social-oriented than revelatory. No question about it. Regardless of their backgrounds. Things were real when people did them, and what people do has to relate to food, shelter, economics, employment, creativity, etc." Marty Lee and Eric Noble, "Interview of Peter Berg and Judy Goldhaft, April 29, 1982." www.diggers.org. Accessed July 26, 2015. The actor Peter Coyote, an original Digger, has a memoir that captures the political intentionality of much of their activity: Peter Coyote, *Sleeping Where I Fall: A Chronicle* (San Francisco: Counterpoint, 1999). Other anarchist and direct-action community groups, most notably New York's Up Against the Wall Motherfuckers, often displayed a connection between avant-garde theater and poetry circles and political action. For the Situationists, see Guy Debord, *Definitions Internationale Situationiste #1* (Paris, June 1958). http://www.cddc.vt.edu/sionline/si/definitions.html. Accessed July 16, 2015. They were masters of the semiotics of both street theater and the *mot*: founder Peter Berg (1937–2011), later a highly influential environmental activist, said, "We were doing a piece of theater called the Diggers . . . and it involved the audience." Berg, quoted in Gitlin, *The Sixties*, 223. For 1970s utopian group communities that emerged from 1960s activist groups, see, for example, The Farm (Tennessee), Lama (New Mexico), and the Elf-Lore Family (Indiana). Although, despite this continuity, *something*—perhaps simply naive optimism—did end after Altamont: an oft-quoted passage from Hunter S. Thompson's *Fear and Loathing in Las Vegas*, probably the most eloquent elegy for the decade ever written, captures the sense of despair that would supplant Sixties idealism: "You could strike sparks anywhere. There was a fantastic universal sense that whatever we were doing was right, that we were winning. And that, I think, was the handle—that sense of inevitable victory over the forces of Old and Evil. Not in any mean or military sense; we didn't need that. Our energy would simply prevail. There was no point in fighting—on our side or theirs. We had all the momentum; we were riding the crest of a high and beautiful wave. / So now, less than five years later, you can go up on a steep hill in Las Vegas and look West, and with the right kind of eyes you can almost *see* the high-water mark—that place where the wave finally broke and rolled back." Thompson, *Fear and Loathing in Las Vegas: A Savage Journey to the Heart of the American Dream* (New York: Vintage, 1998), 22–23.

15. Joseph Campbell, panel discussion with Jerry Garcia and Mickey Hart, "From Ritual to Rapture, from Dionysus to the Grateful Dead," November 1, 1986, Palace of Fine Arts, San Francisco. Transcribed at http://www.sirbacon.org/joseph_campbell.htm. Accessed July 16, 2015. Campbell goes on to explicitly link dancing crowds at Dead shows to the

multisensory religious festivals of Russian Orthodox Easter, the Virgin of Guadeloupe, and Hindu Puri.

16. For archetypal examples of such dancing, see the "rock concert films" (a new genre) *Monterey Pop* (https://youtu.be/IjmUZHshDbg?t=1h9m27s, accessed September 15, 2015), which also includes a brief shot of the Merry Prankster's customized school bus called "Furthur") and *Woodstock* (a montage of dancers appears at 6:42 in Santana's "Soul Sacrifice"). "Dance" as semiotic Sign also played a key role in Sixties activist rhetoric, especially by political speakers who sought to frame its bodily "freedom" and "liberation" to the alienation and authoritarianism they excoriated in middle-class culture. For examples of such rhetoric, see the Yippies' January 16, 1968, manifesto, probably authored by Jerry Rubin, which claims that "there are 500,000 of us dancing in the streets, throbbing with amplifiers and harmony," in David Farber, *Chicago '68*, 17; John Schultz, *No One Was Killed: The Democratic National Convention*, August 1968, 48, 138; and Bruce M. Tyler, "The Rise and Decline of the Watts Summer Festival, 1965 to 1986," *American Studies* 31/2 (Fall 1990), 62.

17. Michael J. Kraemer identifies the political connotations of free-form dancing, but also emphasizes the individual, rather than collective, nature of that experience "Participants at the Acid Tests constituted a public life that was intensely dialectical: it drew on the technologies and ideologies of Cold War America and even exaggerated them, but it also sought to turn them toward a new sense of citizenship. *The dance floor itself became a public space of reshaped personal politics*." Kramer, *The Republic of Rock: Music and Citizenship in the Sixties Counterculture* (New York: Oxford University Press, 2013), 53. Emphasis added.

18. Craig Calhoun, "Occupy Wall Street in Perspective," *British Journal of Sociology* 64/1 (March 2013), 29. Emphasis added.

19. For other "occupation actions," see, for example, the October 1964 Free Speech protests at U.C. Berkeley; the October 1967 March on the Pentagon, which Norman Mailer memorialized in *The Armies of the Night* (New York: New American Library, 1968); the 1968 student occupation at Columbia, protesting university policies on Defense Department research and its uneasy relationship with the minorities that surrounded its campus; and the May 1969 occupation of "People's Park" near the U.C. Berkeley campus, all of which turned, at least in part, upon activists' physical occupation of contested public spaces, often in conditions of considerable personal risk.

20. The deaths of Martin Luther King Jr. and Robert Kennedy; the Tet Offensive; assaults on Black Panther sites in Oakland, Cleveland, and Chicago; and Black Power protests at the Mexico City Olympics are only a small selection of geopolitical events that massively impacted public perceptions of order/disorder in this year. Some of the most powerful eyewitness writing about Chicago '68 comes from "gonzo" journalist Hunter S. Thompson; see Thompson, *Kingdom of Fear: Loathsome Secrets of a Star-Crossed Child in the Final Days* (New York: Simon and Schuster, 2003), 78–83.

21. *Washoi* snake-dancing had received international media attention in 1960, when U.S. President Dwight Eisenhower's visit to Anpo was disrupted by a student group called Zengakuren. See Mark Kurlansky, *1968: The Year That Rocked the World* (New York: Random House, 2005), 83.The technique has continued to be employed in Japanese street demonstrations; see Jordan Sand, *Tokyo Vernacular: Common Spaces, Local Histories, Found Objects*

(Berkeley: University of California Press, 2013), 37; for the practice's origins in Shinto processionals, see Scott Schell, *The Rousing Drum: Ritual Practice in a Japanese Community* (Honolulu: University of Hawaii Press, 1999), 31–32. "Wa-shoi" is a rhythmic chant (often equated to "heave-ho!") and has traditionally been used to coordinate concerted movement within physical work.

22. The so-called "Walker Report," sponsored by the National Commission on the Causes and Prevention of Violence, described the CPD's indiscriminately violent response—beating, tear-gassing, and arresting reporters, hippies, and bystanders—as a "police riot." See http://www.fjc.gov/history/home.nsf/page/tu_chicago7_doc_13.html. Accessed July 16, 2015.

23. Influential leaders in Women's Rights, for example, specifically cited encounters with the pervasive sexism in "The Movement" as essential to their own political maturation. See, for example, J. Zeitz, "Rejecting the Center: Radical Grassroots Politics in the 1970s—Second-Wave Feminism as a Case Study," *Journal of Contemporary History* 43/4 (October 2008), 678. Linda Gordon has argued for the necessity of reconceiving a model of the New Left "that began with civil rights and proceeded through the student movement, the anti–Vietnam War movement, and the women's and gay liberation. None of these were simply "identity politics," although all—including even students—were fighting for rights and recognition that had been denied them. All were connecting their own experience with global injustice." Linda Gordon, "Socialist Feminism: The Legacy of the 'Second Wave,'" *New Labor Forum* 22/3 (Fall 2013), 23.

24. A few members of the earlier gay advocacy organizations (particularly in D.C. and New York) had proposed borrowing tactics from the Civil Rights movement but by and large, the confrontational street actions of the late '60s Gay Rights movement were undertaken by younger people who had learned their tactics in the antiwar and hippie communities. See, for example, Anthony Ashbolt, "'Go Ask Alice': Remembering the Summer of Love Forty Years On," *Australasian Journal of American Studies* 26/2 (December 2007), 36–37.

25. Havelock Ellis, in the 1890s, identifies "inverts" "gathered in clubs that, according to one observer, 'were really dance halls attached to saloons, which were presided over by [invert] waiters and musicians." Greg Sprague, "On the 'Gay Side' of Town: The Nature and Structure of Male Homosexuality in Chicago, 1890–1935," 7; quoted in Kevin J. Mumford, "Homosex Changes: Race, Cultural Geography, and the Emergence of the Gay," *American Quarterly* 48/3 (September 1996), 398.

26. For additional examples into the 1960s, see Simon Hall, "The American Gay Rights Movement and Patriotic Protest," *Journal of the History of Sexuality* 19/3 (September 2010), 550–551; Peter Boag, "'Does Portland Need a Homophile Society?' Gay Culture and Activism in the Rose City between World War II and Stonewall," *Oregon Historical Quarterly* 105/1 (Spring 2004); Justin David Suran, "Coming Out against the War: Antimilitarism and the Politicization of Homosexuality in the Era of Vietnam," *American Quarterly* 53/3 (September 2001), n78; David A. Reichard, "'We Can't Hide and They Are Wrong': The Society for Homosexual Freedom and the Struggle for Recognition at Sacramento State College, 1969–71," *Law and History Review* 28/3 (August 2010), n34.

27. See "Levee Life: Haunts and Pastimes of the Roustabouts," in Lafcadio Hearn and Simon J. Bronner, *Lafcadio Hearn's America* (Louisville: University Press of Kentucky, 2002), 48–49.

28. For a fascinating and insightful chronicle of the impact that WWII service had in formulating one city's postwar gay consciousness, see Boag, "'Does Portland Need a Homophile Society?" 7–14.

29. Analogous postwar experience likewise fueled the literary Beat movement, whose members, many of them openly gay or bisexual, espoused liberation from normative gender expectations, as they did from other bourgeois values.

30. For Owney Madden and the Cotton Club, see Cary D. Wintz and Paul Finkelman, *Encyclopedia of the Harlem Renaissance: K-Y* (New York: Taylor and Francis, 2004), 762–763; the Tijuana Club, see Jason Berry, Jonathan Foose, and Tad Jones, *Up from the Cradle of Jazz: New Orleans Music since World War II* (Lafayette: University of Louisiana Press, 2009), 49; for Almack's, see Christopher J. Smith, *The Creolization of American Culture: William Sidney Mount and the Roots of Blackface Minstrelsy* (Urbana: University of Illinois Press, 2013), 95–98.

31. At the time, it was illegal for adults to appear in public wearing less than three items of clothing appropriate to their physical gender or for same-sex dance partners to touch one another; rather like Jim Crow in the U.S. South, obsessive patrolling of identity behavior was a common feature of antigay police enforcement. So venues like Stonewall in which same-sex dancing or creative transvestism could take place were both rare and cherished.

32. See David Carter, *Stonewall: The Riots That Sparked the Gay Revolution* (New York: St Martin's, 2004); Donn Teal, *The Gay Militants* (New York: St Martin's, 1971); Boag, "Does Portland Need a Homophile Society?"; Duberman and Kopkind, "The Night They Raided Stonewall," 120–147; the documentaries *Before Stonewall* (1984, dir. Robert Rosenberg and Greta Schiller), *After Stonewall* (1999, dir. John Scagliotti); *Stonewall Uprising* (2010, Kate Davis and David Heilbroner), based upon Carter's book; and U.S. President Barack Obama's acknowledgment of Stonewall as a Civil Rights moment of equal import to Selma 1964 (African American) and Seneca Falls 1848 (women's rights), in his Second Inaugural Address (2012).

33. Only a very few photographs of that night's riot are extant—the subsequent three days of street protests and crowd actions are much better documented. But those few photographs do tend to support the idea that it was "street kids" who were literally at the forefront of the crowd. See, for example, http://n.pr/1LiE38V. Accessed July 18, 2015. In a related observation, Judith Bettelheim has identified drag and transvestism as "subversive places where societal norms are questioned and challenged." Bettelheim, "Women in Masquerade and Performance," *African Arts* 31/2, Special Issue: Women's Masquerades in Africa and the Diaspora (Spring 1998), 69.

34. Michael Fader's eloquence comes through even more clearly in the full quote: "We all had a collective feeling like we'd had enough of this kind of shit. It wasn't anything tangible anybody said to anyone else, it was just kind of like everything over the years had come to a head on that one particular night in the one particular place, and it was not an organized demonstration. . . . Everyone in the crowd felt that we were never going to go back. It was like the last straw. It was time to reclaim something that had always been taken from us.

. . . All kinds of people, all different reasons, but mostly it was total outrage, anger, sorrow, everything combined, and everything just kind of ran its course. It was the police who were doing most of the destruction. We were really trying to get back in and break free. And we felt that we had freedom at last, or freedom to at least show that we demanded freedom. We weren't going to be walking meekly in the night and letting them shove us around—it's like standing your ground for the first time and in a really strong way, and that's what caught the police by surprise. There was something in the air, freedom a long time overdue, and we're going to fight for it. It took different forms, but the bottom line was, we weren't going to go away. And we didn't." Carter, *Stonewall*, 160.

35. The hard-won wisdom of this strategic use of media visibility was borne out when all three papers provided extensive coverage, not all of it dismissive or homophobic. See http://www.columbia.edu/cu/lweb/eresources/exhibitions/sw25/case1.html. Accessed July 18, 2015.

36. Duberman and Kopkind, "The Night They Raided Stonewall," 136. The next day, as the public protests continued in the riot's aftermath, the revolutionary dancing continued: "On the Saturday when the fearless chorus line of queens insisted on yet another refrain, kicking their heels high in the air as if in direct defiance, the TPF moved forward, ferociously pushing their nightsticks into the ribs of anyone who didn't jump immediately out of their path" (140).

37. For example, Jacobs describes Pueblo Indian clowns mocking 1920s BIA attempts to control sexual references in sun dancing: "In general, the clowns' skirts and antics created a carnival-like occasion in which the social order was turned upside down." Margaret D. Jacobs, "Making Savages of Us All: White Women, Pueblo Indians, and the Controversy over Indian Dances in the 1920s," *Frontiers: A Journal of Women Studies* 17/3 (1996), 193.

38. Henry Louis Gates Jr., *The Signifying Monkey: A Theory of African American Literary Criticism* (New York: Oxford University Press, 1988).

39. The newly founded Gay Liberation Foundation "borrowed tactics from and aligned themselves with black and antiwar demonstrators with the ideal that they 'could work to restructure American society,' and "took on causes of the Black Panthers, marching to the Women's House of Detention in support of Afeni Shakur, and other radical New Left causes." *Gay Liberation at 40* (New York: PediaPress), 40. http://bit.ly/1LiNq8D. Accessed July 18, 2015. Afeni Shakur (born Alice Faye Williams), became a member of the Black Panther Party in 1964 and was arrested in April 1969, charged with criminal conspiracy. She is the mother of assassinated political and gangsta rapper Tupac (1971–1996).

40. As Mumford says, and as we have seen in concert saloons, working-class theaters, and NOLA tricolor balls for over a century before Stonewall, "Contacts between African Americans and homosexuals in speakeasies constituted direct cultural exchange through the creation of sexualized social practices. . . . African American cultural practices, especially dance, shaped homosexuality not in some abstract, indistinct way, but directly through the communal molding of dance forms that were often indistinguishable from sexual intercourse." Mumford, "Homosex Changes," 406–407.

41. Philadelphia and New York were centers of this groove-oriented dance music, whose production and presentation was as much the responsibility of disco record producers and nightclub DJs as it was of the singers and players.

42. For a good summary, see Frank Hoffman, *Survey of American Popular Music*. http://www.shsu.edu/lis_fwh/book/hybrid_children_of_rock/Disco2.htm. Accessed July 18, 2015. See also Mark Jacobson, "What Everyone Gets Wrong about '70s New York," *New York* (September 29, 2015).

43. Gillian Frank, "Discophobia: Antigay Prejudice and the 1979 Backlash against Disco," *Journal of the History of Sexuality* 16/2 (May 2007), 291.

44. Ibid., 276, 284, 287; Nadine Hubbs, "'I Will Survive': Musical Mappings of Queer Social Space in a Disco Anthem," *Popular Music* 26/2 (May 2007), 231.

45. Ken McLeod, "Space Oddities: Aliens, Futurism and Meaning in Popular Music," *Popular Music* 22/3 (October 2003), 350. See also Frank, "Discophobia," 283.

46. McLeod, "Space Oddities," 352. See also Damien Ridge, David Plummer, and David Peasley, "Remaking the Masculine Self and Coping in the Liminal World of the Gay 'Scene,'" *Culture, Health & Sexuality* 8/6 (November–December 2006), 502: "The all-night, high technology, drug enhanced, rapid beat dancing at raves and dance parties can also be interpreted as ritual: 'immersion and renewal through altered [trance-like] states.'"

47. See new signings, massive stadium concerts, expanding profits, market share, impact of corporate acquisitions. It should also be noted that, despite perceived contrasts of style and audience demographics, an investigation of heavy metal community similar to the present discussion of punk rock yields surprisingly close parallels of ethos and experience. For a good discussion of community and the carnivalesque in (more recent) metal, see Karen Bettez Halnon, "Heavy Metal Carnival and Dis-alienation: The Politics of Grotesque Realism," *Symbolic Interaction* 29/1 (Winter 2006), 33–48.

48. It is no coincidence that many of the New York bands, like groups associated with the early Sixties "British Invasion," often came out of visual arts, university, and/or performance poetry settings.

49. Though punk's audiences were overwhelmingly white and primarily male, the story of black and female punk rockers—in the United States, Detroit's Death (an African American family band) and female-fronted groups like Blondie and Patti Smith Group; in the U.K., Siouxsie and the Banshees, the Slits, and the collaborations between punks and West Indian reggae artists—is an important and under-documented history.

50. See the lyrics to "Complete Control": "They said we'd be artistically free / When we signed that bit of paper / They meant let's make a lotsa mon-ee / An' worry about it later." Joe Strummer, "Complete Control," *The Clash* (London: CBS 82000, S CBS 82000), 1977. Additionally under-documented is the impact of immigrant and working-class status among British punks: most notoriously, Sex Pistols' front man John Lydon, the son of Irish immigrants, whose onstage persona of "Johnny Rotten" intentionally tapped into venerable British tropes of the "wild Irish."

51. In 1978, RAR hosted a protest march and an open-air concert in Hackney, which drew more than 100,000 attendees. This politicized punk stance continued in the early '80s and was appropriated with considerable success by white-power skinheads in the 1990s.

52. For example: Black Flag, Fear, and the Circle Jerks were from SoCal; the Bad Brains and Minor Threat from D.C.; Hüsker Dü from Minneapolis; the Meat Puppets from Phoenix; and the Butthole Surfers from San Antonio.

53. A seminal resource in the period was the DIY resource guide, published by the fanzine *Maximum Rock-N-Roll* and the East Palo Alto Amoeba Collective, called *Book Your Own Fucking Life* (Cicero, Ill.: Rocco Publishing, 2004).

54. Paul Gilroy provides a good overview of the interplay between the West Indian and punk dance scenes in 1970s England, in "Black and White on the Dance Floor," in "*There Ain't No Black in the Union Jack": The Cultural Politics of Race and Nation*. http://bit.ly/1dUfQHg. Accessed August 24, 2014. A good study of U.K. punk's carnivalesque radical agendas is Jones, "Anarchy in the UK," 25–36.

55. Craig T. Palmer, "Mummers and Moshers: Two Rituals of Trust in Changing Social Environments," *Ethnology* 44/2 (Spring 2005), 147.

56. Joe Ambrose, *Moshpit: The Violent World of Mosh Pit Culture* (London: Omnibus Press, 2009), 3–4, quoted in Palmer, "Mummers and Moshers," 155.

57. Not only by the media—for whom it came to stand for hardcore's "savagery"—but also by some participants; MacKaye decried the "Rambo punks" who, taking off from media portrayals, later began to come to shows expressly to behave violently. For "Rambo punks," see Brock Ruggles, "Not So Quiet on the Western Front: Punk Politics during the Conservative Ascendancy in the United States, 1980–2000," PhD dissertation, Arizona State University, 2008, 208. http://bit.ly/1fFSF52. Accessed July 19, 2015. See Michael Azerrad, *Our Band Could Be Your Life*: "When it started, hardcore dancing was only *stylized* violence, an expression of the clamor and aggression of the music, and of the participants' adolescent inner tumult. . . . But as time went on, the difference between fighting and dancing became extremely hard to discern. . . . Hardcore dancing became like sumo wrestling, with beefy contestants marching into the ring, defying all comers to knock them out. A whole new crop of kids had come in, attracted by the music, media hype about punk aggression, even the misleading term 'slam dancing.'" Azerrad, *Our Band Could Be Your Life: Scenes from the American Indie Underground* (Boston: Back Bay Books, 2002), 160.

58. Ibid.

59. Mike Applestein, "Schtick vs. Substance: The Very Uncomfortable Nardwuar Interview with Ian MacKaye," *RFT Riverfront Times* (October 5, 2012). https://www.riverfronttimes.com/musicblog/2012/10/05/schtick-vs-substance-the-very-uncomfortable-nardwuar-interview-with-ian-mackaye. Accessed September 29, 2018.

60. As James Lull comments, "Imagine the trust that exists in the minds of stage divers as they hurl themselves backwards into the crowd." Lull, "Thrashing in the Pit: An Ethnography of San Francisco Punk Subculture," in *Natural Audiences: Qualitative Research of Media and Effects*, T. R. Lindlof, ed. (Norwood, N.J.: Ablex, 1987), 241, quoted in Palmer, "Mummers and Moshers," 158.

61. Fugazi performance, Lafayette Park, January 12, 1991; full video at https://youtu.be/c_5OZOwAhas. Accessed July 17, 2015.

62. As hip hop scholar Tricia Rose says of the parallel idiom of 1980s hip hop, "Oppressed people use language, dance, and music to mock those in power, express rage, and produce fantasies of subversion. These cultural forms are especially rich and pleasurable places where oppositional transcripts or the 'unofficial truths' are developed, refined, and rehearsed." Tricia Rose, *Black Noise: Rap Music and Black Culture in Contemporary America* (Middletown, Conn.: Wesleyan University Press, 1994), 99.

63. The trope ignores, for example, the degree to which New Wave reflected a reengagement by the (predominantly Caucasian) punk scene with contemporary African American dance music. For a good discussion of this dynamic of exchange in New York ca. 1979–1980, see Caroline Polk O'Meara, "The Bush Tetras, 'Too Many Creeps,' and New York City," *American Music* 25/2 (Summer 2007), 204ff. See also Josh Kun, *Audiotopia: Music, Race, and America* (Berkeley: University of California Press, 2005), 119. For more on hip hop's and punk's "network structure" that "avoid[ed] hierarchy while building lateral ties, see Craig Calhoun, "Occupy Wall Street in Perspective," *British Journal of Sociology* 64/1 (March 2013), 36.

64. To provide just a few examples: Fugazi's Ian MacKaye expanded Dischord Records into a home for many bands, several vast archival series documenting the D.C. punk scene over three decades, book publishing, and so on; Black Flag's Greg Ginn continues to run SST, which likewise releases new and archival recordings, DVDs, and promotional merchandise, as well as recordings of his many collaborative projects; and the Minutemen's Mike Watt (after cofounder D Boon was killed in a car accident) has continued to tour, collaborate widely, and author books, as well as compose three operas and a vast and groundbreaking archive/blog.

65. William Maxwell draws an explicit link between hip hop and punk: "Although rap's form and content was shaped by the special experience of young black men within the cities of the Northeast, the code by which it understood its own significance was similar to that of punk. . . . Like early punk, early rap was performed by and for a traditionally voiceless group of lower and working-class urban youth who self-consciously insisted upon their music's marginality and crudeness." Maxwell, "Sampling Authenticity: Rap Music, Postodernism, and the Ideology of Black Crime," *Studies in Popular Culture* 14/1 (1991), 5.

66. Russell A. Potter, *Spectacular Vernaculars: Hip-Hop and the Politics of Postmodernism*, 108. http://bit.ly/1H9q8LR. Accessed July 21, 2015. Emphasis added.

67. A disclaimer is in order here: because this essay is particularly concerned with the ways that 1960s civil rights and antiwar strategies played into the rise of early '70s hip hop consciousness, for reasons of scope and focus only, I omit discussion of the equally significant but historically subsequent West Coast electro-hop and (especially) gangsta, and also 1980s political, conscious, and Afrocentric rap—a large and very important stable of artists. Omitting the righteous roar and Trickster gymnastics of Public Enemy's Chuck D and Flavor Flav, for example, from this discussion pains me—but brevity and historical specificity have their own requirements. See Rose, "Prophets of Rage: Rap Music and the Politics of Black Cultural Expression," in *Black Noise*, 99–145, which uses Public Enemy as a major source for analysis of hip hop's political consciousness.

68. See the vertical housing project as a "neighborhood in the sky," envisioned by the Expressway's architect Robert Moses. https://www.uic.edu/orgs/kbc/hiphop/newyork.htm#birth. Accessed July 20, 2015.

69. http://americanrealities.org/locations/south_bronx/. Accessed July 20, 2015.

70. Joe Flood, "Why the Bronx Burned," *New York Post*, May 13, 2010. http://nypost.com/2010/05/16/why-the-bronx-burned/. Accessed July 20, 2015.

71. A good summary of these losses, especially in public education, is in Katrina Hazzard-Gordon, "Dance in Hip Hop Culture," in William Eric Perkins, ed., *Droppin' Science: Critical Essays on Rap and Hip Hop Culture* (Philadelphia: Temple University Press, 1996), 223–224.

72. For a good summary of the impact of all these societal factors upon the early roots of hip hop, see Jeff Chang, "Necropolis," *Can't Stop Won't Stop: A History of the Hip-Hop Generation* (New York: Macmillan, 2005), 13–20.

73. An excellent summary of the historical interactions of African American and Latino/a dance musics, through hip hop, is Pancho McFarland, "Chicano Rap Roots: Black-Brown Cultural Exchange and the Making of a Genre," *Callaloo* 29/3, Hip-Hop Music and Culture (Summer 2006), 941–944.

74. For the "selector" see Joseph G. Schloss, "'Like Old Folk Songs Handed Down from Generation to Generation': History, Canon, and Community in B-Boy Culture," *Ethnomusicology* 50/3 (Fall 2006), 427.

75. After his death at the hands of police in September 1948, the historical Vincent Martin became a figure in Trenchtown folk legend, as the archetypal "Rude Bwai" ("rude boy") who inspired songs like "Rude Boy" (Johnny Clarke), "Johnny Too Bad" (The Slickers"), "Rudy Got Soul" (Desmond Dekker), and *The Harder They Come*. The film, the first full-length dramatic feature shot on location in Jamaica, made on a shoestring budget, using many nonprofessional actors and a wealth of Trenchtown locations, was premiered at the Venice Film Festival.

76. This recording, and Marley's subsequent career, cemented the status of reggae, particularly as filtered through the cosmology and vocabulary of the syncretic Afro-Protestant religion, Rasta-Far-I, which became emblematic of Third World peoples' aspirations.

77. The proximity of political violence to reggae stares would climax with a failed assassination plot against Marley in December 1976. The "West Indian" émigré population in England increased by 80 percent between 1961–1971, settling in West London throughout the period, and played a key role in the 1970s U.K. punk explosion (see the Clash, "Rudie Can't Fail," *Rude Boy*, earlier). See Richard Dennis and Hugh Clout, "The Inner City," in *A Social Geography of England and Wales: Pergamon Oxford Geographies* (Oxford: Perganon, 2013), 167.

78. A remarkable documentary from the early 1980s depicts Herc driving through his old neighborhood with the two tall speaker columns of a Shure Vocal Master PA blasting from the back seat of his convertible.

79. "What Herc, Flash, and their cohort did was to actualize the immanent possibilities of disco technology." Houston A. Baker Jr., "Hybridity, the Rap Race, and Pedagogy for the 1990s," *Black Music Research Journal* 11/2 (Autumn 1991), 219.

80. For more on the Dozens, see Elijah Wald, *Talking 'Bout Your Mama: The Dozens, Snaps, and the Deep Roots of Rap* (New York: Oxford University Press, 2014).

81. Curiously, despite the flowering of spoken-word-plus-music performance in this period, including the 1970 debut LP by the Last Poets and Gil Scott-Heron's "The Revolution Will Not Be Televised" in the same year, it was not until the late 1980s that the circle

between hip hop toasting and spoken word poetry was closed. Public Enemy's Chuck D situates JB's greater influence specifically in his rhythmic language; see Jeffrey Louis Decker, "The State of Rap: Time and Place in Hip Hop Nationalism," *Social Text* 34 (1993), 63. For more on "slam poetry," see Priya Parmar and Bryonn Bain, "Spoken Word and Hip Hop: The Power of Urban Art and Culture," *Counterpoints* 306, Teaching CITY KIDS: Understanding and Appreciating Them (2007), 131–156. See also Decker, "The State of Rap," 63, on Heron and the Last Poets.

82. Tricia Rose, "Hidden Politics: Discursive and Institutional Policing of Rap Music," in Perkins, *Droppin' Science*, 236.

83. As Theresa A. Martinez puts it, "Oppositional culture can mean everything from extended kinship networks that function in the fact of harsh economic circumstances, to civil rights movements that direct the energies of the group to legal redress of grievances, to finding expression in artistic and cultural mediums that voice or visualize either cultural pride or protest and critique of the dominant culture." Martinez, "Popular Culture as Oppositional Culture: Rap as Resistance," *Sociological Perspectives* 40/2 (1997), 268. See also Decker: "Hip hop nationalists are the most recent in a long line of organic cultural workers who are situated between the intellectual activist and the commercialized entertainer" (60).

84. The Civil Rights activist, author, and scholar Julius Lester actually authored a pamphlet of collected black folktales for use by SNCC members in 1967; see Nick De Genova, "Gangster Rap and Nihilism in Black America: Some Questions of Life and Death," *Social Text* 43 (Autumn 1995), 122. For more on hip hop's evocation of traditional figures from Afro Caribbean folklore, see Yvonne Bynoe, "Getting Real about Global Hip Hop," *Georgetown Journal of International Affairs* 3/1, Special: 9/11: Facing a new threat (Winter–Spring 2002), 79. Or simply watch any Flavor Flav performance. For an excellent survey of the rich historical interplay between African American and Latino music communities, see McFarland, "Chicano Rap Roots," 939–955. For more on gangsta, an originally West Coast response to Bronx styles, typified in the work of N.W.A., Ice T, Schoolly D, and later Tupac Shakur and Biggie Smalls, see Eithne Quinn, *Nuthin' but a "G" Thang: The Culture and Commerce of Gangsta Rap* (New York: Columbia University Press, 2010).

85. This brief summary cannot do justice to the range, scope, and vision of Bambaataa's impact: as DJ, recording artist, talent scout, producer, community organizer, and (in 2012–2015) visiting scholar at Cornell University, where he oversaw the University's Hip Hop Collection, based on materials from his own archive. The architect of an Afrocentric "conscious" (another Jamaican term, conveying "historically aware") approach to hip hop, he was the mentor, among many others, of De La Soul, Queen Latifah, A Tribe Called Quest, and the Jungle Brothers. Disturbingly, while this book was still in production, Donovan / Bambaataa was credibly accused of having molested young members of the Zulu Nation, which he founded. See Dave Wedge, "Afrika Bambaataa Allegedly Molested Young Men for Decades. Why Are the Accusations Only Coming Out Now?" *THUMP* (October 10, 2016). https://noisey.vice.com/en_us/article/8xx5yp/afrika-bambaataa-sexual-abuse-zulu-nation-ron-savage-hassan-campbell. Accessed September 1, 2018. Equally disturbingly, some members of the Zulu Nation's leadership responded to these accusations by attacking or seeking to discredit victims; only after a series of revelations and retrenchments,

and Bambaataa's resignation, did the Nation's leadership acknowledge error. See Marc Hogan, "Zulu Nation Apologizes to Afrika Bambaataa's Alleged Sexual Abuse Victims," *Pitchfork*, June 1, 2016. https://pitchfork.com/news/65868-zulu-nation-apologizes-to-afrika-bambaataas-alleged-sexual-abuse-victims/. Accessed September 1, 2018. Cornell University subsequently disavowed its connection with the hip hop leader. See https://www.library.cornell.edu/about/news/archive/statement-regarding-afrika-bambaataa. Accessed September 1, 2018. Keyes points out the very significant role of Latinos as break-dancers in the early stages; see Cheryl L. Keyes, "At the Crossroads: Rap Music and Its African Nexus," *Ethnomusicology* 40/2 (Spring–Summer 1996), 231.

86. Jeff Chang provides a good survey of this complex boundary-crossing: the ways that the Bronx's Ghetto Brothers and Chicago's Young Lords (both Latino) began to share personnel, off the street and on the dance floor, with Bambaataa's Black Spades and Zulu Nation. See Chang, "Necropolis," 77.

87. An excellent extended analysis of "Apache's" historical and musical impact upon DJs and B-boys is Schloss, "Like Old Folk Songs Handed Down," 411–432. It should be emphasized, however, that hip hop DJs and producers prided themselves on the breadth, diversity, and catholicity of the records they scratched, spun, recorded, and sampled: Bambaataa, for example, was known as "Master of Records" because of his particularly wide and detailed knowledge of recorded music, which expertise began with his mother's record collection. See Afrika Bambaataa with Frank Broughton, "Interview" (Hunt's Point Community Center, Bronx N.Y., 6.10.98), archived at *DJhistory.com*. Accessed July 21, 2015.

88. A good summary of this "Black Nationalist Continuum" from the Victorian period onward is Decker, "The State of Rap," 54–57. Bambaataa had "grown up around the Black Panther Information Center" in the Bronx. His mother and uncle, who raised him together, were both Sixties activists. See Chang, *Can't Stop Won't Stop*, 63, 89, 91, 94–101, 141, 170, 182–183.

89. The Panthers may stand as emblematic of the Black Arts Movement, a loosely organized set of community-based initiatives revolving around music, literature, and entrepreneurship in a number of cities between 1965–1975. Artists in the "loft-jazz" and "free-jazz" movements—the American Association of Creative Musicians (Chicago), Sun Ra's Arkestra (Philadelphia), the Black Artists' Guild (St. Louis), Studio Rivbea (New York)—were particularly closely associated with the Movement. But they do not appear to have played a central role in carrying 1960s Civil Rights thinking into the early hip hop movement. See Parmar and Bain, "Spoken Word and Hip Hop," 138–139. The Nation of Islam provided a more visible and more commonly appropriated hip hop discourse. See Felicia M. Miyakawa, *Five Percenter Rap: God Hop's Music, Message, and Black Muslim Mission* (Bloomington: Indiana University Press, 2005). See also De Genova, "Gangster Rap and Nihilism," 123.

90. Apposite examples might be Martin Scorsese (*Mean Streets*, 1973), Francis Ford Coppola (*The Godfather*, 1972), William Friedkin (*The French Connection*, 1971), John Avildsen (*Joe*, 1970), and Alan J. Pakula (*Klute*, 1971).

91. Ossie Davis's *Cotton Comes to Harlem* (1970), a detective thriller, and Sidney Poitier's *Buck and the Preacher* (1972), a Western parable of black uprising, both reflect these wider trends.

92. In hindsight, it is conventionally understood as the opening salvo in a string of 1970s "Blaxploitation" films of which *Superfly* (1972, about a Robin Hood–like pimp, with a soundtrack by Curtis Mayfield) and *Shaft* (1971, about an unconventional drug-busting black cop, featuring Isaac Hayes's iconic title song) are the landmarks.

93. Huey P. Newton, "He Won't Bleed Me: A Revolutionary Analysis of 'Sweet Sweetback's Baadasssss Song," *Black Panther* 6 (January 19, 1971). Stephen Holden, "Film View: Sweet Sweetback's World Revisited," *New York Times*, July 2, 1995. http://www.nytimes.com/1995/07/02/movies/film-view-sweet-sweetback-s-world-revisited.html. Accessed July 20, 2015. A related example, pertinent to discussion of the French Caribbean in Chapter 4, is 1973's James Bond film *Live and Let Die*, which opens with a New Orleans jazz funeral and includes a good deal of faux-vodou symbolism and folklore, most notably Yaphet Kotto's villainous "Mr Big," whose alter ego is New Orleans spirit religion's "Baron Samedi."

94. "Let us imagine these hip hop principles as a blueprint for social resistance and affirmation: create sustaining narratives, accumulate them, layer, embellish, and transform them. However, be also prepared for rupture, find pleasure in it, in fact, *plan on* social rupture. When these ruptures occur, use them in creative ways that will prepare you for a future in which survival will demand a sudden shift in ground tactics." Rose, *Black Noise*, 39.

95. Robeson Taj Frazier and Jessica Koslow, "Krumpin' in North Hollywood: Public Moves in Private Spaces," *Boom: A Journal of California* 3/1 (Spring 2013), 10. Emphasis added.

96. A fuller version of this anecdote, which began in 2007 as a blog post, may be found at http://coyotebanjo.blogspot.com/2007/07/100-greats-061-public-enemy-greatest.html. Accessed August 30, 2014. Here, I also add a personal admission of guilt: I, too, as a punk rock fan, a year later in Chicago 1978, owned a "Disco Sucks" T-shirt, a possession of which I am now ashamed. At the time, my relationship with the blues of Son Seals and the punk rock of the Clash made it very difficult to relate to the slick production of *Saturday Night Fever* (1977) and the marketing of John Travolta and the Bee Gees. I offer my apologies to my disco brothers and sisters—I learned better, eventually. For more on the racist components of the antidisco backlash ca. 1979, see Frank, "Discophobia" 276–306.

97. Ramsay, quoted in James B. Stewart, "Message in the Music: Political Commentary in Black Popular Music from Rhythm and Blues to Early Hip Hop," *Journal of African American History* 90/3, The History of Hip Hop (Summer 2005), 200.

98. The term *B-boy* appears to be, like so many other seminal aspects of hip hop culture, a product of DJ Kool Herc. See Parmar and Bain, "Spoken Word and Hip Hop," 151. Boom boxes became so emblematic of B-boy culture's assault on public sound that they were eventually banned on the New York subways. See Alexandra Marks, "Sh-sh! This Is New York In the '90s: The $525 Bark," *Christian Science Monitor*, October 17, 1997. https://www.csmonitor.com/1997/1017/101797.us.us.3.html. Accessed August 30, 2014. As Frannie Kelley comments, "Around the time cassettes let break dancers move the party to a cardboard dance floor on the sidewalk, there were boomboxes." Kelley, "A Eulogy for the Boombox," NPR Music Essentials, April 22, 2009.

99. "Dance thus provides a portal to a different organization and assembling of physical space . . . [which] is continuously composed and recomposed by dancers into existence." Frazier and Koslow, "Krumpin' in North Hollywood," 9.

100. Joseph Schloss suggests that B-boying must be present in order for the hip hop complex to be culturally meaningful and "concerned with history, tradition, and community values. Schloss, "Like Old Folk Songs Handed Down," 428. Tricia Rose has a good summary of the multiple sources of the bodily vocabulary: Rose, *Black Noise*, 49.

101. See Chapter 4, n44. For other versions of the sacred circle, see Samuel A. Floyd Jr. "Ring Shout! Literary Studies, Historical Studies, and Black Music Inquiry," *Black Music Research Journal* 22 Supplement: Best of BMRJ (2002), 50; Palmer, "Mummers and Moshers," 38; Katrina Hazzard-Gordan, "Dancing under the Lash: Sociocultural Disruption, Continuity, and Synthesis," in *African Dance: An Artistic, Historical and Philosophical Enquiry*, ed. K. W. Asante (Trenton, N.J.: African World Press, 1996), 107; Hazzard-Gordon on "set de flo'" in "Dancing under the Lash"; Art Rosenbaum, and Margo Rosenbaum, *Shout Because You're Free: The African American Ring Shout Tradition in Coastal Georgia* (Macon: University of Georgia Press, 1988), 20–25. For the Mardi Gras Indians version, see George Lipsitz, "Mardi Gras Indians: Carnival and Counter-Narrative in Black New Orleans," *Cultural Critique* 10, Popular Narrative, Popular Images (Autumn 1988), 113.

102. German B-boy, quoted in Jeff Chang, "It's a Hip-Hop World," *Foreign Policy* 163 (November–December 2007), 65.

103. Chang, "It's a Hip-Hop World," 60. More on the cipher/cypher can be found in Schloss, "Like Old Folk Songs Handed Down," 413.

104. Sally Banes, *Writing Dancing in the Age of Postmodernism* (Middletown, Conn.: Wesleyan University Press, 2011), 145.

105. Thompson finds very strong Kongo and Angolan elements in hip hop dance, but these elements probably filter into the Bronx via Puerto Rico at least as much as Cuba. See Robert Farris Thompson, "Hip Hop 101," in Perkins, ed., *Droppin' Science*, 214–215. Chang has rich material on the historical background of the African American and, especially, Puerto Rican gangs whose turf wars brokered "Hoe Avenue Peace Meeting" (December 1971), transformation to political action groups as The Young Lords and the Zulu Nation set the stage for Herc and the MC's. Chang, *Can't Stop Won't Stop*, 40–65. A great deal of valuable information on the Lords and Nation, and indeed on the early history of hip hop, is actually digital; see, for example, the documentaries *Rubble Kings* (dir. Shan Nicholson, 2010) and the various films discussed in Kimberley Monteyne, *Hip Hop on Film: Performance Culture, Urban Space, and Genre Transformation* (Jackson: University Press of Mississippi, 2013).

106. On the impact of the Nation, see De Genova, "Gangster Rap and Nihilism," 124–125.

107. Thomas F. Defrantz says "theory is, and has always been, embedded within practice," See DeFrantz, "The Black Beat Made Visible: Hip Hop Dance and Body Power," *Carlopies: Theater, Theory, Criticism & Performance*, 67. https://carlopies.wordpress.com/2013/04/06/the-black-beat-made-visible-hip-hop-dance-and-body-power-thomas-f-defrantz/. Accessed May 1, 2015.

108. Schloss, "Like Old Folk Songs Handed Down," 429.

109. "Black social dances physicalize a continuity of *performative oratory* for Africans in diaspora. Dances offer greeting and debate; a mode of cultural identification and recognition, which links African Americans in corporeal orature. Participation in the larger black culture involves the successful attainment of social dances and the invention of individual movement style as a marker of identity. DeFrantz, "The Black Beat Made Visible," 4, 5.

110. "The sound systems that formed the backbone of the burgeoning hip hop scene were identified by their audiences and followers according to the overlapping influences of personae and turf. The territories were tentatively claimed through the ongoing cultural practices that occurred within their bounds and were reinforced by the circulation of those who recognized and accepted their perimeters. . . . Most of the dominant historical narratives pertaining to the emergence of hip hop . . . identify a transition from gang-oriented affiliations (formed around protection of turf) to music and break dance affiliations that maintained and, in some cases, intensified the important structuring systems of territoriality." Murray Forman, "'Represent': Race, Space and Place in Rap Music," *Popular Music* 19/1 (January 2000), 67ff.

111. Tricia Rose provides a powerful reading of the dynamics of containment versus contestation in the public space of a hip hop preconcert but does not address dancing as a significant component in that contestation. See Rose, "'Fear of a Black Planet': Rap Music and Cultural Politics in the 1990s," *Journal of Negro Education* 60/3, Socialization Forces Affecting the Education of African American Youth in the 1990s (Summer 1991), 278.

112. Ronni Armstead, "Las Krudas, Spatial Practice, and the Performance of Diaspora," *Meridians* 8/1, Representin': Women, Hip-Hop, and Popular Music (2008), 130–143. The specific citations are to Michel Foucault, "Of Other Spaces," Jay Miskowiec, trans., *Diacritics* 16 (1986), 22–27; Paul Gilroy, *The Black Atlantic Modernity and Double Consciousness* (Cambridge: Harvard University Press, 1993); R. Murray Schafer, *The Tuning of the World* (New York: Knopf, 1977).The very fact that Armstead is writing about female performers, at another location in the African Diaspora, helps to contextualize Schloss, Rose, and Frazier (the latter discussed later). Her fundamental insight might be said to undergird this entire book: "The creation of sound and music is a powerfully productive tool for the disciplining and organizing of space around particular visual and aural aesthetic principles. . . . *Sound-making is* . . . capable of transgressing seemingly discrete social and spatial hierarchies, *and should be factored more seriously into investigations of resistance*." Armstead, "Las Krudas," 131. Emphasis added.

113. Frazier and Koslow, "Krumpin' in North Hollywood," 1–16. On Los Angeles electro-hop, see Gabriela Jiménez, "'Something 2 Dance 2': Electro Hop in 1980s Los Angeles and Its Afrofuturist Link," *Black Music Research Journal* 31/1 (Spring 2011), 141. A good summary of the origins of krumpin' is Frazier and Koslow. "Krumpin' in North Hollywood," 2–3. Electro-hop is also a primary source influence on rapper and producer Sir Mix-a-Lot, discussed in Chapter 9.

114. In this context we may also recall Breunlin and Regis's discussion of urban landscape in New Orleans second-line consciousness: Rachel Breunlin and Helen A. Regis, "Putting the Ninth Ward on the Map: Race, Place, and Transformation in Desire, New Orleans," *American Anthropologist* New Series 108/4 (December 2006), 753.

115. Frazier and Koslow, "Krumpin' in North Hollywood," 3.

116. Ibid.

117. On "Zip Coon," see Shane White, "A Question of Style: Blacks in and around New York City in the Late 18th Century," *Journal of American Folklore* 102/403 (January–March 1989), 23–25. Ostendorf says, "The emergence of this stereotype at this particular time [Northern emancipation ca. 1800–1820] was a symbolic expression of the fear that *free* blacks, not slaves, instilled in Americans." Berndt Ostendorf, "Minstrelsy & Early Jazz," *Massachusetts Review* 20/3 (Autumn 1979), 582. On free blacks' urban anonymity, see Oscar Reiss, *Blacks in Colonial America* (Jefferson, N.C.: McFarland, 1997), 124. On late-nineteenth-century dandyism, Domosh says, "To see African Americans in clothes clearly unsuited to work must have seemed particularly threatening to whites, who had difficulty fathoming a leisured black class." Mona Domosh, "Those 'Gorgeous Incongruities': Polite Politics and Public Space on the Streets of Nineteenth-Century New York City," *Annals of the Association of American Geographers* 88/2 (June 1998), 220. See also Shane White, "'It Was a Proud Day': African Americans, Festivals, and Parades in the North, 1741–1834," *Journal of American History* 81/1 (June 1994), 32.

118. Webb says, "Racial anxiety has been part and parcel of class anxiety for as long as free blacks have been visible in Western societies." Barbara L. Webb, "The Black Dandyism of George Walker: A Case Study in Genealogical Method," *TDR (1988-)* 45/4 (Winter 2001), 11. See also Ostendorf: "The emergence of [the Zip Coon] stereotype at this particular time was a symbolic expression of the fear which *free* blacks, not slaves, instilled in Americans." "Minstrelsy and Early Jazz," 582.

119. "Black music, as a privileged, while not indexical, mode of black vernacular expression can be read as a meta-narrative of the shifting terrain of political self-consciousness and resistance over time." See Michael Hanson, "Suppose James Brown Read Fanon: The Black Arts Movement, Cultural Nationalism and the Failure of Popular Musical Praxis," *Popular Music* 27/3 (October 2008), 341.

120. "In social dance, the black body achieves a freedom from traditional American strictures defining legitimate corporeality. The dancing black body, responding to and provoking the drumbeat, acts performatively against the common American law of black abjection. 'Speaking well' in terms of black social dance [thus] defies—temporarily—systematized oppression." Thomas DeFrantz, "The Black Beat Made Visible,"10.

121. See Charles Keil, "Participatory Discrepancies and the Power of Music," *Cultural Anthropology* 2/3 (August 1987), 277–278. Paraphrasing Arthur Jafa, Tricia Rose has identified this as "ruptures in line," as part of her identification of African-derived aesthetics of "flow," "layering," and these "ruptures." These values obtain across visual art (graffiti), movement (B-boying), and sound (DJs intercutting records). See Rose, *Black Noise*, 38. See also Barbara Browning on "suspension" and rupture in samba, paraphrased in Schloss, "Like Old Folk Songs Handed Down," 415.

122. See Keil, "Participatory Discrepancies," 277–278.

123. Christopher Small, *Musicking: The Meanings of Performing and Listening* (Middletown, Conn.: Wesleyan University Press, 1998), 13. Emphasis added. See also Christopher Small, *Music of the Common Tongue: Survival and Celebration in African American Music* revised edition (Middletown, Conn.: Wesleyan University Press, 2011), 485.

## Chapter 9. Street Dance and the Dream of Freedom

1. Dorinda Outram, *The Body and the French Revolution: Sex, Class, and Political Culture* (New Haven: Yale University Press, 1989), 1; Stephanie M. H. Camp, "The Pleasures of Resistance: Enslaved Women and Body Politics in the Plantation South, 1830–1861," *Journal of Southern History* 68/3 (August 2002).

2. The bone and ivory flutes and depictions of dancing figures found in the caves of Geissenklösterle, Hohle Fels, and Bocksteinhöhle, in Southwestern Germany, date from this period, in addition to the more recent and well-known (and arguable) depictions of dancing shamans at Lascaux (approximately 15,000 BCE). See Yosef Garfinkel, "Dance in Prehistoric Europe," *Documenta Praehistorica* 37 (2010), 205–214.

3. On ballet as a tool of absolute monarchy in the Sun King's reign, see Mark Franko, "Double Bodies: Androgyny and Power in the Performances of Louis XIV," *TDR (1988-)* 38/4 (Winter 1994), 71–72. In 1985, Campbell (1904–1987), a respected independent scholar of mythology, who by that time had become a minor pop culture celebrity through the alleged influence of his *The Hero with a Thousand Faces* upon George Lucas's *Star Wars* (1977), commented of Grateful Dead rock shows: "The first thing I thought of was the Dionysian festivals, of course. This energy and these terrific instruments with electric things that zoom in. . . . This is more than music. It turns something on in here (the heart?). And what it turns on is life energy. This is Dionysus talking through these kids." Interview at "From Ritual to Rapture, from Dionysus to the Grateful Dead," *San Francisco*, November 1, 1985. ://www.sirbacon.org/joseph_campbell.htm. Accessed January 8, 2016.

4. See the chilling accuracy with which actor Tommy Davidson, at a climactic moment in Spike Lee's film *Bamboozled*, literally assumes the "blackface mask"; see also Chapter 7.

5. David M. Levin says of such socialization through movement, "As we perform the prescribed rituals with greater and greater skill and grace, we are progressively inhabited, correlatively, by a *living, breathing, muscular, and moving understanding* of the visible, legible texts, bearers of our tradition." Levin, *The Body's Recollection of Being* (Boston: Routledge and Kegan Paul, 1985), 209–210, italics original; quoted in Rebecca Sachs Norris, "Embodiment and Community," *Western Folklore* 60/2–3, Communities of Practice: Traditional Music and Dance (Spring–Summer 2001), 116.

6. One of the better theorizations of the meaning and impact of the Occupy movement comes from sociologist Craig Calhoun, who observes: "Occupation was an especially resonant symbolic tactic. It turn[ed] the stranger sociability of the crowd into an organized, located, and more enduring evocation of the people." Calhoun, "Occupy Wall Street in Perspective," *British Journal of Sociology* 64/1 (2013), 28.

7. Ibid.

8. Robert C. Allen, *Horrible Prettiness: Burlesque and American Culture* (Chapel Hill: University of North Carolina Press, 1991), 31.

9. The site was "historically resonant" because it had been the location of the Pangaltı Armenian cemetery and of an Ottoman-era military barracks; the government's plans in 2012 to redevelop the area were seen as attempts to erase elements of the nation's mul-

tiethnic and secular history in favor of a reification of conservative Islamist and ethnic Turkish identity. The initial protest was a peaceful sit-in resisting the cutting of trees in Gezi Park. It quickly escalated into a much more broad-based ritual of protest against the authoritarian government.

10. Deputy Prime Minister Besir Atalay insisted the protests had been incited by "foreign agents" and an international Jewish cabal.

11. Sadly, as of this writing (ca. October 2018), the situation has only further deteriorated into authoritarianism.

12. *Daily Mail* (June 8, 2013). http://www.dailymail.co.uk/news/article-2337922/Turkey-protests-Anti-government-demonstrations-continue-despite-Recep-Tayyip-Erdogans-orders.html#ixzz3wldkVSt6. Accessed January 9, 2016.

13. A brief description of the June 2013 tango protests at Taksim Gezi Park and the social-media–driven worldwide *milongas* (tango dance meetings) organized in solidarity, appears in Melissa A. Fitch, *Global Tangos: Travels in the Transnational Imaginary* (Lewisburg, Ky.: Bucknell University Press, 2015), 157–158. But the events are not theorized.

14. The closing phrase is an intentional evocation (like the subtitle of this final chapter) of the title of Peter Guralnick's magisterial *Sweet Soul Music: Rhythm & Blues and the Southern Dream of Freedom* (New York: Perennial, 1994). As I noted in the Acknowledgments, Guralnick provides not only an inspiring model for writing about popular culture, but also—in this title—captures the realization that popular culture, in the American South, represented an aspirational dream of integration, sharing, and racial justice absent outside the expressive arts. I am indebted to Guralnick for both.

15. See Rob Kemp, "'And I Cannot Lie': The Oral History of Sir Mix-a-Lot's 'Baby Got Back' Video," for a thoughtful, nuanced, and very funny discussion about the making of the track and video, with Mix, Rick Rubin, representatives of Def American, and other contributors. http://www.vulture.com/2013/12/sir-mix-a-lot-baby-got-back-video-oral-history.html. Accessed August 30, 2014.

16. Including some who should have known better: see Clarence Lusane, "Rhapsodic Aspirations: Rap, Race, and Power Politics," *Black Scholar* 23/2, BLACK CULTURE 1993 (Winter/Spring 1993), 41.

17. I will refrain from citing specific 1990s "hair metal" recordings, but a quick search of online video sites, using these artists as keywords, will reveal a host of pulchritudinous examples.

18. A notorious example of dominant-culture repression, voyeurism, and exploitation is the case of the Khoikhoi woman Saartjie "Sarah" Baartman (ca. 1790–1851), whose genetic propensity to *steatopygia* (that is, especially pronounced buttocks) led to her being exhibited across Europe as the "Hottentot Venus" (a racist term and context). White observers of all social classes paid money to indulge sexual voyeurism under the guise of "scientific curiosity." A good analysis of this historical case is Sander L. Gilman, "Black Bodies, White Bodies: Toward an Iconography of Female Sexuality in Late Nineteenth-Century Art, Medicine, and Literature," in Henry Louis Gates Jr., ed., *Race, Writing and Difference* (Chicago: University of Chicago Press, 1985), 223–261.

19. No pun is intended.

20. Janell Hobson, "The 'Batty' Politic: Toward an Aesthetic of the Black Female Body," *Hypatia* 18/4, Women, Art, and Aesthetics (Autumn–Winter 2003), 96–97. Emphasis added. At the time, the white rocker Bruce Springsteen likewise defended "Baby Got Back," as a more realistic portrait of female anatomy than most promotional videos. See http://www.rollingstone.com/music/news/therollingstoneinterviewbrucespringsteen leavesestreet19920806?page=5. Accessed January 12, 2016.

21. Amylia Dorsey-Rivas, quoted in Rob Kemp, "And I Cannot Lie."

22. Anthony Ray, "Baby Got Back," Sir Mix-A-Lot, *Mack Daddy* (Def American DEF 26765 # 1992) (compact disc).

23. Mix describes a good deal of argument between himself and the video crew, who had costumed the dancers in much more stereotypically provocative and objectified ways. See Kemp, "And I Cannot Lie."

24. Adam Bernstein: "We let each dancer freestyle, so I would edit in shots coordinated with the song wherever appropriate. One dancer did that great flying kick, and it made sense to sync that shot with the kungfu movie *Whopppish!* sound in the track."

25. "Baby Got Back" may even be parsed as a kind of semiotic debate between two couture designers' aesthetics: Gaultier's statuesque Aryanism (found not only in Madonna's *Blonde Ambition* costuming but also in a reference to the notorious metallic bustier within "Back") and Jean-Paul Goude's aesthetic, which, as video director Adam Bernstein put it, "happened to be ass-obsessed."

26. The quoted conversation was in 1992, and confirms that Mix and the creative staff understood "Baby" as a political song *even before it appeared on MTV*. Mix even objected, during the video shoot, to the original costuming of some of the dancers, telling the director, "This song is called 'Baby Got Back,' not 'Baby's a Ho,'"—for which he was thanked by the dancers—and a visual of the cover of Cosmo is rendered as Cosmo-pygian. A reference to the adjective "callipygian." See Kemp, "Oral History."

27. Dorsey-Rivas, "And I Cannot Lie."

28. See Kemp, "Oral History." Emphasis added.

29. It is not immediately apparent whether the call for onstage dancers was a spontaneous decision, although the amount of stage apron left open, and the clear sight lines, suggest advance planning. What could not have been known—and, it in fact appears, was significantly underestimated—was the immediacy, scope, and energy of the response: these ladies are not playin'.

30. http://www.zennie62blog.com/2014/06/13/whos-the-woman-in-sir-mix-a-lot-baby-got-back-video-shawn-bounds-68806/. Accessed September 16, 2016.

31. Hundreds of comments on the original Seattle Symphony YouTube upload, from commenters self-identifying as many different ethnicities, overwhelmingly comment approvingly upon Ms. Bounds and the intensity and authority of her dancing.

32. Also for Mix's interaction: he is in fact very careful during this performance, avoiding the most egregious sexual pantomime and encouraging the audience to sing along—instead of himself—on some of the lyric's most explicit lines. The performance has its especially liminal, even "dangerous" moments—at one point, when another woman,

egged on by a companion, begins to "rub up" her body against Mix's, he slips aside until she is snatched away by that companion.

33. See Christopher Small, *Music of the Common Tongue: Survival and Celebration in African American Music* (Middletown, Conn.: Wesleyan University Press, 2011), 70. As Wendy James put it: "This story of American dance history is not one of total prohibition, but of attempts over three centuries to restrict, reshape, and effectively to co-opt dancing, to co-opt it into the usefully productive rhythms of work." James, "Reforming the Circle: Fragments of the Social History of a Vernacular African Dance Form," *Journal of African Cultural Studies* 23/1 (June 2000), 144.

34. For a more detailed summary of this process, and of its impact upon vernacular culture, see Christopher J. Smith, "Reclaiming the Commons, One Tune at a Time," *New Hibernia Review* 10/4 (2006), 9–20.

35. Slaveholders strove to create controlled and controlling landscapes that would determine the uses to which enslaved people put their bodies. Camp, "The Pleasures of Resistance," 534.

36. The standard text on this interpretation of blackface as two-directional resistance by the white working-class is Eric Lott, *Love & Theft: Blackface Minstrelsy and the American Working Class* (New York: Oxford University Press, 1995).

37. A good source on the dynamics of late-nineteenth-century immigration politics is Daniel R. Roediger, *Working toward Whiteness: How America's Immigrants Became White: The Strange Journey from Ellis Island to the Suburbs* (New York: Basic, 2006).

38. Universities have, for this reason, sometimes experienced subaltern push back similar to that against other dominant-culture institutions, most notably in the mid-1960s (the Berkeley Free Speech Movement, and the various occupations, especially at Columbia, protesting university involvement in Vietnam War R&D) and in the early 2010s, in the wake of the Occupy movement.

39. Phillips said this at various times and in various ways, but a good example is this one: "Yes, the long memory is the most radical idea in this country. It is the loss of that long memory which deprives our people of that connective flow of thoughts and events that clarifies our vision, not of where we're going, but where we want to go." Bruce Phillips with Rosalie Sorrels, *The Long Memory* (Red House Records SKU: RHR-CD-83, 1996).

40. See Philip Norman, *Shout! The Beatles in Their Generation* (New York: Simon and Schuster, 2011). http://bit.ly/1mNbZAi. Accessed January 9, 2016. Emphasis added. Another version of the same Lennon quote is: "It's pretty hard when you are Caesar and everyone is saying how wonderful you are and they are giving you all the goodies and the girls, it's pretty hard to break out of that.'" Interview, Tariq Ali and Robin Blackburn January 21, 1971, *Red Mole*. http://www.beatlesinterviews.org/db1971.0121.beatles.html. Accessed January 9, 2016.

# Index

**CHRISTOPHER J. SMITH** is a professor, chair of musicology, and founding director of the Vernacular Music Center at the Texas Tech University School of Music. He is the author of the award-winning book *The Creolization of American Culture: William Sidney Mount and the Roots of Blackface Minstrelsy*.

**MUSIC IN AMERICAN LIFE**

Only a Miner: Studies in Recorded Coal-Mining Songs *Archie Green*
Great Day Coming: Folk Music and the American Left *R. Serge Denisoff*
John Philip Sousa: A Descriptive Catalog of His Works *Paul E. Bierley*
The Hell-Bound Train: A Cowboy Songbook *Glenn Ohrlin*
Oh, Didn't He Ramble: The Life Story of Lee Collins, as Told to Mary Collins *Edited by Frank J. Gillis and John W. Miner*
American Labor Songs of the Nineteenth Century *Philip S. Foner*
Stars of Country Music: Uncle Dave Macon to Johnny Rodriguez *Edited by Bill C. Malone and Judith McCulloh*
Git Along, Little Dogies: Songs and Songmakers of the American West *John I. White*
A Texas-Mexican *Cancionero*: Folksongs of the Lower Border *Américo Paredes*
San Antonio Rose: The Life and Music of Bob Wills *Charles R. Townsend*
Early Downhome Blues: A Musical and Cultural Analysis *Jeff Todd Titon*
An Ives Celebration: Papers and Panels of the Charles Ives Centennial Festival-Conference *Edited by H. Wiley Hitchcock and Vivian Perlis*
Sinful Tunes and Spirituals: Black Folk Music to the Civil War *Dena J. Epstein*
Joe Scott, the Woodsman-Songmaker *Edward D. Ives*
Jimmie Rodgers: The Life and Times of America's Blue Yodeler *Nolan Porterfield*
Early American Music Engraving and Printing: A History of Music Publishing in America from 1787 to 1825, with Commentary on Earlier and Later Practices *Richard J. Wolfe*
Sing a Sad Song: The Life of Hank Williams *Roger M. Williams*
Long Steel Rail: The Railroad in American Folksong *Norm Cohen*
Resources of American Music History: A Directory of Source Materials from Colonial Times to World War II *D. W. Krummel, Jean Geil, Doris J. Dyen, and Deane L. Root*
Tenement Songs: The Popular Music of the Jewish Immigrants *Mark Slobin*
Ozark Folksongs *Vance Randolph; edited and abridged by Norm Cohen*
Oscar Sonneck and American Music *Edited by William Lichtenwanger*
Bluegrass Breakdown: The Making of the Old Southern Sound *Robert Cantwell*
Bluegrass: A History *Neil V. Rosenberg*
Music at the White House: A History of the American Spirit *Elise K. Kirk*
Red River Blues: The Blues Tradition in the Southeast *Bruce Bastin*
Good Friends and Bad Enemies: Robert Winslow Gordon and the Study of American Folksong *Debora Kodish*
Fiddlin' Georgia Crazy: Fiddlin' John Carson, His Real World, and the World of His Songs *Gene Wiggins*
America's Music: From the Pilgrims to the Present (rev. 3d ed.) *Gilbert Chase*
Secular Music in Colonial Annapolis: The Tuesday Club, 1745–56 *John Barry Talley*
Bibliographical Handbook of American Music *D. W. Krummel*
Goin' to Kansas City *Nathan W. Pearson Jr.*
"Susanna," "Jeanie," and "The Old Folks at Home": The Songs of Stephen C. Foster from His Time to Ours (2d ed.) *William W. Austin*
Songprints: The Musical Experience of Five Shoshone Women *Judith Vander*

"Happy in the Service of the Lord": Afro-American Gospel Quartets in Memphis *Kip Lornell*

Paul Hindemith in the United States *Luther Noss*

"My Song Is My Weapon": People's Songs, American Communism, and the Politics of Culture, 1930–50 *Robbie Lieberman*

Chosen Voices: The Story of the American Cantorate *Mark Slobin*

Theodore Thomas: America's Conductor and Builder of Orchestras, 1835–1905 *Ezra Schabas*

"The Whorehouse Bells Were Ringing" and Other Songs Cowboys Sing *Collected and Edited by Guy Logsdon*

Crazeology: The Autobiography of a Chicago Jazzman *Bud Freeman, as Told to Robert Wolf*

Discoursing Sweet Music: Brass Bands and Community Life in Turn-of-the-Century Pennsylvania *Kenneth Kreitner*

Mormonism and Music: A History *Michael Hicks*

Voices of the Jazz Age: Profiles of Eight Vintage Jazzmen *Chip Deffaa*

Pickin' on Peachtree: A History of Country Music in Atlanta, Georgia *Wayne W. Daniel*

Bitter Music: Collected Journals, Essays, Introductions, and Librettos *Harry Partch; edited by Thomas McGeary*

Ethnic Music on Records: A Discography of Ethnic Recordings Produced in the United States, 1893 to 1942 *Richard K. Spottswood*

Downhome Blues Lyrics: An Anthology from the Post–World War II Era *Jeff Todd Titon*

Ellington: The Early Years *Mark Tucker*

Chicago Soul *Robert Pruter*

That Half-Barbaric Twang: The Banjo in American Popular Culture *Karen Linn*

Hot Man: The Life of Art Hodes *Art Hodes and Chadwick Hansen*

The Erotic Muse: American Bawdy Songs (2d ed.) *Ed Cray*

Barrio Rhythm: Mexican American Music in Los Angeles *Steven Loza*

The Creation of Jazz: Music, Race, and Culture in Urban America *Burton W. Peretti*

Charles Martin Loeffler: A Life Apart in Music *Ellen Knight*

Club Date Musicians: Playing the New York Party Circuit *Bruce A. MacLeod*

Opera on the Road: Traveling Opera Troupes in the United States, 1825–60 *Katherine K. Preston*

The Stonemans: An Appalachian Family and the Music That Shaped Their Lives *Ivan M. Tribe*

Transforming Tradition: Folk Music Revivals Examined *Edited by Neil V. Rosenberg*

The Crooked Stovepipe: Athapaskan Fiddle Music and Square Dancing in Northeast Alaska and Northwest Canada *Craig Mishler*

Traveling the High Way Home: Ralph Stanley and the World of Traditional Bluegrass Music *John Wright*

Carl Ruggles: Composer, Painter, and Storyteller *Marilyn Ziffrin*

Never without a Song: The Years and Songs of Jennie Devlin, 1865–1952 *Katharine D. Newman*

The Hank Snow Story *Hank Snow, with Jack Ownbey and Bob Burris*

Milton Brown and the Founding of Western Swing *Cary Ginell, with special assistance from Roy Lee Brown*
Santiago de Murcia's "Códice Saldívar No. 4": A Treasury of Secular Guitar Music from Baroque Mexico *Craig H. Russell*
The Sound of the Dove: Singing in Appalachian Primitive Baptist Churches *Beverly Bush Patterson*
Heartland Excursions: Ethnomusicological Reflections on Schools of Music *Bruno Nettl*
Doowop: The Chicago Scene *Robert Pruter*
Blue Rhythms: Six Lives in Rhythm and Blues *Chip Deffaa*
Shoshone Ghost Dance Religion: Poetry Songs and Great Basin Context *Judith Vander*
Go Cat Go! Rockabilly Music and Its Makers *Craig Morrison*
'Twas Only an Irishman's Dream: The Image of Ireland and the Irish in American Popular Song Lyrics, 1800–1920 *William H. A. Williams*
Democracy at the Opera: Music, Theater, and Culture in New York City, 1815–60 *Karen Ahlquist*
Fred Waring and the Pennsylvanians *Virginia Waring*
Woody, Cisco, and Me: Seamen Three in the Merchant Marine *Jim Longhi*
Behind the Burnt Cork Mask: Early Blackface Minstrelsy and Antebellum American Popular Culture *William J. Mahar*
Going to Cincinnati: A History of the Blues in the Queen City *Steven C. Tracy*
Pistol Packin' Mama: Aunt Molly Jackson and the Politics of Folksong *Shelly Romalis*
Sixties Rock: Garage, Psychedelic, and Other Satisfactions *Michael Hicks*
The Late Great Johnny Ace and the Transition from R&B to Rock 'n' Roll *James M. Salem*
Tito Puente and the Making of Latin Music *Steven Loza*
Juilliard: A History *Andrea Olmstead*
Understanding Charles Seeger, Pioneer in American Musicology *Edited by Bell Yung and Helen Rees*
Mountains of Music: West Virginia Traditional Music from *Goldenseal* *Edited by John Lilly*
Alice Tully: An Intimate Portrait *Albert Fuller*
A Blues Life *Henry Townsend, as told to Bill Greensmith*
Long Steel Rail: The Railroad in American Folksong (2d ed.) *Norm Cohen*
The Golden Age of Gospel *Text by Horace Clarence Boyer; photography by Lloyd Yearwood*
Aaron Copland: The Life and Work of an Uncommon Man *Howard Pollack*
Louis Moreau Gottschalk *S. Frederick Starr*
Race, Rock, and Elvis *Michael T. Bertrand*
Theremin: Ether Music and Espionage *Albert Glinsky*
Poetry and Violence: The Ballad Tradition of Mexico's Costa Chica *John H. McDowell*
The Bill Monroe Reader *Edited by Tom Ewing*
Music in Lubavitcher Life *Ellen Koskoff*
Zarzuela: Spanish Operetta, American Stage *Janet L. Sturman*
Bluegrass Odyssey: A Documentary in Pictures and Words, 1966–86 *Carl Fleischhauer and Neil V. Rosenberg*

That Old-Time Rock & Roll: A Chronicle of an Era, 1954–63 *Richard Aquila*
Labor's Troubadour *Joe Glazer*
American Opera *Elise K. Kirk*
Don't Get above Your Raisin': Country Music and the Southern Working Class *Bill C. Malone*
John Alden Carpenter: A Chicago Composer *Howard Pollack*
Heartbeat of the People: Music and Dance of the Northern Pow-wow *Tara Browner*
My Lord, What a Morning: An Autobiography *Marian Anderson*
Marian Anderson: A Singer's Journey *Allan Keiler*
Charles Ives Remembered: An Oral History *Vivian Perlis*
Henry Cowell, Bohemian *Michael Hicks*
Rap Music and Street Consciousness *Cheryl L. Keyes*
Louis Prima *Garry Boulard*
Marian McPartland's Jazz World: All in Good Time *Marian McPartland*
Robert Johnson: Lost and Found *Barry Lee Pearson and Bill McCulloch*
Bound for America: Three British Composers *Nicholas Temperley*
Lost Sounds: Blacks and the Birth of the Recording Industry, 1890–1919 *Tim Brooks*
Burn, Baby! BURN! The Autobiography of Magnificent Montague *Magnificent Montague with Bob Baker*
Way Up North in Dixie: A Black Family's Claim to the Confederate Anthem *Howard L. Sacks and Judith Rose Sacks*
The Bluegrass Reader *Edited by Thomas Goldsmith*
Colin McPhee: Composer in Two Worlds *Carol J. Oja*
Robert Johnson, Mythmaking, and Contemporary American Culture *Patricia R. Schroeder*
Composing a World: Lou Harrison, Musical Wayfarer *Leta E. Miller and Fredric Lieberman*
Fritz Reiner, Maestro and Martinet *Kenneth Morgan*
That Toddlin' Town: Chicago's White Dance Bands and Orchestras, 1900–1950 *Charles A. Sengstock Jr.*
Dewey and Elvis: The Life and Times of a Rock 'n' Roll Deejay *Louis Cantor*
Come Hither to Go Yonder: Playing Bluegrass with Bill Monroe *Bob Black*
Chicago Blues: Portraits and Stories *David Whiteis*
The Incredible Band of John Philip Sousa *Paul E. Bierley*
"Maximum Clarity" and Other Writings on Music *Ben Johnston, edited by Bob Gilmore*
Staging Tradition: John Lair and Sarah Gertrude Knott *Michael Ann Williams*
Homegrown Music: Discovering Bluegrass *Stephanie P. Ledgin*
Tales of a Theatrical Guru *Danny Newman*
The Music of Bill Monroe *Neil V. Rosenberg and Charles K. Wolfe*
Pressing On: The Roni Stoneman Story *Roni Stoneman, as told to Ellen Wright*
Together Let Us Sweetly Live *Jonathan C. David, with photographs by Richard Holloway*
Live Fast, Love Hard: The Faron Young Story *Diane Diekman*
Air Castle of the South: WSM Radio and the Making of Music City *Craig P. Havighurst*
Traveling Home: Sacred Harp Singing and American Pluralism *Kiri Miller*
Where Did Our Love Go? The Rise and Fall of the Motown Sound *Nelson George*

Lonesome Cowgirls and Honky-Tonk Angels: The Women of Barn Dance Radio *Kristine M. McCusker*
California Polyphony: Ethnic Voices, Musical Crossroads *Mina Yang*
The Never-Ending Revival: Rounder Records and the Folk Alliance *Michael F. Scully*
Sing It Pretty: A Memoir *Bess Lomax Hawes*
Working Girl Blues: The Life and Music of Hazel Dickens *Hazel Dickens and Bill C. Malone*
Charles Ives Reconsidered *Gayle Sherwood Magee*
The Hayloft Gang: The Story of the National Barn Dance *Edited by Chad Berry*
Country Music Humorists and Comedians *Loyal Jones*
Record Makers and Breakers: Voices of the Independent Rock 'n' Roll Pioneers *John Broven*
Music of the First Nations: Tradition and Innovation in Native North America *Edited by Tara Browner*
Cafe Society: The Wrong Place for the Right People *Barney Josephson, with Terry Trilling-Josephson*
George Gershwin: An Intimate Portrait *Walter Rimler*
Life Flows On in Endless Song: Folk Songs and American History *Robert V. Wells*
I Feel a Song Coming On: The Life of Jimmy McHugh *Alyn Shipton*
King of the Queen City: The Story of King Records *Jon Hartley Fox*
Long Lost Blues: Popular Blues in America, 1850–1920 *Peter C. Muir*
Hard Luck Blues: Roots Music Photographs from the Great Depression *Rich Remsberg*
Restless Giant: The Life and Times of Jean Aberbach and Hill and Range Songs *Bar Biszick-Lockwood*
Champagne Charlie and Pretty Jemima: Variety Theater in the Nineteenth Century *Gillian M. Rodger*
Sacred Steel: Inside an African American Steel Guitar Tradition *Robert L. Stone*
Gone to the Country: The New Lost City Ramblers and the Folk Music Revival *Ray Allen*
The Makers of the Sacred Harp *David Warren Steel with Richard H. Hulan*
Woody Guthrie, American Radical *Will Kaufman*
George Szell: A Life of Music *Michael Charry*
Bean Blossom: The Brown County Jamboree and Bill Monroe's Bluegrass Festivals *Thomas A. Adler*
Crowe on the Banjo: The Music Life of J. D. Crowe *Marty Godbey*
Twentieth Century Drifter: The Life of Marty Robbins *Diane Diekman*
Henry Mancini: Reinventing Film Music *John Caps*
The Beautiful Music All Around Us: Field Recordings and the American Experience *Stephen Wade*
Then Sings My Soul: The Culture of Southern Gospel Music *Douglas Harrison*
The Accordion in the Americas: Klezmer, Polka, Tango, Zydeco, and More! *Edited by Helena Simonett*
Bluegrass Bluesman: A Memoir *Josh Graves, edited by Fred Bartenstein*
One Woman in a Hundred: Edna Phillips and the Philadelphia Orchestra *Mary Sue Welsh*
The Great Orchestrator: Arthur Judson and American Arts Management *James M. Doering*

Charles Ives in the Mirror: American Histories of an Iconic Composer *David C. Paul*
Southern Soul-Blues *David Whiteis*
Sweet Air: Modernism, Regionalism, and American Popular Song *Edward P. Comentale*
Pretty Good for a Girl: Women in Bluegrass *Murphy Hicks Henry*
Sweet Dreams: The World of Patsy Cline *Warren R. Hofstra*
William Sidney Mount and the Creolization of American Culture *Christopher J. Smith*
Bird: The Life and Music of Charlie Parker *Chuck Haddix*
Making the March King: John Philip Sousa's Washington Years, 1854–1893 *Patrick Warfield*
In It for the Long Run *Jim Rooney*
Pioneers of the Blues Revival *Steve Cushing*
Roots of the Revival: American and British Folk Music in the 1950s *Ronald D. Cohen and Rachel Clare Donaldson*
Blues All Day Long: The Jimmy Rogers Story *Wayne Everett Goins*
Yankee Twang: Country and Western Music in New England *Clifford R. Murphy*
The Music of the Stanley Brothers *Gary B. Reid*
Hawaiian Music in Motion: Mariners, Missionaries, and Minstrels *James Revell Carr*
Sounds of the New Deal: The Federal Music Project in the West *Peter Gough*
The Mormon Tabernacle Choir: A Biography *Michael Hicks*
The Man That Got Away: The Life and Songs of Harold Arlen *Walter Rimler*
A City Called Heaven: Chicago and the Birth of Gospel Music *Robert M. Marovich*
Blues Unlimited: Essential Interviews from the Original Blues Magazine *Edited by Bill Greensmith, Mike Rowe, and Mark Camarigg*
Hoedowns, Reels, and Frolics: Roots and Branches of Southern Appalachian Dance *Phil Jamison*
Fannie Bloomfield-Zeisler: The Life and Times of a Piano Virtuoso *Beth Abelson Macleod*
Cybersonic Arts: Adventures in American New Music *Gordon Mumma, edited with commentary by Michelle Fillion*
The Magic of Beverly Sills *Nancy Guy*
Waiting for Buddy Guy *Alan Harper*
Harry T. Burleigh: From the Spiritual to the Harlem Renaissance *Jean E. Snyder*
Music in the Age of Anxiety: American Music in the Fifties *James Wierzbicki*
Jazzing: New York City's Unseen Scene *Thomas H. Greenland*
A Cole Porter Companion *Edited by Don M. Randel, Matthew Shaftel, and Susan Forscher Weiss*
Foggy Mountain Troubadour: The Life and Music of Curly Seckler *Penny Parsons*
Blue Rhythm Fantasy: Big Band Jazz Arranging in the Swing Era *John Wriggle*
Bill Clifton: America's Bluegrass Ambassador to the World *Bill C. Malone*
Chinatown Opera Theater in North America *Nancy Yunhwa Rao*
The Elocutionists: Women, Music, and the Spoken Word *Marian Wilson Kimber*
May Irwin: Singing, Shouting, and the Shadow of Minstrelsy *Sharon Ammen*
Peggy Seeger: A Life of Music, Love, and Politics *Jean R. Freedman*
Charles Ives's *Concord*: Essays after a Sonata *Kyle Gann*
Don't Give Your Heart to a Rambler: My Life with Jimmy Martin, the King of Bluegrass *Barbara Martin Stephens*

Libby Larsen: Composing an American Life *Denise Von Glahn*
George Szell's Reign: Behind the Scenes with the Cleveland Orchestra *Marcia Hansen Kraus*
Just One of the Boys: Female-to-Male Cross-Dressing on the American Variety Stage *Gillian M. Rodger*
Spirituals and the Birth of a Black Entertainment Industry *Sandra Jean Graham*
Right to the Juke Joint: A Personal History of American Music *Patrick B. Mullen*
Bluegrass Generation: A Memoir *Neil V. Rosenberg*
Pioneers of the Blues Revival, Expanded Second Edition *Steve Cushing*
Banjo Roots and Branches *Edited by Robert Winans*
Bill Monroe: The Life and Music of the Blue Grass Man *Tom Ewing*
Dixie Dewdrop: The Uncle Dave Macon Story *Michael D. Doubler*
Los Romeros: Royal Family of the Spanish Guitar *Walter Aaron Clark*
Transforming Women's Education: Liberal Arts and Music in Female Seminaries *Jewel A. Smith*
Rethinking American Music *Edited by Tara Browner and Thomas L. Riis*
Leonard Bernstein and the Language of Jazz *Katherine Baber*
Dancing Revolution: Bodies, Space, and Sound in American Cultural History *Christopher J. Smith*

The University of Illinois Press
is a founding member of the
Association of American University Presses.

University of Illinois Press
1325 South Oak Street
Champaign, IL 61820-6903
www.press.uillinois.edu